The Many Lives of
Yang Zhu

SUNY series in Chinese Philosophy and Culture
———————
Roger T. Ames, editor

The Many Lives of
Yang Zhu

A Historical Overview

Edited by

Carine Defoort

and

Ting-mien Lee

Cover image designed by Tingmien Lee based on the idea of "a man whose look is unclear."

Published by State University of New York Press, Albany

© 2022 State University of New York

All rights reserved

Printed in the United States of America

No part of this book may be used or reproduced in any manner whatsoever without written permission. No part of this book may be stored in a retrieval system or transmitted in any form or by any means including electronic, electrostatic, magnetic tape, mechanical, photocopying, recording, or otherwise without the prior permission in writing of the publisher.

For information, contact State University of New York Press, Albany, NY
www.sunypress.edu

Library of Congress Cataloging-in-Publication Data

Names: Defoort, Carine, editor. | Lee, Ting-mien, editor.
Title: The many lives of Yang Zhu : a historical overview / Carine Defoort and Ting-mien Lee.
Description: Albany : State University of New York Press, [2022] | Series: SUNY series in Chinese Philosophy and Culture | Includes bibliographical references and index.
Identifiers: ISBN 9781438490397 (hardcover : alk. paper) | ISBN 9781438490410 (ebook) | ISBN 9781438490403 (pbk. : alk. paper)
Further information is available at the Library of Congress.

10 9 8 7 6 5 4 3 2 1

Contents

Introduction: Being and Becoming: The Many Portrayals of
Yang Zhu   1
    Carine Defoort and Ting-mien Lee

1. Five Pre-Republican Portrayals of Yang Zhu   19
    Carine Defoort

I. From Warring States to Wei-Jin

2. Yang Zhu and Mozi as Critics of Unification Warfare   47
    Ting-mien Lee

3. Beyond Mencius's Portrayal of Yang Zhu and Mozi:
A Zhuangzian-Han Feizian Yang-Mo   79
    Yao-cheng Chang

4. Deconstructing "Hedonism": Understanding Yang Zhu
in the *Liezi*   105
    Erica Brindley

II. From Tang to Ming

5. Yang Zhu's Role in Tang-Song Proto-*daotong* Discourse   135
    John Makeham

6. Yang Zhu's Role in the Construction of Zhu Xi's *Daotong* 161
   John Makeham

7. Plucking Hairs and Shaving Heads: Li Zhi's Repudiation of Yang Zhu 191
   Esther Sunkyung Klein

III. From the Qing Dynasty Onward

8. The Birth of the Image of the "Egoist-Epicurean Philosopher" Yang Zhu during the Meiji Period 227
   Masayuki Sato

9. Struggling between Tradition and Modernity: Liang Qichao's Portrayal of Yang Zhu in the Early Twentieth Century 259
   Xiaowei Wang

10. Feng Youlan and Yang Zhu: The Shifting Discursive Space (1920–80) 289
    Xiaoqing Diana Lin

11. Three Dimensions of Yang Zhu Research in the Twentieth Century: Hu Shi, Meng Wentong, and Guan Feng 319
    Feng Cao

About the Contributors 341

Index 345

Introduction

Being and Becoming: The Many Portrayals of Yang Zhu

CARINE DEFOORT AND TING-MIEN LEE

Like almost all Chinese masters, Yang Zhu 楊/陽朱 (also called Master Yang 楊子 or Mr. Yang 楊生, fl. ca. 350 BCE) is hardly known in the field of philosophy in general. But in overviews of Chinese philosophy more specifically, he plays a certain role. There he is heralded as the founder of Yangism (*Yang Zhu xuepai* 楊朱學派) and the early promoter of egoism, individualism, and hedonism. He is said to have defended bodily integrity under the motto "for oneself" (*wei wo* 為我) against the moral duty or political pressure to sacrifice oneself for others. According to one of Yang's contemporary rivals, Mencius 孟子 (Mengzi, 372–289 BCE), Yang's ideas were immensely popular in his day. Unlike other early Chinese masters, Yang Zhu has no book compiled and transmitted under his name. The modern Chinese novelist Lu Xun 魯迅 (1881–1936) jokingly provided an explanation for this:

> Yangzi certainly did not write anything. This is really "for oneself." Because if he had made a book for others to read, he would have ended up acting "for others."
>
> 楊子就一定不著. 這才是'為我.' 因為若做出書來給別人看, 便變成'為人'了.¹

And this would, of course, have gone against his deepest conviction. Academics, however, are less prone to joking during working hours: since Yang Zhu was launched as a "Chinese philosopher" about one century ago, the scarcity of evidence for his life and thought has been considered a serious problem. This is because academic training in Chinese philosophy largely relies on reconstruction of the early thinkers' lives and thought based on textual evidence.

In the case of Yang Zhu, no text has been explicitly associated with him, aside from some loose statements attributed to him and one rather incoherent chapter entitled "Yang Zhu" in the *Liezi* 列子 (ca. 300 CE), a book that postdates him more than six centuries. A second type of material consists of a few scraps of early (Warring States and Han) writings that explicitly mention Yang Zhu. They portray him either negatively, in a fixed pair with Mozi 墨子 (fl. ca. 430 BCE) (e.g., in *Mencius*, *Zhuangzi* 莊子, *Han Feizi* 韓非子), or neutrally, in longer lists of masters (e.g., in *Lüshi chunqiu* 呂氏春秋, *Huainanzi* 淮南子). Scholars of the early twentieth century have added a third type of source material to Yang Zhu studies, attributing some passages from early sources (e.g., *Lüshi chunqiu*, *Zhuangzi*) to Yang Zhu's followers on the basis of their content and terminology, even though he is never mentioned there. The most commonly used evidence for such attributions are expressions such as "keep intact one's inborn nature" 全性, "preserve the genuine" 保真, "do not allow one's body to be ensnared by things" 不以物累形, "nurture one's life/inborn nature" 養生/性, do not "harm" 害/傷 it, "value oneself" 貴己 and, less favorably, "for oneself" 為我. The most commonly selected passages occur in *Han Feizi* 50 "Eminent Learnings" 顯學, in five *Lüshi chunqiu* chapters (1/2 "Taking Life as Basic" 本生, 1/3 "Valuing the Self" 重己, 2/2 "Honoring Life" 貴生, 2/3 "Essential Desires" 情欲, and 21/4 "Being Attentive to Aims" 審為) and four *Zhuangzi* chapters (28 "Yielding the Throne" 讓王, 29 "Robber Zhi" 盜跖, 30 "Discourse on Swords" 說劍, and 31 "Old Fisherman" 漁父). The reliance on these three types of textual material has been inherited by modern Yang Zhu scholars in their project of discovering the historical Yang Zhu and reconstructing his original thought.

Far from intending to remedy this dearth of reliable material, the current volume treats this lack of information as a feature rather than a bug. It illustrates how this biographical and bibliographical void has allowed the figure of Yang Zhu to incorporate a wide variety of visions and concerns across more than twenty centuries. Our alternative approach relies upon but also differs from previous scholarship. Prior to the Republican period, there were only occasional statements about Yang Zhu. A strong scholarly interest in Yang Zhu's thought only emerged in the twentieth century. In addition to his appearance in overviews of Chinese philosophy[2] and studies about individualism,[3] there has been a growing, but still limited, pool of scholarly work on Yang Zhu. For Western readers specifically, the increase has been remarkable, beginning with Alfred Forke's monograph of 1912[4] up through the more recent work of scholars such as John Emerson,[5] Attilio Andreini,[6] and Ranie Villaver.[7] An even stronger proliferation can be seen in Japan and China, thus far culminating in the work of He Aiguo 何愛國[8] and in workshops[9] dedicated to Yang Zhu.[10]

In Western academia, by far the most influential scholar in this respect has been A. C. Graham (1919–91). Inspired by two Chinese scholars, Feng Youlan 馮友蘭 (1895-1990) and Guan Feng 關鋒 (1919–2005), he identified the five *Lüshi chunqiu* chapters and four *Zhuangzi* chapters cited above as containing Yangist source material. He also confirmed portions of the *Liezi*, specifically from the "Yang Zhu" chapter, as authentic testimonies of pre-Qin thought.[11] Graham's interest in both the *Mozi* and the *Zhuangzi* had called his attention to the shadowy figure Yang Zhu. Along with Mo Di 墨翟, Yang had traditionally figured as a heterodox master; and aligned with Zhuang Zhou, he had been considered a Daoist. But Graham gave him an even greater role as the inventor of the notion of "inborn nature" (*xing* 性) and consequently as the instigator of a major philosophical debate in the fourth century BCE. "Little as we know directly about Yang [Z]hu, it seems that his intervention provoked a metaphysical crisis which threatened the basic assumptions of Confucianism and Mohism and set them on new courses."[12] It is hence only "with the appearance of rival doctrines" that Chinese philosophy became lively and sophisticated for Graham.[13] This portrayal of Yang Zhu and his role in the growth of Chinese philosophy, although based on little evidence, has been very influential in Western academia.[14]

The dominant trend since the twentieth century has consisted in identifying Yang Zhu's original thought in extant sources, reconstructing it as a systematic theory, and comparing it with possible equivalents in other cultures (e.g., hedonism). Without precluding such philosophical endeavors, the authors of this volume have chosen not to join this trend. Our project instead is to describe and situate the various reconstructions of Yang Zhu's thought in Chinese history. It illustrates that today's diligent search for firm textual evidence and a philosophical theory is largely the result of the most recent and currently dominant reconstruction of Yang Zhu. Rather than discussing Yang Zhu within the confines of that or any other specific historical frame, this volume tries to broaden the lens and retrieve a variety of paradigms in which Yang Zhu has played a role. This not only leads to more multifarious presentations of Yang Zhu but also to the contexts that shaped them. More generally, the remarkable dearth of textual material for this figure represents the almost "nothing" out of which early Chinese philosophers such as Yang Zhu have been fruitfully "created."

This introduction reviews the eleven Yang Zhu portrayals presented in the current volume. It then concludes with some reflections on Yang Zhu as an extreme case of the more general scholarly predicament with respect to the reconstruction of early Chinese philosophy. All of the portrayals have to some extent been created and re-created in a multiplicity of historical contexts. Despite (but also thanks to) the lack of textual evidence, Yang Zhu represents the undetermined dimension and creative potential of all ancient Chinese philosophers who are now studied, even the most well-attested and supposedly unshakable ones—such as Confucius, Zhuangzi, and Mozi.

1. A Selection of Yang Zhu Portrayals

This volume is chronologically ordered. Following a general overview, it contains three parts: part 1 covers Warring States to the Wei-Jin dynasties, part 2 from Tang to Ming, and part 3 from the Qing dynasty onward. In the introductory chapter, Carine Defoort traces the consecutive emergence and lasting influences of five major Yang Zhu portrayals preceding the creation of him as an ancient philosopher in the Republican period. First, in the late Zhou dynasty, he was primarily seen as a debating rival and secondarily as a defender of physical integrity. Combined, these two characteristics constituted the core of what gradually grew into an enduring interest in the lineage to which Yang Zhu belonged. From the Han dynasty onward, Yang Zhu became part of a rhetorical trope based on Mencius's negative portrayal of him alongside Mo Di. However, like Mencius, these two figures constituted the least informative parts of the trope. Mencius and Yang-Mo, respectively, were no more than slots where debaters could enter their own contemporary heroes and enemies. The third Yang Zhu portrayal, in the Wei-Jin period, pictures him as a prominent figure in his own right, most notably in the *Liezi* chapter named after him. By emancipating Yang Zhu from the Mencian Yang-Mo trope, this portrayal differs remarkably from previous and subsequent ones. It was later retrieved in the late Qing dynasty and played a major part in twentieth-century research. Even though in the fourth portrayal, from the Song onward, reflections on Yang's thought mostly reverted to the shadow of Mohist and Confucian thought, they also became increasingly sophisticated. Few of these Neo-Confucian reflections have been adopted in the field of Chinese philosophy, especially when compared with Kang Youwei's influence. Kang's remarks on Yang Zhu represent the fifth and last portrayal before the latter came to be treated seriously as a philosopher. This late Qing reformer portrayed Confucius among a wealth of rivals, including Yangzi, who all confirmed the sage's status as China's major reformer.

The first part of this volume contains three chapters, which cover the Warring States period (475–221 BCE) up to the Wei-Jin dynasties (220–420 CE). The first two, by Ting-mien Lee and Yao-cheng Chang, respectively, focus on the *Mencius* and other early (pre-Han and Han) sources. While Lee presents an alternative reading of Mencius's criticism of Yang and Mo by rereading the *Mencius* along with less familiar sources, Chang suggests an alternative to the Mencian portrayal of Yang and Mo on the basis of the *Zhuangzi* and *Han Feizi*. The third chapter by Erica Brindley turns to the *Liezi*, in which Yang Zhu is portrayed in his own right apart from Mozi.

By confronting the currently dominant interpretation of Mencius's criticism, Lee demonstrates that due to the dearth of textual evidence, this portrayal of Yang Zhu as Mencius's rival is inevitably speculative and open to radical challenge. In her alternative reading, Mencius does not criticize Yang and Mo for their opposite scope of moral concern—ranging from "for oneself" to "care for all"—but for their shared opposition to his advocacy of the war to end all wars. For Yang Zhu and Mozi, military unification is not the right way to restore peace and order. Yang Zhu argues that wars and interstate power struggles would naturally stop if no one would be willing to sacrifice oneself by participating in them. Mohists believe wars would stop if everyone would be willing to sacrifice oneself rather than others. Rather than defending this alternative reading as the correct interpretation of the debate between Mencius, Mozi, and Yang Zhu, Lee's construction is meant to shock the reader out of all-too-familiar lines of interpretation.

Chang's focus is not on interpreting Mencius's criticism but rather on reconsidering the long-standing fixation with this criticism and highlighting an alternative, often neglected, yet significant portrayal of Yang and Mo. While Mencius seems to depict Yang Zhu and Mozi as advocates of extreme forms of egoism and altruism, they are depicted in other early texts as deploying extraordinary but futile skills in manipulating language. This portrayal of Yang and Mo as debaters not only differs from the Mencian portrayal of them as promoters of certain ethical perspectives but also figures into Mencius's own use and defense of *bian* 辯 against his rivals. It does not criticize Yang Zhu or Mozi for their pernicious perspectives but rather for their useless skills: the *Zhuangzi* suggests that they lost their inborn nature, while the *Han Feizi* thinks that their skills do not contribute to the prosperity of the state. Drawing on the Yang-Mo discourses in *Zhuangzi* and *Han Feizi*, Chang offers an alternative methodological perspective on these non-Mencian Yang-Mo descriptions in early texts. He considers them a product of a dynamic development in a highly open and fluid textual culture rather than, as is usually assumed, the expression of a dominant and stable Mencian depiction of Yang and Mo.

Erica Brindley's chapter tries to identify the type of hedonism that can be attributed to the "Yang Zhu" chapter of the *Liezi* and the book as a whole: it is not just the enjoyment of immediate physical pleasures but rather a deeper understanding of what enhances authentic pleasure in life. Her analysis suggests that simple pleasures of immediate and physical joys cannot fully encapsulate the hedonism and conception of pleasure in the "Yang Zhu" chapter. Its conception of pleasure should be understood within the web constituted by the concepts of nature, destiny, joy, life, freedom, possession, reputation, and so on. By focusing on the themes of "life over death," "reality over pretense or reputation," "internal, not external," and "freedom," she argues that the philosophical orientation of Yang Zhu's hedonism echoes simple or popular hedonism in its advocacy of indulgence in sensual pleasures, but it does not always prioritize sensory pleasure as the ultimate life goal. The pursuit of the most authentic and unadulterated forms of enjoyment of life points to hedonism in a deeper philosophical sense. The *Liezi*'s Yang Zhu figure in general expresses an appreciation of vitality and freedom in each living moment and considers that sort of joy to be the highest good in life.

The second part covers the period from the Tang (618–907) to the Ming (1368–1644) dynasty. It also contains three chapters, two of which are by John Makeham and one by Esther Klein. They represent two ends of a spectrum between serious speculation and literary ploys: at one end, Makeham's chapters show Yang Zhu's role in the gradual construction of the *daotong* 道統 (succession of the Way) lineage; at the other end, Klein's contribution on the iconoclast Li Zhi 李贄 (1527–1602) portrays a more surprising, personal, and ambiguous treatment of Yang Zhu.

Makeham's first chapter depicts the gradual emergence of a proto-*daotong* discourse preceding Zhu Xi's 朱熹 (1130–1200) construction of his own orthodoxy. In this discourse the negative image of Yang Zhu plays a notable role. Makeham identifies and examines key themes that emerged in the course of four centuries, across a broad range of literary genres including letters, reading notes, essays, prefaces, postfaces, tomb inscriptions, epitaphs, laudations, and commentaries written by important intellectuals of the period, such as Han Yu 韓愈 (768–824), some proponents of *guwen* 古文 (ancient-style learning), and the Cheng brothers (Cheng Hao 程顥 [1032–1085] and Cheng Yi 程頤 [1033–1107]). Yang Zhu was not a central figure in the process of *daotong* construction at that time, but his appearances in the Confucian discourses that appropriated the Mencian rhetoric indicate certain key steps in the *daotong* construction. Han Yu, for example, portrayed the Daoists and Buddhists as latter-day Yangists and Mohists and hence more dangerous than the erstwhile Warring States masters Yang and Mo. Later advocates of *guwen* adopted the same rhetorical strategy, while the Cheng brothers and their disciples eventually removed Han Yu himself from the lineage of orthodox transmission.

Makeham's second chapter goes on to explore the role that Zhu Xi accorded to Yang Zhu in his notion of *daotong*. It shows how Zhu's appropriation of the negative image of Yang and Mo was further developed in his critiques of Daoism and, even more so, of Buddhism. Makeham's analysis casts light on the importance of this critical dimension of Zhu Xi's project. By promoting and excluding certain figures, Zhu Xi presented himself as the legitimate heir to the succession of the true Way. As Makeham's previous chapter has illustrated, the Cheng brothers' criticisms of Yang Zhu and Mozi elaborated on the idea that a small diversion could develop disastrous consequences. In this respect, the brothers held that both Yang Zhu and Mozi came from the Confucians, initially only differed slightly from Mencius but nevertheless had led to terrible heresies under their followers. Zhu Xi, however, refuted this judgment. He argued that Yang Zhu's teaching was derived from Laozi's and that

Buddhism was an even more deviant version of extreme Yangism and Mohism. For Zhu Xi, it was through Buddhism that Yang and Mo had been perpetuated. By re-narrating the intellectual affiliation of Yang Zhu and Mozi, Zhu Xi formulated his particular account of *daotong*, which identified Daoism and Buddhism not only as "the other" but also as the latter-day incarnation of Yang and Mo. He moreover suggested that Ouyang Xiu 歐陽修 (1007–1072), Wang Anshi 王安石 (1021–1086), and Su Shi 蘇軾 (1037–1101) all lost the Way of Confucius.

Klein's chapter shows how surprisingly seldom the notorious iconoclast and individualist Li Zhi referred to Yang Zhu. When he did, the allusions were unclear and therefore are all the more alluring and pregnant with possible interpretations. As a notorious individualist or egoist, Li might strike many scholars as "a Yang Zhu type": he resigned from office to pursue intellectual pleasures, refused to respect social norms, and advocated perspectives that certainly could be labeled as "for oneself." In spite of superficial similarities, however, Li Zhi's references to Yang Zhu tend to be negative. An intriguing example is found in his "Self-Evaluation" 自贊, one of Li's best-known pieces of work. By contextualizing the piece within Li Zhi's life experiences and the intellectual traditions that might have shaped his thought, Klein explores potential readings of the "Self-Evaluation" and analyzes the significance of its Yang Zhu references. Her close analysis suggests that Li Zhi's disapproval of Yang Zhu was meant to signal that he was *not* acting merely for himself; instead, he viewed himself as a man who contributed to the realm.

The third and last part of this volume, covering from the Qing (1644–1911) into the twentieth century, contains four chapters that focus on the emergence and changing visions on Yang Zhu as a philosopher. The first chapter is by Masayuki Sato on the scholarship related to Yang Zhu in Japan during the Meiji period (1868–1912). The Japanese scholarship constructed some crucial stepping-stones for Yang's entrance into the world of philosophers. Xiaowei Wang's analysis of Liang Qichao's 梁啟超 (1873–1929) deployment of Yang Zhu describes a second important step from Japan to China. Then follows Diana (Xiaoqing) Lin's description of five stages in Feng Youlan's evolving views of Yang Zhu. Feng Cao's chapter concludes the volume by presenting three important scholars' contributions to Yang Zhu study: Hu Shi 胡適 (1891–1962), Meng Wentong 蒙文通 (1894–1968), and Guan Feng.

Sato's chapter is an overview of the discourse on Yang Zhu produced in the last decades of the Meiji period. It illustrates how young intellectuals of the time began to interpret and elaborate on the thought of Yang Zhu, often called "Master Yang" (Yōshi 楊子), in the scholarly framework of "philosophy." The discipline of "Chinese philosophy" or "Eastern Philosophy" was institutionalized in the 1880s at Tokyo University. Sato analyzes lecture transcripts of the courses delivered in the philosophy department, notes taken by students, and subsequent articles and monographs on Chinese or Eastern philosophy. Yang Zhu played a significant role in those writings even though he had been a marginal figure throughout Chinese history. Not only was Yang Zhu often mentioned among other well-known Warring States thinkers, he also enjoyed much philosophical attention. He appeared in almost every history of Chinese philosophy written in Japanese. Being studied under the disciplinary category of philosophy, he was even treated by some scholars as the founder of a "Yang Zhu school," which was associated with distinctive philosophical perspectives.

In China, pre-Republican portrayals of Yang Zhu were generally negative. This changed in the twentieth century, and Liang Qichao was one of the important Chinese intellectuals contributing to this change. Inspired by Japanese intellectuals, in 1902 Liang became the first Chinese scholar to call Yang Zhu a philosopher (*zhexuejia* 哲學家). He was also the first Chinese intellectual to depict Yang Zhu as an advocate of the notion of "rights." This depiction led to the portrayal of Yang Zhu as an individualist in the May Fourth period. While some scholars have noted Liang's contribution to the shift from a negative to a positive evaluation of Yang Zhu, little attention has thus far been paid to the specific complexities of Liang's new portrayal of Yang Zhu in light of his sociopolitical agenda. Xiaowei Wang's contribution not only traces the various steps of Liang's refiguration of Yang Zhu between 1896 and 1904 but also brings out the wavering and tensions between Yang's supposed pernicious world weariness and his laudable promotion of rights.

Next, Diana Lin outlines five stages of Feng Youlan's assessments of Yang Zhu, from the 1920s to the 1980s. Similar to Liang Qichao, Feng's descriptions and evaluations of Yang Zhu vary in accordance with the changing conditions of his personal experiences and the sociopolitical situation. Yang Zhu does not play a significant role in the first stage and is nonjudgmentally described as a hedonist in Feng's 1923 PhD dissertation. The second stage depicts Yang Zhu as an egoist, whose idea of self-preservation, according to Feng's 1931 *History of Chinese Philosophy*, proposes a balanced life approach for mankind to adopt. It also constructs an extensive genealogy of Daoism, assigning Yang Zhu the role of Daoist founder associated with a wide range of primary texts. During wartime in the 1940s, Feng's assessment of Yang Zhu entered the third stage. He criticized Yang's philosophy for being selfish and discouraging individuals from contributing to the nation. The fourth stage was Marxist: Feng applied the idea of the declining slave-owning class in portraying Yang Zhu. The last stage, as presented in Feng's *New History of Chinese Philosophy*, is marked by harsher criticism of Yang Zhu. Echoing the first stage, it depicts him as a pernicious hedonist. After going through experiences related to the Gang of Four during the last years of the Cultural Revolution, Feng had come to consider Yang Zhu's hedonism reprehensible. Lin's analysis of Feng's five stages shows that despite shifts in his views, Feng's concern throughout remained centered on the relationship between individual and society.

The last chapter, by Feng Cao, argues that Hu Shi, Meng Wentong, and Guan Feng represent three different directions in the study of Yang Zhu. While Hu showcased him as a model of modernity with imported notions of "individualism" and "self-awareness," Meng drew on a wide variety of early sources and figures to reconstruct a large network of lineages surrounding him, and Guan used Marxist class analysis to shape him into a representative of the small craftsmen such as Mozi. Guan has also exerted influence upon the Western scholarship through A. C. Graham's research on Yangism. Cao's analysis of the three scholars' Yang Zhu research shows not only their different interpretations or characterizations of Yang Zhu's "philosophy" but also the different approaches they envisaged to tackle the intellectual and social situations they were facing. For Hu Shi, the essential aspect of modernity was the pursuit of independent thought and the individual's status, which echoes the ethos of the May Fourth movement. Guan Feng was one of the leading scholars who applied Marxism to the study of Yang Zhu. As for Meng Wentong, according to Cao, his approach was an attempt to appropriate positivism to conduct scientific research on Chinese philosophy. Such case studies illuminate how modern scholars, motivated by their pursuit of modernity or ideological integrity, deployed and reshaped the philosopher Yang Zhu.

2. To Be or to Become: That Is the Question

The eleven contributions to this volume present a wealth of information. However, they do not add up to a complete and reliable picture of who the historical Yang Zhu was and what he really thought. In line with Roger Ames's insistence, inspired by the American pragmatist John Dewey (1859–1952),[15] on "becoming" rather than "being," the current volume tries to establish Yang Zhu's successive *becomings*, rather than aiming at a consensus on who he might have *been*. This approach of unfolding Yang's process of "becoming" is not only provoked by the remarkable dearth of information about the original figure but also by the potential we see in it for the study of early masters in general. Those masters who have books named after them—Mozi, Laozi 老子, Mencius, Xunzi 荀子, Guanzi 管子, Han Feizi, and so on—or who are closely associated with one, as Confucius is with the *Lunyu* 論語, also underwent an ongoing process of becoming during the vicissitudes of Chinese history. Yang Zhu's extreme case therefore is highly illuminating and instructive in terms of forming an approach to the uncertainties in the field of Chinese philosophy. Our ignorance about the early masters is inevitable, but it has a positive side: it is the source of endless potential for new portrayals. Yang Zhu represents this potential more than well-attested masters. We elaborate on this predicament in three ways.

First, "being" and "becoming" are not mutually exclusive but rather intricately related. We have hardly any textual testimony about who Yang Zhu really was, let alone an autobiography (and even that would have been merely one of the portrayals, albeit a privileged one). Yet there is some point in trying to identify the oldest surviving portrayal of who he was. Mark Cskiszentmiahlyi's effort with Confucius is an example of such attempt. His identification of the historical figure behind the wealth of later portrayals is short, tentative, and relies on those portions of the *Lunyu* that he considers old and apparently not influenced by Han ideology.[16] We have no reason to deny the historical existence of Yang Zhu, though the scarcity of textual support means that any conclusion about Yang Zhu must be even more limited and tentative. We offer two conjectures. Considering the chronology of the portrayals, we have more reasons to believe that Yang Zhu was among the earliest masters who challenged the status quo with argumentation (*bian*) than to believe that he invented the notion of individual rights or represented the class of slave owners. His resort to argumentation is not only attested in the oldest sources uninfluenced by later or foreign ideologies, but even in different and seemingly unrelated ones: the *Mencius* as well as the *Zhuangzi-Han Feizi* portrayal discussed by Yao-cheng Chang. Second, since various early sources identify Yang Zhu with ideas concerning "oneself" (我/己) and "body" (身) or "life" (生), we can suppose that he argued for physical integrity or health against social duties, participation in warfare, or political aggrandizement. His ideas may have influenced later authors, stretching from those recorded in some *Lüshi chunqiu* chapters to the biography of Mao Zedong's personal doctor.[17] The fact that his name was not mentioned by them does not necessarily deny his possible influence. But due to the scarceness of evidence, both characteristics can only tentatively be associated with the historical figure Yang Zhu.

Our second point relates to "being" or Yang Zhu as a historical figure: namely, who he really was. While it is natural that scholars who quote or refer to Yang Zhu think of the person who lived in the past (slightly before Mencius), we are also aware of the fact that any portrayal of this person is to some extent a construction. The supposed historical figure differs in character and importance depending on the portrayal to which it belongs. The notion of a historical Yang Zhu may have had some relevance for all those who referred to him, but it might not have been a crucial matter for most premodern scholars. It is, for example, hard to identify the real opponent behind Mencius's polemic statements,[18] and the Zhuangzian-Han Feizian cluster does not seem particularly interested in the real Yang Zhu. Nor does the oft-quoted Yang-Mo trope, which uses Mencius's statement as a rhetorical tool to label Confucian opponents—Daoists, Buddhists, Christians, or even other Confucians. Likewise, Kang Youwei's presentation of Yang Zhu, along with other masters, basically served to uncover the real Confucius rather than the real Yang Zhu. Later portrayals of Yang Zhu in the context of China's nation building, the May Fourth movement, or the advocacy of Marxist ideology, were also not all primarily driven by curiosity about the historical figure. Interest in the textual basis for reconstructing the *Liezi*, and hence also in Yang Zhu, initially emerged among textual scholars, especially in the Qing dynasty. Of the twenty-four opinions on this matter that Yang Bojun 楊伯峻 (1909–1992) collected in his *Liezi* edition, only six predate the Qing. The dominant view among these scholars, including Yang Bojun himself, was that the *Liezi*—and also the "Yang Zhu" chapter—was at the earliest a Wei-Jin text.[19] It is only with the emergence of Yang Zhu as a philosopher that this interest also turned into some sort of obsession: Who was this person? When and where did he live? And most of all: Is the *Liezi* a reliable source for reconstructing Yang Zhu's thought? The urge to identify one individual personality behind a reliable set of texts therefore seems to be part of the modern academic philosophical endeavor. In China as well as in the West, this paradigm has come to dominate much of Yang Zhu research. Almost every academic discussion of Yang Zhu is nowadays steered toward these questions.[20] Because of its current dominance and despite its relatively recent date, the emergence of and variations in the philosophical portrayal have received more attention in this volume (four chapters for one century) than the preimperial and imperial ones (seven chapters for more than twenty centuries). Our study of Yang Zhu is therefore also an attempt to historically situate the philosophical portrayal of early Chinese masters in general.

The third and final reflection about Chinese masters through the study of Yang Zhu concerns their "becoming." While our approach may not offer the clearest possible presentation of an ancient philosopher's thought, we gain a variety of other insights. We could speculate on the textual passages that are selected or overlooked in the various portrayals. Anecdotes about Yang Zhu "lamenting at a crossroads" (*Xunzi*, *Huainanzi*, *Lunheng*) or "lodging in the inn" (*Zhuangzi*, *Han Feizi*), for instance, have thus far received little attention. Another interesting issue is how the various portrayals relate to each other, for example, how Song and Ming scholars enhanced the Mencian trope or how Kang Youwei revived early textual evidence. Some contributions also show how political or intellectual contexts fed into the evolving portrayals of Yang Zhu, going from his negative role in the *daotong* construction to a more diverse one in nation-building projects and perceived class struggles. The most striking is the question about the many other possible Yang Zhu portrayals that can be retrieved and studied. One could, for example, trace the consecutive opponents attacked through the framework of Yang-Mo, going from Daoists and Buddhists to Christians and even rival Confucians. How to understand the Song-Ming association of Yang Zhu with *yi* 義 or with an extreme that guides us away from the perfect "middle"? What were the growing pains of the Daoist lineage into which Yang Zhu was increasingly but differently incorporated? And what degree of variety did the Marxist views allow, positioning Yang Zhu in the declining slave owners' class (Feng Youlan) or the rising class of small craftsmen (Guan Feng)? A wealth of Chinese intellectuals are discussed in relation to Yang Zhu.[21] Each of them could be singled out and made the focus of one's research, as Esther Klein shows with Li Zhi. Through her analysis of Li's very sporadic and unclear references to Yang Zhu, we get to know Li Zhi much better than Yang Zhu. Narrowing the focus thus allows one to broaden the scope, especially with a figure such as Yang Zhu who always seems to have functioned as a "secondary figure," ceding the main stage to others.[22] As a result, the information contained in this book will not satisfy one's hunger for the "authentic" Yang Zhu but hopefully will whet the appetite for more knowledge about Chinese intellectual history and the construction of philosophy in it.

These three characteristics of Yang Zhu research presented in terms of "being" and "becoming" do not concern only him but the whole field of early Chinese masters. They keep our interest lively and the conversation going. Our gratitude goes to our interlocutors: the authors of this volume, the participants of the workshop organized at the University of Leuven in the spring of 2019, and the various reviewers of our work: Roger Ames, Attilio Andreini, Steve Angle, Erica Brindley, Feng Cao, Yaocheng Chang, Chen Shaoming, Paul Goldin, Hao Sutong, Esther Klein, Li Lanfen, Diana Lin, Liu Gusheng, Philippe Major, John Makeham, Yuri Pines, Thomas Radice, Masayuki Sato, Nicolas Standaert, Paul van Els, Xiaowei Wang, Wu Xiaoxin, Yves Vendé, and the two anonymous reviewers of this volume. We also thank Flanders Research Foundation for their support,[23] Bobby Carleo for his painstaking proofreading of the whole manuscript, and the staff of SUNY press. Without their precious contribution and generous support, this volume would not have been possible.

This volume was conceived before the worldwide pandemic hit, and manifestations of climate change struck hard around the globe. The authors revised their contributions in the years 2020 and 2021, as they were confronted head on with these disasters. With nature fighting back, humankind slowly became aware of the often implicit choices that had hitherto shaped our lifestyles. How much of the climate must be sacrificed before some of those choices are reconsidered? These are the types of questions that are associated with Yang Zhu: What are the priorities in life? How much value is attributed to good health? What are we willing to sacrifice in return? What is worth fighting for? Is our body given a voice in crucial decisions? Yang Zhu's inspiration has become increasingly relevant, regardless of the historical figure and the coherence of his original insights. For us he is the sum of all past and present Yang Zhu figures. We hope that future generations will continue creating powerful portrayals of him that contribute to a world in which we can and want to live.

Notes

1. Lu Xun 魯迅, *Collected Works of Lu Xun* 魯迅全集, 18 vols. (Beijing: Renmin wenxue chubanshe, 2005) 3:538.

2. See, e.g., Hu Shi 胡適, *Zhongguo zhexueshi dagang* 中國哲學史大綱 [*Outline of the History of Chinese Philosophy*] (Beijing: Dongfang chubanshe, 1995 [1919]), 155–62; Feng Youlan 馮友蘭, *Zhongguo zhexue shi: Juan yi* 中国哲学史: 卷一 (*A History of Chinese Philosophy, vol. 1*) (Beijing: Zhonghua, 2015 [1931]), 147–56; Benjamin Schwartz, *The World of Thought in Ancient China* (Cambridge, MA: Harvard University Press, 1985), 175–79; A. C. Graham, *Disputers of the Tao: Philosophical Argument in Ancient China* (Chicago and La Salle, IL: Open Court, 1989), 53–64; Chad Hansen, *A Daoist Theory of Chinese Thought: A Philosophical Interpretation* (New York: Oxford University Press, 1992), 154–57, 162; Bryan Van Norden, *Virtue Ethics and Consequentialism in Early Chinese Philosophy* (New York: Cambridge University Press, 2007), 200–11.

3. Compared to general overviews of Chinese philosophy, Yang Zhu's role is more prominent in studies of the Chinese notion of individualism. See, e.g., Donald Munro, ed., *Individualism and Holism: Studies in Confucian and Taoist Values* (Ann Arbor: University of Michigan Press, 1985); Erica Brindley, *Individualism in Early China: Human Agency and the Self in Thought and Politics* (Honolulu: University of Hawai'i Press, 2010).

4. Alfred Forke, trans., *Yang Chu's Garden of Pleasure*, with introduction by Hugh Cranmer-Byng (London: Murray, 1912). A later but undated work (postdating WWII) was by the Dutch poet and China aficionado, Jef Last, *Het ware boek der volkomen leegte. Bloemlezing uit de geschriften van Liéh Tze en Yang Tsjoe* (Deventer: Kluwer). See also Aloysisus Chang, *A Comparative Study of Yang Chu and the Chapter on Yang Chu* (New York: St. John's University Press, 1969).

5. John Emerson, "Yang Chu's Discovery of the Body," *Philosophy East and West* 46, no. 4 (1996): 533–66.

6. Attilio Andreini, *Il pensiero di Yang Zhu (IV secolo a.C.) attraverso un esame delle fonti cinesi classiche* (Trieste: Edizione università di Trieste, 2000).

7. Ranie Villaver, "Does Guiji Mean Egoism?: Yang Zhu's Conception of Self," *Asian Philosophy* 25, no. 2 (2015): 216–23. His doctoral dissertation was also dedicated to Yang Zhu: Ranie Villaver, "Zhuangzi's Scepticism in Light of Yangist Ideas" (PhD diss., University of New South Wales, 2012).

8. He Aiguo 何愛國, *Xiandaixing de bentu huixiang: Jindai Yang Mo sichao yanjiu* [Local echoes of modernity: A study on the modern thought trends of Yang Zhu and Mozi] (Guangzhou: Shijie tushu chuban Guangdong, 2015). He has also dedicated several articles to Yang Zhu.

9. In the summer of 2017, Tsinghua and Wuhan Universities co-organized a workshop titled "The Value of Life and Respect for Humans: Academic

Forum on Yang Zhu's Human Centered Thought" 生命的价值和人的尊严：杨朱的人本主义学术论坛.

10. Discussion of early Japanese and Chinese scholarship related to Yang Zhu is contained in the current volume as well as in a recent issue of the journal *Contemporary Chinese Thought* dedicated to him. See Xiaowei Wang and Carine Defoort, eds., "How Yang Zhu Became a Philosopher: A Selection of Yang Zhu Scholarship in the PRC," *Contemporary Chinese Thought* 50, no. 3–4 (2019).

11. Summarized in Graham, *Disputers of the Tao*, 55, 60. See also A. C. Graham, "The Right to Selfishness: Yangism, Later Mohism, Chuang Tzu," in Munro, *Individualism and Holism*, 73–84, esp. 73–75. For more on Feng Youlan, see chapter 10 by Diana Lin; for Guan Feng, see chapter 11 by Feng Cao.

12. A. C. Graham, *Later Mohist Logic, Ethics, and Science* (Hong Kong: Chinese University Press, 1978), 16.

13. Graham, *Disputers of the Tao*, 59.

14. See, e.g., Van Norden, *Virtue Ethics and Consequentialism*, 200–11; and Karyn Lai, *An Introduction to Chinese Philosophy* (Cambridge: Cambridge University Press, 2008), 46–47.

15. See Roger T. Ames, "Reconstructing A. C. Graham's Reading of *Mencius* on *xing* 性: A Coda to 'The Background of the Mencian Theory of Human Nature' (1967)," in *Having a Word with Angus Graham: At Twenty-Five Years into His Immortality*, ed. Carine Defoort and Roger T. Ames (Albany: State University of New York Press, 2018), 185–213.

16. Mark Csikszentmihalyi, "Confucius," in *The Rivers of Paradise: Moses, Buddha, Confucius, Jesus, and Muhammad as Religious Founders*, ed. David Noel Freedman and Michael James McClymond (Grand Rapids, MI: Eerdmans, 2001), 233–308. The suggestions about the possibly historical Confucius are on 265–73.

17. Mao's doctor Li Zhisui (1919–1995) is one of the many testimonies of what some scholars might want to identify as Yangist priorities and cautions. See Li Zhisui, *The Private Life of Chairman Mao: The Memoirs of Mao's Personal Physician* (New York: Random House, 1994).

18. See Carine Defoort, "Unfounded and Unfollowed: Mencius' Portrayal of Yang Zhu and Mo Di," In Defoort and Ames, *Having a Word with Angus Graham*, 165–84.

19. Yang Bojun 杨伯峻, *Liezi jishi* 列子集釋 [Collected explanations of the *Liezi*] (Beijing: Zhonghua, 1996 [1979]). These views on the *Liezi*'s authenticity were collected in the third appendix (pp. 287–348), which was first published as an article in 1956. It was later included in the book in 1957 and revised in 1978. Linguistic features and the absence of citations in extant pre-Qin sources convinced Yang Bojun that the *Liezi* did not even contain many (if any) pre-Qin fragments (348).

20. For China see, e.g., Liu Gusheng and Li Haijie, "The Thought of Yang Zhu in the History of Laozi's Thought: Along with a Discussion of the

Authenticity of the *Liezi*," *Contemporary Chinese Thought* 51, no. 3–4 (2019): 75–91. For the West, see A. C. Graham presented above.

21. Other figures whose Yang Zhu portrayal is worth studying are Yu Xin 庾信 (513–581), Han Yu 韓愈 (768–824), Li Ao 李翺 (772–841), Lu Zhongxuan 盧重玄 (8th c.), Lu Xisheng 陸希聲 (?–895), Sun Fu 孫復 (992–1057), Shi Jie 石介 (1005–1045), Du Mo 杜默 (1019–1085), Wang Anshi 王安石 (1021–1086), Chen Jingyuan 陳景元 (1025–1094), Feng Xie 馮澥 (1060–1140), Shi Yaobi 史堯弼 (1118–1157), Lu Jiuyuan 陸九淵 (1139–1193), Lin Xiyi 林希逸 (1193–1271), Chen Zhensun 陳振孫 (1179–1262), Wu Cheng 吳澄 (1249–1333), Zhu Dezhi 朱得之 (16th c.), Wu Yu 吳虞 (1872–1949), Gu Shi 顧實 (1878–1956), Yan Fu 嚴復 (1854–1921), Jiang Weiqiao 蔣維喬 (1873–1958), Tang Yue 唐鉞 (1891–1987), Bi Yongnian 畢永年 (1869–1902), Chen Li 陳澧 (1810–1882), Gao Xu 高旭 (1877–1925), Cai Yuanpei 蔡元培 (1868–1940), Zhang Zhidong 張之洞 (1837–1909), Yan Fu 嚴復 (1854–1921), Chen Sanli 陳三立 (1853–1937), Guo Moruo 郭沫若 (1892–1978), Yang Daying 楊大膺 (1903–1977), Chen Cisheng 陳此生 (1900–1983), Gu Jiegang 顧頡剛 (1893–1980), Tao Xisheng 陶希聖 (1899–1988), Xiong Meng 熊夢 (1902–1983), Lü Simian 呂思勉 (1884–1957), Du Guoxiang 杜國庠 (1889–1961), Hou Wailu 侯外廬 (1903–1987), Zhao Jibin 趙紀彬 (1905–1982), Cao Bohan 曹伯韓 (1897–1959), Ji Wenfu 嵇文甫 (1895–1963), etc. Most of these figures are mentioned in the current volume and in *Contemporary Chinese Thought* 51, no. 3–4 (2019).

22. Chen Shaoming, "A Secondary Figure in the 'World of Classics': An Analysis of Yang Zhu's Image," *Contemporary Chinese Thought* 51, no. 3–4 (2019): 92–103.

23. The FWO project G060817N: "Mozi and Yang Zhu from Heretics to Philosophers: Caught in Another Web? The Genealogy of 'Chinese Philosophy' in Three Major Steps."

Chapter 1

Five Pre-Republican Portrayals of Yang Zhu

CARINE DEFOORT

Introduction

In the world of Chinese philosophy, Yang Zhu 楊朱 figures as the founder of Yangism or the Yangist school (*Yang Zhu xuepai* 楊朱學派) and the leader of those who would never sacrifice their physical integrity, least of all for a ruler or a state.[1] Since the large-scale establishment of universities in China roughly one century ago, he has been discussed in academic circles as a proto-Daoist, Daoist, hedonist, individualist, egoist, Epicurean, hermitist, anarchist, pessimist, fatalist, naturalist, sophist, socialist, liberal, democrat, nationalist, humanist, atheist, populist, and materialist.[2] This variety of labels attests to a shared set of expectations, namely that Yang Zhu's thought is consistent and that it can be reconstructed on the basis of early sources. However, due to a striking dearth of textual evidence, we only have a few scraps of information. In the *Mencius* 孟子 and some other early texts, he has been associated with such expressions as "for oneself" (為我) and "honoring the self" (貴己).[3] These scraps have been variously kneaded into coherent portrayals of the historical figure that rescue his authentic ideas from the vicious misrepresentations of opponents and have been enhanced with sources that contain no reference to Yang Zhu. All this has been supported by textual research attesting to the early dates and authenticity of reliable texts for determining Yang Zhu's thought system.[4]

This modern portrayal has become so dominant that we tend to overlook its relatively recent emergence and historical contingency. Rather than the portrayal itself, its pre-Republican layered genealogy is the subject of this chapter.[5] I distinguish five portrayals emerging in chronological order: Yang Zhu as a rival in argumentation (late Zhou), a heretic (Han), a prominent figure (Wei Jin), a master with deficient thoughts (Song), and a political reformer (late Qing). Portions of preceding portrayals contributed to later stages and got entangled with newly emerging ones. By thus disentangling premodern portrayals of Yang Zhu we can highlight the different fragments that constitute the current supposedly coherent portrayal of this early thinker.[6] The clustering of the previous portrayals in twentieth-century academia has led to a relatively flat figure. It is as if one first takes away all the different tastes from a rich meal by brewing them into one stew, in this case of the Western philosophical cuisine. But how was Yang Zhu savored before being brought to taste with such foreign herbs? Which previous ingredients have been relinquished or preserved? How can older portrayals be revived? And how might he taste in the future when current intellectual constellations are being reshuffled again?

The historical approach to the figure of Yang Zhu is not new. Previous portrayals have been identified as testimonies of their own times rather than of the original thinker who lived in the Warring States era. The Fudan historian and Yang Zhu scholar He Aiguo, for instance, has argued that the portrayal of Yang Zhu in the Republican period substantially differed from the real pre-Qin figure and basically responded to early twentieth-century needs. But he is convinced that during the pre-Qin period a clearly identifiable and authentic Yang Zhu lineage thrived and was ultimately absorbed by Daoism after the Han dynasty.[7] Li Yucheng also sees evidence of a pre-Qin historical figure but argues that already after the Han, "most Yang Zhu portrayals were created on the basis of needs of the times."[8] This chapter takes the argument one step further by tracing all Yang Zhu portrayals as products of their own times, even in pre-Qin times. This does not entail any statement about the presumably historical figure, which I consider beyond the scope of this research and also, I believe, beyond our capacity to rediscover. This could, to some extent, be said about any master or philosopher; however, with a figure who has left hardly any written trace, the historicity of his portrayals is all the more striking. The dearth of textual evidence therefore makes Yang Zhu a fascinating case study of intellectual history and its layered construction of important figures. Unraveling these layers adds more to the figure of Yang Zhu than his exclusive evaluation in terms of philosophical stances.

1. Yang Zhu as a Disputer

If we collect the scraps of evidence that probably date from the Warring States era (475–221)—allowing for a degree of uncertainty in dating matters—the most striking Yang Zhu portrayal is that of an opponent or rival. The fact *that* Yang Zhu disagreed is better attested than *what* he argued for. Roughly simultaneously, the defense of self-preservation and resistance to any type of physical or personal sacrifice—the core of the current philosophical portrayal—became increasingly associated with him.

First, Yang as a rival is best known from the book *Mencius*, in which he appears three times. The shortest of these passages begins as follows:

> When deserting Mo, they invariably turn to Yang; when deserting Yang, they invariably turn to the Ru.
>
> 逃墨必歸於楊; 逃楊必歸於儒

This statement suggests that the followers of Mo, Yang, and the Ru were more or less identified as groups that one could join or desert. It does not say how they were organized nor what was at stake, but adherents were clearly wanted. What follows is probably a piece of advice to his fellow Ru:

> When they turn to [us], then we simply accept them
>
> 歸斯受之而已矣

Mencius criticizes the argumentative strategies used by some Ru:

> Those who nowadays argue with Yang and Mo, are like chasing strayed pigs: having led them into the pigsty, they then also tie them up.
>
> 今之與楊墨辯者如追放豚: 既入其苙, 又從而招之 (7B26)[9]

Short and unconnected as it stands, like every passage in book 7, this fragment leaves many questions open. While the statement may reliably express the view of Mencius or of those who attributed it to him, we do not know how representative it was in his time. Its content is even less clear: What sort of people or opinions were seen as turning from Mo to Yang, and then to Ru? Did Mencius insist on this specific sequence of changing allegiances, or did he merely portray a situation of continuous switches in various directions? What precisely did "turn to" mean? What was at stake? How conscious were these people of their changing alliance? Did they actively choose a new label, or was it attributed to them by others? These are some of the questions that can be asked about the alliance with Yang discussed in this passage.

The passage does contain a clue that resonates in other early mentions of Yang Zhu, namely the use of argumentation or debate (*bian* 辯). Mencius seems to agree with the policy of accepting adherents into the "pigsty" of Confucianism, but he objects to keeping them there with arguments. We know from another *Mencius* passage that he was struggling with this issue and that he claimed to use *bian* only as a last resort. When a disciple confronted him with his reputation of being fond of arguing, Mencius responded:

> The statements of Yang Zhu and Mo Di fill the world. All statements in the world either turn to Yang or to Mo. . . . If the ways of Yang and Mo do not stop, Confucius' Way will not be visible. This means that wrong theories mislead the people and totally block humaneness and righteousness. When this happens, beasts are led to eat people, and people will end up eating each other. I fear this. . . . Why would I be fond of arguing? I simply have no choice. One who is able to stop Yang and Mo with words is the follower of the sages.
>
> 楊朱墨翟之言盈天下. 天下之言不歸楊, 則歸墨. . . . 楊墨之道不息, 孔子之道不著. 是邪說誣民, 充塞仁義也. 仁義充塞, 則率獸食人, 人將相食. 吾為此懼 . . . 豈好辯哉? 予不得已也. 能言距楊墨者, 聖人之徒也. (3B9)

Other early sources also present Yang as one among the rivals associated with this contested notion of *bian*. This portrayal occurs in the *Han Feizi* ("Eight Theories" 八說) and the *Zhuangzi*, where Yang and Mo are criticized as debaters ("Ghostless Xu" 徐無鬼) whose mouths should be shut with clamps ("Ransacking Coffers" 胠篋) and who parade with useless debates on hard and white, same and different, or right and wrong ("Webbed Toes" 駢拇).[10] What Yang Zhu argued for seems unclear or irrelevant. Along with others, he was criticized more for his self-confident reliance on argumentation than for the specific views he defended.

A second characteristic of Yang Zhu's oldest portrayal is his conviction. Two *Mencius* passages identify him with the motto "for oneself" (*wei wo* 為我), opposed to Mozi's promotion of "inclusive care" (*jian ai* 兼愛). In the dialogue partly quoted above, Mencius accuses them of, respectively, not respecting their lord (*wu jun* 無君) or father (*wu fu* 無父), which is something for "birds and beasts" (是禽獸也), resulting in a terrifying dehumanization and a risk of cannibalism (3B9). In the other passage, Mencius claims that if Yang Zhu "could have benefited the world by pulling out one hair, he would not have done it" (拔一毛而利天下, 不為也), while Mozi would have sacrificed all his body hair to benefit the world (7A26).

We can conclude that the three mentions of Yang Zhu in the book *Mencius*, or perhaps in its latest layers,[11] combine two major characteristics of the earliest portrayal, namely *that* he argued and *what* he argued for. He is perceived as a rival promoting ideas that threatened Confucius's Way. The three passages attest to the emergence of rivaling alliances in preimperial China but not quite to an intellectual scene teeming with already full-fledged lineages (*jia* 家), nor to a clear division between Confucian orthodoxy and its opposition. It was the beginning of something that would gain importance over time, namely Yang Zhu's affiliation. Since this has become a core component of the current portrayal, I conclude this first layer with a quick overview of the lineages that were associated with him throughout history up to the twentieth century.

The case of Yang Zhu shows that the existence of "lineages" or "schools" is not an either-or matter but rather a gradual, messy, and hard to reconstruct phenomenon. Some textual evidence suggests that there was no awareness of Yang Zhu fitting into any type of grouping during the last centuries before the beginning of the common era. He is not mentioned even once in chapters that nowadays are often identified as Yangist: for example, in the *Lüshi chunqiu*'s "Taking Life as Basic" 本生, "Valuing the Self" 重己, "Honoring Life" 貴生, "Essential Desires" 情欲, and "Being Attentive to Aims" 審為; nor in the *Zhuangzi*'s "Yielding the Throne" 讓王, "Robber Zhi" 盜跖, "Discourse on Swords" 說劍, and "Old

Fisherman" 漁父.¹² Equally remarkable is his absence from early overviews of the intellectual scene such as the *Xunzi*'s "Against the Twelve Masters" 非十二子 and "Dispelling Blindness" 解蔽, *Han Feizi*'s "Eminent Learnings" 顯學, *Zhuangzi*'s "The World" 天下, *Huainanzi*'s "Overview of the Essentials" 要略, *Shiji*'s "Preface of the Grand Scribe" 太史公自序, and *Hanshu*'s "Treatise on Art and Literature" 藝文志.

But some groupings were gradually emerging, and a certain depiction of Yang valuing himself became incorporated into sets of rivaling views. The *Lüshi chunqiu*, for instance, contains a list of ten personalities with their priorities. Among these figures is Mr. Yang 陽生 honoring the self (貴己) ("No Duality" 不二).¹³ The *Huainanzi* describes an even more elaborate scene in which four masters—Kongzi, Mozi, Yangzi, and Mengzi—promote some values and attack each other. In this Han description of the intellectual past, Master Yang is said to have rejected Mozi's "inclusive care," "elevating the worthy" (尚賢), "supporting ghosts" (右鬼), and "rejecting fate" (非命). He is in turn attacked by Mencius for promoting "keeping one's nature intact" (全性), "preserving the genuine" (保真), and "not allowing things to entangle one's body" (不以物累形) ("Boundless Discourses" 氾論). In another *Huainanzi* chapter, Yang occurs in a list of four figures who all preach just one part of the total solution seen from their particular background ("Activating the Genuine" 俶真). And when Yang Xiong 揚雄 (53 BCE–CE 18) criticizes a list of seven figures, he puts Zhuangzi and Yangzi together as "wild and without rules" (蕩而不法) ("Five Hundred [Years]" 五百).

The trend of associating Yang Zhu with lineages and allies gained momentum after the Han dynasty. The strongest association—and the one that has survived the ages—was with Daoism (道家/流), whether represented by Laozi, Liezi, Zhuangzi, Daoism, pure conversations (*qingtan* 清談), or longevity practices (*xiulian* 修煉). This was clearly the case in the *Liezi*'s "Yang Zhu" chapter, discussed below. The Song dynasty (960–1279) further confirmed the Daoist connection. In a response to the question of why Mencius had not opposed Laozi, who presumably preceded the hardly known Yang Zhu and whose followers were perceived as more threatening, the standard answer was that "Yang Zhu's learning came from Laozi" (楊朱之學出於老子) and that "in refuting Yang Zhu, Mencius actually refuted Zhuangzi and Laozi" (孟子闢楊朱，便是闢莊老了).¹⁴ Other alliances were sometimes suggested, none of which have made it into the currently dominant portrayal. Among them was the association of Mozi with the Daoists and Yang Zhu with the Confucians.[15] Zhu Xi 朱熹 (1130–1200) also put forward an alliance with two types of Buddhism, namely Zen learning (*chan xue* 禪學) and mendicant orders (*xingbushi* 行布施), respectively evolving from Yang Zhu and Mo Di.[16] He moreover rejected Cheng Yi's 程頤 (1033–1107) suggestion that Yang and Mo derived from sublineages within Confucianism, from Zixia 子夏 (Bu Shang 卜商, Shang 商) and Zizhang 子張 (Zhuansun Shi 顓孫師, Shi 師) respectively.[17] Yet another association was of Yang Zhu with Yanzi 顏子 (Yan Yuan/Hui 顏淵/回) living in a narrow alley (居陋巷) versus Mozi with Yu 禹 (and sometimes Hou Ji 后稷) passing his home thrice without entering while laboring for the people of the world. Zhu Xi considered the association of Mozi with the Great Yu partly acceptable but not the comparison of Confucius's beloved disciple with Yang Zhu.[18]

Hence, from the Zhou dynasty onward, Yang Zhu's supposed affiliation was characterized by the fact *that* he argued (his verbal combativeness) as much as what he argued *for* (the actual content of his arguments). His belonging to the Daoist lineage became increasingly complex. Even occasional challenges to a particular affiliation of Yang Zhu were evidence of the urge to locate him in one of the rivaling lineages and to take his stance on being "for oneself" seriously. If his oldest portrayal contains indications of the earliest emergence of the notion of lineages—which, I believe, it does—then argumentation (*bian*) resides at its very core. Apparently for Mencius, recourse to argument and debate was a sensitive matter in need of defense. It may have indicated the bankruptcy of more elevated modes of persuasion such as moral example or education. In later Yang Zhu portrayals *bian* seems to have been a less sensitive issue; in the philosophical sphere it even became a core asset.

2. Yang Zhu as a Heretic

When during the Han dynasty—not before that time[19]—authors began to cite Mencius's portrayal of Yang and Mo, they picked up Yang Zhu's oppositional dimension rather than his ideas. They did not particularly engage in reflection about self-preservation versus political devotion. The combined threat of Yangzi and Mozi became a rhetorical trope used to construe the model of a courageous worthy person versus his dangerous and wicked enemies. Mencius stood for the former, Yang and Mo for the latter. The reluctant but necessary use of *bian* due to the moral urgency of the situation was part of this trope. Content wise, this portrayal was very meager and negative.

The initial building blocks of the trope came from the *Mencius*: with Yang and Mo "totally blocking humaneness and righteousness" (充塞仁義) and "Confucius' Way not being visible" (孔子之道不著), Mencius "simply had no choice" (不得已). The true "follower of the sages" (聖人之徒) had to continue their civilizing mission through an "ability to stop Yang and Mo with words" (能言距楊墨). Hence, he claimed:

> I also wish to correct the hearts of others, end incorrect theories, stop biased behavior, and banish lewd expressions in order to carry on the work of the three sages.
>
> 我亦欲正人心, 息邪說, 距詖行, 放淫辭, 以承三聖.

The three exemplary figures that Mencius singled out for emulation all had restored order in the fashion fitting their age: the legendary Great "Yu repressing the floods" (禹抑洪水), "the Duke of Zhou annexing the Yi and Di [barbarians]" (周公兼夷狄), and "Confucius completing the *Spring and Autumn [Annals]*" (孔子成春秋) (3B9).

As a trope, this portrayal was fixed and enhanced by Yang Xiong, who would later gain an important position in some constructions of the succession of the Way (*daotong* 道統).

> When in antiquity Yang and Mo blocked the road, Mencius spoke up and refuted them, thus opening up [the road]. Since afterwards people have been blocking the road [again], I humbly compare myself with Mencius.
>
> 古者揚墨塞路, 孟子辭而闢之, 廓如也. 後之塞路者有矣, 竊自比於孟子. (*Fayan* 法言, "Our Masters" 吾子)[20]

Some portions of this statement also became part of the often repeated stereotype that Yang and Mo blocked the "road" (路), that Mencius "spoke up and refuted them" (辭而闢之), "thus opening up [the road]" (廓如也),[21] and that he "humbly compared himself with Mencius" (竊自比於孟子). This last line may have been an echo of Confucius's claim that he did not create but only transmitted, "humbly comparing myself to our Lao Peng" (竊比於我老彭) (*Lunyu* 7.1). Even though Yang Xiong was sometimes (halfheartedly) included or excluded in the *daotong*, it is interesting to see that his wording contributed to the trope, even when used by those Neo-Confucians who excluded him from the succession of the Way (e.g., the Cheng brothers).[22]

Thus emerged Yang Zhu's second portrayal, namely as a rhetorical trope, which was initially not exclusively Confucian.[23] Gradually, as a series of scholars claimed their place in the Confucian line of orthodoxy, Mencius and his two rivals increasingly became empty signifiers. The trope gained momentum in the Tang dynasty (916–907), with Han Yu 韓愈 (768–824) as its next architect. In his eyes, Mencius had courageously tried to defend the Way against Yang and Mo, and Yang Xiong had tried to restore it, but then disaster struck. Echoing Mencius's complaints about changing alliances between Mo, Yang, and Ru (7B26), Han stated:

> Those discussing morality, if they did not join Yang, they joined Mo; if not Mo, then Lao; if not Lao then Fo, invariably going from one to the other.
>
> 其言道德仁義者不入于楊則入于墨，不入于墨則入于老，不入于老則入于佛。入于彼必出于此。[24]

The addition of Lao and Fo (sometimes Shi 釋), representing Daoism and Buddhism, respectively, was neither casual nor arbitrary, since "the harm of Shi and Lao exceeded that of Yang and Mo" (釋老之害過於楊墨). For Han Yu, Daoism and Buddhism were the real problem; and he was the savior of his own age.

> I am less worthy than Mencius. He could not save [the Confucian Way] before it went lost. And I now wish to restore it after its destruction. Alas! How poorly did I estimate my force. Now seeing the danger in which I am, nobody can save me from death. But if thanks to me this Way could be more or less transmitted, I would not at all mind to die for it.
>
> 韓愈之賢不及孟子。孟子不能救之於未亡之前。韓愈乃欲全之於已壞之後。嗚呼其亦不量其力。且見其身之危，莫之救以死也。雖然使其道由愈以粗傳，雖滅死，萬萬無恨。[25]

At this stage, the Mencian trope had become the core of an emerging Ru orthodoxy, with new building blocks added by Han Yu, such as "How poorly did I estimate my force!" (其亦不量其力).[26] The empty signifiers were filled on both ends of the trope: on the one side, Han Yu added himself behind Mencius and Yang Xiong in an increasingly clear defense of Confucian orthodoxy. On the other side, he replaced Yang and Mo with worse villains, namely Lao and Fo.

From the Song dynasty onward, we encounter growing variation on both ends of the trope: moral heroes and wicked enemies. New courageous defenders of Confucius's Way were added, often by their disciples. For instance, Ouyang Xiu 歐陽修 (1007–1072) was paired with Han Yu.[27] Zhang Zai 張載 (1020–1077) "simply had no choice but to speak up" (言不得已而云) to refute the "statements of Buddha and Laozi" (浮屠老子之言).[28] The same went for Zhou Dunyi 周敦頤 (1017–1073), Cheng Hao 程顥 (1032–1085), and Cheng Yi, according to Hu Hong 胡宏 (1102–1161).[29] The list of opponents also increased. Lu Jiuyuan 陸九淵 (1139–1193), for instance, gave the label "Yang and Mo" to those opportunistic office seekers who merely repeated Ru classics for the sake of passing the exams.[30] Wang Yangming 王陽明 (1472–1529) "simply had no choice" but to refute "the current theories that venerate Zhu [Xi]" (今日之崇尚朱之說).[31] And so did the critics of Christianity in defense of the indigenous tradition.[32] Their opponents were associated with Yang and Mo, who were increasingly identified as "heretics" (*yiduan* 異端),[33] an equally vague label used to identify enemies.[34]

This variety of new villains was accompanied by the explicit acknowledgment that Yang and Mo were themselves actually no longer the problem. They had been threats in the past but were now courageously and effectively discarded. The real problem at present lay with Daoists, Buddhists, other Confucians, Christians, egoists, and indiscriminate philanthropists. The Cheng brothers, for example, repeatedly pointed out that "harms like those of Yang and Mo no longer exist in the current generation" (如楊墨之害在今世則已無之), and even that "the harm of theories like Daoism is in the end small" (如道家之說其害終小). "Only Buddhist learning" was seen as a threat because "now everybody discusses it, abundantly and overwhelmingly, so that its harm is unlimited" (今則人人談之，瀰漫滔天，其害無涯).[35] The identification of the specific threat was never determined once and for all. Yan Yuan 顏元 (1635–1704), for example, was of the opinion that "while the harm of [Daoist] immortals and Buddhism was worse than Yang and Mo, the disaster of the study of the pattern (*lixue*, a strain of Neo-Confucianism) was more disruptive than [Daoist] immortals and Buddhism" (仙佛之害甚於楊墨, 理學之禍烈於仙佛).³⁶ The Yang-Mo trope had thus become a powerful but empty mechanism to discard any threat in the promotion of one's own views, deployed not only against outsiders but also close opponents, including fellow Confucians.

As a mechanism, the Yang-Mo trope has not survived the introduction of philosophy in China: at least professional academics no longer use to it today to express their moral stance against social threats. But due to the long dominance of Confucianism, its original content, namely the opposition to Yang and Mo, has been so deeply entrenched in the minds of scholars that its influence has lingered. Mencius's negative image of the two opponents may have softened a bit, but its rhetorical form has endured as a frame of thought, even for those modern scholars who have taken up the defense of Mozi and Yang Zhu.³⁷ The opposition of Yang and Mo, on the one hand, and Ru, on the other, has therefore continued to shape most narratives of early Chinese thought. This is understandable since the only statement that the consecutive users of the trope more or less share is their rejection of Yang and Mo. One could therefore deduce that this was a widely shared philosophical view. This deduction is, however, misleading because this shared content carries the least importance. Yang and Mo as villains constitute no more than a common trope, the content of which is sometimes even explicitly played down. What really counts is where these claims differ: who made the statement, against whom, for what reason—in short, who gets to belong to the real succession of the Way.

3. Yang Zhu as a Prominent Figure

While further enhanced in the Song dynasty, the rhetorical trope also began to feed into real reflections about Yang and Mo (see section 4). But before that came a remarkable portrayal that seems somewhat disconnected on both ends: from the preceding rhetorical trope as well as from the following Song reflections. It occurs in the book *Liezi* (ca. 300 CE). Whether written, forged, collected, or edited and commented on by Zhang Zhan 張湛 (d. 360 CE) or his contemporaries, this book in eight chapters gives a surprisingly prominent position to Yang Zhu no less than six centuries after his supposed lifetime.³⁸ Not only does it contain the sole chapter in the entire Chinese corpus explicitly named after him (chapter 7); it also portrays him in other parts of the book (in chapters 2, 4, 6, and 8). While there is a generally recognized breach between the pre-Qin Yang Zhu and the figure in the *Liezi*,[39] the latter is itself quite incoherent. The stories in which he appears within the whole book and even within the chapter named after him convey different and sometimes even conflicting messages.[40] I therefore consider this the portrayal of "a prominent figure," refraining from a more specific label in terms of hedonism, anarchism, Daoism, or egoism.

As a rule, the Yang Zhu figure in the *Liezi* is almost unconnected to the trope in which he is criticized along with Mozi in the previous portrayal. The only exception is, interestingly, the most often quoted statement attributed to him. It concerns Yang's unwillingness to sacrifice a single strand of hair for the whole world. A tentative translation goes as follows:

> Since Bocheng Zigao would not benefit (from?) others (material things?) at the cost of one hair, he renounced his state and retired to plough the fields. Since the Great Yu did not preserve even his own person for his own benefit, he worked to drain the flood until his whole body was limping and emaciated. If men from antiquity could have benefited (from?) the world by the loss of one hair, they would not have given it; if the world had been given to them alone, they would not have taken it. If nobody would lose one hair, and nobody would benefit (from?) the world, the world would be well ordered.

> 伯成子高不以一毫利物，舍國而隱耕。大禹不以一身自利，一體偏枯。古之人損一毫利天下不與也，悉天下奉一身不取也。人人不損一毫，人人不利天下，天下治矣。[41]

I refrain here from discussing this statement's date (between late Zhou and the Wei-Jin period), authenticity (whether or not it reflects the historical Yang Zhu's thought), and interpretation ("to benefit" versus "to benefit from").[42] While echoing the Mencian portrayal, the passage does not mention Mencius. Compared to the trope, there are important differences: the author takes Yang Zhu seriously, exclusively opposes him to Mo and not to Ru, provides him with a defense, and locates him in a clear lineage. This is apparent in the following debate between some

Yangists and Mohists about the willingness to sacrifice body parts. The Mohist master Qinzi 禽子 (Mozi's disciple Qin Guli 禽滑厘) first challenges Yang Zhu, who is, in turn, defended by his own disciple, Mengsun Yang 孟孫陽. The debate concludes with a stalemate between the two views in terms of distinct lines of allies. On the Mohist side, this passage presents Great Yu 大禹 as a model, Mo Di 墨翟 as a master, and Qin Guli as disciple and master (Qinzi). On the other side, the hermit Bocheng Zigao 伯成子高 figures as model,[43] Yang Zhu as a master, and Mengsun Yang as disciple, with Lao Dan 老聃 and Guan Yin 關尹 as authorities.[44]

In general, the prominent figure of Yang Zhu in the *Liezi* stands out as rather disconnected from earlier as well as later portrayals. The only exception, namely these passages about sacrificing hair, have some connection with both: they echo Mencius's portrayal and are quoted by Song and Ming scholars (although rarely).[45] Whenever the latter happens, it is again in line with the rhetorical trope, not the new content initiated in the "Yang Zhu" chapter. Echoes of the *Liezi*'s Yang Zhu figure only emerged in the late Qing dynasty (the fifth portrayal) and moved to center stage in the Republican era.

4. Yang Zhu as a Misleading Master

When the Mencian trope eventually gave rise to a variety of reflections in the Song dynasty, most scholars showed no particular interest in the actual thought of Yang or Mo but merely used them to defend and refine their interpretation of the Confucian Way.[46] Buddhism was an important trigger for the emergence of this new portrayal of Yang Zhu; Mohism was a necessary detour. To make a long story short, influenced by Buddhist ideals of supporting sentient beings, some early Neo-Confucians praised the notion of humaneness (*ren* 仁) in terms that resonated with the Mohist ideal of "inclusive care."[47] Some even believed that after the decline of Mohism, Mozi's ideal had survived in the Buddhist notion of "great compassion" (大悲).[48] The ensuing debate ended up entailing Mo Di's twin heretic Yang Zhu.[49]

The twins Yang and Mo did not arouse equal interest. While Yang Zhu was almost always paired with Mozi, the latter sometimes independently triggered reflection and discussion, with the former following suit. The dominant interest in Mozi appeared, for instance, when Yang Shi 楊時 (Guishan 龜山, 1053–1155) expressed his admiration for Mozi who "simply did not want his supplies to be scant" (濟不欲寡而已). Yang Shi argued that this altruistic ambition resembled the generally praised Great Yu and Hou Ji (Lord of Millet), who suppressed the floods and fed the hungry, respectively. He then briefly added the less important parallel case of Yang Zhu resembling Yan Hui living a simple life.[50] A second example was triggered by Han Yu's praise for Mozi in his short text "Reading Mozi" 讀墨子. More specifically, he had stated that Mozi's "inclusive care" resembled and supported Confucius's "all-round care and loving humaneness, acting as a Sage by broadly supplying for the sentient beings" (泛愛親仁以博施濟衆為聖).[51] This was a disturbing statement from the Song Confucians' hero.[52] Neither totally agreeing nor disagreeing, Cheng Yi pointed out that Mozi was perhaps almost too dedicated to humaneness (仁), while his heretic counterpart had an equally strong sense of righteousness (義).[53] Such examples give the impression that discussion of Yang Zhu was initially considered less important: he was included as a counterpart of Mo Di. The Neo-Confucian comments about him seem to be steered by the attempt to position themselves in relation to Mohism, which in turn was seen in relation to Buddhism.

The new portrayal was accompanied by more textual evidence. While Mencius's three Yang Zhu passages still constituted the major textual material, there existed also a *Mozi* edition.[54] Cheng Yi sometimes refers to it, for example, when pointing out that "the book *Mozi* is not all that much about inclusive care" (墨子之書未至大有兼愛之意).[55] Moreover, other passages from the *Mencius* and the *Lunyu* triggered reflections on Yang, even though they did not mention him. There exists one *Mencius* dialogue discussing Mohism independently from Yang Zhu, in which the master accuses the Mohists of using "two roots" rather than one (3A5). This dialogue may have inspired the recurrent Neo-Confucian claim that Mencius had attacked Mozi—and Yang Zhu in his tracks—at the roots.[56] Other inspiring *Mencius* passages were Mencius's claim to understand the hidden intricacies of four kinds of speech (2A2) and the disdain that he shared with Confucius for the morally mediocre "village worthy" (鄉原) (7B37). Among the *Lunyu* passages were (tentatively translated): "To work on *yiduan*, this causes real damage" (攻乎異端斯害也已) (*Lunyu* 2.16), "As for Shi, he overshoots the mark and as for Shang, he falls short" (師也過商也不及) (*Lunyu* 11.16), "While curbing oneself, return to rituals" (克己復禮) (*Lunyu* 12.1), "learning for oneself" (學者為己) versus "learning for [the eyes of] others" (學者為人) (*Lunyu* 14.24), "six statements and six delusions" (六言六蔽) (*Lunyu* 17.7), and "the village worthy is virtue's thief" (鄉原德之賊也) for stealing the appearance of worthiness (*Lunyu* 17.11).[57] This cluster of textual references fed reflection on Yang Zhu as a master with his own, albeit deficient, ideas.

A detailed study of all the Song-Ming reflections concerning Yang Zhu would lead too far into the intricacies of Neo-Confucian thought.[58] One idea, for example, was that Yang and Mo were not as terrible as Mencius had claimed but that his harsh criticism was nevertheless warranted in order to stop their disastrous influence.[59] To some extent this may have resulted from their role as irrelevant, empty signifiers in the trope. Mozi was now appreciated for his altruism and humaneness, while Yang Zhu was consistently—but somewhat less elaborately—attributed a sense of right or righteousness.[60] These similarities to Ru values made them all the more alluring and hence threatening to Confucianism. Wang Yangming, for instance, argued,

> The two masters were also worthies of their time. If they had lived in Mencius' days, he certainly would also have considered them worthies. Mozi's "inclusive care" simply overshot the mark in implementing goodness while Yang Zhu's "for oneself" simply overshot the mark when implementing rightness.
>
> 二子亦當時之賢者. 使與孟子並世而生, 未必不以之為賢. 墨子兼愛行仁而過耳楊子為我行義而過耳.[61]

Echoing *Lunyu* 11.6, some Neo-Confucians argued that while Mozi had overshot the mark, Yang Zhu had fallen short.[62] An implication of this archery metaphor was the conviction that even a minor deviation at the beginning (e.g., in Yang and Mo's own deeds or words) could lead to an increasing and disastrous divergence of paths (their later or unworthy followers).[63] Only Mencius had been alert enough to hear the germinating sounds of disaster in what seemed like very attractive variations of his own beliefs.[64] This speculation allowed some Neo-Confucians to divert the major blame from Yang and Mo to their later followers.[65]

These are only some of the wealth of reflections engendered by one clichéd portrayal. A few Song ideas have shaped modern views of Yang and Mo, such as their respective association with "righteousness" and "humaneness." But not many of the Song debates have survived in current Yang Zhu research, probably because the Song focus of interest was not Yang Zhu to begin with. Most Song reflections were replaced by the tsunami of Western notions such as individual rights and liberty, which rescued Yang and Mo from their traditional predicament as mere heretics or deficient masters.

5. Yang Zhu as Reformer

The philosophical reading of Yang Zhu in the Republican era was preceded by one more important portrayal shaped by Qing scholars. I focus here on someone who was influenced by Western thought but not yet abundantly, nor in the explicitly comparative and borrowing fashion of the Republic, namely Kang Youwei 康有為 (1858–1927). He shaped the last important portrayal of Yang Zhu on the verge of the creation of Chinese philosophy.[66] In his eyes, the Confucian *daotong* corpus of Old Texts was based on the fabrications of Liu Xin 劉歆 (ca. 50 BCE–23 CE) in support of the political system of Wang Mang's 王莽 (45 BCE–23 CE) short-lived Xin 新 Dynasty (9–23 CE). Fortunately, according to Kang, Confucius had hidden a reformist ideal in the original New Texts, waiting to be decoded. His *Study of Confucius as a Reformer* 孔子改制考 (1897), written when Kang was himself also preparing fundamental reforms for China, contained a fleshed-out portrayal of Yang Zhu as one of the less important Zhou masters objecting to Confucius's suggestions for political reform and for a "doctrine," "teaching," or "religion" (*jiao* 教).

Kang's novel views somewhat reshuffled all the previous Yang Zhu portrayals. Those closely connected with the succession of the Way—the rhetorical trope and Neo-Confucian reflections—somewhat lost their dominance. But Kang's Yang Zhu portrayal preserved traces of the heretic promoting being "for oneself" in opposition to "inclusive care," as well as reflections on extreme views that overshoot or fall short in either humaneness or righteousness. The oldest portrayal of Yang Zhu as an opponent using argumentation fitted nicely in Kang's claim that all masters had competed with Confucius in presenting their views on reforms. Hence, the lively Zhou debates among masters began to overshadow the age-old opposition between *daotong* and heresy. Finally, thanks to textual research supplanting Song and Ming speculations, an impressive array of sources, including the *Liezi*, contributed to his portrayal.[67] From this source may have come Kang's shift from the opposition of Yang-Mo versus Ru toward the opposition between Yang and Mo. The two major characteristics of this fifth portrayal were Kang's insistence on Yang Zhu's institutional vision and on his belonging to an intellectual lineage. Combined, they supported his view that all masters responded to Confucius's proposals for reform.

Kang argued that Yang was one of the many reformers who attributed their projects to the exemplary past. "Yang Zhu made being 'for oneself' a core rule; what he said about indulging in desires was the task, as well as not pulling out one hair to benefit the world. He attributed them all to antiquity." (楊朱以為我為宗旨; 所言以縱欲為事, 拔一毫利天下不為而皆托之於古)[68] Kang's identification of Yang Zhu with being "for oneself" and with the unwillingness to sacrifice even a single follicle of hair was inspired by the *Mencius*, further elaborated upon with references to the *Liezi*, also identified as the source of his hedonism. Examples of "Yang Zhu changing the system" (楊子改制) were that "like Mozi, he was in favor of frugal burials" (與墨子薄葬同) and that "he sang when presiding at a funeral, which did not accord with Confucius' system" (臨喪而歌, 必非孔子之制), but rather with Laozi.[69] Together Laozi and Yang Zhu stood for self-care (為我, from Yang Zhu) and "inhumaneness" (不仁, from *Laozi*).[70]

The content of Yang Zhu's thought was thus closely connected to his belonging to the Daoist lineage against not just Confucianism but even more against Mohism. Based on *Mencius* 7B26, Kang portrayed Yang and Mo as two legs of a tripod: "Since they saw Confucius as creating and installing a religion, Yang and Mo stood in a tripod relation with him. Hence they simply had some followers deserting and others turning to them." (以其為孔子創立之教, 楊墨鼎立. 故其門下有逃有歸耳)[71] This tripod was a step away from the Mencian cliché and somewhat more in line with the *Liezi* portrayal: Kong stood closer to Mo than to Yang. "Mozi came from Confucius's followers" (墨子本孔子後學),[72] while "Yang Zhu was a disciple of Laozi" (楊子為老子弟子). The former two supported "humaneness" and wanted to rescue their age, as did Kang in his own days; the latter two promoted the opposite.[73] "Even though forming three [lineages], they actually were two" (則雖三而實為二焉). While "Ru and Mo had flourished in the Warring States era" (在戰國儒墨最盛), in "the early Han, Laozi was the most flourishing, Confucians did well, and Mohism had disappeared" (至於漢初, 老氏最盛, 儒學駸駸其間, 而墨亡矣). The competition between the two survivors had eventually enabled Confucianism and Daoism to live on.[74] It was even "thanks to this after-effect of Yang Zhu that Lao's learning could spread throughout the world" (楊朱得此後勁，老學所由遍天下哉).⁷⁵ For Kang, Yang was not just one of Laozi's disciples but the influential leader of his worst sublineage, representing egoistic hedonism leading to social disruption.

Inspired by previous portrayals and based on an exceptionally wide variety of extant sources, Kang's portrayal was again very different. As Wei Yixia points out, he was not interested in getting to know Yang Zhu for his own sake but in establishing a variety of responses to Confucius's proposal of a state religion (*guojiao* 國教).⁷⁶ Yang's thought and affiliation both remained secondary to this aim. The focus was not on Yang Zhu but on Laozi, or actually on the latter's relation to Confucius: since Mencius criticized Yang (never Lao) and since Yang was Laozi's direct disciple, they were all more or less contemporaries, along with Zisi 子思. This chronology clearly set Confucius apart as the first and most important reformer in Chinese history.⁷⁷ Kang did not even pretend to objectively and coherently interpret Yang Zhu as a philosopher in his own right, a portrayal that would soon emerge.

Envoy: Yang Zhu as a Philosopher

The five selected Yang Zhu portrayals constitute a dense cluster of historical and partial visions. More portrayals could be analyzed and connections between them further unraveled. This is actually what the chapters in this volume all do. The quantity and diversity of visions of such a minor figure—one with hardly any textual testimony—is truly remarkable. Some of their characteristics have survived better than others. Yang Zhu's label "for oneself," his unwillingness to sacrifice even a single hair, and his oppositional stance all date from the Zhou dynasty. The rhetorical trope reinforced his opposition but is no longer functional in the current academic discourse. Even though it has lost its generic function in defending a moral stance, the trope's content has survived in the form of philosophy. The seventh chapter of the *Liezi* has contributed to the current portrayal of Yang Zhu as an interesting master in his own right and part of a respectable lineage. From the many Song-Ming views about Yang, relatively little specific content has been transmitted. Finally, Kang Youwei's reinvigoration of the pre-Qin portrayal, his use of a range of textual evidence including the *Liezi*, his attempt to knead statements about Yang Zhu into one coherent vision, his elaboration of Yang's lineage, and his insistence on Confucius's priority have all contributed to the booming field of philosophical portrayals from the Republic onward.

As for the primary sources, *Mencius* and *Liezi* have contributed most to current portrayals of Yang Zhu as a philosopher: the former negatively and heavily supported by a long Confucian tradition; the latter positively by defending Yang Zhu against Mohists. Current specialists of Daoism and Yang Zhu's philosophy understandably prefer the latter. From the Republican era also dates the academic view that the original Yang Zhu did not resist "benefitting" the world but "taking benefit from" it, that the *Liezi* passages predate Mencius and were misrepresented by him,[78] that the *Liezi* is an authentic testimony of pre-Qin thought, and that Yang Zhu and Liezi are historical figures of the Daoist lineage.[79] These traits, among others, characterize much of the current Yang Zhu portrayal.

As long as Yang Zhu as philosopher is presented as just one portrayal among the many, namely one that is appropriate for the twentieth century but also borrows from older versions, I have nothing to object to. But when this specific portrayal is presented as the only authentic, historically reliable, and philosophically relevant object of research, we end up with an impoverished vision. One selective mixture from various texts and periods is then promoted as the only real Yang Zhu. As a result, many facts risk being overlooked, such as the fact that Mencius's portrayal was unheeded before the Han dynasty, that it initially survived as a relatively empty rhetorical trope, that the notion of lineages gradually took shape, that Yang Zhu was emancipated from Mozi in the *Liezi*, and that he was opposed to the pairing of Kong and Mo by Kang Youwei. We can also conclude that in the various pre-Republican Yang Zhu portrayals, something else was at stake—whether it was various authors' changing opponents, competing visons of the succession of the Way, or the status of Confucius in relation to Laozi. Each portrayal tells us a bit about Yang Zhu and much about a variety of tensions, times, and concerns throughout Chinese history. In that sense, Yang Zhu has always been, as Chen Shaoming put it, a secondary figure.[80]

Notes

1. This chapter is a revised version of Carine M. G. Defoort, "Five Visions of Yang Zhu: Before He Became a Philosopher," *Asian Studies* 8, no. 2 (2020): 235–56. This research was supported by the FWO project G060817N: "Mozi

and Yang Zhu from Heretics to Philosophers: Caught in Another Web? The Genealogy of 'Chinese Philosophy' in Three Major Steps."

2. See, for example, Hu Shi 胡適, *Outline of the History of Chinese Philosophy* 中國哲學史大綱 (Beijing: Dongfang, 1995 [1919]): 155–62; Feng Youlan 馮友蘭, *The History of Chinese Philosophy* 中國哲學史, 2 vols. (Beijing: Zhonghua, 2015 [1931 + 1934]), 1:147–56; A. C. Graham, *Disputers of the Tao: Philosophical Argument in Ancient China* (La Salle, IL: Open Court, 1989), 53–64.

3. The early sources are *Zhuangzi* 莊子, *Han Feizi* 韓非子, *Lüshi chunqiu* 呂氏春秋, *Huainanzi* 淮南子, and—for those who consider this an early source—the *Liezi* 列子. No complete book has been named after Yang Zhu. See also this volume's introduction.

4. For a summary, see this volume's introduction and Xiaowei Wang and Carine Defoort, "How Yang Zhu became a Philosopher: A Selection of Yang Zhu Scholarship in the PRC," *Contemporary Chinese Thought* 50, no. 3–4 (2019): 69–74.

5. For the construction of Yang Zhu as a philosopher in Japanese and Chinese Republican sources, see the chapters by Sato, Wang, Lin, and Cao in this volume.

6. Anecdotes having to do with Yang Zhu are not discussed since they have a limited role in the current portrayal: for example, "lodging in the inn with a pretty and ugly lady" (*Zhuangzi, Han Feizi*), "lamenting at a crossroads" (*Xunzi, Huannanzi, Lunheng*), as "the brother of Yang Bu who hit a dog" (*Han Feizi*), and the "cold intestines" (冷肠) versus the Mohist "hot stomach" (热腹) (*Yanshi jiaxun*). See Li Yucheng 李玉诚, "The Emergence and Evolution of Yang Zhu as 'Heretic' Symbol" 杨朱'异端'形象的历史生成, *Shehui kexue luntan* 社会科学论坛 3 (2017): 51–61, esp. 57. For a translation, see *Contemporary Chinese Thought* 50, no. 3–4 (2019): 119–32. For anecdotes including Yang Zhu, see the chapter by Lee in this volume.

7. He Aiguo 何愛國, *Local Echoes of Modernity: A Study on the Modern Thought Trends of Yang Zhu and Mozi* 現代性的本土迴響：近代楊墨思潮研究 (Guangzhou: Shijie tushu chuban Guangdong, 2017), 2–41, 87–160. See also He Aiguo, "From 'Beast' to 'Philosopher of Rights': On the Newly Shaped Modern Structure of Yangism," *Contemporary Chinese Thought* 50, no. 3–4 (2019): 104–118.

8. Li, "The Emergence and Evolution of Yang Zhu," 51–60.

9. I follow the popular interpretation of *zhao* 招 (recruit) as *juan* 罥 (tie up). See Jiao Xun 焦循, *True Meaning of the* Mencius 孟子正義 (Beijing: Zhonghua: 1991 [1825]): 997–99.

10. For more on these passages, see the chapter by Chang in this volume.

11. This is argued in Bruce Brooks and Taeko Brooks, "The Nature and Historical Context of the *Mencius*," in *Mencius: Contexts and Interpretations*, ed. Alan Chan (Honolulu: University of Hawai'i Press, 2002), 242–81, esp. 242–43. The three explicit mentions of Yang in the *Mencius* exclusively occur in books 3 and 7, as does Mencius's explicit self-designation as Ru. Bruce and Taeko

Brooks suggest that the sharp awareness of rivaling allegiances belongs to the latest layer of the book, just before the final conquest of Lu in 249 BCE. Most scholars, however, read them as representative of Mencius's thought in general.

12. For the identification of Yang Zhu's thought with these chapters, see Graham, *Disputers of the Tao*, 55.

13. Unlike the *Lüshi chunqiu* itself, the Eastern Han scholar Gao You 高誘 (168–212) connects this in his commentary to the claim in *Mencius* 7A26 that "Yangzi would not pull out one hair to save the world." See Chen Qiyou 陳奇猷, *Annotated Edition of the* Lüshi chunqiu 呂氏春秋校釋, 2 vols. (Shanghai: Xinhua shudian, 1984), 2:1127.

14. See, for example, Zhu Xi 朱熹, *Collected Works of Zhuzi* 朱子大全, 27 vols. (Shanghai: Shanghai guji, 2010), 18:3900.

15. Wang Anshi 王安石 (1021–1086) was inspired by *Lunyu* 14.24 (quoted in Li, "The Emergence and Evolution of Yang Zhu," 59).

16. Zhu, *Collected Works of Zhuzi*, 18:3924.

17. Inspired by *Lunyu* 11.16 (Zhu, *Collected Works of Zhuzi*, 15:1411). See also Makeham's second chapter in this volume.

18. Zhu, *Collected Works of Zhuzi*, 16:1963. This association had been suggested by Cheng Yi's student, Yang Shi (see the fourth portrayal).

19. For the argument that this portrayal went unheeded until the Han dynasty, see Carine Defoort, "Do the Ten Mohist Theses Represent Mozi's Thought? Reading the Masters with a Focus on Mottos," *Bulletin of the School of Oriental and African Studies* 72, no. 2 (2014): 337–70, esp. 354–57.

20. *Fayan*, 2.5/22. See Michael Nylan, *Exemplary Figures* 法言 (Seattle and London: University of Washington Press, 2013), 35. All quotes of Chinese masters texts refer to Lau Dim-Cheuk, *ICS Ancient Chinese Texts Concordance Series* (Hong Kong: Commercial Press, 1993–2002) except in the case of well-established references as for such easily available sources as the *Lunyu*, *Mencius*, and *Laozi*.

21. For this expression, "lui rendant son ampleur" (or "in this displaying true greatness") see Béatrice L'Haridon, *Maîtres Mots* (Paris: Belles Lettes, 2010), 20 and Nylan, *Exemplary Figures*, 35.

22. For the various reconstructions of *daotong*, with or without Yang Xiong and others, see Makeham's two chapters in this volume.

23. Another Han example of this trope is in *Lunheng* 論衡, "Responding about Creating [this book]" 對作. Wang Chong 王充 (27–100 CE) did not identify with the Ru tradition.

24. See his "Tracing the Way" 原道 (of 805 CE). Zhou Qicheng 周啓成 et al., eds., *Newly Translated Literary Collection of Mr. [Han] Changli* 新譯昌黎先生文集, 2 vols. (Taipei: Sanmin, 2011), 4–9.

25. "Letter to minister Meng Jian," in, for example, Zhou, *Newly Translated Literary Collection*, 374–76; and Li, "The Emergence and Evolution of Yang Zhu," 58.

26. For example, Wang Yangming in Wang Shouren 王守仁, *Complete Collection of Wang Yangming* 王陽明全集, 2 vols. (Shanghai: Guji, 1992), 1:78.

27. By, for example, Wang Yangming: "As for the mistakes of those two [Lao and Fo] and Yang and Mo, respectively, Mencius refuted them first, and masters such as Han [Yu] and Ou[yang Xiu] refuted them later" (若夫二氏與楊、墨之非, 則孟子闢之於前, 韓、歐諸子闢之於後). See Wang, *Complete Collection*, 1:862.

28. See Fan Yu 范育 in his preface to "Rectifying Ignorance" 正蒙. Zhang Zai 張載, *Collection of Zhang Zai* 張載集 (Beijing: Zhonghua, 1985), 5.

29. Hu Hong 胡宏, *Collection of Hu Hong* 胡宏集 (Beijing: Zhonghua, 1987), 161, 158.

30. Lu Jiuyuan 陸九淵, *Collection of Lu Jiuyuan* 陸九淵集 (Beijing: Zhonghua, 1980), 150. For more examples, see Li, "The Emergence and Evolution of Yang Zhu," 59–60.

31. See his *Instructions for Practical Living* 傳習錄 in Wang, *Complete Collection*, 1:77.

32. See, for example, Yang Guangxian 楊光先 (1597–1669) in *Rejecting Heresies* 辟邪论 (1659), collected in his *I Simply Have No Choice* 不得已 (1664). For this and other examples, see Yang Hongfan 杨虹帆, "Discussion of Two Types of 'I Simply Have No Choice'" 两种"不得已"之辩 (Master's thesis, Shanghai Normal University, 2013), 14–15. For a similar use of the trope by Inoue Tetsujirō 井上哲次郎 (1856–1944) against his own "egoistic" and "indiscriminatingly philanthropic" contemporaries, see chapter 8 in this volume by Sato.

33. Probably inspired by *Lunyu* 2.16. This label had been applied to Yang and Mo by Zhao Qi 趙岐 (d. 201 CE) in his *Mencius Topics and Expressions* 孟子題辭. But the label only became prominent later. See Li, "The Emergence and Evolution of Yang Zhu," 54, 57.

34. For the vagueness of this label, see Xiao Yongming 肖永明 and Zhang Jiankun 张建坤, "Interpretation of the *Lunyu* and the Evolution of Ru Learning: Using the 'Attack Heresies' Section as an Example" 《论语》诠释与儒学演进——以"攻乎异端"章的诠释史为例, *Journal of Hunan University* 31, no. 1 (2017): 5–11.

35. Cheng Hao and Cheng Yi, *Collection of the Two Cheng Brothers* 二程集, 4 vols. (Beijing: Zhonghua, 1981), 1:3.

36. See, for example, Yan Yuan attacking the Cheng-Zhu and Lu-Wang schools, quoted in Xiao Yongming 肖永明, "Theories about 'Heresies' in Ming and Qing and Different Directions in Academic Constructions: A Study Focusing on the Theories of 'Heresies' by Yan Yuan, Chen Que, Wang Fuzhi and Fang Yizhi" 明清之际"异端"论与学术建构的不同取向——以颜元、陈确、王夫之、方以智的"异端"论为中心的考察, unpublished PowerPoint presented at the University of Pennsylvania at a workshop on the notion of "heresies," 2018, 6–8.

37. On the endurance of this Mencian frame, see the chapter by Chang in this volume.

38. I bypass debates on the dates and authenticity of (portions of) the *Liezi*. The *Liezi* editor, Yang Bojun, considered it a post-Han text, while A. C. Graham identified a mix of pre-Han and post-Han material. See Yang Bojun 楊伯峻, *Collected Explanations of the* Liezi 列子集釋 (Beijing: Zhonghua, 1996 [1979]), 5. For other views, see A. C. Graham, *The Book of Lieh-tzŭ: A Classic of Tao* (New York: Columbia University Press, 1990 [1960]), 12; and Liu Gusheng 刘固盛 & Li Haijie 李海杰, "The thought of Yang Zhu in the history of Laoxue learning: Along with a discussion of the authenticity of *Liezi*" 老学史中的杨朱思想———兼论《列子》书非伪, *Hunan Daxye xuebao* 32, no. 1 (2018): 35–42; for a translation, see *Contemporary Chinese Thought* 50, no. 3–4 (2019): 75–91.

39. For example, Feng, *Zhongguo zhexue shi*, 1:149, 154; and see the chapter by Lin in this volume.

40. See Brindley's chapter in this volume.

41. *Liezi* 7: 41/18–20; see also Graham, *The Book of Lieh-tzŭ*, 148–49 and the alternative translation by Lee in this volume.

42. For this last debate, see Carine Defoort, "The Profit that does not Profit: Paradoxes with *li* in Early Chinese Texts," *Asia Major* 21, no. 1 (2008): 153–81, esp. 173–76. For the former debates, see Liu and Li, "The Thought of Yang Zhu in the History of Laoxue."

43. This figure is known from the *Zhuangzi*, "Heaven and Earth" 天地, where he refuses to serve and retreats to till the land.

44. This vision of two elaborate lineages is one of the reasons I tend to agree with a post–Warring States date for at least this portion of the "Yang Zhu" chapter. For another argument, see Carine Defoort, "Unfounded and Unfollowed: Mencius' Portrayal of Yang Zhu and Mo Di," in *Having a Word with Angus Graham: At Twenty-Five Years into His Immortality*, ed. Carine Defoort and Roger T. Ames (Albany: State University of New York Press, 2018), 165–84, esp. 175–77.

45. See, for example, Zhu, *Collected Works*, 16:1962.

46. William Lyell considered this the second stage in the Neo-Confucian use of the Yang Mo symbol, namely for the sake of the "systematization of beliefs." He calls the first stage the "assertion of orthodoxy," coinciding with what I identified as the rhetorical trope. See William Lyell, "The Birth and Death of the Yang-Mo Symbol" (Master's thesis, University of Chicago, 1962), 92.

47. See Zhang Zai's claim in "Sincere and Enlightened" 誠明 that "knowledge must be all-round, care must be inclusive" (知必周知，愛必兼愛) and his "Western Inscription" 西銘 about "the people and I being one family, others and I joined together" (民吾同胞，物吾與也). See, respectively, Zhang, *Collection*, 21, 62. For the discussion, see Feng, *Zhongguo zhexue shi*, 2:744–46.

48. Zhu, *Collected Works*, 18:3953.

49. For example, between Cheng Yi and Yang Shi; see Lyell, "The Birth and Death," 46–47. Another, secondary Buddhist inspiration may have been the

perceived similarities between some types of Buddhism and Yang Zhu's supposed support for hermits and nonworldliness.

50. Quoted in Zhu, *Collected Works*, 7:743–44; see also Zhu, *Collected Works*, 14:635–36.

51. See Zhou, *Newly Translated Literary Collection*, 35–36, 37–38; and Makeham's chapter in this volume.

52. This praise was indeed inconsistent with Han Yu's generally negative and standard mentions of Mozi along with Yang Zhu. For this schizophrenic portrayal, see Carine Defoort, "The Modern Formation of Early Mohism: Sun Yirang's *Exposing and Correcting the* Mozi," *T'oung Pao* 101, no. 1–3 (2015): 208–38, esp. 224–27.

53. See, for example, Cheng, *Collection of the Two Cheng Brothers*, 1:231–32.

54. Respect for the Song taboo on *kuang* 匡 (of the first Song emperor, Zhao Kuangyin 趙匡胤, 927–979) suggests that the *Mozi* was included in the now lost Song *Daozang*.

55. See, for example, Cheng, *Collection of the Two Cheng Brothers*, 1:171. He also refers to the book *Mozi* when checking Mencius's claims. See also Cheng, *Collection of the Two Cheng Brothers*, 1:231, where he slightly misrepresents Mencius, since the latter made his claim about the Mohist Yi Zhi, not about Mozi.

56. See, for example, Hu Hong on Zhang Shi 張栻 (1133–1180), in Hu, *Collection of Hu Hong*, 339.

57. I do not go into the long tradition of interpreting and translating all these statements. See also in Li, "The Emergence and Evolution of Yang Zhu," 59 and Xiao and Zhang, "Interpretation of the *Lunyu*."

58. For further reflection on this and other Neo-Confucian views on Yang Zhu, see Makeham's second chapter in this volume.

59. For Hu Hong's initial puzzlement of Mencius's criticism, see Hu, *Collection of Hu Hong*, 281–82.

60. Cheng, *Collection of the Two Cheng Brothers*, 1:231–32.

61. Wang, *Complete Collection*, 1:77.

62. For example, Zhu, *Collected Works*, 7:392–93.

63. This metaphor connects nicely with early Yang Zhu passages presenting him weeping at the crossroads because minor decisions can have major results.

64. Cheng, *Collection of the Two Cheng Brothers*, 1:231.

65. See, for example, Cheng, *Collection of the Two Cheng Brothers*, 1:171.

66. Wei Yixia 魏义霞, "Yang Zhu in the Eyes of Kang Youwei" 康有為視界中的楊朱, *Jiang Huai luntan*, no. 4 (2017): 40–45, esp. 40. For a translation, see *Contemporary Chinese Thought* 50, no. 3–4 (2019): 133–43.

67. Along with its precedent *Study of Xin Learning as Forgeries* 新學偽書考 (1891). *Confucius as a Reformer* contains a remarkable variety of early references to Yang Zhu, weeping at a crossroads, singing at a burial, describing the vagueness of the past, denying the importance of a reputation, etc.

68. Kang Youwei 康有為 et al., *Complete Collection of Kang Youwei* 康有為全集, 12 vols. (Beijing: China Renmin University Press, 2007), 3:41.

69. Kang, *Complete Collection*, 3:25. He also enhanced older attempts to identify lesser known figures in relation to Yang Zhu, such as Yang Ziju 陽子居 in the *Zhuangzi*, Yuan Rang 原壤 in the *Lunyu*, Zi Sanghu 子桑戶 in *Shuoyuan*, or Mengsun Yang 孟孫陽 and Xin Duzi 心都子 in the *Liezi*. See Kang, *Complete Collection*, 3:72–73.

70. See *Laozi* 5 about "Heaven and earth" (天地) as well as the "sage" (聖人) being "inhumane" (不仁) and using others as "strawdogs" (芻狗).

71. Kang, *Complete Collection*, 3:88, echoing *Mencius* 7B26, quoted above.

72. Kang, *Complete Collection*, 3:16.

73. Kang, *Complete Collection*, 3:58.

74. Kang, *Complete Collection*, 3:206.

75. Kang, *Complete Collection*, 3:59.

76. Wei, "Yang Zhu in the Eyes of Kang Youwei," 40. For a translation, see *Contemporary Chinese Thought* 50, no. 3–4 (2019): 143.

77. See, for example, Kang, *Complete Collection*, 2:142–43, in the lecture notes of 1896 *Wanmu caotang koushuo* 萬木草堂口說: "Yang Zhu, Laozi's disciple, lived in Mencius' time, which shows that Confucius came before Laozi" (老子之弟子楊朱, 生當孟子時, 可知孔子在老子之先) and "Yang Zhu was a contemporary of Zisi" (楊朱子思同時).

78. For these arguments by scholars such as Men Qiming 門啟明 and Gu Jiegang 顾颉刚, see Defoort, "The Profit That Does Not Profit," 173–76.

79. For an example of this trend, see Liu and Li, "The Thought of Yang Zhu in the History of Laoxue."

80. Chen Shaoming, "A Secondary Figure in the 'World of Classics': An Analysis of Yang Zhu's Image," *Contemporary Chinese Thought* 50, no. 3–4 (2019): 92–103.

I
From Warring States to Wei-Jin

Chapter 2

Yang Zhu and Mozi as Critics of Unification Warfare

Ting-mien Lee

Introduction

Contemporary study of classical Chinese philosophy is predominantly a project of reconstructing early masters' thought and their disputes with each other based on existing sources. To reconstruct Mozi's thought and Mohist debates with other masters, for example, scholars rely on the book *Mozi* 墨子 and the texts that mention Mozi, Mohists, or Mohism. Yang Zhu is generally considered important in the picture of classical Chinese philosophy because Mengzi 孟子 harshly criticized him along with Mozi and claimed that their views were influential. However, the extant sources on Yang Zhu are extremely scarce. There is no classical text named after him, nor is any classical quote explicitly attributed to him. As a result, the currently dominant portrayal of Yang Zhu's thought (and his quarrels with Mengzi and Mohists) is largely based on the popular interpretation of the two *Mengzi* fragments that criticize Yang Zhu. With such little textual basis, the portrayal is inevitably speculative, and we thus should allow for possible alternatives. To explore one such possibility, I first describe the currently dominant portrayal of Yang Zhu. Then, without denying its plausibility, I offer an alternative by taking into account other early textual fragments.

The two *Mengzi* fragments read:

> The sage king has not arisen, and territorial rulers perpetrate whatever evils they please. Advisors who do not hold offices make arbitrary suggestions, amongst which the words of Yang Zhu and Mo Di are the most prevalent. The suggestions [one can hear these days] are views either of Yang or of Mo. Now, Yang's suggestion is to "care for oneself," which is tantamount to turning one's back on one's ruler. Mo's suggestion is to "care for all," which is tantamount to turning one's back on one's father. But to acknowledge neither ruler nor father is to be in the state of a beast. . . . If the principles of Yang and Mo be not stopped, and the principle of Kongzi not set forth, then those perverse opinions will delude the people, and the path of benevolence and righteousness will be blocked.

聖王不作，諸侯放恣，處士橫議，楊朱、墨翟之言盈天下。天下之言，不歸楊，則歸墨。楊氏為我，是無君也；墨氏兼愛，是無父也。無父無君，是禽獸也。……楊墨之道不息，孔子之道不著，是邪說誣民，充塞仁義也。(*Mengzi* 3B9)[1]

> Mengzi said, "Yangzi advocates 'care for oneself.' Though he might have benefited all under Heaven by plucking out a single hair, he would not have done it. Mozi advocates 'care for all.' If by rubbing smooth his whole body from the crown to the heel he could have benefited all under Heaven, he would have done it. Zimo holds a medium between these. By holding to that medium, he is closer to what is right. But by holding to it without leaving room for the exigency of the circumstance, it is the same as their holding to their singular (principle)."

孟子曰：「楊子取為我。拔一毛而利天下，不為也。墨子兼愛。摩頂放踵利天下，為之。子莫執中，執中為近之，執中無權，猶執一也」。(*Mengzi* 7A26)

The fragments suggest a debate between Mengzi, Yang Zhu, and Mozi. The popular understanding of this debate sees Yang Zhu and Mozi as advocates of mutually opposed ethical views concerning human relations.

According to this interpretation, Yang Zhu advocated that one should care exclusively for oneself, and Mozi argued that one should care inclusively for all. Mengzi, by contrast, held a middle position between the two extreme views. This middle position, Mengzi believed, is the path of "benevolence" (*ren* 仁) and "righteousness" (*yi* 義).[2]

The popular interpretation of Mengzi's criticisms is influential in Yang Zhu studies as well as in Mohist studies. In the case of Yang Zhu, because it remains unclear what textual fragments faithfully present Yang Zhu's thought, it is tempting to speculate about his thought based mainly on these *Mengzi* fragments. Mohist scholars have the text *Mozi* to rely on; this gives Mohism a better opportunity to speak for itself (assuming that the *Mozi* is a reliable source of Mohism).[3] However, the *Mengzi* had a significant influence even upon Mohist studies, despite the existence of the book *Mozi*.[4] As a result, many scholarly discussions of Yang Zhu and Mozi are to a certain extent responses to Mengzi's criticisms:[5] they often revolve around the question of whether Mengzi's harsh rebukes of Yang Zhu and Mozi are fair.[6] The existing answers to the question reflect two major opinions. One opinion holds that Yang Zhu and Mozi somehow "deserve" the criticisms, at least from Confucian ethical perspectives. According to this opinion, Yang Zhu's thought is problematic because it yields a form of selfish egoism (or hedonism), while Mozi is reprehensible for advocating "impartial care" (*jian ai* 兼愛), which violates the Confucian ethical norm of partiality and gradation of love, namely that one has greater moral obligations to one's own parents.[7] The other opinion holds that Mengzi misinterprets (or intentionally misrepresents) Yang Zhu and Mozi. He fails to apprehend Yang Zhu's philosophy of nourishing life and refusing to take office,[8] and he misunderstands or wrongly presents Mozi's idea of "impartial care."[9]

While the two types of opinions exhibit divergent evaluations of Yang Zhu and Mozi, both of them accept the aforementioned popular interpretation of the *Mengzi* fragments. According to the interpretation, that Mengzi criticizes Mozi for embracing the idea of caring for all and Yang Zhu for advocating the idea of caring for oneself only suggests that Yang Zhu and Mozi represent (or were manufactured by the *Mengzi* as representing) two irreconcilable extreme perspectives regarding one's moral obligation toward others. Yang Zhu scholars, therefore, often characterize Yang Zhu's thought as opposing Mozi's.

This popular interpretation of the *Mengzi* fragments is plausible. There are, however, other ways for one thinker to disagree with another.

It is also possible that Yang Zhu's thought is antithetical to Mozi's in other ways. So far, scholars have not yet explored other possibilities in detail and length. This chapter invites the reader to consider an alternative interpretation of the quarrels between Mengzi, Yang Zhu, and Mozi. In this alternative interpretation, Mengzi promotes war for unification as a solution to constant interstate wars, whereas Yang Zhu and Mozi oppose this solution by resorting to two seemingly incompatible arguments. Yang Zhu argues that wars would naturally stop if no one sacrificed one's own physical integrity or life by participating in wars. Mozi argues that wars would naturally stop if everyone would be willing to care for others and even sacrifice one's own life (instead of urging others to sacrifice their lives) to stop wars. This interpretation also squares with other (less often quoted in the context of Yang Zhu research) *Mengzi* fragments. Moreover, it sheds light on the peculiar resonance between the "Da qu" 大取 (Greater selection) chapter of the *Mozi* and Mengzi's criticisms of Yang Zhu and Mozi; and it shows how Mengzi's criticisms of Yang Zhu and Mozi connect to early juxtapositions of Yang Zhu and Mozi.

Briefly, this experimental interpretation yields an alternative portrayal of Yang Zhu that coheres with the textual web constituted by the two Yang Zhu fragments in the *Mengzi*, Mengzi's political advice recorded in the *Mengzi*, a later Mohist text, and early discourses that mention Yang Zhu and Mozi in conjunction. This demonstrates the tentative and speculative nature of the dominant portrayal of Warring States Yang Zhu. It thus gives rise to the question of to what extent the contemporary portrayal of Yang Zhu is, in essence, like the various portrayals of Yang Zhu throughout Chinese history (as depicted in other chapters of this volume), a projection of a modern-day intellectual agenda. To buttress the understanding of Mengzi as a philosopher of relational ethics, for example, scholars portray Yang Zhu as an advocate of the unfathomably radical view that one has no moral obligations toward others. Once this interpretation of Mengzi is not taken for granted, many alternative reconstructions of Yang Zhu may emerge.

1. Mengzi's Advocacy of Unification Warfare and the Notion of *Quan* 權

The popular interpretation holds that Yang Zhu and Mozi represent (or are understood by Mengzi as representing) two irreconcilable and extreme perspectives regarding one's moral obligation toward others. However, as Mengzi does not claim that Yang Zhu's and Mozi's views are irreconcilable, it is also possible that they merely differ in terms of how they defend their shared view. Yang Zhu and Mozi, for example, might share the view that war should not be a solution to constant interstate wars. Mengzi, however, advocated this solution.

As I have argued elsewhere, the *Mengzi*'s "benevolence and righteousness" discourses resemble those in some military texts. Their "benevolence and righteousness" sometimes refers to morality in the context of war. It may refer to the tactic of displaying morality, such as minimal or restricted use of violence or merciful acts. Displaying morality is a core tactic because the war they discuss is often war for unification and regime change. This enterprise is not just a small-scale military operation to seize a piece of territory; instead, it is about seizing all under Heaven, namely the utmost power. Thus, to achieve this goal, one should win over the hearts of the people to create allies and ensure little resistance in the long process.[10] Yang Zhu and Mozi, however, do not believe that unifying all under Heaven *via* war is the right path. This brings us to another key notion, *quan* 權 (weighing, expediency, or expedient measure).

In addition to the "benevolence and righteousness" discourses, the resemblance of Mengzi's and early military discourses about *quan* is also noteworthy. The notion of *quan*, intriguingly, is also important in the *Mozi* and the early textual fragments that are associated with Yangist ideas. In line with Carine Defoort, I believe that early "*quan*" discourses are the textual milieu and intellectual context of Mengzi's criticisms of Yang Zhu and Mozi.[11] My hypothesis is that because Mengzi advocates unification war (with restricted use of violence) as an "expedient measure" to end the chaos of the Warring States, he criticizes Yang Zhu and Mozi for their opposition to this "expedient measure."

The echoes between the *Mengzi*, the *Liutao* 六韜 (Six Bow Cases), and the *Sima fa* 司馬法 (Sima's Principles of War) in terms of the view of seeing war as means to achieve moral ends is perhaps not coincidental. In the classical period, these three works were perceived to be similar in terms of their intellectual affiliation: they were classified either as Confucianism or as classicism.

The *Sima fa* is classified under the category of classicism (*liu yi* 六藝, often rendered as "six arts") in the bibliographical chapter of the *Hanshu* 漢書 (The Book of Han).[12] The opening paragraph of the *Sima fa* applies *quan* to war as a measure of restoring order:

> In antiquity, using benevolence as the foundation and employing righteousness to govern the people was regarded as the standard. When using the standard failed to meet the expected results, then [the ruler would resort to] expediency. [The norms regulating] expediency come from warfare; they do not come from the accordance with humanity. For this reason, if one kills to give peace to the people, then killing them is permissible; if one attacks another state to care for its people, then attacking it is permissible. If one starts a war to stop a war, then even starting a war is permissible.

> 古者，以仁為本以義治之之為正。正不獲意，則權。權出於戰，不出於中人。是故，殺人安人，殺之可也；攻其國愛其民，攻之可也。以戰止戰，雖戰可也。[13]

According to the *Sima fa*, ruling in accordance with benevolence and righteousness is the traditional standard way of governance, but this does not mean that a ruler should apply the standard universally whatever the circumstances are. The "standard" means the practice for ordinary situations. When the standard way fails to maintain order, a ruler will resort to expedient measure (*quan*): namely, killing some people and attacking some states. Doing so is not incompatible with the standard way if the situation requires expedient measures to bring about peace and care for (*ai* 愛) the people.

Similar perspectives appear in the *Liutao*, a military text purportedly composed in the Warring States period[14] and classified under the category of Confucianism (*rujia* 儒家) in the *Hanshu*.[15] The *Liutao*'s "benevolence and righteousness" does not always imply "no killing" or "no wars"; in some contexts, it has the connotation of "killing less" or "killing specific targets only." Such a connotation comes from a military tactic of showing the aggressor's moral superiority through sparing innocent lives or announcing that the ruler of the besieged territory is the only target. The aim of such tactics is to make the people of the besieged territory give up fighting for their ruler or even turn against him:

> Do not kill those who surrender and do not slay captives. Display benevolence and righteousness to them; bestow generous virtues to them. Cause his soldiers and commoners to say: "The guilt lies with one man." In this way, the world will become harmonious and submissive.

降者勿殺，得而勿戮。示之以仁義，施之以厚德。令其士民曰：
「罪在一人」。如此，則天下和服。¹⁶

Displaying "benevolence and righteousness" means the invading troops will send a clear message that they will kill only the ruler of the invaded territory and those who try to defend him. In other words, it implies neither "no killing" nor "no wars"; it means restricted use of violence instead. This practice is also prescribed in the *Mengzi*, the Zhongshan 中山 bronze inscriptions, and the *Lüshi chunqiu* 呂氏春秋 (Mr. Lü's spring and autumn annals).¹⁷ Such use of "benevolence and righteousness" often appears in early discussions about warfare for reuniting all under Heaven. An obvious example is the *Liutao*, which records how Taigong 太公 instructed King Wen 文王 and King Wu 武王 to create allies, attract the people to their side and eventually subvert the Shang dynasty. It is the warfare of vanquishing all other states and eventually overcoming the Son of Heaven; to use its own expression, it is the enterprise of *qu tianxia* 取天下 (seizing all under Heaven).¹⁸ This is also the solution that the *Mengzi* advocates. The *Mengzi* holds that the way to end the Warring States situation is to reunite all states under a new sovereign. He thinks the Zhou dynasty should have collapsed and a new king should have already been installed:

> When Mengzi left Qi, Chong Yu questioned him upon the way, saying, "Master, you seem to have an unhappy countenance. But formerly I heard you say, 'The superior man does not murmur against Heaven or hold grudges against men.'" Mengzi said, "That was one time, and this is another. Every five hundred years, there must arise a new King, and during that time there must be those whose names are known to their generation for their accomplishments. From the founding of the Zhou dynasty to now, it has been more than seven hundred years. . . . It may be that Heaven does not yet desire to pacify all under Heaven; if it desires to pacify all under Heaven, who besides me in the present time is there to help do it? Why would I be unhappy?"

孟子去齊。充虞路問曰：「夫子若有不豫色然。前日虞聞諸夫子曰：『君子不怨天，不尤人。』」曰：「彼一時，此一時也。五百年必有王者興，其間必有名世者。由周而來，七百有餘歲矣。……夫天未欲平治天下也；如欲平治天下，當今之世，舍我其誰也？吾何為不豫哉？」(2B13)¹⁹

Mengzi does not try to help the Zhou restore power; instead, he looks for a state ruler with potential to become the new king, whom he will assist to "become the King of all under Heaven" (*wang tianxia* 王天下). This is an enterprise equivalent to the *Liutao*'s "seizing all under Heaven." Mengzi is also akin to the Taigong depicted in the *Liutao*; the only difference is that he never found a King Wen. In addition to sharing the *Liutao*'s advocacy of subversive war of reunification, the *Mengzi* also shares the peculiar use of "benevolence": in the *Mengzi*, too, the notion does not necessarily imply "no killing" or "no wars."

For Mengzi, to become the founding father of a new dynasty, one cannot avoid participating in wars. Thus, the candidate must have strong military prowess and at the same time show moral superiority and charisma because his enemies (all other states and the central authority of the Zhou dynasty), when put together, must be more powerful than an individual state. As it is stated in the *Mengzi*:

> He said, "If the people of Zou and the people of Chu fought, who does your Majesty think would win?" [King Xuan of Qi said,] "The people of Chu would win." [Mengzi replied,] "So the small definitely cannot match the big, the few definitely cannot match the many, the weak definitely cannot match the strong. Within the four seas there are nine divisions of territory that have a thousand *li* square. All of Qi, taken together, is one of them. How is one subjugating eight different from Zhou's matching Chu? We still must return to the basic approach. Suppose your Majesty were to bestow benevolence in governing; this will cause all under Heaven who serve others to all want to take their place in Your Majesty's court.... All under Heaven who are aggrieved by their rulers will wish to come and complain to your Majesty. If it were like this, who could stop it"?

> 曰：「鄒人與楚人戰，則王以為孰勝？」曰：「楚人勝。」曰：「然則小固不可以敵大，寡固不可以敵眾，弱固不可以敵彊。海內之地方千里者九，齊集有其一。以一服八，何以異於鄒敵楚哉？蓋亦反其本矣。今王發政施仁，使天下仕者皆欲立於王之朝 ⋯⋯ 天下之欲疾其君者皆欲赴愬於王。其若是，孰能禦之？」(1A7)

By bestowing "benevolent governance," Mengzi argues, a ruler of a "small state" such as Qi can still win over the people of other states, and his becoming the utmost power cannot be stopped. Qi was of course not a "small" state; it was one of the most powerful states at the time. It could, however, be said to be "small" in the context of unification warfare because in this context its enemy is the rest of all under Heaven. As the enemy is powerful, Qi could not win with pure force; it had to resort to benevolence. This explains the story about Mengzi encouraging Qi to attack the state of Yan 燕. As he puts it, this is a good opportunity for the king of Qi to become the founder of a new dynasty (1B10, 1B11).[20] A related point appears in *Mengzi* 1A5. By practicing benevolent governance, it says, a state ruler can order his people to fight other states.[21] In addition, practicing benevolence does not necessarily require the ruler to have the moral virtue of *ren*. For the *Mengzi*, not indulging in slaughtering suffices for a territorial ruler to be a candidate for the would-be king.

> Mengzi went to see King Xiang of Liang. After coming out from the meeting, he said to some people, "When I looked at him from a distance, he did not appear like a sovereign; when I came close to him, I saw nothing venerable about him. Abruptly he asked me, 'How can all under Heaven be settled?' I replied, 'It will be settled by being united.' 'Who can unite it?' I replied, 'He who takes no pleasure in killing people can unite it.'"
>
> 孟子見梁襄王。出，語人曰：「望之不似人君，就之而不見所畏焉。卒然問曰：『天下惡乎定？』吾對曰：『定於一。』『孰能一之？』對曰：『不嗜殺人者能一之』。」 (*Mengzi* 1A6)

Not enjoying killing is an important virtue for the new king of all under Heaven because he has to launch wars and sanction killing, which are necessary expedient measures. As the *Sima fa* holds, it is permissible to kill for the sake of maintaining peace and to attack other states to care for the people. Therefore, the ideal candidate for the would-be king should be someone whose military prowess is powerful enough to conquer other states even though he does not take pleasure in slaughter; he should be a merciful man who cannot bear to see massive causalities. Hence, "He who takes no pleasure in killing people can unite it [all under Heaven]."

Nonetheless, how could it be permissible for the ruler of a state, without the authorization of the Son of Heaven, to invade other states to care for their people? It violates ritual propriety. In our time, the question may sound like this: how could one justify an invasion of a country by claiming that it is aimed at the welfare of the people of the invaded country? Mengzi employs an interesting "drowning sister-in-law" analogy to answer this question (*Mengzi* 4A17). Physical contact with your sister-in-law is ritually inappropriate. Yet, if she is drowning, "rescuing her with your hands is expediency." Some might believe that with this analogy, the *Mengzi* is just talking about Confucian ritual protocols. That is, however, unlikely. The *Mengzi* immediately continues with Chunyu Kun 淳于髡 saying, "[Now] all under Heaven is drowning, it must be rescued." It seems that Mengzi disagrees with Chunyu, but he continues to clarify that what he objects to is the idea of saving the world with *bare hands*. Rescuing all under Heaven, or becoming the king of all under Heaven, is an enterprise much more complex than saving a drowning person; one cannot accomplish this with bare hands. As explained previously, early strategy for unification tends to emphasize that one could not accomplish it with pure force (bare hands). The close association of unification warfare and the drowning people analogy appears in another passage of the *Mengzi*:

> Mengzi replied: "With a territory that is only a hundred *li* square, it is possible to become the King. If Your Majesty applies a benevolent governance to the people . . . then [your people] can be employed to make clubs to beat the strong helmets and sharp weapons of the troops of Qin and Chu. . . . As they [Qin and Chu] are sinking and drowning their people, should Your Majesty go forth and conquer them, who will be a match for you? Thus, it is said: 'Benevolence has no match.' I beg your Majesty not to doubt it!"
>
> 孟子對曰：「地方百里而可以王。王如施仁政於民 …… 可使制梃以撻秦楚之堅甲利兵矣。…… 彼陷溺其民，王往而征之，夫誰與王敵？ 故曰：『仁者無敵。』 王請勿疑！」 (1A5)[22]

Mengzi says that the "drowning" people are waiting for a savior, that is, they are looking for a benevolent man to eradicate the regime that is maltreating them.[23] Therefore, a state ruler who seems to be benevolent enough would definitely be welcomed.

Mengzi's idea of unification war as an expedient measure is obviously incompatible with the views ascribed to Mozi and Yang Zhu. Here, "Mozi" and "Yang Zhu" serve as labels for the perspectives that early authors attributed to them.[24] The surviving literature suggests that both, directly or indirectly, oppose wars. They either argue against wars or passively refuse to take office or work for any rulers' ambition of expanding territory and power.[25] In addition, both defend their antiwar perspectives by drawing on the norms of "benevolence," "righteousness," "caring/love" (*ai*), or "benefiting all under Heaven" (*li tianxia* 利天下). This is perhaps why Mengzi criticizes them. As the *Mengzi* shares with the *Sima fa* an idea of *quan* that sees killing people and launching wars as expedient measures, it criticizes Yang Zhu and Mozi for failing to appreciate the importance of *quan*. According to *Mengzi* 7A26, Mengzi is unhappy with Yang Zhu and Mozi because they select (*qu* 取) the principles of "care for oneself" and "care for all" respectively and their adhering to these principles allows no expedient measures. In the passage, Mengzi does not say that the "crime" of Yang Zhu and Mozi is promoting extreme ethical views; instead, he censures them for selecting a singular principle concerning the benefit of all under Heaven and holding exclusively to that principle (*zhi yi* 執一). He considers holding on to one principle vicious because many tasks such as killing people and invading other states cannot be done; it leaves no room for expedient measures. For this reason, adherence to one principle "injures" the right path (*zei dao* 賊道, Mengzi 7A26). Mengzi's path of benevolence and righteousness, as previously mentioned, is to have a territorial ruler conquer and reunify other states and then establish a new dynasty. If Yang Zhu's and Mozi's principles flourish, as *Mengzi* 3B9 states, no one would accept this remedy. Under Yang Zhu's and Mozi's principles, many necessary undertakings cannot be accomplished.

2. Later Mohist Reclarification of the *Mengzi*'s Terminologies

In the above interpretation, Mozi's principle would obviously undermine Mengzi's approach. The *Mozi* expresses a salient voice against large states' aggression toward small states. The anecdote of Mozi rescuing Song from Chu's invasion, for example, illustrates that Mozi's principle of benefiting the world intends to stop wars and to save weak states from being militarily annexed by powerful states. When Mozi learned that Chu was about to attack Song, he traveled ten days to meet the king of Chu and risked his life trying to persuade the king not to invade Song (*Mozi* 50 Gongshu). In this regard, Mozi indeed blocks Mengzi's "path" because he selects and holds on to an antiwar principle of seeking to make the world a better place; this principle would not allow attacking other states as an expedient measure.

The contrast between Mozi's and Mengzi's perspectives on warfare is thus much sharper than that between their perspectives concerning relational ethics. Scholars have noticed that the ethical perspectives in the *Mengzi* and the *Mozi* are essentially compatible: the *Mozi* does not repudiate "Confucian" norms such as filial piety, benevolence, or righteousness.[26] The tension between their perspectives on warfare is, however, intense. Despite the diversity of thought presented in the *Mozi*,[27] Mohist authors are generally against military annexation. By contrast, the *Mengzi*'s advocacy of unification war is a prescription of ongoing active military annexation until all states are eventually unified under one man. This might be the reason why Mengzi complains about Mozi, saying that his thesis would "delude the people, and the path of benevolence and righteousness will be blocked."

Let us advance this line of interpretation further to include later Mohists in the debate and suppose that later Mohists were aware of Mengzi's criticism of Mozi. Intriguingly, a later Mohist text, the "Da qu," counters the criticism by undermining Mengzi's use of the following terms: *quan* 權 (expediency), *qu* 取 (select), *zhi* 執 (hold to), *ze* 擇 (choose between), *li tianxia* 利天下 (benefit the world), *shi* 事 (undertaking), and *bu de yi* 不得已 (cannot but/be compelled to). Like other later Mohist texts, the "Da qu" is cryptic.[28] However, by reading it as a response to Mengzi, we may find it more intelligible. It analyzes almost all the key terms Mengzi uses to defend the approach of unification war and to attack Yang Zhu and Mozi. As the "Da qu" is a very short essay, this intensive concern with Mengzi's terminology is probably not a coincidence.

Mengzi's criticisms of Yang Zhu and Mozi, as discussed earlier, deploy the terms and expressions of "*qu*" (select), "*li tianxia*" (benefit all under Heaven), "*zhi*" (hold to), and "*quan*" (expediency). He criticizes Yang Zhu and Mozi for selecting and holding to one principle, consequently allowing no room for expedient measures. As Mengzi censures Mozi for leaving no room for *quan* practices, the "Da qu" devotes a paragraph to clarifying this notion.

The "Da qu" does not deny the importance of *quan*. It approves the values of *quan* and illustrates that the *Mengzi* and the *Sima fa* misuse (or abuse) the notion. The *Sima fa* suggests that *quan* as expedient measures can deviate from the standard principle (*zheng* 正). The *Mengzi* expresses a similar view; it says that holding to one principle allows no room for *quan* practices. As both the *Sima fa* and *Mengzi* consider *quan* a convenient approach that implies a suspension of standard principles, the "Da qu" chapter claims the opposite. It states, "*quan* is *zheng*" (*quan, zheng ye* 權, 正也). Which means, expedient measures should also be in accordance with the standard. There are no circumstances in which expedient measures deviate from the standard.

The "Da qu" explains this point by clarifying that the basic meaning of "*quan*" is "weighing." The act of weighing, sometimes, aims to measure what is lighter and heavier to make a decision regarding what to take or to discard. It thus has the connotation of "choosing between" and takes on the derivative connotations of "sacrificing" and "expediency." One can be said to make an expedient decision when weighing the options and sacrificing some over others for maximizing benefits or minimizing losses.

It may seem that the *Mengzi* and the *Sima fa* use the term "*quan*" correctly. Killing some people to bring about peace and restore order for all the people of the entire realm sounds like a necessary sacrifice or expedience measure. However, the "Da qu" points out that it is a manipulation and abuse of the term "*quan*" by emphasizing an important linguistic convention that regulates the use of "*quan*": you can only weigh things that belong to you against each other. The *Mengzi* and the *Sima fa* violate this convention by applying *quan* to sacrificing *others*' lives or physical integrity. The "Da qu" introduces the notion of *ti* 體 (a body) to explain this linguistic convention:

> Weighing light and heavy among the things that one considers parts of a body is what we call quan.
>
> 於所體之中而權輕重，之謂權。[29]

The term *quan* means "expediency" when it refers to the activity of measuring which part of a body (*ti*) is lighter or heavier than another part of the body, determining which is more important. Only things that are parts of one body can be weighed against one another. For example, you cannot weigh your finger against a stranger's and decide whose finger is more important. One cannot violate this same-body principle in applying the notion of *quan*.[30] The "Da qu" continues to illustrate the principle by drawing the analogy of sacrificing a finger for one's wrist:

> Cutting off a finger to keep the wrist is selecting the greater among the benefits and selecting the lesser among the harms. Selecting the lesser among the harms is not selecting harms, but rather selecting benefits. [The principle that determines] what one selects is what one should hold to.
>
> 斷指以存腕，利之中取大，害之中取小也。害之中取小也，非取害也，取利也。其所取者，人之所執也。[31]

Following the same-body principle, what this passage considers are one's own body parts, not someone else's. It lays out the standard principle that everyone would hold on to in selecting what to protect or sacrifice: one will choose the greater benefit over the lesser and the lesser harm over the greater. Following this principle, everyone in the aforementioned situation would decide to sacrifice a finger if it will save the wrist by doing so. This is not because the person wants to lose the finger but because he wants to keep his wrist. We would therefore tend to say that one makes the decision to save the wrist rather than one makes the decision to lose a finger. Moreover, we would say so because the finger and the wrist in this case are constituent parts of *the same body*. The wrist is more important than the finger because the finger cannot be kept while losing the wrist. Whoever owns the body would so select and hold to this principle. With this example, the "Da qu" repudiates the view that *quan* implies deviation from the standard principle. It is obvious that Mengzi would follow this principle under any circumstances to make decisions regarding which part of the body to keep or sacrifice.

To buttress the view against the *Mengzi* and the *Sima fa*, the "Da qu" goes on to illustrate how this principle applies to acts of weighing that concern the benefit of *all under Heaven*. As Mengzi criticizes Yang Zhu and Mozi for holding to one principle of benefiting all under Heaven, leaving no room for expedient measures, the "Da qu" invites the reader to consider the following situation.

> When a man encounters a robber, if he can save his life by cutting off a finger, then doing so is to pursue [the greater] benefits. That he encounters a robber is a harm. Whether he cuts off a finger or a wrist, it makes no difference to the benefits of all under Heaven, so there is nothing [for him] to choose between.
>
> 遇盜人，而斷指以免身，利也；其遇盜人，害也。斷指與斷腕，利於天下相若，無擇也。³²

If a man runs into a robber and must sacrifice a finger in order to save his life, then his decision of sacrificing a finger in exchange for his life is choosing the greater benefit for himself, as the same-body principle dictates. We would not say that he chooses harm because he does not want any harm if he has a choice. In this case, the obvious harm is him unfortunately running into a robber; he certainly does not desire it. Interestingly, the "Da qu" brings up the benefit of all under Heaven, saying that whatever this man's decision is, his decision is irrelevant to the benefit of all under Heaven. This statement is puzzling, as it does not fit the context. It also sounds morally incorrect to Mohists, who advocate the idea of inclusive care and are supposed to hold that everyone's well-being matters for the sake of the benefit of all under Heaven.³³ The puzzle can be solved by the same-body principle. The man's finger or wrist is an integral part of his own body, not anyone else's. His choice of keeping a finger or a wrist of his own would not add or reduce the benefit of others. Therefore, he cannot claim that he is making the choice to benefit all under Heaven. As the "Da qu" concludes, "There is nothing for him to choose between" for the benefit of all under Heaven.

However, why does the "Da qu" chapter emphasize this trivial truth? The answer lies in the expression "choosing between" (*ze* 擇), which is also a term Mengzi uses in selling the ideal of unifying all under Heaven under one man.

The "Da qu" discusses not only the terms "select," "hold to," and "benefit of all under Heaven" that Mengzi uses to criticize Mozi but also the expression "choosing between" that Mengzi uses to praise the king of Qi's benevolence so as to encourage the king to unify all under Heaven. The *Mengzi* records a conversation between Mengzi and King Xuan of Qi in which King Xuan expresses his ambition:

King Xuan of Qi asked, "May I hear stories about Duke Huan of Qi and Duke Wen of Jin?" Mengzi replied, "The followers of Zhongni [Confucius] did not speak of stories about Huan and Wen, therefore the stories were not transmitted to later generations. [Therefore,] your servant has not heard them. If you will have me speak, how about I speak of *wang* [true kings]?"

齊宣王問曰：「齊桓、晉文之事可得聞乎？」孟子對曰：「仲尼之徒無道桓、文之事者，是以後世無傳焉。臣未之聞也。無以，則王乎？」(1A7)

King Xuan of Qi expresses his interest in learning how Duke Huan of Qi and Duke Wen of Jin became *ba* 霸 (hegemons, overlords). Mengzi, however, suggests he strives to become the king of all under Heaven rather than a mere superpower. King Xuan asks Mengzi how he could have the *de* 德 (virtue, charisma) required to achieve such a big goal. Mengzi tells the king that it is possible because he already knows the art of "protecting the people" (*bao min* 保民). The king is perplexed. Mengzi reminds him of an earlier event. Earlier, the king saw an ox being prepared for a sacrificial ceremony and decided to have a sheep killed instead. This shows that the king has the potential to become the new king because he is benevolent enough: the king felt compassion for the ox and chose to have a smaller animal, a sheep, killed instead. Killing a small one instead of a large one (*yi xiao yi da* 以小易大) indicates that the king of Qi is capable of mastering the art of benevolence (*ren shu* 仁術), as Mengzi says, otherwise "what was there to choose between" (*he ze yan* 何擇焉). The "Da qu," however, mocks Mengzi, saying that for the victim animal, there is nothing for it to choose between (*wu ze ye* 無擇也). As many scholars have already noted, Mengzi does not praise the king for not killing any sacrificial animals, nor does he suggest the king not kill any (Van Norden 2011: 94). He suggests the king stay away from the kitchen so as to not witness the slaughtering of the sacrificed. By doing so, the king can retain the reputation of being benevolent: not only does he not witness any slaughtering event, but he also displays his virtue by minimizing the sacrificed.

To follow Mengzi's prescription of becoming the king of all under Heaven, a state ruler needs to engage in wars, sacrificing his people and killing others. These are expedient measures. However, a ruler has a better opportunity if he is merciful and takes no pleasure in slaughtering. Displaying moral superiority is strategically crucial because even the ruler of the most powerful state cannot conquer the rest of the world purely with hard power; he must attract the people of other states to his side with the art of benevolence. For Mengzi, the king of Qi is a good candidate because the king bothers to *choose between* which to sacrifice.

The expression "choosing between" in the "Da qu" case, therefore, has two layers of reference. One refers to the one-body principle (*ti*), the other to Mengzi's ox-sheep argument. According to the one-body principle, whether the victim chooses to let the robber take his finger or his life is irrelevant to other people's bodies. Therefore, there is no greater benefit or lesser harm for him to *choose between* for the sake of the benefit of *all under Heaven*. Mengzi's ox-sheep argument, by contrast, does not consider the victim's decision but the robber's instead. It is tantamount to praising a robber for his bothering to choose between taking a finger or the life of his victim.

The robber analogy might have been folklore in the Warring States. In the *Zhuangzi*, the "great robber" symbolizes a ruler who aspires to possess greater power and territory while at the same time seeking to win the moral reputation of benevolence and righteousness.[34] King Xuan of Qi has the features of a "great robber." Thus, it is likely that the "Da qu" deploys this robber analogy to ridicule Mengzi for his helping robbers acquire the utmost power. Mengzi applauds a robber's choice of killing the smaller amount of people and presents this choice as "benevolent," and he thinks he is rescuing all under Heaven (through sacrificing fewer people). Nonetheless, the sacrificed have no choice. As the "Da qu" chapter suggests, if you unfortunately have a ruler who aspires to seize all under Heaven and you are forced to go to war, you would not be said to "benefit all under Heaven" by sacrificing a finger, an arm, or your life for his wars of unification. The reason is simple: he is a robber and an obvious danger to human society. "That one encounters a robber is a harm," as the "Da qu" holds. For this reason, "there is nothing there to choose between." Additionally, Mengzi cannot be said to rescue all under Heaven by persuading robbers to initiate wars as an expedient measure. A power-hungry man who desires to launch wars to annex all other states must drive people to battle that will inevitably incur causalities. Therefore, the "Da qu" continues to say:

> Killing one person to maintain [one's possession of] all under Heaven, this is not killing one person to benefit all under

Heaven. [However, if you] kill yourself to maintain [one's possession of] all under Heaven, this is killing oneself to benefit all under Heaven.

殺一人以存天下，非殺一人以利天下也。殺己以存天下，是殺己以利天下。³⁵

As the "Da qu" states, killing one person to possess the highest power cannot be said to be "killing one person to benefit all under Heaven." This echoes its previous statement that whether the victim of a robber loses a finger or wrist makes no difference to the benefit of all under Heaven. If you unfortunately run into a ruler and must sacrifice yourself for his ambition, whether you sacrifice yourself does not benefit all under Heaven; you only satisfy the desire of the ruler. For the same reason, Mengzi cannot argue that a ruler can benefit all under Heaven *via* war of unification if this approach implies having even one person killed in such a war. If a strategist wants to sell the idea of a unification war, he must volunteer to sacrifice himself for the battle rather than other people. You can claim to be killing for the benefit of all under Heaven only if you kill yourself, but not others. This is another principle that regulates *quan* acts (expedient measures). One could harm oneself to practice *quan*, but not others. The principle is also stated in the *Gongyang zhuan* 公羊傳 (The Gongyang commentary on the Spring and Autumn annals).

> What is *quan*? *Quan* is to derive some good only after going against *jing*. There is no call for applying *quan* except in cases of life or death. Practicing *quan* has its proper way, namely, one degrades or harms oneself in order to practice *quan*, but one does not injure others in order to practice *quan*. To kill others in order to survive, to bring about doom for others' [states] so that one's own may be preserved—the noble man does not do this.³⁶

權者何？權者反於經，然後有善者也。權之所設，舍死亡無所設。行權有道，自貶損以行權，不害人以行權。殺人以自生，亡人以自存，君子不為也。

According to this principle, practicing *quan* as an expedient measure means to sacrifice one's own benefits. Killing others for self-serving reasons clearly violates the principle. This coheres with Mohist principles of *quan*, as the "Da qu" says a person can benefit all under Heaven by killing himself but not others. But Mengzi not only distorts the value of *quan* but also distorts the value of righteousness. The "Da qu" goes on:

> To weigh light and heavy among the things that belong to one's undertakings is what we call "pursuit." Undertaking one's own pursuit is not right. [In doing things that are not right,] select the less among the harms for the sake of doing the righteous in one's pursuit is not doing something righteous.
>
> 於事為之中而權輕重之謂求。求為之，非也。害之中取小，求為義非為義也。[37]

Mengzi's criticism of Mozi is correct in a way. By holding fast to the view against military aggression, Mozi would prevent many undertakings (*shi* 事) from being carried out. Yet, Mengzi's understanding of *quan* and righteousness is wrong. According to the "Da qu," *quan* means "to weigh light and heavy among the things that one considers parts of the same body." One can apply *quan* to situations in which he reluctantly has to decide which part of his own body will be sacrificed, but he cannot apply the notion to situations in which he decides what undertakings are to be done for his own or someone else's pursuits (*qiu* 求). He can be said to be righteous if he sacrifices himself for others. However, he is not righteous if he carries out some undertakings for certain ends. The undertakings Mengzi has in mind include sending troops into battle and conquering other states to satisfy his and the territorial ruler's ambitions. Thus, they cannot be said to be pursuing righteousness. Accordingly, Mengzi cannot accuse Mozi of blocking the path of righteousness because the path is by definition not righteous.

The "Da qu" explains the conceptual relationship between "undertaking" and "righteousness" in the context of defining *quan* because Mengzi's criticism of Yang Zhu and Mozi refers to the notion of undertaking (*shi*). Mengzi complains that the popularity of their views blocks the path of benevolence and righteousness. He says once their views are in people's minds, the ruler's undertakings will be jeopardized (*zuo yu qi xin, hai yu qi shi* 作於其心，害於其事) (*Mengzi* 3B9). Mengzi is right. Mozi's followers would not partake of any military aggression. However, what is jeopardized, the "Da qu" argues, is not the pursuit of righteousness but only power-hungry rulers' and their strategists' pursuit of their own ambitions.

The "Da qu" analyzes all the important terms Mengzi uses to attack Mozi, including the intriguing expression "being compelled to" (*bu de yi* 不得已). It occurs in *Mengzi* 3B9 where Mengzi complains that since Yang Zhu's and Mozi's views are extremely detrimental yet very popular, even though he dislikes engaging in disputes, he cannot but appeal to disputation to show that their views are wrong. "I am compelled to do so" (*yu bu de yi ye* 予不得已也), he says. The expression is not a technical term, but the "Da qu" devotes two lines to it, explaining that Mengzi's use of the expression is also problematic:

> Selecting greater benefits among benefits is not "being compelled to." But selecting lesser harms among harms, this is being compelled to.
>
> 利之中取大，非不得已也。害之中取小，不得已也。³⁸

The "Da qu" indicates that according to the linguistic convention, people do not use the expression "being compelled to" in circumstances of selecting among benefits. Suppose I give you two options: an award of $50 and an award of $10,000. In this case, you would not say, "I am compelled to select the $10,000 award." No one can "be compelled to" select a greater benefit over a lesser benefit. Only in a situation of choosing between harms, such as being forced to choose between losing a finger or a wrist, can one say, "I am compelled to lose a finger." By clarifying the convention regulating the use of "being compelled to" in the context of running into a robber, the "Da qu" insinuates that Mengzi applies the expression wrongly.

Mengzi debates with Yang Zhu and Mozi because he wishes to serve an aspirant for the highest power (a great robber). Thus, he objects to Yang Zhu and Mozi in attempting to sell his proposal to territorial rulers for the opportunity of becoming chief counselor to the founding father of a new dynasty—to use Mengzi's term, the advisor of the king-to-be (*wang zhe shi* 王者師). Therefore, Mengzi could not "be compelled to" debate with them; because choosing to gain benefits is not something one can "be compelled to" do.

Mengzi should not apply this phrase to his engagement in debate with Yang Zhu and Mozi; rather, he should apply it to his service to robbers. The territorial rulers to whom Mengzi provides strategic guidance are robbers; they pursue self-aggrandizement at the cost of human casualties. In this sense, Mengzi himself runs into robbers. Running into a robber, as the "Da qu" suggests, is obviously harmful. If the robbers ask Mengzi to go to battle, this could be a situation to which Mengzi can apply the expression "being compelled." Only in such situations can Mengzi say that he "is compelled to" lose a finger, a wrist, or his life because this is a matter of choosing between lesser or greater harms. To have an opportunity to "be compelled to" do something, therefore, Mengzi should volunteer to go to war himself. Mengzi can then be compelled to decide what part of his own body to sacrifice for the satisfaction of the robber's great desire (*da yu* 大欲).

3. Revisiting the Yang Zhu Fragments and Early Juxtaposition of Yang Zhu and Mozi

In the alternative interpretation of Mengzi's criticism of Yang Zhu and Mozi, the quarrels between Mengzi and Mohists revolve around the question of whether military aggression is a justified expedient measure to restore peace and order. This interpretation can also make sense of the perspectives ascribed to Yang Zhu and early juxtaposition of Yang Zhu and Mozi.

Angus C. Graham and other scholars have argued that the fragments attributed to Yang Zhu generally present an antiwar perspective as well as a view against involvement in the pursuit of political success. This is why Mengzi criticizes Yang Zhu together with Mozi: both share an antiwar position and think that driving people to battle for political struggles cannot be said to benefit all under Heaven. Their shared perspectives explain the terminological resonance between the "Da qu" and the Yang Zhu textual fragments.

The "Da qu" emphasizes that *quan* can be applied only to one's act of weighing the lighter and the heavier among things that belong to one's own *ti* (body). For example, you cannot help me by sacrificing someone else's fingers because the fingers do not belong to you or me. Therefore, one cannot argue that unifying the world *via* war is *quan* (an expedient measure) that serves as a means to benefit all under Heaven. You cannot sacrifice your neighbor's fingers to keep your wrist, nor can you benefit all under Heaven by having someone else killed and still call this an action of *quan*. The key terms, "select" (*qu*) and "body" (*ti*), intriguingly occur in the "Yang Zhu" chapter of the *Liezi* 列子 (Master Lie).

> Yang Zhu said: "Bocheng Zigao refused to benefit others with one hair; he renounced his state and retired to plough the fields. Yu the Great did not keep even his physique for his own benefit, so his entire body was depleted. For a man of ancient times, benefiting all under Heaven at the cost of one hair is something that should not be approved[39]; serving his physique with the entirety of all under Heaven is something that should not be selected."

> 楊朱曰：「伯成子高不以一毫利物，舍國而隱耕。大禹不以一身自利，一體偏枯。古之人，損一毫利天下，不與也，悉天下奉一身，不取也。[40]

The paragraph attributes to Yang Zhu a statement concerning the benefits to oneself and others, which mentions "body," the act of "selecting," and the enterprise of "benefiting all under Heaven." The statements suggest that one should not benefit all under Heaven with one hair and that one should not select the option of being benefited with all under Heaven either.[41] Both principles sound extreme. However, reading the statement in light of the "Da qu" chapter of the *Mozi*, it does not sound so odd. According to the "Da qu," one can only benefit one's own *ti* (body) by keeping or sacrificing parts from one's *ti*. Following this same-body principle, Yang Zhu is right here to state that one cannot be said to sacrifice a single hair from one's body to benefit others' bodies nor utilize others to serve one's own body.[42]

Nevertheless, this statement of Yang Zhu's view differs from the "Da qu." The "Da qu" holds that although one cannot sacrifice others to benefit all under Heaven, one can still sacrifice oneself to benefit all under Heaven. Thus, instead of advising a territorial ruler to send his people to battlefields, Mengzi should encourage the ruler to sacrifice himself for the benefit of all under Heaven. This is a better approach to win the hearts of the people. This approach reminds us of Yu the Great 大禹, the legendary king who did not found a new dynasty through military operations.

The *Liezi*, therefore, attributes to Mohists this remedy for the chaos of the Warring States: the good model is not King Tang 湯王 or King Wu but Yu the Great instead.[43] The model of Yu the Great differs from that of King Tang and King Wu. Tang and Wu resorted to military coups and wars for unification. Yu the Great, however, devoted himself to flood control; he worked so hard that he had all the hairs on his legs rubbed off. While the *Mozi* does not explicitly advocate this model of regime change, the Mohist antiwar perspective and positive remark about Yu the Great together yield advocacy of such an approach, in contrast to Mengzi. Mengzi's approach encourages territorial rulers to emulate King Tang and King Wu to conquer and reunite all under Heaven. The Mohist approach promotes the ideal of Yu the Great, who works extremely hard to benefit all under Heaven without having people killed.

Briefly put, Mohists disagree with Mengzi because they think a ruler should not send others to war in the name of righteousness and to benefit all under Heaven. Yet, the ruler can choose to sacrifice himself to benefit all under Heaven. As the "Da qu" says, "[If you] kill yourself to maintain [your possession of] all under Heaven, this is killing oneself to benefit all under Heaven." The Yang Zhu portrayed in the *Liezi* is stricter in terms of the same-body principle that one can only use one's own body parts to benefit oneself. Therefore, the *Liezi* paragraph arranges for a Mohist disciple to ask the following question:

> Qinzi asked Yang Zhu: "If by discarding one hair of your body, you can save a generation, would you do it?" Yangzi said: "A generation certainly cannot be saved by one hair." Qinzi said: "If it can be saved this way, would you do it?" Yangzi did not reply.
>
> 禽子問楊朱曰：「去子體之一毛，以濟一世，汝為之乎？」楊子曰：「世固非一毛之所濟。」禽子曰：「假濟，為之乎？」楊子弗應。

Intriguingly, the notion of the body, *ti*, is invoked again in Qinzi's question concerning whether Yang Zhu would discard one hair of his *ti* to benefit the rest of the world. The occurrence of *ti* is not grammatically necessary. Qinzi could put his question as follows: "If by discarding one of your hairs (*qu zi zhi yi mao* 去子之一毛) you could save all under Heaven, would you do it?" However, his question is this: "If by discarding one hair of *your body* (*qu zi ti zhi yi mao* 去子體之一毛), you can save all under Heaven, would you do it?"

A possible explanation is that *ti* is invoked here to reinforce the same-body principle that dictates *quan* practices and to highlight the difference between Yang Zhu's and Mohist positions. For Mohists, if one can sacrifice a hair from one's own body to benefit others, one should do it. As we have seen, the "Da qu" chapter also advocates the principle that one can sacrifice oneself for the sake of all under Heaven. This principle can override the same-body principle. By contrast, Yang Zhu subscribes strictly to the same-body principle; that is, only things from the same body can be weighed against each other or benefit each other. Therefore, the hair from a body cannot be weighed against, or benefit, the totality of other bodies. This is why the Yang Zhu in the *Liezi* says that his hair cannot benefit others. For this reason, whatever one sacrifices for a ruler's unification war, it cannot ultimately benefit others.

Yang Zhu's steadfast position against one's participation in wars resonates with the *Han Feizi* 韓非子 (Master Han Fei) fragment that states, "There is a man who on principle refuses to enter a city that is in danger, to take part in a military campaign, or in fact to exchange so much as a hair of his shin, though it might bring the greatest benefit to the world."[44] Following Men Qiming (1934), I believe this *Han Feizi* fragment refers to a Yang Zhu position. As the "Da qu" argues that there is nothing righteous in serving a robber's desires, Yang Zhu goes further to argue that there is nothing righteous in participating in war.

The alternative interpretation of the quarrels between Mengzi, Mozi/Mohists, and Yang Zhu/Yangists can also make sense of early discourses that juxtapose Yang Zhu and Mozi. Mengzi's criticisms of Yang Zhu and Mozi are not the only early fragments that pair Yang Zhu and Mozi. The pairing of "Yang" and "Mo" occurs also in several pre-Han and Han texts. More importantly, as we will continue to see, other early texts couple Yang Zhu with Mozi not because Yang and Mo advocate two mutually opposed ethical views (as is suggested by the popular reading of the *Mengzi*) but because the two thinkers share some concerns, opinions, or features.

The early textual fragments (postdating the compilation of the *Mengzi*) that juxtapose Yang Zhu and Mozi often suggest that the two masters are similar in certain ways. Some fragments are more or less a repetition of Mengzi's criticisms of Yang Zhu and Mozi, which were discussed earlier. Some allude to the anecdotes about Yang Zhu and Mozi sharing a certain melancholy on how a minimal divergence could result in enormous deviation. The theme of the anecdotes echoes other fragments that group Yang Zhu and Mozi because both thinkers are capable of seeing far beyond the surface of things.

The anecdotes about Yang Zhu and Mozi shedding tears over the deviation caused by slight variations appear in several early texts, such as the *Xianzhi fu* 顯志賦 (Expressing my aspirations), the *Fengsu tongyi* 風俗通義 (Comprehensive meaning of customs and mores), and the *Lunheng* 論衡 (Balanced discourses). The *Lunheng*, for example, mentions the anecdotes twice. On one occasion, it says:

> Mozi wept over plain silk; Yangzi wept over by-roads. It is because they mourned the loss of the original, and grieved over having gone astray from the real.
>
> 墨子哭於練絲；楊子哭於歧道。蓋傷失本，悲離其實也。

In these anecdotes, Yangzi and Mozi express their sadness over the reality that a minor difference can lead to outrageous deviation from the right path. Yang Zhu's anecdote concerns the scenario of confronting a fork in the road, in which the choice one makes can result in enormously different results. As to Mozi's anecdote, it is narrated in the *Mozi* as well as in the *Lüshi chunqiu*. According to the narratives, Mozi feels sorrow when he sees a silk-dyeing scene. He then laments that once the plain silk is dyed, it can no longer return to its original color. The third group of Yang and Mo juxtapositions resonates with the anecdotes about Yang Zhu's and Mozi's shared melancholy on slight differences that lead to major deviations. It suggests that both Yang and Mo have keen insights into the initial and insignificant cause of the deviation from the right path that is nonetheless difficult for the mediocre to detect. This depiction of Yang Zhu and Mozi is reminiscent of the stories about their sensitivity to subtle differences that would eventually lead things astray. Because both Yang Zhu and Mozi are capable of identifying slight differences that would eventually lead to disasters, they cannot help crying when they notice them.

Taking just a glance at early Yang-Mo discourses, we might find them unrelated to each other. The *Mengzi*'s criticisms of them, the anecdote about their sadness and the praise of their keen insight do not seem to constitute a unified picture of Yang Zhu and Mozi. However, they can be understood in light of each other by putting aside the popular interpretation of Mengzi's criticism of Yang and Mo. The popular interpretation suggests that Yang Zhu and Mozi stand for two polar outlooks concerning relational ethics and that they do not prevent slight differences from causing deviance from the right path promoted by Mengzi. Yang and Mo are sometimes the very cause of the deviances, and they block the right path to achieving order. Nonetheless, other early Yang-Mo discourses suggest that Yang Zhu and Mozi share concerns and are capable of detecting and feeling sad about subtle deviations from the right path. This puzzle can be solved by the alternative interpretation of the *Mengzi*, the "Da qu," and the *Liezi* fragments. In this interpretation, Yang Zhu and Mozi do not advocate two extreme and irreconcilable ethical views. Instead, both adhere to an antiwar position and the same-body principle. They share the views that war cannot be an expedient measure to restore order and peace and that no one can sacrifice anybody else to achieve the goal. Holding to the principle, Yang and Mo are sensitive to abuses of the norms of benevolence, righteousness, expediency and so on. A subtle abuse of ethical terminology, such as *quan* (weighing/expediency), *zheng* (standard), and *li tianxia* (benefiting all under Heaven), contains some slight deviations from the standard meanings of the terms, but this abuse does tremendous damage to important moral values. The ethical terms "benevolence" and "righteousness," when applied by the *Mengzi* and *Sima fa* in relation to expedient measures (such as sanctioning killing and launching wars), differs from their standard meanings. They do not imply "no killing" or "no wars"; instead, they refer to bringing about peace, caring for the people, and putting an end to wars *via* killing at least some people and launching wars against other states. This "subtle" adaptation of terminology loses the original meaning (*shi ben* 失本) and deviates from the real meaning (*li shi* 離實) of benevolence and righteousness. Yang Zhu and Mozi "weep over" this because it can be exploited by violent men (*bao ren* 暴人, a term used in the "Da qu" and the *Zhuangzi*) and lead to serious deviation from the path, namely, manipulating morality to justify what cannot be justified.

Conclusion

According to the popular interpretation, Mengzi denounces Yang Zhu and Mozi because they advocate certain ethical views that are antithetical to the Confucian norm that one has a moral responsibility to society, and that responsibility should be graded and in proportion to one's relation with others. To promote Confucian ethics, Mengzi criticizes Yang Zhu for his refusal to fulfill any moral duties to the society and Mozi for his perspective that one has equal moral obligations to all. This interpretation presents Yang Zhu and Mozi as two extreme opposite views regarding relational moral obligation. However, if we consider different textual fragments inside and beyond the *Mengzi*, we may come up with other possible interpretations.

This chapter considers the view on warfare in the *Mengzi*, the "Da qu" chapter of the *Mozi*, and early discourses that juxtapose Yang Zhu and Mozi to explore an alternative interpretation. In this alternative interpretation, Mengzi criticizes Yang Zhu and Mozi not because of their extreme views regarding relational ethics but because of their shared antiwar perspective. Mengzi believes that the right path to restore order and peace is to reunite all states under a new sovereign through wars. For him, it is an expedient measure (*quan*). Yang Zhu's and Mozi's principles, however, do not allow such an expedient measure. The notion of *quan* sometimes implies unavoidable necessary sacrifices, which one must make in order to maintain a greater good. This is why Mengzi could exploit the positive connotation of *quan* by applying it to using war to stop war. To counter Mengzi's rhetoric, later Mohists point out an essential principle that regulates *quan* practices, namely, the same-body principle. According to this principle, only the owner of a body can weigh parts of the same body against one another and decide which part to sacrifice. Following this principle, launching wars to annex other states cannot be *quan* because it implies killing others to enhance one's personal power: the persons being killed are not connected to the one who is pursuing the utmost power and trying to seize all under Heaven. For this reason, the "Da qu" states that this is not *quan* and is not righteous. In addition to the same-body principle, Mohists also promote the principle of self-sacrifice. The *Mozi*, for example, depicts Master Mozi as a man who prepares to sacrifice his own life to save a small state under the threat of a powerful state's military invasion. The "Da qu" accordingly states that one can say one sacrifices oneself to benefit all under Heaven, whereas one cannot say that one sacrifices another person to benefit all under Heaven. In this regard, Yang Zhu adheres more strictly to the same-body principle. According to the fragments attributed to Yang Zhu, one cannot sacrifice a single hair of one's own body to benefit others and, in similar vein, one's own body cannot benefit from others' sacrifices.

In this alternative interpretation, Yang Zhu and Mozi share an antiwar position, but they differ in terms of their arguments and their solutions to the Warring States chaos. For Mengzi, an ambitious ruler who does not enjoy killing is benevolent and is qualified to be the new king because he bothers to choose between killing less or more. For

Mozi and Mohists, however, only those who truly sacrifice themselves to benefit all under Heaven can be a qualified candidate for the ultimate throne. Yu the Great, therefore, is better than King Tang and King Wu as a model founder of a new dynasty. A power-hungry and warlike robber cannot be a candidate for king-to-be; even if the robber takes only your finger and mercifully spares your life, he is not a sage and cannot be said to benefit all under Heaven. For Yang Zhu, Yu the Great is still not a model because he sacrifices himself for all under Heaven. Despite the differences, Yang Zhu and Mozi share concern regarding the subtle manipulation of positive notions such as *quan*, righteousness, and benefiting all under Heaven. The subtle manipulation is slight and seems insignificant, but its undesirable consequences can be extreme. As thinkers who detect the subtlety of sneaky manipulations of the ethical values, Yang Zhu and Mozi inevitably feel sorrow and try to scrutinize and reclarify the meaning of the ethical terms.

Notes

1. In this chapter, translations of the *Mengzi* fragments are mine. I have benefited from the translations offered in Philip J. Ivanhoe and Bryan W. Van Norden, eds., *Readings in Classical Chinese Philosophy* (Indianapolis: Hackett, 2001).

2. Some argue that the Mengzi portrayal is in some sense a distortion of Mozi's or Yang Zhu's views that is manufactured by the author(s) of the Mengzi. See, for example, Thomas Radice, "Manufacturing Mohism in the Mencius," *Asian Philosophy* 21, no. 2 (2011): 139–52, and Attilio Andreini, "The Yang Mo 楊墨 Dualism and the Rhetorical Construction of Heterodoxy," *Asiatische Studien-Études Asiatiques* 68, no. 4 (2014): 1115–74.

3. For example, Tomas Radice (2011) draws on the *Mozi*'s discourses about filial piety to illustrate in what sense Mengzi "manufactured" a Mohism that refuses to prioritize the moral obligation of caring for one's own father.

4. Carine Defoort, "The Modern Formation of Early Mohism: Sun Yirang's Exposing and Correcting the Mozi." *T'oung Pao* 101, no. 1–3 (2015): 208–238.

5. Imperial Chinese scholars, for example, often describe Yang Zhu and Mozi in Mengzi's terms and disparage their thought as heresies; see Carine Defoort, "The Modern Formation of Early Mohism."

6. For some examples, see Angus C. Graham, *The Book of Lieh-Tzŭ: A Classic of Tao* (New York: Columbia University Press, 1960) and D. C. Lau, trans., *Mencius* (Harmondsworth, UK: Penguin, 1970), 29–31.

7. See, for example, Daniel A. Bell, "Reconciling Confucianism and Nationalism," *Journal of Chinese Philosophy* 41, no. 1–2 (2014): 33–54.

8. See, for example, Erica Brindley, *Individualism in Early China: Human Agency and the Self in Thought and Politics* (Honolulu: University of Hawai'i Press, 2010); Ranie Villaver, "Does Guiji Mean Egoism? Yang Zhu's Conception of Self," *Asian Philosophy* 25, no. 2 (2015): 216–23.

9. See, for example, Thomas Radice, "Manufacturing Mohism in the Mencius" and Attilio Andreini, "The Yang Mo 楊墨 dualism and the rhetorical construction of heterodoxy."

10. I am aware that this interpretation of the *Mengzi* is controversial and thus requires a convincing argument. I have argued its plausibility in other essays. Given the focus of the current chapter is on Yang Zhu and Mozi, I will not repeat the details of those arguments but only brief summaries of relevant ones. I recommend reading this chapter together with the following essays: Ting-mien Lee, "'Benevolence-Righteousness' as Strategic Terminology: Reading Mengzi's 'Ren-Yi' through Strategic Manuals," *Dao* 16, no. 1 (2017): 15–34; "Humaneness, Rightness, and Universal Love in the *Zhuangzi*'s 'Way of Heaven': An Ethical Conception or a Strategem of the Counselor to the Emperor" 《莊子天道》中的"仁義"與"兼愛"：倫理學的概念抑或帝王師的謀略," in *Academia Ethica* 伦理学术 vol. 6, *Hegel's Theory of Justice and Post-Conventional Ethics* 黑格尔的正义论与后习俗伦理, ed. Deng Anqing 鄧安慶 (Shanghai: Shanghai Jiaoyu chubanshe, 2019), 269–83; "To Become the King of All under Heaven: Mengzi as a Strategist of Regime Subversion," in *Critique, Subversion, and Chinese Philosophy: Socio-Political, Conceptual, and Methodological Challenges*, ed. Hans-Georg Moeller and Andrew Whitehead (London: Bloomsbury, 2021), 89–98.

11. Carine Defoort, "Heavy and Light Body Parts: The Weighing Metaphor in Early Chinese Dialogues," *Early China* 38 (2015); see also Griet Vankeerberghen, "Choosing Balance: Weighing (quan) as a Metaphor for Action in Early Chinese Texts," *Early China* 30 (2005): 47–89.

12. Ban Gu 班固, *Hanshu* 漢書 (Beijing: Zhonghua, 1964), 1709.

13. The translation is slightly adapted from Ralph D. Sawyer and Mei-chün Sawyer, *The Seven Military Classics of Ancient China Including the Art of War* (New York: Basic Books, 1993), 126.

14. Regarding the dating of the *Liutao*, see Ralph D. Sawyer and Mei-chün Sawyer, *The Seven Military Classics of Ancient China Including the Art of War*, 35–37; Alastair Iain Johnston, *Cultural Realism: Strategic Culture and Grand Strategy in Chinese History* (Princeton, NJ: Princeton University Press, 1998), 43; and Yang Chaoming 楊朝明, "Guanyu *Liutao* chengshu de wenxianxue kaocha" 關於六韜成書的文獻學考察, *Zhongguo wenhua yanjiu* 中國文化研究 1 (2002): 58–64.

15. Ban, *Hanshu*, 1725.

16. My translation follows Sawyer and Sawyer, *The Seven Military Classics of Ancient China Including the Art of War*, 87.

17. Lee, "'Benevolence-Righteousness' as Strategic Terminology."

18. Lee, "'Benevolence-Righteousness' as Strategic Terminology."

19. Translation adapted from Ivanhoe and Van Norden, *Readings in Classical Chinese Philosophy*, 126.

20. Lee, "'Benevolence-Righteousness' as Strategic Terminology."

21. The *Mengzi* 1A5 paragraph will be cited and discussed later in this essay.

22. Translation adapted from Angus C. Graham, *Disputers of the Tao: Philosophical Argument in Ancient China* (La Salle, IL: Open Court, 2003), 113–14.

23. This is why the *Lüshi chunqiu* says, "The more the people have suffered from poverty and distress, the easier [one can] become their [new] King" (民之窮苦彌甚，王者之彌易); see Zhang Shuangdi 張雙棣, *Lüshi chunqiu yizhu* 呂氏春秋譯注 (Changchun: Jilin wenshi chubanshe, 1987), 581.

24. Many scholars of Chinese philosophy try to tackle the issue of authorship and thought/text attribution. For a good example, see Esther Klein, "Were There 'Inner Chapters' in the Warring States? A New Examination of Evidence about the Zhuangzi," *T'oung Pao* 96, no. 4 (2010): 299–369.

25. Graham, *Disputers of the Tao*, 53–64.

26. In addition to Radice's explicit arguments, many scholars have noted that the *Mozi* shares many moral terms or norms with other Confucian texts; see, for example, Thomas Radice, "Manufacturing Mohism in the Mencius"; Tang Junyi 唐君毅, "Zhongguo zhexue yuan lun: yuandao pian juan yi" 中國哲學原論：原道篇卷一, vol. 14, *Tang Junyi quanji* 唐君毅全集 (Taipei: Xuesheng shuju, 1986), 159; Graham, *Disputers of the Tao*, 34–47; Dan Robins, "The Mohist and the Gentlemen of the World," *Journal of Chinese Philosophy* 38, no. 3 (2008): 385–402; and Dan Robins, "Mohist Care," *Philosophy East and West* 62, no. 1 (2012): 60–91.

27. Carine Defoort and Nicolas Standaert, *The Mozi as An Evolving Text: Different Voices in Early Chinese Thought* (Leiden: Brill, 2013), 35–67.

28. Later Mohist texts are generally cryptic because they are corrupted. Scholars have made attempts to reconstruct and collate them. A. C. Graham's *Later Mohist Logic, Ethics, and Science* (Hong Kong: Chinese University Press, [1978] 2003) is considered the best reconstruction, but his interpretation of the texts remains questionable; see Jane Geaney, "A Critique of A.C. Graham's Reconstruction of the 'Neo-Mohist Cannons,'" *Journal of the American Oriental Society* 119, no. 1 (1999): 1–11. The task of editorial reconstruction is particularly difficult because the texts' intellectual context is still unclear and thus difficult to decipher.

29. Translation adapted from Ian Johnston, *The Mozi: A Complete Translation* (Hong Kong: Chinese University Press, 2009), 580–81.

30. Compare my interpretation with Carine Defoort, "Heavy and Light Body Parts," 60.

31. I follow Sun Yirang's reconstruction; Sun Yirang 孫詒讓, *Mozi jiangu* 墨子閒詁 (Beijing: Zhonghua shuju, 2007), 404.

32. Sun, *Mozi jiangu*, 404.

33. By saying that Mohist thinkers advocate the norm of inclusive care, however, I do not suggest that they consistently used the expression "inclusive care" or that they shared systematic views or prescriptions that were closely associated with the norm of inclusive care. For a detailed analysis, see Defoort and Standaert, *The Mozi as an Evolving Text*, 35–67.

34. A clear example is the "Qu Qie" 胠篋 chapter of the Zhuangzi, which mentions the usurpation of Qi by Tian and alludes to Tian as a great robber. See Brook Ziporyn, *Zhuangzi: The Essential Writings: With Selections from Traditional Commentaries* (Indianapolis: Hackett, 2009), 63.

35. Sun, *Mozi jiangu*, 404.

36. See Paul R. Goldin, "The Theme of the Primacy of the Situation in Classical Chinese Philosophy and Rhetoric," *Asia Major* 18, no. 2 (2005): 1–25, especially 20n55.

37. Sun, *Mozi jiangu*, 404.

38. This quote follows the Daozang edition.

39. I translate the word *yu* 與 here as "approve/agree" instead of "give."

40. Translation adapted from Andreini, "The Yang Mo Dualism," 1132.

41. The principle might be interpreted differently if we consider the semantic ambiguity of the word *li* 利. This chapter does not discuss alternative readings grounded on the interpretation of *li* as "benefiting from" or "enjoying the benefit of" because its goal is to explore the possibility of a specific interpretation, namely, a unification warfare interpretation that understands *li tianxia* 利天下 as strategic jargon. See Carine Defoort, "The Profit That Does Not Profit; and Lee, "'Benevolence-Righteousness' as Strategic Terminology."

42. Compare my interpretation with Graham, *Disputers of the Tao*, 46–47.

43. Many scholars hold that differing from Confucianism, Mohism promotes Yu the Great as the sage king model rather than King Tang and King Wu. For an example, see Tang, "Zhongguo zhexue yuan lun: yuandao pian juan yi," 158.

44. Burton Watson, trans., *The Work of Han Fei Tzu* (New York: Columbia University Press, 1984), 122.

Chapter 3

Beyond Mencius's Portrayal of Yang Zhu and Mozi

A Zhuangzian-Han Feizian Yang-Mo

Yao-cheng Chang

Introduction

Yang Zhu 楊/陽朱 (fl. ca. 350 BCE) and Mozi 墨子 (or Mo Di 墨翟, ca. 479–391 BCE) are most famously paired in the *Mencius* 孟子 as prominent preachers of extreme doctrines, "acting for oneself" (*wei wo* 為我) and "caring equally for all" (*jian ai* 兼愛) respectively.[1] In this characterization, Mencius foresees how their teachings and practices could become a potent threat to the upright way of Confucius. The same pair of thinkers is also presented in other early texts such as the *Zhuangzi* 莊子 and *Han Feizi* 韓非子 as specializing in the ineffectual activity of *bian* 辯 (dispute, debate, argue), which causes harm to society in a very different way.[2] These divergent paths of portraying Yang Zhu and Mozi in early texts are the main focus of this chapter.[3] There are two issues that might affect how this phenomenon is perceived. The first issue is the fact that Mencius's portrait, the most influential and philosophically substantial source of information about the coupling of Yang-Mo, has overshadowed the others for so long.[4] Consequently, when other descriptions of Yang-Mo are brought into academic discussion, the primary purpose is generally to fit these "minor" descriptions into the frame of Mencius's portrayal.[5] Unlike the studies that only highlight Mencius's portrayal, this paper also looks at how Yang-Mo is used as a trope in non-Mencian contexts. The second issue is the fact that some discussions of the matter are driven by concerns about the dates and authenticity of transmitted sources. In this regard, the non-Mencian depictions of Yang-Mo are often read as inauthentic, second-rate imitations of Mencius's portrayal. Instead of asking which portrayal is more authentic or which comes first, this chapter is more concerned about how different authors craft and develop the trope of Yang-Mo in a variety of modes that best meet their rhetorical needs. As a consequence, the paper invites readers to put Mencius's portrayal temporarily on hold and to consider another, often neglected portrayal of Yang-Mo. This alternative portrayal is suggested by several early descriptions in which non-Mencian elements figure prominently, such as the theme of fruitlessness (*wu yong* 無用) and the combination of Yang-Mo and Zeng-Shi (Zeng Can 曾參 and Shi Qiu 史鰌).[6] To fully explore this topic, the paper first provides a methodological reflection on the treatment of divergent portrayals, followed by a rereading of passages where Yang and Mo are unconventionally presented as useless disputers. The textual aspect of the Yang-Mo passages is then reconsidered with reference to recent studies of authorship and textuality, especially the concept of open versus closed texts.

1. How to Treat Contradictory Portrayals?

Portrayals of early figures occur in pairs, lists, or groups that are not always entirely mutually consistent. This can complicate attempts to reconstruct historical images of these persons. For instance, we base our understanding of Socrates's beliefs and philosophical views on portrayals by his contemporaries, such as Plato, Xenophon, and Aristophanes, which taken together seem contradictory.[7] Our knowledge of Yang and Mo as a prominent pair of masters can likewise be disturbed by a bewildering array of early portrayals that do not strongly corroborate each other. One way to understand these possible inconsistencies is to consider them a matter of accuracy: they are all intended to be accounts of historical figures, but some are more accurate than others; some are merely misrepresentations. In doing so, Mencius's portrayal may, on the basis of an overall picture, turn out to be the most accurate; most extant portrayals of Yang-Mo in history are primarily in line with it. Or we can consider that not all portrayals are meant to be faithful. Portrayals could be disparate since some of them, to different degrees, are meant as literary or rhetorical devices, furnished with various elements that produce a different impact. Some descriptions become more influential than others, thereby followed by more repetition or imitation.[8] On top of all this, the variance of portrayals may also, to a certain extent, reveal the bias of the authors.

Among the portrayals of Yang-Mo in early texts, there are signs of significant divergence, notably between the depiction based on the *Mencius* and another group of descriptions distributed in the *Zhuangzi* and *Han Feizi*. In the latter group, Yang and Mo are described as the duo-maestros of unprofitable disputation rather than as the greatest threats to Confucius's Way. Furthermore, the Yang-Mo duo is often paired with prominent figures in other spheres such as painting, music, and moral practices. These descriptions, however, have frequently been regarded as inaccurate or second-rate copies of Mencius's portrayal. Such a reading could be the consequence of not only the impact of the long-dominant Mencian portrayal but also a strong expectation of accuracy for judging dissimilar portrayals. By perceiving all portrayals of Yang-Mo equally and to some extent rhetorical, this chapter aims to shift from concern with the authenticity of portraits of Yang-Mo to their rhetorical functions. This allows us to better explore how the combination of Yang-Mo is used differently as a trope when applied in a context that is somewhat different from the *Mencius*. This non-Mencian use of Yang-Mo can still be traced on the basis of the coherent descriptions from *Zhuangzi* chapter 8 ("Webbed Toes" 駢拇), chapter 10 ("Ransacking Coffers" 胠篋), chapter 12 ("Heaven and Earth" 天地), and *Han Feizi* chapter 47 ("Eight Persuasions" 八說).[9]

2. The Portrait of Yang-Mo as Disputers of Useless Words

The early non-Mencian portrayal based on the descriptions in the *Zhuangzi* and *Han Feizi* (henceforth the Zhuangzian-Han Feizian portrayal) is first marked by its distinctive emphasis on the futility and unprofitability of the disputations of Yang-Mo.[10] In *Zhuangzi* chapter 8, the images of having "webbed toes" (*pianmu* 駢拇) and "extra fingers" (*zhizhi* 枝指) are used as metaphors for the fanatical obsession with artificial standards and skillfulness that corrupt people's "inborn nature" (*xing* 性).¹¹ Prominent figures in different fields are chosen as illustrations: Li Zhu 離朱 is obsessed with his examination and classification of colors and patterns, Music Master Kuang 師曠 with that of sounds, and Zeng-Shi with morality. Having "webbed toes" in their obsession with useless "disputation" (*bian* 辯), the likes of Yang and Mo also lose their inborn nature:

> Are those who have webbed toes in their disputation not artfully maneuvering the phrases as if stacking balls on top of each other or tying knots, sending their minds wandering amid the "hard and white" and the "same and different," and arduously praising those useless words? That is exactly what [the likes of] Yang and Mo do.
>
> 駢於辯者，纍瓦[丸]結繩竄句，遊心於堅白、同異之間，而敝跬譽無用之言非乎？而楊墨是已。¹²

Yang Zhu and Mozi here are depicted as manipulating words like stacking balls and tying knots, which display flashy but useless skillfulness. Instead of advocating the subversive ideas of "acting for oneself" and "caring equally for all," they are portrayed as the thinkers disputing over theses such as the nature of "hard and white" (*jianbai* 堅白) and "same and different" (*tongyi* 同異).

A cautious distrust of this description may arise out of the traditional attribution of the two theses to other figures.¹³ For example, Qian Mu 錢穆 (1895–1990), who considered Mencius's statement about Yang and Mo's success to be an exaggeration,¹⁴ argued that the Yang-Mo coupling in this *Zhuangzi* description should be understood as a contingent outcome of Mencius's portrayal.¹⁵ Considering Yang as a meaningless constituent, he proposed to read this passage as a description of the later Mohists instead of Yang-Mo.¹⁶ Qian's reading is an illustration of a general attitude toward this description: a lack of appreciation of its uniqueness and informativeness due to Mencius's influence and to a preoccupation with factuality. Although recognizing the rhetorical nature of Mencius's portrayal, he was still enthralled by a plausible explanation of this description on a sound "factual" basis. This determined his opinion of what a proper portrayal of Yang-Mo should be. However, an alternative explanation could be that both portrayals attribute to Yang-Mo the doctrines the authors perceive as the most destructive or problematic. "Hard and white" and "same and different" are the doctrines representing ineffectual logic chopping, while "acting for oneself" and "caring for all" are the opposite ends of the spectrum from extreme egoism to altruism.

3. Yang-Mo as Disputers versus Zeng-Shi as Practitioners

The second feature of the Zhuangzian-Han Feizian portrayal is Yang-Mo's recurrent attachment to another pair of figures, Zeng Can (ca. 505–432 BCE) and Shi Qiu (or Shi Yu 史魚, ca. 534–493 BCE). The former was a disciple of Confucius, famous for his practice of "filial piety" (*xiao* 孝), and the latter was a minister of Wei 衛 who was considered the embodiment of "moral uprightness" (*zhi* 直) or "loyalty" (*zhong* 忠). These two figures are depicted in *Zhuangzi* chapter 8 as those who "have extra fingers in their humaneness" (*zhi yu ren* 枝於仁) by "pulling up virtues and blocking the inborn nature in exchange for a good name, thus making the people of the world trumpet and drum forth in pursuit of some unreachable standards" (擢德塞性以收名聲，使天下簧鼓以奉不及之法).[17] In contrast with the disputers Yang and Mo, who express their pursuit of useless distinctions through words, the practitioners Zeng and Shi express the pursuit of moral standards through their deeds. The two pairs, therefore, are often juxtaposed with each other. For example, in *Zhuangzi* chapter 10, although mixed with other "experts" such as Li Zhu and Music Master Kuang, Yang-Mo and Zeng-Shi are closely tied with each other in the same sentence:

> Only when the (virtuous) deeds of Zeng and Shi are pared back, the (eloquent) mouths of Yang and Mo are gagged, and humaneness and righteousness are discarded will the virtues of all under the heaven begin to merge in obscurity.
>
> 削曾史之行，鉗楊墨之口，攘棄仁義，而天下之德始玄同矣。[18]

In *Zhuangzi* chapter 12 the pair of Zeng-Shi is first contrasted with the tyrant Jie 桀 and Robber Zhi 盜跖 in terms of morality, followed by a remark on Yang-Mo a few lines later:

> Though there may be a divergence in the practice of righteousness between [the tyrant Jie] and [Robber] Zhi, on the

one hand, and Zeng and Shi, on the other hand, they are the same in terms of having lost their original nature.... Yet Yang and Mo went striding around thinking that they had attained something, but that is not what I would call attainment. If what you attain brings confinement, then can that be attainment? If so, then the dove or the owl in a cage may also be said to be attainment.

[桀]跖與曾史，行義有閒矣，然其失性均也……而楊墨乃始離跂自以為得，非吾所謂得也。夫得者困，可以為得乎？則鳩鴞之在於籠也，亦可以為得矣。[19]

The combination of Yang-Mo and Zeng-Shi also appears in *Han Feizi* chapter 47.[20] Here the disputatious intellects of Yang Zhu and Mozi are contrasted with the virtuous practice of Bao Jiao 鮑焦 and Hua Jiao 華角. The contrast between these two pairs is implicitly associated with another contrast between the intellects of Kong 孔 and Mo 墨 and the practice of Zeng and Shi:

What only incisive intellects can understand should not be made an order, because the people are not all incisive. What only the worthies can practice should not be made a law, because the people are not all worthy. Yang Zhu and Mo Di are universally regarded as men of incisiveness. Regardless of how incisive, they should not be promoted as officials because they intervened in the turmoil in their time yet did not solve it in the end. Bao Jiao and Hua Jiao are universally regarded as worthies. Regardless of how worthy, they could not be turned into farmers and warriors because Bao Jiao dried up to death like a tree while Hua Jiao drowned himself in a river. Therefore, the intelligent make full use of their disputation to investigate what the ruler wants to investigate; the able make full use of their conduct to practice what the ruler values as meritorious. Now that the rulers of this time consider useless debates incisiveness and honor unprofitable activities, is has become impossible to achieve wealth and strength for the state. The erudite, learned, disputatious, and intelligent people are like Kong [Qiu] and Mo [Di]. However, since Kong and Mo never engaged in agricultural work, what does the state gain from them? People who cultivate filial piety and reduce their desires are like Zeng [Can] and Shi [Qiu]. However, since Zeng and Shi never engaged in warfare, how does the state benefit from them?

察士然後能知之，不可以為令，夫民不盡察。賢者然後能行之，不可以為法，夫民不盡賢。楊朱、墨翟，天下之所察也，干世亂而卒不決，雖察而不可以為官職之令。鮑焦、華角，天下之所賢也，鮑焦木枯，華角赴河，雖賢不可以為耕戰之士。故人主之所察，智士盡其辯焉。人主之所尊，能士盡其行焉。今世主察無用之辯，尊遠功之行，索國之富強，不可得也。博習辯智如孔、墨，孔、墨不耕耨，則國何得焉？修孝寡欲如曾、史，曾、史不戰攻，則國何利焉？[21]

In this *Han Feizi* passage, Yang Zhu and Mozi are also portrayed as the most illustrative examples of incisive intellects who attempted to solve the problems of their time by useless disputation and Zeng and Shi as the examples of moral practitioners. Although Yang-Mo is not tied up with Zeng-Shi here, their roles of disputers and practitioners remain the same.[22]

The common feature shared by these passages from the *Zhuangzi* and *Han Feizi* is that Yang-Mo always plays the role of distinguished disputers and Zeng-Shi of famous moral practitioners. As opposed to the theme of Mencius's portrayal of Yang-Mo, namely the perilousness of Yang-Mo's teachings, these descriptions of Yang-Mo (together with Zeng-Shi) present the motif of their futility and unprofitability. The descriptions in the *Zhuangzi* further emphasize that they have lost their inborn nature while those in the *Han Feizi* highlight that they contribute nothing to the prosperity of the state. The fact that the same view of Yang-Mo as useless disputers is described in different ways in different texts might be a sign that this Yang-Mo portrayal was open to interpretation in its wide circulation. The fluid descriptions were probably the result of re-using a basic portrayal adapted to fulfill the needs of different authors. This could explain why among different textual styles there are several shared formulaic elements, such as the pairing of Yang-Mo and Zeng-Shi, the roles of eloquent disputers and moral practitioners, and the theme of uselessness. This textual fluidity will be discussed in the next section. Moreover, the non-Mencian and Mencius's portrayals of Yang-Mo are both linked to an even more fundamental theme: disputation. When accused of being "fond of disputation" (*hao bian* 好辯), Mencius perceives his "refuting Yang-Mo with words" (言距楊墨) as a means to preserve the way of the sage (*Mencius* 3B9). He also says that "those who nowadays argue with Yang-Mo are like chasing strayed pigs" (今之與楊墨辯者如追放豚; *Mencius* 7B26). Mencius has no choice but to refute the corruptive words of Yang-Mo, which makes him also engage in the activity of *bian*. By contrast, what is condemned in the *Zhuangzi* and *Han Feizi* is the activity of *bian* itself, and Yang-Mo specialize in it. This shows a strong association between Yang-Mo and disputation—they are either rivals that need to be refuted through disputation or themselves the very representation of disputation. It also suggests that there might be a common source from which the respective portrayals are derived in the context of their rhetorical needs.

One last topic is the interchangeability of names used to connote useless debate. The activity of *bian* tends to be linked to a particular group of thinkers in early texts. The role of useless disputers does not seem to be exclusively played by Yang-Mo. Several early texts not only share the same motif (uselessness) but also a similar disputers-practitioners contrast, in which Yang-Mo is replaced by similar actors such as Gongsun Long, Huizi, the pair of Ru and Mo, Shen [Dao] 慎到 and Mo, and Hui Shi and Deng Xi 鄧析. All these actors play the role of disputers and are sometimes related to the vague thesis of the "hard and white." This disputers-practitioners contrast also sometimes extends to a wider contrast between maestros classified in different spheres (sometimes corresponding to the classification of organs such as ears, eyes, hands, and mouths), containing famous figures such as Li Zhu, Music Master Kuang, and Carpenter Chui (see Appendix).

One may consider the non-Mencian descriptions of Yang-Mo less informative because the role of disputers can be played by other figures, too; the roles themselves thus seem more important than the actual figures, who turn out to be replaceable. Their informational value is then diminished by the likelihood that they are not intended as a faithful portrayal of Yang-Mo but rather represent a recurrent theme contingently presented in the shape of Yang-Mo. However, an alternative way to look at the matter would be that all those different uses of Yang-Mo are tropes of trouble and disputation. They can be allied to other tropes, such as the contrast between debaters and practitioners, to form a new mode of portrayal. This also applies to the "unique" Mencian portrayal of Yang Zhu promoting "for oneself" and "not pulling out a hair" (7A26) and Mozi "caring equally for all" and "wearing [oneself] smooth from the crown to the heels" (摩頂放踵; 7A26). The metaphors of pulling out hair and wearing oneself smooth to save the world are, in fact, also not exclusive to Yang-Mo and could be linked to the early Chinese trope of weighing and comparing one's body parts and the entire world.[23]

The two abovementioned traits—the theme of futility and the pairing of Yang-Mo with Zeng-Shi—define a type of Yang-Mo portrayal that is distinguishable from Mencius's characterization. But how do we further explain their similarities in a textual respect? This leads us to ask about the textual relations between these early portrayals of Yang-Mo.

4. Interrelations between the Early Mentions of Yang-Mo

Mencius's portrayal of Yang-Mo is more widely studied than the others, not only for its philosophical innovation and its influence on later development of Confucian thought but also for its supposed temporal priority. Qian Mu explicitly articulated this supposition as early as 1935.[24] Being one of the scholars who noticed the mentions of Yang-Mo in the *Zhuangzi*,[25] he explained this commonly shared topic as "merely owing to the fact that the text [*Zhuangzi*] came after the *Mencius* and adopted the name of Yang-Mo" (特其書出《孟子》後，襲用楊墨之名).[26] What Qian expressed here was and has largely remained a prevalent opinion. It relies on the view of the *Mencius* as a highly reliable text that can be ascribed to authors of the middle Warring States, namely Mencius and his followers. As for the *Zhuangzi*, its Outer and Miscellaneous Chapters are supposed to be produced by many hands of late Warring States or Western Han writers.[27] These opinions together could lead to the conclusion that the Yang-Mo passages in the Outer Chapters of the *Zhuangzi* (chapters 8, 10, 12) are later texts that might have been influenced by the ones in the *Mencius* (3B9, 7A26, 7B26). The same holds for the Yang-Mo passage in the even more reliably dated late Warring States text *Han Feizi* (chapter 47).[28] The interrelations between those Yang-Mo passages, however, can be revisited in the light of some recent studies. To argue that the mentions of Yang-Mo in the *Mencius* may not necessarily be the origin of the others, I discuss three points: the complex composition of the *Mencius*, the location of the Yang-Mo passages in the remarkably homogeneous part of the *Zhuangzi*, and the concept of "open textual culture" as a useful analytical tool.

It is a popular opinion that the *Mencius* is a more reliable source of Warring States thought than most transmitted texts. The reason behind this, as Michael Hunter has pointed out, is perhaps the consistency of the *Mencius* in thought and language.²⁹ However, some scholars consider the composition of the *Mencius* no less complex than other transmitted texts. For example, Bruce and Taeko Brooks argue that the *Mencius* can be more plausibly seen as consisting of different layers due to its seeming inconsistencies. In their view, the Yang-Mo passages, which occur in books III and VII of *Mencius*, belong to the latest layer of the text (just before the Chu 楚 conquest of Lu 魯 in 249 BCE), while most scholars regard them as representative of the historical Mencius himself, who lived much earlier.³⁰ Michael Hunter also contends that at least some portions of the received *Mencius* can be dated to the Han period.³¹ Even though their views of the dates might also, to differing degrees, be problematic, these considerations are sufficient to appreciate the likelihood that the Yang-Mo passages in the *Mencius* may not necessarily predate and thus influence those in the *Zhuangzi* and *Han Feizi*.

The second point is about the location of the Yang-Mo passages in the received *Zhuangzi*. Compared to the *Mencius* and *Han Feizi*, the received *Zhuangzi* is more obviously an assembly of different groups of material. The division of the *Zhuangzi* into different sections, such as "inner," "outer," and "miscellaneous," has played an essential role in its complex textual history, and the Inner Chapters are conventionally viewed as comprising a more authentic section. Scholars adopting this view, like Qian Mu, might perceive the Yang-Mo passages in the *Zhuangzi*, which are located in the non-Inner Chapters, as less reliable records of the thought of the historical Zhuangzi (ca. 369–286 BCE), who is supposed to have lived approximately at the same time as Mencius.³² However, this view has been challenged by recent studies such as the work of Esther Klein.³³ If the Inner Chapters are not necessarily more privileged, the location of the Yang-Mo passages in the Outer Chapters of the *Zhuangzi* should no longer be a valid reason for considering them less reliable or less important.

Scholars have also noted that the three mentions of Yang-Mo in *Zhuangzi* chapters 8, 10, and 12 come from a group of texts that are generally considered among the most coherent parts of the received *Zhuangzi*.³⁴ Going by similarities in terms and topics, many scholars believe that this homogeneous corpus could be attributed to a single (group of) author(s).³⁵ This homogeneity encourages scholars to treat this group of texts as a coherent textual unit. Most of their discussions rest upon the belief that texts with similar traits can be dated to the same period. Accordingly, they tend to perceive similar phrases (such as "Yang-Mo") and textual parallels³⁶ found in presumably more reliable texts (such as the *Han Feizi*) as evidence by which to determine the date of this textual unit.³⁷ However, as Esther Klein has pointed out, the complex nature of the received *Zhuangzi* as a compiled, edited, and often rearranged text suggests the possibility that its coherence and consistency may be due to the editing process.³⁸ We should avoid over-interpreting the textual consistency as a sign of single authorship that dates the entire textual group to the same period. An alternative is to consider these similarities the result of compilation in which similar texts were selected, assembled, or edited on the basis of their primitive forms. To more clearly explain what I mean by "primitive forms," I refer to the concept of "open text."

Qian Mu considered the mentions of Yang-Mo in the *Zhuangzi* to be the "adoption and continuation" (襲用) of Mencius's original pairing of Yang-Mo. However, this kind of thinking, according to Du Heng's research, is perhaps a view "applying the logic of closed texts onto a largely open textual culture."³⁹ In her dissertation, Du pointed out that there are two different ways of imagining early textual cultures: namely, a world of "open texts," whose contents are substantially fluid and adaptable, and that of "closed texts," whose contents are already "packaged together and stabilized as an integral whole."⁴⁰ A text is "open" when "the majority of its users are not preoccupied with its faithful reproduction," whereas a text is "closed" when "the majority of textual producers are concerned with its accurate replication."⁴¹ As a result, concepts such as "authenticity," "citation," and "imitation" of a text are only meaningful in a closed textual culture. Du also identified the problem that the current view of early texts has been influenced to a degree by how closed texts are expected to behave, even though preimperial Chinese texts were mostly open and did not circulate like modern books.

An alternative way to view the mentions of Yang-Mo in early texts can largely benefit from insights formulated by Du Heng on the nature of open versus closed texts. The Yang-Mo passages in the *Zhuangzi* and *Han Feizi*, as explored in the previous section, were very likely once open texts since there are many formulaic repetitions among them and similar passages in other early texts. A possible way to imagine the formative history of these Yang-Mo passages from their primitive forms as a "primordial soup"⁴² of open texts to their final form as closed texts goes as follows. In table 1, I distinguish between four different stages of development. At the first stage, there were independently circulating textual units about thinkers associated with disputation; some users-producers of these open texts specified these disputers as Yang-Mo. Next, these Yang-Mo open texts were adapted into two different types, namely, the portrayal of Yang-Mo as a dangerous threat and that as unprofitable disputers; these may have been the sources of what are known as, respectively, Mencius's portrayal and the Zhuangzian-Han Feizian portrayal of Yang-Mo. The third stage is a transitional period when these Yang-Mo texts were adapted and packaged with other texts to form different kinds of relatively stabilized texts (namely, Confucian and the so-called Daoist and Legalist texts). That is to say, they were gradually finalized as the form that is perhaps very close to their current form in the received texts. I call the texts at this stage closing texts because they might not yet have been considered by their composers and users as closed texts attributable to particular authors. In the final stage, they were eventually completely closed with the help of not only the functioning of "para-text" (namely, author name and chapter and book title) but also accredited repetitions (namely, references and citations) from other texts.[43]

Table 3.1

Primordial soup of open texts (pre-Imperial China)	Open texts about Yang-Mo (or other thinkers) associated with disputation		
	Open texts about Yang-Mo as dangerous debating rivals	Open texts about Yang-Mo (or other thinkers) as unprofitable disputers	
Closing texts (relatively stabilized packaged texts)	Closing texts about Yang-Mo as threats to the Confucian Way	Closing texts about Yang-Mo as maestros disturbing the inborn nature	Closing texts about Yang-Mo as maestros contributing little to the state's prosperity
Closed texts (Imperial China)	Yang-Mo passages as the part of the *Mencius* (3B9, 7A26, 7B26); with accredited repetitions in the *Fayan*, *Lunheng*, and *Fengsu tongyi*	Yang-Mo passages as the part of the *Zhuangzi* (chap. 8, 10, 12)	Yang-Mo passage as the part of the *Han Feizi* (chap. 47)

To reconsider the question of whether the mentions of Yang-Mo in the *Mencius* influenced those in the *Zhuangzi* and *Han Feizi*, it seems that we should not regard the interrelations between them as what has been described as "reception" or "intertextuality." In the alternative model, the interrelations already occurred at the stage when they were open. Therefore, the best possible deduction is that some preexisting open texts about Yang-Mo already existed before the compilation of these received texts. We should admit some degree of uncertainty about the various dates of these emerging texts and our inability to answer the question of which Yang-Mo portrayal is the earliest and most original.[44] With this admission, our readings of the Yang-Mo passages in the *Zhuangzi* and *Han Feizi* will be less troubled by the seductive but indeterminable question of whether these mentions of Yang-Mo came after and have been influenced by the ones in the *Mencius*.

Conclusion

This chapter begins with a call for a new understanding of the largely overlooked portrayals of Yang-Mo in the *Zhuangzi* and *Han Feizi* as a developing trope in early Chinese texts. The Zhuangzian-Han Feizian Yang-Mo is unique because of the accusation of useless verbal disputation and the coupling of sophistries debaters with moral practitioners. During the reexamination, we also realized that the reading of these Yang-Mo portraits could be affected by the profound and variegated influences of Mencius's depiction. Characterizing Yang-Mo as sophistries-debaters may be the result of the unconscious acceptance of Mencius's depiction of them as advocates of extreme egoism and altruism. Or, like Qian Mu, we might be suspicious of this portrayal but still acknowledge its special status as the prototype for other early descriptions. These influences have marginalized a unique type of Yang-Mo portrayal that once dynamically circulated in an open textual culture. Like the blind men figuring out the nature of an elephant, we can learn when open to a variety of views and experiences. It is certainly unwise to privilege one individual's perception without accepting new experience, especially in the case of learning about and conceptualizing a historical pair of masters from the remote past for whose existence there is so little textual evidence.

Appendix: Fragments with the Shared Motif of Uselessness and the Shared Contrast of "Disputers-Practitioners" or "Disputers-Practitioners-Experts"

Text	Disputatious intellects	(Im)moral practitioners	Other maestros
Zhuangzi 8 "Webbed Toes"	Yang and Mo (disputation, the "hard and white" and the "same and different")	Zeng and Shi (humaneness 仁); Bo Yi and Robber Zhi	Li Zhu (keen eyesight 明); Music Master Kuang (keen hearing 聰)
	Going awry and indulging in humane and righteous deeds and being crafty in the use of keen hearing and eyesight 淫僻於仁義之行、多方於聰明之用; humane and righteous conduct 仁義之操; practices of perversity and excess 淫僻之行		
Zhuangzi 10 "Ransacking Coffers" 胠篋	The mouths of Yang and Mo 楊墨之口	The deeds of Zeng and Shi 曾史之行	The ears of the blind-musician Kuang 瞽曠之耳 (keen hearing); the eyes of Li Zhu 離朱之目 (keen eyesight); the fingers of Carpenter Chui 工倕之指 (dexterity 巧)
	[Only when] humaneness and righteousness are discarded will the virtues of all under the heaven begin to merge in obscurity. 攘棄仁義, 而天下之德始玄同		
Zhuangzi 11 "Preserving and Accepting" 在宥	All the Ru and Mo arouse 儒墨畢起; it was then that Ru and Mo started striding around and flipping back their sleeves among fetters and manacles 儒墨乃始離跂攘臂乎桎梏之間	The deeds of Robber Zhi and Zeng and Shi; on the lower part there were Jie and Zhou, on the upper part there were Zeng and Shi 下有桀跖 上有曾史	

Text	Disputatious intellects	(Im)moral practitioners	Other maestros
Zhuangzi 12 "Heaven and Earth" 天地	Yang and Mo went striding around thinking that they had attained something 楊墨乃始離跂自以為得	Though there may be a divergence in the practice of righteousness between Jie and Zhi and Zeng and Shi, they are the same in terms of having lost their inborn nature 跖與曾史, 行義有間矣, 然其失性均	
Han Feizi 41 "An Enquiry about Disputes" 問辯	Although their sayings are extremely incisive 言雖至察; regarding convoluted as accurate and broad culture as discrimination 以難知為察, 以博文為辯; the words of the "hard and white" and the "widthlessness" 堅白無厚之詞	Although their deeds are highly determined 行雖至堅; considering eccentricity as worthy and opposition to superiors as resilience 以離群為賢, 以犯上為抗; men wearing the garments of Ru and girding the swords of the cavaliers 儒服帶劍者	
Han Feizi 47 "Eight Theories"	Yang Zhu and Mo Di (incisive 察, understanding 知); the intelligent 智士; useless debates; Kong and Mo (erudite, learned, disputatious, and intelligent 博習辯智)	Bao Jiao and Hua Jiao (worthy 賢, practicing 行); the able 能士; unprofitable activities 遠功之行; Zeng and Shi (cultivating filial piety and reducing desires 修孝欲寡)	

continued on next page

Text	Disputatious intellects	(Im)moral practitioners	Other maestros
Xunzi 8 "The Teachings of the Ru" 儒效	What gentlemen would call "wise/ disputatious/incisive" . . . Causing Shen [Dao] and Mo [Di] to make no progress in disseminating their doctrines, or causing Hui Shi and Deng Xi not to insinuate artfully their investigations. 君子之所謂知/辯/察者……慎墨不得進其談，惠施鄧析不敢竄其察	What gentlemen would call "worthy" 君子之所謂賢者	
Zhuangzi 2 "Qiwu lun" 齊物論	Huizi 惠子 (leaning against the parasol trees 據梧)		Zhao Wen 昭文 (playing zither 鼓琴) Master Kuang (beating rhythm with a stick 枝策)
	三子之知幾乎……以堅白之昧終 The intelligence of these three masters was virtually complete. . . . Some ended their days in obscure discussion of the "hard and white."		
Huainanzi 11 "Placing Customs on a Par" 齊俗	Gongsun Long, who always refutes a disputation and counters an argument, who differentiates between the same and the different and the hard and the white, cannot share his course with the masses 公孫龍折辯	The Northerner Wu Ze, who condemned Shun and threw himself into the abyss of Qingling, cannot serve as the model of the world. 北人無擇非舜而自投清泠之淵，不可以為世儀	Chang Hong and Music Master Kuang, who foretell the fortune and predicts without failure, cannot share the same job as the masses. Luban and Mozi, who carved the wood to make a kite and flew it and the kite did not

Text	Disputatious intellects	(Im)moral practitioners	Other maestros
	抗辭，別同異，離堅白，不可與眾同道也		come down for three days, cannot not be made carpenters. 萇弘師曠，先知禍福，言無遺策，而不可與眾同職。魯般墨子以木為鳶而飛之，三日不集，而不可使為工也。

Notes

1. The translation of *jian ai* as "caring equally for all" might not adequately represent the Mohist view as seen in the text *Mozi*. On the basis of the three chapters of *Mozi* titled "Jian'ai," this term would be better rendered as "inclusive care" or "caring inclusively." However, this translation might represent the view of the *Mencius*, in which *jian ai* is related to the image of "benefiting the world by wearing off one's hairs" (摩頂放踵利天下; 7A26).

2. Apart from the three mentions in the *Mencius* (3B9, 7A26, 7B26), there are ten more mentions of Yang-Mo in other pre-Qin and Han texts—three in the *Zhuangzi* (chap. 8, 10, 12), one in the *Han Feizi* (chap. 47), one in the *Hanshu* 漢書 ("Yang Xiong Zhuan" 揚雄傳), one in the *Fayan* 法言 (chap. 2), three in the *Lunheng* 論衡 (chap. 84), and one in the *Fengsu tongyi* 風俗通義 (chap. 7). Half of these mentions are more or less repetitions of Mencius's portrayal, which leads to the impression that the early descriptions of Yang-Mo are probably derived from Mencius's exaggeration. Yang Zhu and Mozi together are also sometimes affiliated with a group of thinkers, such as mentioned in the *Zhuangzi* chapter 24, *Huainanzi* 淮南子 chapter 13, and *Zhonglun* 中論 chapter 11.

3. An earlier version of this chapter appeared in 2021 as "An Exceptional Portrait of Yang Zhu and Mozi: Beyond the Mencian Track" in *Asian Studies* 9, no. 1: 203–224. This research was supported by the FWO project G060817N: "Mozi and Yang Zhu from Heretics to Philosophers: Caught in Another Web? The Genealogy of 'Chinese Philosophy' in Three Major Steps."

4. Scholars' views of Yang-Mo have been so shaped by the *Mencius* that even those who find fault with its viewpoint are still largely indebted to or

framed by it. They might reject the informative, descriptive, evaluative, or interpretive stance of Mencius's portrayal—the proclaimed popularity of Yang-Mo, the mottos ascribed to them, and Mencius's interpretation and disapproval of these mottos—yet accept some aspects of it, such as its originality, the pairing of Yang-Mo, the opposition between them, and even their existence.

5. For scholars who have paid attention to the coupling of Yang-Mo in early texts but discussed the coupling primarily in the Mencian frame, see William Lyell, "The Birth and Death of the Yang-Mo Symbol" (Master's thesis, University of Chicago, 1962); Kano Naoki 狩野直喜, "Mencius and Yang-Mo" 孟子與楊墨, trans. Liang Weixian 梁韋弦, *Qiqihar Shifan Xueyuan xuebao* 齊齊哈爾師範學院學報 1 (1987): 33–39, and Antillio Andreini, "The Yang Mo 楊墨 Dualism and the Rhetorical Construction of Heterodoxy," *Asiatische Studien-Études Asiatiques* 68, no. 4 (2014): 1115–74. For more recent examples, see Zhang Hao 張浩, "Yang Zhu xuepai: baijia zhengming de qidongzhe—jian lun Zhuangzi ruogan pianmu de niandai wenti" 楊朱學派：百家爭鳴的啟動者—兼論《莊子》若干篇目的年代問題 [Yangist School, the Initiator of the Hundred Schools: With a Discussion on the Dates of Several Zhuangzi Chapters], *Wen shi zhe* 文史哲 344 (2014): 29–36; and Shi Chao 石超, "Meng Zhuang pi Yang Mo xintan—jian lun Ru Dao shenti guan zhi chayi" 孟、莊闢楊墨新探—兼論儒道身體觀之差異 [A New Investigation into Mencius' and Zhuangzi's Rejection of Yang-Mo: With a Discussion of the Difference in Confucian and Daoist Views of Body], *Yantai Daxue xuebao* 煙臺大學學報 28, no. 1 (2015): 13–18.

6. For the pronunciation of Zengzi's given name, Shen or Can 參, see Takigawa's commentary in his *Shiki kaichû kôshô* 史記會注考證 67.32. Takigawa Sukenobu 瀧川資言, *Shiki kaichû kôshô* (first published in 1934; Chinese reprint, Beijing: Shinshijie chubanshe, 2009).

7. This inconsistency is called the "Socrates problem," which is presently deemed a task that is "not amenable to a satisfactory solution," but still "useful to identify the principal obstacles and pitfalls that render the discovery of a solution improbable, or even impossible." See Louis-André Dorion, "The Rise and Fall of the Socratic Problem," in *The Cambridge Companion to Socrates* (Cambridge: Cambridge University Press, 2010), 1–23, esp. 1.

8. Mencius's portrayal had an enormous influence on later scholars since at least the Song dynasty (960–1279) onward. The image of Mencius's Yang-Mo was repeatedly imitated by several later Confucians, including Yang Xiong 揚雄 (ca. 53 BCE–18 CE), Wang Chong 王充 (ca. 27–100), Han Yu 韓愈 (ca. 768–824), Zhu Xi 朱熹 (ca. 1130–1200), and Wang Yangming 王陽明 (ca. 1472–1529). The image served as a recurrent trope by which the tasks of later Confucians were compared to that of Mencius, who attempted to rescue the precarious intactness of Confucius's Way from the increasing threat of heresy. For research on the image of Mencius's Yang-Mo and the later Confucian uses of this image, see Lyell, "The Birth and Death of the Yang-Mo Symbol," and Andreini, "The Yang Mo Dualism."

9. The term "Yang-Mo" appears thrice in the *Zhuangzi* (8/22/3–19; 10/25/12–20; 12/34/3–9). "Yang" is also mentioned together with four other debating rivals in the "Xu Wugui" 徐無鬼 chapter (24/69/19–23): "There are four positions of Ru, Mo, Yang, and Bing [i.e., Gongsun Long 公孫龍]. Adding you, master [i.e., Huizi 惠子], it makes five." (儒、墨、楊、秉四、與夫子為五) Other Yang Zhu stories in the *Zhuangzi* include an anecdote about Yangzi 陽子, who was lodging in the inn with two concubines—one who was attractive and one who was not (20/56/9–11)—and two dialogues between Lao Dan 老聃 and Yang Ziju 陽子居, which is believed to be another name for Yang Zhu (7/20/19–23; 27/80/26–27/81/4). In one of these Yang Ziju passages, Yang Ziju's question receives the same criticism from Lao Dan as the "disputers" (辯者) do in another *Zhuangzi* passage (12/31/15–20).

10. Two Yang-Mo passages in the *Mencius* (3B9 and 7B26) also explicitly mention the topic of disputation. However, their mentioning of Yang-Mo's disputation is outlined in a very different scenario: namely, Yang-Mo and their followers as dangerous opponents with whom the Confucians must dispute. For a discussion of this resonant theme of disputation, see Defoort's paper in the present volume.

11. For a detailed discussion of the themes of artificial standards and inborn nature, see Giacomo Baggio, "The Four Primitivist Chapters of the *Zhuangzi*: A Text Ahead of Our Time," *CSRCA Newsletter* (2014): 13–18.

12. All my translations from the *Zhuangzi* are largely based on Victor H. Mair, *Wandering on the Way: Early Taoist Tales and Parables of Chuang Tzu* (Honolulu: University of Hawai'i Press, 1998) and Brook Ziporyn, *Zhuangzi: The Essential Writings with Selections from Traditional Commentaries* (Indianapolis: Hackett, 2009).

13. The two theses are more famously attributed to other "sophistries-debaters." A more likely member of these debaters is Gongsun Long 公孫龍 (ca. 320–250 BCE), who was said to "excel at the disputation on 'the hard and white'" (善為堅白之辯) in *Shiji* 76 (平原君虞卿列傳). He was also said to dispute both theses in *Shiji* 74 (孟子荀卿列傳), *Huainanzi* 11 ("Equalizing the Customs" 齊俗訓), and *Zhuangzi* 17 ("Autumn Floods" 秋水). Another connection is that there is a chapter called "On the Hard and White" 堅白論 in the received text named after Gongsun Long. One other candidate is Hui Shi 惠施 (or Huizi 惠子, ca. 370–310 BCE), who is said to be obsessed with the "hard and white" in *Zhuangzi* chapter 2 and chapter 5. In *Zhuangzi* chapter 33, he is also said to "have the proper understanding of the disputers" (曉辯者) and share in their delight in sophistries.

14. In the Song dynasty, the Confucian scholar Hu Hong 胡宏 (1105–1161) already expressed doubt about Mencius's depiction of Yang-Mo. See Wu Renhua 吳仁華, ed., *Hu Hong ji* 胡宏集, vol. 2 (Beijing: Zhonghua shuju 中華書局, 1987), 281–82. Also see Li Yucheng 李玉誠, "Yang Zhu 'yiduan' xingxiang de lishi shengcheng" 楊朱'異端'形象的歷史生成 [The emergence and evolution of Yang Zhu as

heretic symbol], *Shehui kexue luntan* 社會科學論壇 3 (2017): 51–61. In the 1930s, the authenticity of Mencius's portrayal was intensely questioned in the "Doubting Antiquity" (*yigu* 疑古) movement by several articles published in the magazine *Gushi bian* 古史辨 [Debates on ancient history], esp. vol. 4 (first published in 1933). However, by only questioning or attacking Mencius's portrayal, these doubts also stayed in his confines. They, to some extent, have narrowed the current vision, causing other early descriptions of Yang-Mo to fade into oblivion. See Gu Jiegang 顧頡剛, "Cong Lüshi chunqiu tuice Laozi zhi cheng shu niandai" 從呂氏春秋推測老子之成書年代 [Inferring the dates of the *Laozi* from the *Lüshi chunqiu*], in *Gushi bian* 4 (1982), 465–520; Tang Yue 唐鉞, "Yang Zhu kao" 楊朱考 [An investigation of Yang Zhu], in *Gushi bian* 4 (1982): 540–53; and Men Qiming 門啟明, "Yang Zhu pian he Yangzi zhi bijiao yanjiu" 楊朱篇和楊子之比較研究 [A comparative study on the "Yang Zhu" chapter and Yangzi], in *Gushi bian* 4 (1982), 592–610.

15. Qian Mu, *Xianqin zhuzi xinian* 先秦諸子繫年, first published in 1935, reprinted in *Qian Binsi xiansheng quanji* 錢賓四先生全集, vol. 5. (Taibei: Lianjing chuban, 1994), esp. 285–87.

16. In Qian's opinion, Yang merely serves as a meaningless constituent so as to follow Mencius's combination. He also considered Mo here as unrelated to the early Mohists, who normatively advocated the core Mohist doctrines such as "caring equally for all." Alternatively, it refers to the later Mohists, who developed delicate linguistic techniques in the descriptive analysis of Mohist theories and engaged themselves in the discussion of the "hard and white." Qian's impression is probably based on *Zhuangzi* chapter 33 ("Tianxia" 天下), in which some of the later Mohist schools are depicted as "denouncing each other with the disputations about the 'hard and white' and the 'same and different'" (以堅白、同異之辯相訾; *Zhuangzi* 33/98/23–25). This impression may also be enhanced by some relevant passages from the so-called Mohist Canons (*Mojing* 墨經).

17. Lau Dim-Cheuk, ICS Ancient Chinese Texts Concordance Series (Hong Kong: Commercial Press, 1993–2002), *Zhuangzi* 8/22/8–9.

18. *Zhuangzi* 10/25/17.

19. *Zhuangzi* 12/34/6–7. Going by the fragments in Cheng Xuanying's 成玄英 *Zhuangzi* commentary and *Zhuangzi* chapter 11, Liu Shipei 劉師培 argued that Jie 桀 is missing in front of Zhi 跖.

20. By the 1930s, Luo Genze 羅根澤 had already pointed out that the term "Zeng-Shi" only appears in the four Outer Chapters of the *Zhuangzi* and several chapters of the *Han Feizi* (some of which also contain the combination of Yang-Mo). Luo argues that these passages in the *Zhuangzi* and *Han Feizi* are very likely to be composed by the same author or school. "Apart from these fragments, few have mentioned Zeng and Shi. Therefore, we have great reason to suspect that these fragments are written by a single hand or school." (除此數篇外，很少提到曾史的，則這幾篇的同出一派或一人之手，是有極大嫌疑的) See Luo Genze, *Zhuzi kaosuo* 諸子考索 (Beijing: Renmin chubanshe, 1958), 287. The

passages that contain Zeng-Shi are from *Han Feizi* chapter 26, chapter 38, and chapter 46. However, putting aside the enthusiasm for tracing authorship and dates of transmitted texts, these passages might be more safely seen as different early fragments sharing the same textual pattern.

21. *Han Feizi* 47/140/9–14. This rendition is modified from W. K. Liao, *The Complete Works of Han Fei Tzu: A Classic of Chinese Political Science* (London: Arthur Probsthain, 1959) and a translation provided by Christoph Harbsmeier's *Thesaurus Linguae Sericae* (http://tls.uni-hd.de/home_en.lasso).

22. Yang-Mo and Ru-Mo are related here in terms of both being disputatious intellects. In other texts, it seems that sometimes Ru-Mo and Yang-Mo are interchangeable. There are similar expressions in *Zhuangzi* 11 and 12 (*Zhuangzi* 11/27/11–12, 12/34/6–7), where both Ru-Mo and Yang-Mo are portrayed as "starting to stride around" (乃始離跂). In a quoted passage from *Zhuangzi* 10 that appears in Lu Zhongxuan's 盧重玄 Tang dynasty *Liezi* commentary, the role of Yang-Mo seems to have been replaced by Ru-Mo, which is different from the received *Zhuangzi*: "Hence the *Zhuangzi* says: 'If we glue up the eyes of Li Zhu, then all the people of the world will acquire keen vision. If we break the fingers of Carpenter Shu, then all the people of the world will be skillful. If one wants to bring together the learning of Ru and Mo, feeling confident about one's judgment of right and wrong and regarding oneself as profuse . . .'" (故莊子曰：膠離朱之目，故天下皆明矣；戾工輸之指，故天下皆巧矣。合儒墨之學，矜是非之名以為富……). See Yang Bojun 楊伯峻, *Liezi jishi* 列子集釋 [Collected commentaries on the *Liezi*] (Beijing: Zhonghua, 1979). Moreover, Chu Boxiu 褚伯秀 (fl. ca. 1246), in his compiled annotation to the *Zhuangzi*, replaced the pair of Ru-Mo with Yang-Mo in his commentary on *Zhuangzi* chapter 11: "For this very reason we know that what is called sagacious, wise, humane, and righteous may serve as foot chains and manacles; Zeng and Shi and Yang and Mo may also be the useful tools of Jie and Zhou" (由是知世所謂聖知仁義未必不為桁楊椄桔，曾史楊墨未必不為桀跖利器). See Chu Boxiu, *Nanhua zhenjing yihai zuan wei* 南華真經義海纂微 [Implications of the vast compiled profundities on the *Zhuangzi*] (Taipei: Shangwu yinshuguan, 1983).

23. For the discussion of Yang Zhu and the image of hair, see Carine Defoort, "Unfounded and Unfollowed: Mencius's Portrayal of Yang Zhu and Mo Di," in *Having a Word with Angus Graham: At Twenty-Five Years into His Immortality*, ed. Carine Defoort and Roger T. Ames (Albany: State University of New York Press), 165–84.

24. One other reason might be that Mencius's portrayal is more arresting and better known than the other ones. Esther Klein's insight into the Inner Chapters of *Zhuangzi* is perhaps also applicable in this case. For scholars working on early texts, it is important to consider insightful and refined works as masterpieces by great masters of those times. It is natural to presume Mencius's ingenious portrayal to be the origin of the relatively less elegant descriptions of

Yang-Mo in other texts. However, "a work of genius can arise in almost any time." The elegance of a portrayal could also be a result of later refinement of primitive ones. See Esther Klein, "Were There 'Inner Chapters' in the Warring States? A New Examination of Evidence about the Zhuangzi," *T'oung Pao* 96, no. 4 (2011): 299–369, esp. 306.

25. Several scholars in history have noticed that Yang Zhu and Mozi are paired in the *Zhuangzi* as well. The Song dynasty *Zhuangzi* commentator Lin Xiyi 林希逸 (1193–1271) pointed out that "Mencius castigates Yang and Mo, and it is frequent that this text [the *Zhuangzi*] also uses the term 'Yang-Mo' to refer to them together" (孟子闢楊墨, 此書亦以楊墨兼言者屢矣). See *Nanhua zheng jing kouyi* 南華真經口義 [Vernacular exegesis of the *Zhuangzi*], in *Wu qiu bei zhai Zhuangzi jicheng chu bian* 無求備齋莊子集成初編, vol. 7–8 (Taipei: Yiwen yinshuguan, 1972), 148. In the Yuan dynasty, Jin Luxiang 金履祥 (1232–1303) in his commentary on Zhu Xi's *Mengzi ji zhu* 孟子集注 also noted that "the text *Zhuangzi* as well often speaks of the disputation of Yang and Mo" (莊子書亦盛言楊墨之辨). See Jing Luxiang, *Mencius jizhu kaozheng* 孟子集注考證 [Study of the collected commentaries on the *Mencius*] (Beijing: Zhonghua, 1991), 31.

26. Qian, *Xianqin zhuzi xinian*, 286.

27. It is widely accepted that the relatively more coherent Inner Chapters, which are supposed to be the work of Zhuangzi (ca. 369–286 BCE) himself, is a more reliable source of Warring States thought than the other parts of the received *Zhuangzi*. For a reflection of this prevalent opinion, see Klein, "Were There 'Inner Chapters' in the Warring States?"

28. According to Bertil Lundahl, there is a group of chapters for which there is external evidence in the *Shiji* 史記 and *Huainanzi* to support Han Fei's (ca. 281–233 BCE) authorship. These "safest" chapters include chapters 11, 12, 22, 30–39, 49, 50. Connecting to the theme of "self-defeating behavior," which is brought up in chapter 49, and echoing the topics of several of these "safest" chapters, *Han Feizi* 47, "Eight Persuasions" 八說, is widely regarded as a chapter written by Han Fei himself. See Bertil Lundahl, *Han Fei Zi: The Man and the Work* (Stockholm: Institute of Oriental Languages Stockholm University, 1992), 139–69.

29. D. C. Lau considers the *Mencius* "extraordinarily well preserved," and A. C. Graham believes that it is "unusual among the early philosophical texts in raising no problems of authenticity." See Michael Hunter, "Did Mencius Know the *Analects*?," *T'oung Pao* 100, no. 1–3 (2014): 33–79, esp. 58–59.

30. Bruce E. Brooks and Taeko A. Brooks, "The Nature and Historical Context of the Mencius. Mencius," in *Mencius: Contexts and Interpretations*, ed. Alan K. L. Chan (Honolulu: University of Hawai'i Press, 2002), 242–81, esp. 242–43, 256–58.

31. Hunter, "Did Mencius Know the *Analects*?," 74–75.

32. Qian mistrusted the Yang-Mo passages in the *Zhuangzi* since they all belong to the Outer and Miscellaneous Chapters, which are clearly not written

by a single hand and in a single period. By contrast, the Inner Chapters, which are considered to be written by Zhuangzi himself, seem more reliable and only mention the pair of Ru-Mo. Qian, *Xianqin zhuzi xinian*, 285.

33. Esther Klein proposed the possibility that the Inner Chapters did not exist before Liu An's 劉安 (ca. 179–122 BC) compilation of the *Huainanzi*, for most of the textual parallels of the *Zhuangzi* found in other earlier texts are from the Outer and Miscellaneous rather than the Inner Chapters. See Klein, "Were There 'Inner Chapters' in the Warring States?"

34. As A. C. Graham pointed out, "Within the medley of a book called *Chuang-tzu*, there is one other writer with an identity as distinctive as that of the Chuang-tzu who wrote the *Inner Chapters*. He is the author who wrote the first three *Outer chapters* (Chapters 8–10) and the introductory essay of the fourth, whom we shall call the 'Primitivist.'" See A. C. Graham, *Chuang-Tzu: The Inner Chapters* (London: George Allen & Unwin, 2001), 197.

35. Many scholars have agreed that there is a homogeneous corpus attributable to a single (group of) author(s), though their opinions differ in terms of content and date. See Luo, *Zhuzi kaosuo*, 284–88; Guan Feng 關鋒, *Zhuangzi wai za pian chutan* 莊子外雜篇初探 (A Preliminary Survey on the Outer and Miscellaneous Chapters of *Zhuangzi*), reprinted in *Zhuangzi zhexue taolunji* 莊子哲學討論集 (Beijing: Zhonghua, 1961), 319–58; Zhang Hengshou 張恆壽, *Zhuangzi xintan* 莊子新探 [A new investigation into the *Zhuangzi*] (Wuhan: Hubei renmin chubanshe, 1983); A. C. Graham, "How Much of *Chuang Tzu* Did Chuang Tzu Write?," reprinted in *Companion to Angus C. Graham's Chuang Tzu: The Inner Chapters*, ed. Harold D. Roth (Honolulu: University of Hawai'i Press, 2003), 58–103; Liu Xiaogan, *Classifying the Zhuangzi Chapters* (Michigan: University of Michigan Center for Chinese, 2003), 84–88, 134–47; and Baggio, "The Four Primitivist Chapters of the *Zhuangzi*."

36. One example of textual parallels in terms of this group of texts and Yang-Mo passages is Li Xueqin's 李學勤 recent paper on the Guodian 郭店 manuscript *Yucong IV* 語叢四. In this bamboo manuscript, there are phrases similar to the ones in *Zhuangzi* chapter 10, a short *Zhuangzi* chapter containing the pairing of Yang-Mo. Li argues that the parallel passage in *Yucong IV* is an excerpt from *Zhuangzi* chapter 10. This parallel hence suggests that the received *Zhuangzi* chapter 10 was not composed later than 300 BCE (the date of the Guodian manuscript), which is very close to Mencius's lifetime (d. ca. 289 BCE). See Li Xueqin, "Looking at the 'Qu Qie' Chapter of the *Zhuangzi* from the *Guodian Yucong IV* Bamboo Slip Manuscript," *Bamboo and Silk* 1 (2018): 337–46.

37. A sentence from *Zhuangzi* chapter 10 was used by Graham as proof that this coherent group of *Zhuangzi* passages was composed after the Qin unification (221 BCE): "Tian Cheng Zi in one morning killed the ruler of Qi and stole his state . . . for twelve generations his family held possession of the state of Qi" (田成子一旦殺齊君而盜其國……十二世有齊國). See Graham, "How Much

of *Chuang Tzu* Did Chuang Tzu Write?," 84. In contrast, Li Xueqin counts the twelve generations from Chen Wan 陳完 (b. 706 BCE) to the Tai Gong He 太公和 (r. 386–384 BCE). For another example, Luo Genze and Giacomo Baggio have determined the date of this group by its textual correspondence with the *Han Feizi* and the *Shangjunshu* 商君書, whose composition can perhaps be more safely dated to the late Warring States period. See Luo, *Zhuzi kaosuo*, 284–88, and Baggio, "The Four Primitivist Chapters of the *Zhuangzi*," 13–18.

38. "It is true that part of a compilation can become coherent and representative because it was first written by a single person and then served as the inspiration for the rest of the text. Yet it is equally possible that the most coherent and representative part of a compilation can be produced by an editor who had access to the entire work and selected from it (and/or was inspired by it) to create a coherent and representative subset." Klein, "Were There 'Inner Chapters' in the Warring States?," 310.

39. Du Heng, "The Author's Two Bodies: Paratext in Early Chinese Textual Culture" (PhD diss., Harvard University, 2018), 25.

40. Du, "The Author's Two Bodies," 23. Du borrowed and modified these terminologies from Gerald Bruns. In Brun, closed texts are "the results of an act of writing that has reached a final form." See Gerald L. Bruns, "The Originality of Texts in a Manuscript Culture," *Comparative Literature* 32 (1980): 113–29, esp. 113.

41. Accordingly, the users-producers of open texts are mainly interested in "making use of pre-existing texts to fulfill different needs in their own contexts." The users of closed texts, instead, are absorbed in "preserving the text itself, often associating it with an earlier production context (real or imagined)." See Du, "The Author's Two Bodies," 11.

42. In Du's words, "a primordial soup teeming with independently circulating textual units, whose size ranges from short aphorisms to chapter-length compositions." Du, "The Author's Two Bodies," 4.

43. Du uses "para-text" to refer to "the textual elements that produce the body authorial." These elements are often devices that are "employed to identify, circumscribe, and stabilize a textual unit against the backdrop of ever present tendencies toward variation," which reflects "the wishes and efforts of the human agents involved the textual productions in any medium." This term was coined by Gérard Genette. In his original use, it refers to the textual elements, such as the title, author name, and preface, that surround the main text. See Du, "The Author's Two Bodies," 2, 26–27; Du Heng, "The Author's Two Bodies: The Death of Qu Yuan and the Birth of Chuci zhangju," *T'oung Pao* 105 (2019): 259–314, esp. 264; and Gérard Genett, *Paratexts: Thresholds of Interpretation*, trans. Jane E. Lewin (Cambridge: Cambridge University Press, 1997), 1–2.

44. Even if we were able to answer the question of whether the Yang-Mo in the *Zhuangzi* postdates that in the *Mencius*, the premise that the earlier

instance of a term is the source of the latter one would still be problematic because it is equally possible that they are unrelated incidents or joint effects of a common cause—perhaps the real prominence of these two schools at that time is the common cause of the mentions of Yang-Mo in different texts (but for some reason the numbers of mentions are limited). In any case, it seems that it is nearly impossible to prove that the Yang-Mo in the *Zhuangzi* is influenced by that in the *Mencius*.

Chapter 4

Deconstructing "Hedonism"
Understanding Yang Zhu in the *Liezi*

Erica Brindley

Introduction

Nowhere in the early textual record do we have more extensive collected materials explicitly concerning the figure of Yang Zhu than in the reputedly forged third- to fourth-century CE compilation, the *Liezi*. In chapter 7 of the book, dedicated to Yang Zhu's alleged sayings, the author(s) focus a good deal on what A. C. Graham calls "Yangist hedonism."[1] In this discussion of the main themes of the "Yang Zhu" chapter, I examine the nature and extent of these hedonistic themes, questioning whether the orientation in the chapter is rightfully understood as hedonistic. I suggest that "hedonism" as a term, while helpful, must nonetheless be used with caution and only with an eye to a deeper understanding of a cluster of important concepts in the chapter concerning life and death (*sheng si* 生死), reality (*shi* 實), reputation and false pretense (*ming* 名 and *wei* 偽), internal and external (*nei wai* 內外), and freedom or letting go (*si* 肆). This last concept reflects a particular flavor of freedom that diverges from the typical Daoist notions that became popular through Zhuangzian lineages, which are otherwise dominant in other parts of the *Liezi*. This analysis ultimately shows how all these concepts come together to form a "joy-in-life" (*le sheng* 樂生) philosophy that recasts Yang Zhu in a distinctive Wei-Jin-era light.

Since there is very little evidence concerning the historical Yang Zhu, and since there is no significant body of writings that we can attach to him with certainty, I will not try to uncover the "true" Yangzi or "original" Yangist philosophy apart from what we can know about his thinking from certain Warring States and early Han sources. Rather, this analysis focuses on what Yang Zhu stood for in the *Liezi* chapter and the text of the *Liezi* as a whole.

1. Recent Studies on Pleasure, Hedonism, and *Carpe Diem* in Premodern China

In this chapter we will define simple hedonism as an attitude of enjoying life to the fullest, especially in carnal, sensory ways. To designate a larger philosophical orientation, I use the following definition instead: *Hedonism is an orientation that promotes pleasure and the complete fulfilment of one's sensory desires as the ultimate good and goal in life.*[2] Is there something in the "Yang Zhu" chapter that resembles either simple or philosophical hedonism? And if the latter, what kind of philosophy is it? While it is beyond the scope of this article to analyze the history of the notion of "hedonism" in ancient Greece and even modern times in Euro-American philosophy, it behooves us to take a quick look at the ways in which a couple recent scholars of premodern Chinese literature and philosophy have understood "hedonism" and similar ideas concerning the pursuit of pleasure.

In Euro-American scholarship on the classical Chinese corpus, discussions of "hedonism" beyond those brief comments found in A. C. Graham's translation of the *Liezi* are mostly restricted to discussions of indulgent sentiments displayed in medieval poetry or discussions of activities that are pleasurable to the senses, such as sex, eating, drinking, music-making, and other such arts. Such discussions are usually distinct from scholarly accounts of *le* 樂 ("joy," "pleasure") in the philosophical literature. This divergence between philosophical discussions of pleasure and hedonism can be attributed to the unique way that hedonism is generally understood in Western academia, in both scholarly and non-scholarly contexts.

Anne Birrell's account of Han-period ballads from the Han Bureau of Music (*Yue fu* 樂府) highlights what she calls a *carpe diem* approach to life that is reflected in some poems of the collection. She easily moves from her description of *carpe diem* attitudes to the notion of hedonism, at times equating the terms.[3] For Birrell, hedonism is an approach found in some poems that urges us, because of our temporary existence in life, to indulge, or even inundate, the senses with pleasurable feelings from merrymaking activities and objects (drinks, sex, etc.). Intriguingly, the Han ballads that she examines in her chapter on the *carpe diem* theme might justifiably be considered to be lyrical companions to some of the prose passages typically labeled as "hedonistic" in the *Liezi*'s "Yang Zhu" chapter, which we examine below.[4] That there are literary and philosophical texts that rejoice and promote sensory indulgence should not come as a surprise, since they are bound to show up in any period or place. But what interests us here is whether these attitudes can be tied to a deeper philosophy or tradition of hedonism and just what such a philosophy or tradition might entail.

Michael Ing has noted that Birrell and other scholars of Chinese poetry usually highlight these examples because they fit what he thinks is a simple or popular understanding of hedonism. This popular hedonism, Ing states, "advocates an amoral (if not immoral) indulgence in sensual pleasures given the inevitability of death and the brevity of life" and neglects broader discussions of hedonism as a viable philosophical stance.[5] It is important to distinguish between hedonistic attitudes or inclinations, on the one hand, and a philosophy on the other. What Ing is calling "popular hedonism" seems a lot like a general ethos or attitude, one that is echoed in current standard dictionary definitions of the term "hedonism." Such definitions often stress the pursuit of pleasures via one's senses or desires without relating such a pursuit to any larger philosophical discourse on hedonism. Notably, what we will look for and test in the "Yang Zhu" chapter of the *Liezi* is whether the writing points to something more than the type of popular hedonism that is evinced in the Han ballads and other such celebrations of quick enjoyments.

In her recent book on "pleasure thinkers" in the ancient and medieval traditions, Michael Nylan neither discusses Yang Zhu as a figure nor the "Yang Zhu" chapter in the *Liezi*. Her omission of Yang Zhu seems intentional. For her, "hedonism," as understood in the West, is characterized by the "pleasure-pain dichotomy," whereas the "pleasure calculus in classical Chinese" revolving around the concept of *le* is utterly disinterested in such a dichotomy.[6] Moreover, for Nylan, "pleasure" in ancient and medieval China denoted long-term relational pleasures, obtained through assiduous effort at converting "the *consuming* pleasures—those that expend vast wealth, time, and physical energy—into *sustaining* pleasures that could support, rather than deplete or corrupt the polity, the family, or the body."[7]

By framing "pleasure calculus" as such, Nylan can exclude the pursuit of short-term or immediate pleasures from her account of pleasure.

To my mind, Nylan's definition of *le* is not comprehensive for the Chinese case. To state that Yang Zhu or those associated with his name should not be associated with a "pleasure calculus" is an odd interpretive choice. This is especially the case, as we will see, since the figure of Yang Zhu seems to have evolved in early history to be linked precisely to *le*, vitality, enjoyments, and other clearly pleasure-related activities. What happens, for example, when immediate or short-term pleasures are considered to be the only means of attaining long-term gratification? What about those instances in which *le* as a "quick enjoyment" is deemed to be the highest form of attainment and means to ultimate vitality and the ultimate good and goal in life?

2. The Chapter's Various Types of Hedonism

A. C. Graham refers to the author of this chapter as a "hedonist" who expresses a philosophy "in which everything is familiar, and we follow effortlessly every turn of the thought without ever sensing elusive differences of preconception which obscure the point."[8] He goes on to juxtapose what he considers to be an original Yangist philosophical orientation—one that rejects external possessions and benefits as harmful to the body—with the hedonism presented in the "Yang Zhu" chapter. But what Graham calls "hedonism" is easy to understand and translate across radically different cultures precisely because it is the "popular hedonism" that we have outlined above. Is the "hedonism" of the "Yang Zhu" chapter really just popular hedonism, or is there a larger philosophy associated with it? And is Graham correct to suppose that there is an original Yangist position (starting with Yang Zhu in the Warring States period) that is distinguishable from the approaches we find in the "Yang Zhu" chapter of the *Liezi*? In what follows, I will explore the limits of popular hedonism in this chapter to see if it makes sense to understand it as such and to gauge the extent to which we might associate this understanding of hedonism with a version of Yang Zhu that predated the third- to fourth-century CE compilation of the *Liezi*.

To simplify our discussion of the seventeen or so stories (depending on how one slices the chapter) in the *Liezi*, I refer to the stories by number as they appear in the online version of the Chinese Text Project.[9] This is also the numbering I use in the following Table, which charts at a glance what the author(s) wished for us both to avoid and embrace, singling out encouragements that clearly point to key elements of our working definition of simple/popular hedonism: the pursuit of quick enjoyments and fulfilling one's sensory pleasures and desires.

Table 1. *Liezi*, "Yang Zhu" Chapter 7: What to Avoid and What to Embrace (Two Types)

Yang Zhu Story	Avoidances (what not to worry about)	Encouragements (Clearly pointing to quick enjoyments and sensory pleasure): *simple/popular hedonism*	Encouragements (Other: relaxation, freedom, joy, fulfilling life and one's nature, basic comforts): *life-affirming, philosophical hedonism*
Story 1	Reputation 名, which wears away the body and scalds the heart-mind 苦其身燋其心		
Story 2	External motivators such as punishments and rewards 刑賞, reputation and laws 名法, empty praise 虛譽, enduring glory 餘榮, one's fated allotment of years 年命多少	Enjoyments of the ears and eyes 為聲色爾美厚聲色, 當身之娛, utmost joy in the present 當年之至樂, giving oneself up to the moment 自肆於一時, following what moves the heart 從心而動, not going against what one naturally likes 不違自然所好, following the roaming of one's nature 從性而游, not going against what all creatures like 不逆萬物所好	

continued on next page

Yang Zhu Story	Avoidances (what not to worry about)	Encouragements (Clearly pointing to quick enjoyments and sensory pleasure): *simple/popular hedonism*	Encouragements (Other: relaxation, freedom, joy, fulfilling life and one's nature, basic comforts): *life-affirming, philosophical hedonism*
Story 3	Worrying about what comes after death 遑死後		Gravitate towards one's present life 趣當生
Story 4	Sagely purity and probity 清貞 that bring about starvation and the diminishment of one's clan 餓死, 寡宗		Desires 欲, feelings 情
Story 5	Poverty 窶 that takes away from one's life 損生, and prosperity 殖 that weighs down one's body 累身		Enjoying life 樂生, easing the body 逸身
Story 6	Wasteful expenditures on the dead		Taking care of the life and the living; easing those who toil, filling the bellies of those who starve, warming those who are cold, helping those who are poor makes ends meet 使逸, 饑能使飽, 寒能使溫, 窮能使達
Story 7	The many restraints 諸閼 on one's sensory desires, which are the rulers of great oppression 廢虐之主; Worrying about burial practice 送死 and death 死	Nourishing life 養生, to unfetter it 肆之, indulging the ears, eyes, nose, mouth, and intent 恣耳, 恣目, 恣鼻, 恣口, 恣意	

Yang Zhu Story	Avoidances (what not to worry about)	Encouragements (Clearly pointing to quick enjoyments and sensory pleasure): *simple/popular hedonism*	Encouragements (Other: relaxation, freedom, joy, fulfilling life and one's nature, basic comforts): *life-affirming, philosophical hedonism*
Story 8	The idea that health is important 性命之重 and ritual and propriety are valuable	Being fond of and drinking lots of wine 禮義之尊好酒, being fond of and having lots of sex 好色; Exhausting a life's delights 盡一生之歡, 窮當年之樂	
Story 9		Everything that the people desire to do 生民之所欲為, everything that human intent wishes to amuse itself with 人意之所欲玩者; attaining that which the feelings desire, the ears wish to hear, the eyes long to see, and the mouth craves to taste 至其情所欲好, 耳所欲聽, 目所欲視, 口所欲嘗	
Story 10	Valuing life and cherishing the body 貴生愛身, prolonging life 久生	Using up one's desires 究其所欲 and waiting for death 俟於死	Letting go and allowing life to happen 廢而任之(生)
Story 11			Not even for the sake of a single hair, benefitting other things 不以一毫利物, Not even for the sake

continued on next page

Yang Zhu Story	Avoidances (what not to worry about)	Encouragements (Clearly pointing to quick enjoyments and sensory pleasure): *simple/popular hedonism*	Encouragements (Other: relaxation, freedom, joy, fulfilling life and one's nature, basic comforts): *life-affirming, philosophical hedonism*
Story 11 (cont'd.)			of one's body, gaining benefit for the self 不以一身自利
Story 12	Reputation 名, letting ritual and propriety bring misery to oneself 以禮義自苦	Indulging in all the amusements of the ears and eyes 恣耳目之所娛 exhausting all that one's intents and thoughts want to do 窮意慮之所為, making merry until death 熙熙然以至於死; unleashing one's passions 肆情, giving free rein to one's desires 縱欲	
Story 13			Ruling the world is like rolling it in the palm of one's hand 治天下如運諸掌
Story 14	Reputation 名譽, bodily and spiritual toil 苦其神形		Seeking the joy/pleasure in life 生之樂
Story 15	Possessing one's body 有其身, possessing external things 有其物, lopsidedly possessing one's body and external things 橫私天下之身, 物		Preserving oneself 存我, completing one's life and body 全生身, treating one's body and external things as what is common to all 公天下之身公天下之物

Yang Zhu Story	Avoidances (what not to worry about)	Encouragements (Clearly pointing to quick enjoyments and sensory pleasure): *simple/popular hedonism*	Encouragements (Other: relaxation, freedom, joy, fulfilling life and one's nature, basic comforts): *life-affirming, philosophical hedonism*
Story 16	Worrying about the four affairs, long life, reputation, official position, and material gain 壽, 名, 位, 貨, 貴, inclining toward nobility 矜貴, wanting power 要勢, coveting wealth 貪富		Not going against fate 不逆命, being in accord with the people 順民, keeping the regulation of one's fate under one's own control 制命在內; enjoying the simple comforts of the peasant 野人之所安, 野人之所美
Story 17	An insatiable nature 无猒之性, worrying about one's reputation for loyalty and duty being loyal, dutiful 忠名義名, worry and misery, which violate our natures 憂苦 犯性者	A fine house, 豐屋, beautiful clothes 美服, 厚味, strong tastes 姣色, good-looking people	Ruler and minister are both safe 君臣皆安, external things and the self both receive benefits 物我兼利, being relaxed and joyful, which accord with our natures 逸樂順性者

The table above provides the frequency and textual locations in which quick enjoyments and pleasurable activities are promoted in the chapter, as opposed to more general types of desired pursuits that do not necessarily involve sensory pleasure, such as joy, relaxation, and fulfilling basic needs and emotions. One sees that just over half of the stories in the chapter—at least eleven of seventeen, and arguably more—do not prioritize sensory pleasure as the highest end. The main goals of these passages concern completing, preserving, and following one's nature, destiny, joy, life, and body (*xing, ming, le, sheng, shen* 性, 命, 樂, 生, 身). One notes the high intensity of passages clustered together (stories 7–10) that do prioritize indulgences in sensory pleasure and the fulfillment of desires.[10] Intriguingly, this same cluster of four stories is noteworthy for the fact that no single passage starts with either the formulation, "Yang Zhu said/asked," or "Yang Zhu travelled in/went to see."[11] Every other story in the chapter makes use of such a format.

The table also points to at least three different strands of writing in the "Yang Zhu" chapter: (1) Stories 1–6 (except for 2). These stories are not overtly hedonistic in a simple, popular way. Nor are they clearly hedonistic in a deeper, more philosophical sense. Instead, they revolve around the concepts of reputation, the real versus fake (or pretense), life and death, and worrying about externalities such as death and moral reputation instead of enjoying life and the present moment.

(2) Stories 2, 7–10, and 12, maybe 17. These passages explicitly promote the pursuit of hedonistic, sensual pleasures, expressing a simple/popular hedonism. They take the concepts of the "utmost joy" 至樂 and "nourishing life" 養生 in a clearly material and sensory-oriented way. These are concepts that also happen to be the thematic focus in parts of the *Zhuangzi* ("Utmost Joy" is the title of chapter 18). A new metaphor of liberation: unfettering, unleashing, and letting go (*si, zong, fei* 肆, 縱, 廢) presents itself alongside acts of indulging, reaching the limits of, using up, and exhausting (*zi, jin, qiong, jiu* 恣, 盡, 窮, 究) resources such as joy, lust, desire, delight, and the passions. The sharp contrast between what is meant by "utmost joy" in the *Zhuangzi* and these stories suggests that these writings may have emerged from a similar milieu of debate on the concept, perhaps during the early Han.[12]

(3) Stories 11 and 13–16, maybe 17. These stories contain concepts and terms that echo the concerns of Warring States thinkers (ca. fourth to third century BCE). These include notions such as the cultivation of one's spirit, body, and nature (*shen, shen, xing* 神, 身, 性) and an aversion to things that burden our lives, such as possessions, reputation, and profit. The vocabulary of inner and outer, public and private interest, self (*wo* 我) versus other things (*wu* 物), and "inclusive benefit" (兼利) is reminiscent of debates that we find flourishing in passages from the Mohists, Mencius, and parts of the *Zhuangzi*. The shared vocabulary and way of discussing this cluster of concepts suggests that these six stories may have been formulated as early as the fourth century BCE.

I have tried to explain the three varied and discrete sections of this chapter as arising from different intellectual contexts and time periods. To be sure, there is probably much more to the picture. While a satisfactory explanation for the chapter's varied content may still elude us, we can nonetheless ask ourselves what the compiler aimed to accomplish with it. Why collect this particular group of stories and sayings—some of which are attributed to Yang Zhu, others involving Yang Zhu or his disciple Mengsun Yang, and others not explicitly mentioning Yang Zhu but touting the virtues of simple hedonism—in a single chapter titled "Yang Zhu"? The evidence we have concerning the figure of Yang Zhu prior to the Han period suggests that thought associated with Yang Zhu did not necessarily contain hedonistic elements, nor did it emphasize the pursuit of joy.[13] Perhaps by the compiler's day, Yang Zhu had already changed into a figure associated with unbridled joy and the sensory pleasures in life. Or was it the compiler of this *Liezi* chapter who created the new image of Yang Zhu according to his own understanding and fancy? My analysis suggests that the answer may be the latter.

3. Aspects of Philosophical Hedonism in the Chapter

In order to come to grips with these questions, and to begin answering whether the hedonism in the Yang Zhu is anything more than simple, popular hedonism, let us discuss four main themes that seem to reverberate throughout the chapter: (1) life over death; (2) reality over pretense or reputation; (3) internal, not external; and (4) freedom. It is through a deeper understanding of these philosophical concepts that we begin to appreciate the way hedonism as a notion fits in.

Life over death: As for valuing life over death, the relevant words are *sheng/si* (life and death 生/死) and *shen* (body/person 身). At times, the term "nourishing" (*yang* 養) appears, especially in relation to life (*yang sheng* 養生) in story 7 (a dialog between Yanzi and Guan Zhong); it is at least superficially reminiscent of "Nourishing Life," chapter 3 of the *Zhuangzi*. But it is also clearly an activity that one should engage in involving one's physical body and concrete, material person. While one might think that the hedonistic approach would value long life, or that good health would be an important part of the practice of nourishing life, the general recommendation in the chapter is not to worry about such things, as consideration of health and long life is rooted in an externality that causes internal harm and anxiety. We see this in the following passage:

Whether we are worthy or foolish, noble or base, is not of our own doing. And whether we are stinking or rotting, decaying or extinguished is also not of our own doing. Thus, it is not by virtue of life that we live, not by virtue of death that we die, not by virtue of worthiness that we are worthy, not by virtue of foolishness that we are foolish, not by virtue of nobility that we are noble, and not by virtue of baseness that we are base. This being the case, the myriad things are all even in life and death, and even in their worthiness, foolishness, nobility, and baseness. Those who live for ten years die, just as those who live for one hundred years die. The sages and benevolent ones die, just as the evil and stupid die.

賢愚貴賤，非所能也；臭腐消滅，亦非所能也。故生非所生，死非所死，賢非所賢，愚非所愚，貴非所貴，賤非所賤。然而萬物齊生齊死，齊賢齊愚，齊貴齊賤。十年亦死，百年亦死，仁聖亦死凶愚亦死.[14]

The discussion in this passage provides a justification for why our differences (in worthiness, intelligence, long or short life) in life do not matter since we are all fundamentally equal in death. Having set up the logic of our mortal equality and the notion that death is the great leveler, the author goes on to argue his main point, which is a comment on how we should live. "So, relish your present life; why rush [to worry] about the post-mortem?" (且趣當生，奚遑死後)[15] Death in this passage serves as the ultimate ground upon which meaning in life sprouts. It is the reason for, or that which permits and justifies, the underlying *carpe diem* attitude to "relish your present life," expressed at the end of this story.

So far, the program for this author's good life seems very good, indeed, in the sense that we are supposed to enjoy what we are given, whatever it may be, without worrying about morality and a long life. But this does not mean that it should be understood as a form of simple/popular hedonism that merely promotes pleasure and the complete fulfillment of one's desires. Desires and pleasure may, in fact, only be part of the equation. Indeed, a constant refrain in this section of the chapter is not so much a positive promotion of pleasure as much as it is a negative injunction to avoid and disregard things that injure your life. This is clear in the judgment Yang Zhu metes out on Bo Yi in story 4, immediately following the statement above concerning life and death. In this passage, which may very well be intended as a continuation of the previous passage, Yang Zhu states:

> It is not that Bo Yi had no desires; it's that he cherished purity so much that he quit his office and let himself starve to death. It is not that Zhan Li had no emotions; it's that he cherished moral probity so much that he quit his office, was widowed, and neglected his ancestral clan. These cases demonstrate the error of mistaking purity and moral probity as the good.
>
> 伯夷非亡欲，矜清之卸，以放餓死。展李非亡情，矜貞之卸，以放寡宗。清貞之誤善之若此。[16]

Here, the author makes fun of Bo Yi and Zhan Li, who by denying their desires (*yu* 欲) and emotions (*qing* 情), brought suffering on themselves and their loved ones. Preferable to Bo Yi and Zhan Li's methods, the author suggests, are alternative ways of being that engage and presumably implicate the fulfillment of our human desires and emotions. Although this is beginning to hint at a hedonistic injunction for the promotion of pleasure, its scope still seems broader than the mere pursuit of sensory pleasure. After all, fulfilling one's desires and emotions is not tantamount to seeking to promote pleasure exclusively, especially since each person's desires and emotions might be fulfilled differently and not necessarily in ways that please the senses.

Story 5 provides a more positive formulation of what it means more precisely to "relish this present life" as stated above. Just as long life is explicitly not an ultimate goal, neither is wealth or pleasure: "What is acceptable is delighting in life and easing the body. Thus, the one who delights in life is not impoverished, and the one who eases his body is not wealthy." (可在樂生，可在逸身。故善樂生者不窶，善逸身者不殖) The word *yi* 逸, "to ease," literally means to escape or break free from something, and recluses in early China were famously known as *yi min* 逸民 or *yi ren* 逸人, (i.e., people who broke free from society). In this passage, therefore, we might consider the goals of *le sheng* 樂生 and *yi shen* 逸身 to be related: to find pleasure in life is also to harness a relaxed state that comes with breaking free from external constraints and pressures. The constraints mentioned in story 5 are wealth and poverty, but in other parts in the chapter, they include reputation, long life, honor, knowledge, and moral strictures. Clearly, a primary component of this philosophical outlook is much broader than the single-minded pursuit of sensory pleasures; it is the pursuit of a joy that is begotten from the shedding of external constraints and pressures.

In story 6, the emphasis is again not on sensory pleasure per se but on easing the body during this life, of other people as well as of the self. Indeed, this particular viewpoint is more life-affirming than hedonistic:

> Yang Zhu said, "There is an old saying that we should 'Empathize with the living and renounce the dead.' This saying is very true. The way to empathize with others is not simply to feel for them. When they toil, we can bring ease; when they are hungry, we can fill their bellies; when cold, we can warm them; when poor, we can help them get by. The way to renounce the dead is not about refusing to grieve for them. Rather, we should not put pearls or jade in their mouths, dress them in brocades, lay out sacrificial victims, or set up mortuary vessels."

> 楊朱曰：「古語有之：『生相憐，死相捐。』此語至矣。相憐之道，非唯情也；勤能使逸，饑能使飽，寒能使溫，窮能使達也。相捐之道，非不相哀也；不含珠玉，不服文錦，不陳犧牲，不設明器也.[17]

A major aspect of this approach involves not mere benefit to the self, but a socially responsible injunction to help others through material benefits and aid as well.[18] In the Bo Yi and Zhan Li passage (story 4) previously examined, the author also condemns the latter for quitting office, becoming widowed, and neglecting his ancestral clan, all in the name of moral purity. The social dimension of these quotes stands in direct contrast to Mencius's depiction of Yang Zhu as being egoistic, or "for the sake of oneself" (*wei wo* 為我).[19] While we do not know if a Warring States Yang Zhu included this social dimension in his teachings, or if this is but a fabrication of the Han or Wei-Jin periods, at the very least we can say that figures like Yang Zhu, Confucius, Mo Di, and other notable thinkers of the ancient period became stock characters to whom a variety of characteristics and philosophical stances were attributed. For our purposes here, it is enough to note that the figure of Yang Zhu in the *Liezi* cares about the flourishing of life in this world and not the afterlife.

Reality over pretense: In addition to affirming life by musing on life and death, certain authors of the "Yang Zhu" chapter highlight the distinction between reality (*shi* 實) and reputation (*ming* 名, or name). The contrast between reality and reputation, also referred to as false pretense (*wei* 偽), is a prominent theme in the chapter, one that seems to connect the chapter with the equally prominent theme of absolute reality, found throughout the *Liezi*. The pairing of *ming* and *shi* has a long history in early Chinese thought, going back to the theoreticians of statecraft and language/logic, but it seems to have acquired an especially pointed use in this chapter.[20] In this chapter, *ming* almost invariably refers to one's reputation, which while it may have its redeeming qualities, is always condemned. The Yang Zhu of this chapter lambasts reputation not just because it is an externality that is unnecessary for the fulfillment of life and vitality but because it is a deadly poison, worse even than the poison of pretense.

Many stories in the chapter affirm life in a negative way, by opposing what goes against it. Pursuing a reputation is the biggest culprit. Stories 2, 8, 12, 14, 16, and 17 all send the unequivocal message that reputation can actively impede the enjoyment of life (生之樂).[21] Story 1 complicates the notion of reputation while at the same time acknowledging Yang Zhu's disapproval of it. The dialog, featuring Yang Zhu and a certain Mr. Meng in the state of Lu, serves as an extended meditation on reputation. At first, it seems to turn on its head the idea that concern for externalities is necessarily harmful to life, since Yang Zhu admits that reputation brings not only benefit to oneself and one's descendants but to all of one's local affiliations and the larger clan. ("By riding one's reputation, one can bring blessings to one's clan and benefits that include one's local village and community. How much more one's descendants as well!" [乘其名者澤及宗族，利兼鄉黨；況子孫乎]).[22] But as one progresses through the story, the main point switches away from the benefits of reputation to a deeper, cynical realization: that benefit for oneself and one's affiliates is built on pretense, not reality. The takeaway, I think, is for the reader to return to Yang Zhu's early statement in the story: that "reputation wears away at one's body and scalds the heart-mind," and if what you want are benefits from reputation, you are better off peddling a false reputation by pandering to those in power than trying to pursue a real reputation.

The story's allusions to famous historical figures illustrate these points. Yang Zhu raises the contrasting cases of Guan Zhong versus Tian Heng on the one hand, and Yao and Shun versus Bo Yi and Shu Qi on the other. In Guan Zhong's case, he was sincere in his actions as minister to Duke Huan of Qi (d. 463 BCE) yet failed to bring benefit to his descendants. In contrast, Tian Heng, a minister who served as de facto ruler under his puppet, Duke Ping of Qi (d. 456 BCE), relied on pretense yet was able to gain possession of the state of Qi. Notably, this Yang Zhu states, the man who faked his loyalty to Duke Ping passed on the enjoyments [of possessing power in the state] to his descendants, "which has been unbroken to the present day" (子孫享之，至今不絕).[23]

Yao and Shun are similarly criticized. In this story they are not legendary sage heroes but notorious pretenders, in contrast to Bo Yi and Shu Qi, who achieved a reputation but met their end through starvation on Mount Shouyang.[24] By engineering a fake resignation to Xu You 許由 and Shan Juan 善卷, they enjoyed the perks of ruling all under Heaven and being revered by later generations.[25] So, even though story 1 seems to denounce the pursuit of any type of reputation (recall Yang Zhu's pronouncement that "reputation wears away at one's body and scalds the heart-mind"), the subtext signals to the reader that pursuing a false reputation to enjoy riches and power is better than chasing after a reputation of moral purity. How foolish of Guan Zhong, Bo Yi, and Shu Qi!

This complicated introduction to the concept of reputation serves an interesting purpose in the chapter. I believe it subtly endorses a philosophy of material benefit and foreshadows an attitude that embraces enjoyment found in several of the passages that immediately follow. Clearly, nobody would dare argue that Guan Zhong, Bo Yi, and Shu Qi did not make a lasting name for themselves, just as the pretenders they are contrasted with achieved great renown. But to what extent were such pursuits justified? To lead a miserable life, die alone of starvation, and leave nothing for one's progeny is arguably morally worse than not to seek out a moral reputation at all. If one must waste one's time worrying about a reputation, then a preferable way to do so would be through pretense and not moral conviction. The discussion of reputation in story 1 thus warms us to the idea that earning a nice living and enjoying the material, life-affirming rewards of a false reputation is actually a superior choice compared to the choice of a moral reputation that causes suffering.[26] In other words, *don't be a sucker*. Moral reputation is not worth it.

Internal versus external: Another important theme that relates to the authors' critique of reputation concerns the relative value of what is internal versus external. "Ordering what is on the outside" (治外者) is contrasted with "ordering what is on the inside" (治內者), an activity that notably involves one's human nature (*xing* 性). Story 8 sums up the matter:

> The person who is good at ordering what is on the outside does not necessarily bring order to things, but rather, brings hardship to his body. The person who is good at ordering what is on the inside does not necessarily bring disorder to things, but rather, brings ease to his nature.
>
> 夫善治外者，物未必治，而身交苦；善治內者，物未必亂，而性交逸.[27]

Before this concluding remark, however, the story provides quintessential examples of what we readily associate with hedonism: the pursuit of sensory pleasure as the highest good. A brief analysis of how it parses what is internal versus what is external will tell us much about how the author wishes to tie hedonistic views into a larger philosophy of human nature and life.

Story 8 features the moral and responsible Zichan, a sixth-century BCE prime minister of the state of Zheng. The author underscores how Zichan's successes are purely external. They apply to state order but not to his own family, which is revealed to be an utter mess.[28] Zichan's ostensible successes are also expressed in typical social values such as knowledge, foresight, ritual, duty, reputation, and status (智慮禮義名位).[29] Then there are his two brothers, Gongsun Chao 公孫朝 and Gongsun Mu 公孫穆. Each of these is characterized by a different form of excessive behavior and debauched lifestyle. Gongsun Chao drinks incessantly, so much that he has a store of thousands of pots of spirits. When in a stupor, Chao could be on a battleground, with water and fire and clashing swords in front of him, and he would not even be aware of what was happening.[30] Gongsun Mu engages in constant sex with harems of women in the rear palaces, at times emerging only once every three months. He would tempt every beautiful virgin in the village with riches, using a go-between to reach out to her and would only give up if he failed through these means to catch her.[31] From these wonderful descriptions, we sense that everything associated with the staid Zichan are external concerns, while everything associated with the colorful brothers is internal, and hence, desirable. Accordingly, qualities such as knowledge, foresight, ritual, duty, reputation, and status are all external, and appetites for drinking and sex are internal. But is this all there is to the internal?

Various hints throughout the story help us piece together the internal realm that needs fulfillment. When Zichan criticizes the two brothers' actions, he says that they endanger their "natural lifespan" (*xing ming* 性命) by indulging their emotions, cravings, and desires.[32] The brothers' response to Zichan, however, shows us how such an understanding of the internal realm is impoverished:

> For the sake of our desires, we will fully exhaust the delights of this one life, draining the utmost joy from its years. Our only misfortune is a belly too full to drink as much as the mouth would like, potency that gives out before we can fully abandon our passions in sex. We have no time to worry that our reputation is bad and our health and lifespans are in danger.
>
> 為欲盡一生之歡，窮當年之樂，唯患腹溢而不得恣口之飲，力憊而不得肆情於色，不遑憂名聲之醜，性命之危也.[33]

These statements provide us with ample evidence that fulfillment of the internal realm is not about achieving good health and a long life.[34] Indeed, these are considered to be external and inimical to the fulfillment of carnal pleasures. Rather, it is about satisfying one's emotions and nature (*qing xing* 情性) by fulfilling one's desires and cravings, not about correcting or distorting them (literally, "straightening them out" [矯情性]).[35] More specifically, it concerns carnal pleasures and joys associated with fun activities such as drinking and sex.

In story 16, as well, long life, reputation, status, wealth, and the accumulation of goods are mentioned as externalities that might take control of one's life course.[36] There, one formulation of the external-internal dichotomy of authority is provided to us in a helpful quip: "When we can be killed or given life, that which controls our lives is outside us. . . . When nothing in the world counters us; that which controls our lives is within us." (可殺可活，制命在外……天下无對，制命在內)[37] The passage describes two scenarios: the former defined by external worries that stress people out, the latter defined by internal freedoms that allow one to transcend such worries. The point of the ditty is that our lifespans may be controlled by either external affairs or internal freedom. It is only when one

> does not go against one's destined lifespan . . . does not incline towards honor . . . does not want power . . . and does not crave wealth that one does not yearn for long life, reputation, position, and possessions.

> 不逆命，何羨壽？不矜貴，何羨名？不要勢，何羨位？不貪富，何羨貨？[38]

Here, what is internal is defined exclusively in terms of what *is not external* or what *goes against the external*. This is summed up in the ditty's formulation: "when nothing in the world counters us." The defining feature for the good life is, according to story 16, not necessarily the pursuit of one's sensory pleasures. It is all that is internal to our lives, as defined negatively by what should not be controlling us.

The minimal effort to present a positive, exhaustive list of the internalities that should be guiding our lives is repeated in the last story in the chapter, story 17. There, too, the author stresses the importance of denying external things' control over one's life. But intriguingly, the author of this last passage does produce some guiding principles to consider. In a much more modest way than in stories 2, 7–10, and 12, this author presents the following as internal needs and basic desires: "A fine house, beautiful clothes, strong tastes, and good-looking people—if you have these four, why seek anything on the outside?" (豐屋美服，厚味姣色，有此四者，何求於外)[39] The final story in the chapter thus returns to the idea that the fulfillment of such palpable sensory desires is precisely what is meant by the pursuit of one's internal freedoms. Given the placement of this statement at the end of the chapter, as though in direct response to the vague implications of story 16, it appears that the compiler may have been quite consciously trying to promote a hedonistic message associated with Yang Zhu. While it is arguable whether this particular story endorses simple, popular hedonism, as compared to stories 2, 7–10, and 12 in the chapter, it seems clear that the affirmation of sensory pleasures here functions effectively as a reference to the stories with more hedonistic content that appear earlier in the chapter. Story 17, in other words, is the compiler's way of both filling in the blanks left by the predominant emphasis in this chapter on what to avoid, signaling to the reader that sensory pleasure is the most effective way to practice this approach.

<u>Freedom</u>: So far we have seen that the type of philosophical hedonism propounded in the "Yang Zhu" chapter—one that affirms life by emphasizing an awareness of mortality and death—explicitly positions itself against any type of external authority that might possess and overtake our zest for life. It is anti-Confucian in the sense that it rejects the pursuit of moral conventions and goals, anti-Mohist in the sense that it rejects the pursuit of benefit or social good for the sake of social good, and generally anti-"do-gooder" of any sort. And, unlike philosophies that ask us to rely on the so-of-itself of an underlying Dao of the cosmos, this approach urges us to engage in an untethered approach to life without any specific spiritual Dao at the root. I choose the term "untethered" as a translation for the term *si* 肆 because it emphasizes the negative things that hold us back from happiness. *Si* appears only four times in the chapter, but prominently, in conjunction with the pursuit of pleasure and one's abandonment to one's sensory desires (ears, eyes, nose, mouth, body, mind).[40] When we free ourselves in such a way, we are said to "nourish" (*yang* 養) or affirm life. This can be seen in story 7, where Guan Zhong describes this free, untethered state of being: "By ridding yourself of these oppressive masters, you will blithely await death, whether it be for a day, a month, a year, or ten years; this is what I call nourishing [life]" (去廢虐之主，熙熙然以俟死，一日一月，一年十年，吾所謂養).[41]

While freedom, in the sense of being *si*-untethered, is largely defined as an act of breaking free, it is also guided by positive incentives. These are mentioned a few times in the text in relationship to one's bodily senses and desires. In the same story (7), Guan Zhong also links being untethered with the senses and desires in the following manner:

> Yan Pingzhong asked Guan Yiwu about nourishing life. Guan answered, "It is simply a matter of untethering it. Do not block and do not clog." Yan asked further, "What do you mean?" "Indulge in whatever your ears wish to listen to, your eyes to look upon, your nose to turn towards, your mouth to utter, your body to find rest in, your mind to desire and carry out."

> 管夷吾曰：「肆之而已，勿壅勿閼。」晏平仲曰：「其目奈何？」夷吾曰：「恣耳之所欲聽，恣目之所欲視，恣鼻之所欲向，恣口之所欲言，恣體之所欲安，恣意之所欲行。」[42]

Freedom in this scenario is a freedom of the psychological and sensory burdens of life by means of the various internal faculties of the body: the senses, body, and mind. Examples of objects in the world that help complete the freedom of the body are music, good food, fancy clothes and luxurious objects, leisure, and even a good debate about right and wrong. These types of desirable objects and activities bring comfort, joy, pleasure, and perhaps most importantly, a temporary release from our natural cravings. Whereas many moralists might argue that the active pursuit of such goals would only increase one's cravings—or, at the very least, not curb them—this author does not view the fulfillment of these objectives in such a way. Our poison is not the desirable objects; our demons are not our desires. Rather, they are the many worries derived from false goals that divert us from these simple internal needs and desires: reputation, salary, and donating valuables to the dead. Notably, the goal of obtaining lots of money is not explicitly mentioned in the chapter as one of these external goals, although one might assume that it would belong to the same category as reputation—one of the true evils in life.

Freedom in this chapter appears to be deeply linked to play—and play linked to losing awareness of the passage of time. A story that parallels the most hedonistic stories in the chapter, story 9, presents a simple commentary on the pursuit of joy as an activity involving play, amusement, delight, and fun. The protagonist, Duanmu Shu (端木叔, allegedly Zi Gong's descendent), has lived a life out of step with the moral and ritual goals of his time but in tune with his heart's desires and passions. He did not just play lightheartedly; he got the most joy and fun out of every moment of life he was given. And so, without worrying about his health (he did not possess medicines or needles to cure ailments or prolong his life) or other social goals, he achieved the pinnacle of understanding as an "accomplished person" (*da ren* 達人) and "surpassed his ancestors in virtue" (*de* 德).[43]

A whole cluster of terms referring to one's likes and desires, including the verb, "to play" (*wan* 玩), are featured in this story, all driving home the central point about the importance of not wasting joy and delight as our life's most valuable goal. But what happens when we play? During moments of play we feel completely free because, as suggested throughout the "Yang Zhu" chapter, we are not really stressed and worried about winning or achieving certain goals. But another aspect of this freedom is that there is no resistance in the passage of time. We forget about time because we are lost in play and other activities that untether our spirits from time itself. This is best exemplified at the end of story 10, which mentions the act of "allowing life to run its course":

> Being alive, abandon yourself to life and allow it to run its course; exhaust all your desires and wait for death. . . . By never not abandoning oneself and never not allowing it to run its course, what need would you have to delay it or speed it on its way?
>
> 既生，則廢而任之，究其所欲，以俟於死……无不廢，无不任，何遽遲速於其間乎[44]

Here, the link between life and freedom is established through a special connection to time. Waiting, running a course, delaying, speeding up—all of these actions involve our psychological relationship to time. Rushing and delaying the moment are acts that attempt to manipulate time and treat it as an external object. They thus violate the freedom associated with proper enjoyment of life running a course *in its proper time*. When we give ourselves over to the proper rhythm of time, however, we enjoy life in a stress-free manner and do not notice the progression. This is expressed literally in the passage as letting life run its course and, ironically, as "waiting for death." Waiting for death is not a literal waiting but a metaphorical understanding that life is but a special moment that must be lived in the present and not pushed or pulled along in any way.[45]

Conclusion

Having examined four main themes in the chapter, we may now ask whether the Yang Zhu of this *Liezi* chapter promotes a specific philosophy of hedonism, or whether he is merely the poster child for simple, popular hedonism. Is "hedonism" even the right label for such a chapter? As mentioned previously, statements and descriptions in stories 2, 7–10, 12, and possibly story 17 all seem to endorse, at the very least, a simple, popular understanding of hedonism. The unbounded drinking and sex of Zichan's brothers in story 8 certainly look a lot like the pursuit of physical pleasures as an ultimate good. It is probably such passages, among those others listed, that prompted Graham to claim that the chapter was penned by a later hedonist author who differed significantly from the so-called original Yang Zhu of the Warring States period.

The places where the authors in the chapter actually depict examples or provide positive formulations of this hedonistic pursuit, however, are relatively few. Simple, popular hedonism is clearest in about 6 or 7 of the chapter's 17 stories, and of those passages, three (stories 7–9) are not attributed to Yang Zhu as a figure, nor do they make mention of him in any way. Nonetheless, the placement of such passages in a chapter named after Yang Zhu betrays an attempt by the compiler to tie the pursuit of physical pleasures to an overarching Yangist philosophy. In much of the chapter, a negative approach prevails, warning us to beware of external motivations such as reputation, long life, and other thieves of our joy and vitality.[46] But there are moments where the point is precisely to link quick enjoyments to this negative philosophy.

In sum, the simple hedonism that comprises a third of the chapter's stories cannot simply be dismissed as radical sentiments that were inserted haphazardly into a whole. Rather, it makes good sense to view the hedonism in the chapter as the compiler's response to larger questions discussed in the chapter: the relative value of life over death, the problems of reputation and false pretense, the importance of focusing on the internal and going against external controls over our natures, and the ultimate delights of freedom as play. Although this orientation includes elements of simple hedonism, it is not limited to them. These elements of simple hedonism should thus be taken as an integral part of its overarching philosophical outlook.

Rather than characterize this chapter as simple hedonism, we might do better to view it in terms of a deeper philosophical orientation—a "joy/pleasure-in-life" orientation.[47] This emphasizes the two Chinese terms, joy/pleasure (*le*) and life (*sheng*), that are affirmed in the stories and better encapsulate the chapter's resounding proposals to savor delightful, life-giving moments as well as its directives to live freely in time, avoiding the oppression of goals that are extrinsic to happiness. Thinking about the chapter in terms of "joy-in-life" and not simple hedonism allows us to be more open to its various elements, including its valorization of acts of charity and its praise of those who contribute to the welfare of state and society, as well as its promotion of play, delight, and anything fun.

What we learn from this joy-in-life approach appears to complicate Nylan's understanding of the role of *le* in the Chinese tradition. If the Yang Zhu of this chapter recommends anything, it is to pursue *le* in its most authentic, unadulterated forms. There should be no transmuting of less desirable pleasures into superior pleasures and forms of attainment. With the Liezian Yang Zhu, we are introduced to a figure who encourages us to go for the immediate and short-term pleasures as well as whatever else might bring an appreciation of our vitality and freedom in each living moment. Indeed, the *Liezi's* presentation of a semi-forgotten figure recasts him indelibly as a sage who truly understood that the highest good in life is joy.

In addition to the *carpe diem* theme found in Han-era ballads, as well as other more hedonistic attitudes found in earlier texts like the *Lüshi chunqiu* and *Zhuangzi* (especially the Robber Zhi stories), the joy-in-life philosophy presented in the *Liezi* chapter resonates with cultural trends and stories surrounding important Wei-dynasty elites, especially the Seven Sages of the Bamboo Grove (ca. third century CE). Figures such as Ji Kang 嵇康 (223–262 CE), Ruan Ji 阮籍 (210–263 CE), and Liu Ling 劉伶 (ca. 221–300 CE) were known to have survived the treacherous political uncertainties of their time by turning to excessive drinking and other decadent behaviors.[48] With famous poets, musicians, and philosophers like these extolling the virtues of alcoholic spirits, amusement, and laughter as a way of managing the depressing realities of the day, it is no wonder that a chapter such as the "Yang Zhu" chapter of the *Liezi* should arise during the medieval era. Thinkers, writers, and compilers of texts, obsessed as they were with death and mortality, could easily build on stories and sayings associated with figures like Yang Zhu to give an old master a new guise.[49] Paradoxical as it may be, the authors and compiler(s) of the "Yang Zhu" chapter seem to have resuscitated him by drowning him in wine.

Notes

1. The "Yang Zhu" chapter of the *Liezi* is the only chapter in the entire literary tradition of China that explicitly dedicates itself to Yang Zhu. Eleven of the seventeen stories in the chapter begin with the statement, "Yang Zhu said" (楊朱曰), while three others begin with Yang Zhu (or Yangzi) being asked something, going somewhere, or visiting with a ruler. Only three stories in the chapter (stories 7, 8, and 9) do not mention Yang Zhu at all, and instead feature dialogs between famous thinkers or leaders discussing profligates. In this article, I number the stories of this chapter according to divisions that are established in the online Chinese Text Project version of the chapter. See https://ctext.org/liezi/yang-zhu.

2. Deriving from the Greek term *hēdonē* (ἡδονή), meaning "pleasure." Epicurean thought, which "hedonism" is associated with, valued pleasure that

may not derive from virtuous actions and was mostly associated with physical pleasures. For more on Epicurean hedonism, see James Warren, *Epicurus and Democritean Ethics: An Archaeology of Ataraxia* (Cambridge: Cambridge University Press, 2002), 50. The definition that I use above is a reformulation of many basic definitions of "hedonism" in contemporary dictionaries.

 3. Anne Birrell, *Popular Songs and Ballads of Han China* (London: Unwin Hyman, 1988), 78–93.

 4. Birrell, *Popular Songs and Ballads*, 78–83. Intriguingly, Birrell thinks of hedonism as part and parcel of a *carpe diem* attitude and not some larger philosophy, and she links the two themes of immortality and *carpe diem*, claiming that, although they are "intellectually incompatible," they are both "present without one dominating" (82). I do not think that the two orientations (immortality and *carpe diem*) are necessarily contradictory, as they could have both been variations on the theme of maximizing vitality and life to the greatest extent possible.

 5. Michael Ing, "Chapter Three: Immediate Enjoyments" (unpublished manuscript, 2019), 12.

 6. Michael Nylan, *The Chinese Pleasure Book* (New York: Zone, 2018), 41–42.

 7. Nylan, *The Chinese Pleasure Book*, 33, italics in the original.

 8. A. C. Graham, trans., *The Book of Lieh-tzŭ: A Classic of the Tao* (New York: Columbia University Press, 1990), 135.

 9. https://ctext.org/liezi/yang-zhu.

 10. Not part of this cluster but nonetheless sharing this emphasis on sensory pleasures and fulfilling desires are stories 2 and 12.

 11. The exception is story 10, which although it doesn't start with Yang Zhu, features Yangzi's disciple Mengsun Yang asking a question of Yang Zhu. So perhaps story 10 should be counted as a "Yang Zhu" story. It is also interesting to notice the difference in formal features among passages involving Yang Zhu.

 12. The fact that these simple hedonistic sentiments are reminiscent of what Anne Birrell has highlighted as a *carpe diem* theme in Han-era ballads may support a Han dating for this approach to life. Birrell, *Popular Songs and Ballads*, 78–93.

 13. In Erica Brindley, *Individualism in Early China: Human Agency and the Self in Thought and Politics* (Honolulu: University of Hawai'i Press, 2010), 70–74, I provide an overview of what we can know about the thought and figure of Yang Zhu during the Warring States and early Han. There, I evaluate descriptions of Yang Zhu's philosophy found in the *Mencius*, *Lüshi chunqiu*, and *Huainanzi* to theorize about his emphasis on self (*ji* 己, *wo* 我), body (*xing* 形), genuineness (*zhen* 真), and nature (*xing* 性) over and above external things. I conclude that the Yang Zhu of that era seems to have been associated with a cult of bodily (material) vitality that diverged from Zhuangzi's emphasis on ethereal vitality of the spirit.

 14. Story 3, Yang Bojun, ed., *Liezi jishi* 列子集釋 (Beijing: Zhonghua, 1979), 220–21.

15. Yang, *Liezi jishi*, 221.

16. Story 4, Yang, *Liezi jishi*, 221; altered from Graham's translation in Graham, *The Book of Lieh-tzŭ*, 141. Bo Yi and Zhan Li's positions, criticized in this passage, are reminiscent of the passage in *Mencius* 6A10, in which Mencius compares relative desires for fish versus bear paws.

17. Yang, *Liezi jishi*, 222; altered from Graham's translation in Graham, *The Book of Lieh-tzŭ*, 141–42.

18. Several more stories in the chapter reveal a socially oriented sense of justice. Aside from the ones discussed here, stories 11, 15, and 17 speak of bringing order and benefit to state and society, and even story 9, which touts a hedonistic attitude, features a certain Duanmu Shu who gave away all his wealth and belongings at age sixty when he no longer could make good use of them.

19. *Mencius* 3B9; Yang Bojun, ed., *Mengzi yizhu* (Hong Kong: Zhonghua, 1988), 155. Intriguingly, Mencius juxtaposes egoism (*wei wo* 為我) alongside the confirmed tenet of the Mohist school, inclusive caring (*jian ai* 兼愛). It is possible, then, that *wei wo* designates an actual formulation propounded by Yang Zhu and his followers, and if so, the Mencian interpretation of it as "egoistic" would likely be an intentional misunderstanding of how Yang Zhu understood *wei wo*. Certainly, it would not be unreasonable to believe that Yang Zhu's followers, back in Mencius's time, actually endorsed a socially conscious conception of *wei wo*.

20. In late Warring States and Han times, it refers on the one hand to the linguistic or conceptual realm of definitions outlining the boundaries of one's office or duties as opposed to one's performance in that office, and on the other to semantic categories as opposed to the objective realities they depict.

21. Yang, *Liezi jishi*, 234.

22. Yang, *Liezi jishi*, 217. This story's jarring reversals and, at the end, the author's switching of the main point from the pros and cons of reputation to the difference between a true and false reputation, or pretense (*wei*), suggests that the author may have been adding to a preexisting dialog that made a different point.

23. Yang, *Liezi jishi*, 217. This notion that Tian's descendants were enjoying the fruits of Qi "to the present day" is intriguing if one were to consider this passage to be composed in the late Han or Wei-Jin period of the second or third century CE. Perhaps it was intentionally stated in such a way so as to lend historicity and veracity to Yang Zhu's words.

24. Yang, *Liezi jishi*, 217. Notably, Yao and Shun are mocked, separately, in story 12, which is one of the most hedonistic passages that begins with "Yang Zhu said" in the "Yang Zhu" chapter. (As mentioned above, stories 7–10 do not take this format but are equally hedonistic in orientation.)

25. It is noteworthy that in story 3 of the same chapter, Yao and Shun are both classified as "benevolent and sagely" (仁聖).

26. This story can be compared nicely with a story featuring Yang Zhu in the next chapter of *Liezi*, "Explaining Conjunctions": "Yang Chu said: It is not

for the sake of reputation that you do good, but reputation follows. You expect reputation without benefit, but benefit comes. You expect benefit without contention, but contention arrives. Therefore the gentleman must be careful when he does good." (楊朱曰：「行善不以為名而名從之；名不與利期而利歸之；利不與爭期而爭及之：故君子必慎為善」) Yang, *Liezi jishi*, 267; translation from Graham, *The Book of Lieh-tzŭ*, 177.

27. Yang, *Liezi jishi*, 226; Graham, *The Book of Lieh-tzŭ*, 145.
28. Yang, *Liezi jishi*, 225.
29. Yang, *Liezi jishi*, 225.
30. Yang, *Liezi jishi*, 224–25.
31. Yang, *Liezi jishi*, 225. While the name Gongsun Chao appears a couple of times in Warring States texts, once as an important figure in Chu and then twice in association with the state of Wei during Confucius's time, we have no other textual corroboration of the existence of this older brother of Zichan. As for Gongsun Mu, his name only appears in the *Liezi* story.
32. Literally, the criticism reads: "acting on whatever rams against their emotions and indulging in their cravings and desires" (若觸情而動，聃於嗜慾，則性命危矣).
33. Yang, *Liezi jishi*, 226; altered from Graham, *The Book of Lieh-tzŭ*, 145.
34. This apparently contradicts Yang Zhu's lament in chapter 4 of the *Liezi*, in which he sang at the death of Ji Liang, who lived out natural years but cried at the untimely and tragic death of Sui Wu. Yang, *Liezi jishi*, 132.
35. Yang, *Liezi jishi*, 226.
36. See Yang, *Liezi jishi*, 236.
37. Altered from Graham, *The Book of Lieh-tzŭ*, 154.
38. Yang, *Liezi jishi*, 236.
39. Yang, *Liezi jishi*, 238.
40. Story 7 supports this list.
41. Yang, *Liezi jishi*, 223. The story begins with the question of how to nourish life, so life is clearly what is implied in this response.
42. Yang, *Liezi jishi*, 222.
43. Yang, *Liezi jishi*, 229. Consistent with the notion that nourishing life is not about living a long life or being rich and famous, Duanmu Shu leaves behind nothing and donates his pleasurable possessions and treasures when "the main supply-line (literally, the 'tree trunk') of his *qi* was about to be depleted." Yang, *Liezi jishi*, 228.
44. Yang, *Liezi jishi*, 230; adapted from Graham, *The Book of Lieh-tzŭ*, 148.
45. One might compare this idea of not pushing or pulling time to Mencius's famous metaphor of not pulling on sprouts. Both passages demonize a certain kind of human manipulation and interference in a natural process.
46. Indeed, much like the negative version of the Golden Rule that appears in the *Analects*, this negative injunction stresses what not to do and does not

push for the active pursuit of single type of moralistic or hedonistic approach, leaving interpretation open to the individual.

47. Indeed, by including the aspects of simple hedonism into a larger orientation concerning "joy," we can better understand the full meaning of *le* as both joy and pleasure, and not just one or the other.

48. Many Dark Learning (玄學) writings merit further consideration in relationship to the central themes discussed in the "Yang Zhu" chapter of *Liezi*. These include Ji Kang's treatise, "Treatise on Nourishing Life" (養生論); a poem attributed to Ruan Ji, titled "Madness from Wine" (酒狂); and a poem by Liu Ling, titled, "Hymn to the Virtues of Wine" (酒德頌), which glorifies the life of a carefree drunkard who is badgered by two moralists who try to save him. Even the drunken and capacious figure of Liu Ling, who valorized a worry-free life devoid of concerns about health, longevity, and social mores, is reminiscent of the "Yang Zhu" story of Zichan's profligate brothers, as discussed previously. As legend goes, so unattached was Liu from all of these that he had a servant carry around a shovel wherever he went, at the ready to bury him on the spot the moment he keeled over and died.

49. The culture of quick enjoyments or simple hedonism is carried on in the great poetic traditions of the medieval period. Tao Yuanming's (ca. 365–427) writings on wine and enjoyment are a case in point.

II
From Tang to Ming

Chapter 5

Yang Zhu's Role in Tang-Song Proto-*daotong* Discourse

JOHN MAKEHAM

Introduction

Thomas A. Wilson describes the *daotong* 道統 (succession of the Way) concept as signifying "a specific conception of the Confucian past as a singular lineage of sages who were regarded as the sole transmitters of the true Confucian Way."[1] Since Song times it has been employed as a powerful tactic in the retrospective creation of lineages and "schools" and also in the promotion of certain thinkers and the exclusion of others from privileged versions of just who and what constitutes ideological and doctrinal orthodoxy.[2] The concept has continued to be employed for that purpose in modern times.[3] This chapter aims to provide an overview of the prominent role that the negative image of Yang Zhu 楊朱 (and the cognate Yang-Mo 楊墨 [Yang Zhu and Mozi] trope) played in the construction of four centuries of proto-*daotong* discourse before the great Song Neo-Confucian Zhu Xi 朱熹 (1130–1200) began to use the term to construct his own *daotong* orthodoxy. It seeks to do so by identifying and examining key themes that emerged in that long tradition of discourse, across a broad range of literary genres—letters, reading notes, essays, prefaces, postfaces, tomb inscriptions, epitaphs, encomia, and commentaries—and which subsequently also became central to Zhu Xi's appropriation of the *daotong* concept.⁴ The deployment of the negative image of Yang Zhu and the cognate Yang-Mo trope provides a unique perspective—hitherto largely overlooked—from which to observe the unfolding of a range of themes in Tang-Song intellectual history. In particular, this chapter identifies several key themes that subsequently became central to Zhu Xi's appropriation of the *daotong* concept.

1. Han Yu, the Yang-Mo Trope, and Proto-*daotong* Discourse

In the development of pre-Song proto-*daotong* discourse, Han Yu's 韓愈 (768–824) essay "Yuan dao" 原道 (Tracing the Way to its origins), written in 804 or 805, is the best known. Key ideas in that essay, however, had already been adumbrated in conversations with Han's protégé Zhang Ji 張籍 (ca. 767–ca. 830) in 798. In one letter Zhang writes:

> Sir, in recent times I have been instructed by your discourse, in which you maintain that mores today are decadent and no match for those in ancient times. [You further maintain that] this is surely because the Way of the sages has been abandoned. After Confucius passed away, Yang Zhu and Mo Di promoted perverse and strange doctrines, confusing what people heard. Mencius wrote a book, rectifying matters, and so the Way of the sages once more existed in the age. The Qin dynasty destroyed learning, and further, the Han [dynasty] used the techniques of Huang-Lao to instruct people, causing them to be steeped in confusion. Yang Xiong wrote *Model Sayings* to dispute them and so the Way of the sages was still clear. With the demise of Han, the Dharma of the Buddhists from the Western Regions penetrated the Central States. For generations, men of the Central States translated and disseminated it. The techniques of Huang-Lao were passed on, shining brightly. Throughout the realm, anyone who spoke of the good was referring only to these two.

> 頃承論於執事，嘗以為世俗陵靡，不及古昔。蓋聖人之道廢弛之所為也。宣尼沒後，楊朱、墨翟，恢詭異說，干惑人聽，孟子作書而正之，聖人之道，復存於世。秦氏滅學，漢重以黃老之術教

人,使人浸惑,揚雄作《法言》而辨之,聖人之道猶明。及漢衰末,西域浮屠之法,入於中國。中國之人,世世譯而廣之,黃老之術相沿而熾,天下之言善者,唯二者而已矣。

In Han Yu's reported views, the perverse and strange doctrines of Yang Zhu and Mozi are replaced by the aberrant teachings of Huang-Lao and the foreign teachings of Buddhism—with "Huang-Lao" apparently also morphing into a reference to Daoism in a more general sense—and the theme of dynastic decay is linked to the rise of these aberrant teachings. Zhang then exhorted Han to express his views in writing:

> In the nearly one thousand years since Yang Xiong wrote *Model Sayings*, no one but you, sir, has spoken of the Way of the sages. . . . I hope that you will be the successor to the writings of Mencius and Yang Xiong and dispute the doctrines of Yang Zhu, Mozi, Laozi, and the Buddha so that the Way of the sages will again appear in the Tang. How excellent that would be!
>
> 自揚子雲作《法言》,至今近千載,莫有言聖人之道者,言之者惟執事焉耳。. . . 願執事 . . . 嗣孟子、揚雄之作,辨楊、墨、老、釋之說,使聖人之道,復見於唐,豈不尚哉。[5]

This account includes Yang Xiong 揚雄 (53 BCE–18 CE) as a transmitter of the Way of the sages after Mencius. In his "Du Xun" 讀荀 (Reading *Xunzi*) essay, possibly written around the same time as the above correspondence, in the transmission of "the Way of Confucius" Han not only includes Yang Xiong but also Xunzi 荀子 (third century BCE), albeit adding the qualification, "Mencius was the purest of the pure; Xunzi and Yang Xiong were mostly pure but with some slight faults." (孟氏,醇乎醇者也。荀與揚,大醇而小疵。)[6]

By about 804, however, his succession of the Way lineage no longer included Xunzi and Yang Xiong. In "Song Wang Xiucai xu" 送王秀才序 (Valedictory preface for "Flourishing Talent" Wang Xun), Han writes:

> Mencius took Zisi as his teacher, and undoubtedly the learning of Zisi came out of Zengzi. After Confucius passed away, although all of these disciples had some writings, it was the tradition to which Mencius belonged that alone received the

main lineage [of his teachings]. . . . To take the learning of Yang Zhu, Mozi, Laozi, Zhuangzi, or the Buddha as the Way and seek to use this learning to proceed to the Way of the sages is like being cut-off in the arm of a tributary or severed in a pond and yet hope to reach the sea. Hence, one must begin with Mencius if one seeks to behold the Way of the sages.

孟軻師子思，子思之學，蓋出曾子。自孔子沒，群弟子莫不有書，獨孟軻氏之傳得其宗 。. . . 道於楊、墨、老、莊、佛之學，而欲之聖人之道，猶航斷港絕潢，以望至於海也。故求觀聖人之道，必自孟子始。[7]

Mencius's privileged elevation represents a significant change, as does the clustering of Yang, Mo, Lao, Zhuang, and the Buddha, which is contrasted to the Confucius—Zengzi—Zisi—Mencius lineage. Significantly, this lineage also came to feature as a key component of Zhu Xi's *daotong*.[8]

Written in 804 or 805, Han Yu's celebrated "Yuan dao" essay identifies a lineage of Confucian sages and luminaries responsible for handing down the "way and virtue" from antiquity to Mencius. Han relates that after Mencius the transmission became interrupted, implying that he was the first after Mencius to have taken up the mantle of transmission.

After the demise of the Zhou and the passing of Confucius, during the period from the burning of the books in the Qin, [the rise of] Huang-Lao in the Han and [the spread] of Buddhism during in the Jin, Wei, Liang, and Sui, those who spoke of the Way and virtue, humaneness and rightness, were either followers of Yang Zhu or of Mozi, of Laozi or the Buddha. . . .

Today [the Daoist and Buddhist] teachings say, "You must do away with the relation between ruler and minister, abandon the relation between father and son, and cease the path of sustaining livelihoods," in order to seek their so-called pure nirvana. Alas! Their teachings were indeed fortunate to have appeared after the time of the Three Dynasties, thereby avoiding suppression by Yu, Tang, kings Wen and Wu, the Duke of Zhou, and Confucius. We, however, are indeed unfortunate that they did not appear before the Three Dynasties and thus avoided being rectified by Yu, Tang, kings Wen and Wu, the Duke of Zhou, and Confucius. . . .

[Someone asked]: "This Way—what Way is it?"

[I] replied: "It is what *we* call the Way and is not what the Daoists and Buddhists hitherto have called the Way. Yao passed it on to Shun, Shun passed it on to Yu, Yu passed it on to Tang, Tang passed it on to kings Wen and Wu and the Duke of Zhou, the Duke of Zhou passed it on to Confucius, and Confucius passed it on to Mencius. When Mencius died there was nobody to pass it on to. Xunzi and Yang Xiong selected aspects of it, but they were careless; they spoke about it, but it was incomplete.

周道衰，孔子沒，火於秦，黃老於漢，佛於晉、魏、梁、隋之間。其言道德仁義者，不入於楊，則入於墨。不入於老，則入於佛。……今其法曰：「必棄而君臣，去而父子，禁而相生養之道。」以求其所謂清淨寂滅者。嗚呼！其亦幸而出於三代之後，不見黜於禹、湯、文武、周公、孔子。其亦不幸而不出於三代之前，不見正於禹、湯、文武、周公、孔子也。……曰：「斯道也，何道也？」曰：「斯吾所謂道也，非向所謂老與佛之道也。」堯以是傳之舜，舜以是傳之禹，禹以是傳之湯，湯以是傳之文武周公，文武周公傳之孔子，孔子傳之孟軻。軻之死，不得其傳焉。荀與揚也，擇焉而不精，語焉而不詳。[9]

In this essay there is a clear articulation of a core early lineage of sages: Yao—Shun—Yu—Tang—Wen—Wu—Zhou—Confucius, with Mencius being the last transmitter of their teachings.[10] Han Yu intensified the sense of loss brought about by the failure to pass on the Confucian Way after the death of Mencius through his portrayal of the usurpation of "the Way and virtue, humaneness and rightness." Also intensified is the sense of a zero-sum contest between the Confucian Way on the one side and the Daoist and Buddhist "Ways" on the other.[11] And once again, Daoists and Buddhists are portrayed as latter-day Yangists and Mohists, a device that Zhu Xi also came to adopt as a key rhetorical strategy.

In 820, in a letter to Meng Jian 孟簡 (d. 823), Han Yu first affirms the vital role that Mencius played in enabling knowledge of "the Way of the Former Kings" to be kept alive, even though the teachings of Yang Zhu and Mozi had inflicted major harm on "the great Way of the Two Emperors, the Three Kings, and the sages" through the burning of books and burial of scholars in the Qin dynasty and the loss of significant portions of the classical corpus by Han times. Against this background, Han writes:

After the [teachings of] Yang Zhu and Mozi came to prevail, the true Way was abandoned. . . . Since the Han dynasty, large numbers of Confucian scholars have merely been able to undertake minor repairs to the tattered state [of the classical corpus]. No sooner are [the teachings] put in some order than they become lost [again]. This parlous situation is like that of a single strand of hair holding up a thousand *jun* weight: even though [Confucian learning] extends unbroken to present times, it is increasingly hastening towards decline and extinction. And yet, at such a time as this, [there are still people who] sing the praises of Buddhism and Daoism, encouraging all throughout the realm to follow them. Alas! Such inhumanity! . . .

Although Mencius was a worthy and a sage, he did not attain office, and so his words were uttered in vain. Even though they were incisive, of what use were they? And yet, it is due to his words that students today still know to treat Confucius as the founding teacher of our lineage, to honor humaneness and rightness, and to respect kings and to despise hegemons—but that is all. The great norms and great models have all perished and are beyond recovery; destroyed, they cannot be recuperated. What remains is but a tiny fraction. . . . Yet, if it were not for Mencius, we would all be fastening our robes on the left side and babbling in foreign tongues. . . .

The harm that Buddhism and Daoism do is worse than that done by the teachings of Yang Zhu and Mozi. My talents fail to measure up to those of Mencius. Mencius was unable to save [the Way of the Two Emperors, the Three Kings, and the sages] before it was lost, and yet I, Han Yu, seek to keep it intact even after it has been destroyed. Alas! I fail to know my limits or to see the danger I am in. Nobody can save me from certain death! Yet, despite this, if it is possible that the Way can somehow be passed on through me, however crudely, then even if I were to die, I would not have the slightest regret!

夫楊墨行，正道廢……。漢氏已來，羣儒區區修補，百孔千瘡，隨亂隨失，其危如一髮引千鈞，緜緜延延，寖以微滅。於是時也，而唱釋老於其間，鼓天下之眾而從之，嗚呼，其亦不仁甚矣！……孟子雖賢聖，不得位，空言無施，雖切何補？然賴其言，而今學者尚知宗孔氏，崇仁義，貴王賤霸而已。其大經大法，皆亡滅而不救，壞爛而不收，所謂存十一於千百⋯⋯。然向無孟氏，則皆服左衽而言侏離矣。故愈嘗推尊孟氏，以為功不在禹下者，為此也。⋯⋯釋老之害過於楊墨，韓愈之賢不及孟子，孟子不能救之於未亡之前，而韓愈乃欲全之於已壞之後。嗚呼！其亦不量其力且見其身之危，莫之救以死也！雖然，使其道由愈而粗傳，雖滅死萬萬無恨！[12]

The general account is consistent with the "Yuan dao" essay, but the concluding sentence marks a significant new development: Han Yu now insinuates himself as the candidate next in line after Mencius in the transmission of the Confucian Way.[13]

2. Northern Song Developments

Han Yu's proto-*daotong* lineage gained little traction in the Tang. The main exception is the modified version by Pi Rixiu 皮日休 (ca. 834–ca. 884 or ca. 840–ca. 880) in his essay "Shi yuan xi shu" 十原係述 (Account of ten origins), in which Pi also includes Han Yu in the lineage: Duke of Zhou—Confucius—Mencius—Han Yu. "One thousand years after [Mencius] there is only Mr. Changli [Han Yu] [who is the equal of Mencius]" (千世之後，獨有一昌黎先生). Pi even deems Han Yu's attacks on "the teaching from the Western Regions" (Buddhism) to be an achievement on par with Mencius's criticisms of Yang Zhu and Mozi.[14]

In a petition perhaps written circa 863,[15] "Qing Han Wengong peixiang Taixue shu" 請韓文公配饗太學書 (A memorial petition for investing Han Yu as a correlate in the shrine to Confucius at the State Academy), Pi outlined quite a different lineage for "the Way of Confucius," one that includes Wang Tong 王通 (ca. 584–617): Mencius—Xunzi—Wang Tong—Han Yu.[16] *Pizi wensou* 皮子文藪 (Mr. Pi's literary marsh) also includes a memorial, "Qing Mengzi wei xueke shu" 請孟子為學科書 (A memorial petition to have *Mencius* made an official examination text), which lobbies to replace *Zhuangzi* and *Liezi*—both officially prescribed texts—with *Mencius*. *Mencius* was not an officially prescribed text for the civil examinations in the Tang. Indeed, *Mencius* had long been without an official status. During the reign of Han Emperor Wen 文帝 (r. 180–157 BC), the posts of Academicians (*boshi* 博士) for *Lunyu*, *Xiao jing*, *Mencius*, and *Erya* were established but were discontinued when Emperor Wu 武

帝 (r. 141–87 BC) established the posts of Academicians for the Five Classics in 136 BC.[17] Both petitions mark the beginning of a process in which the status of Han Yu and of Mencius increasingly became tied to one another, albeit only really gaining momentum two centuries after Han Yu had died.

Liu Kai 柳開 (947–1000) was the main figure in the early Northern Song period to sing the praises of Han Yu. Dingxiang Warner relates that "so enthralled was he with his idol [Han Yu] that Liu began slavishly emulating Han Yu's literary style in his own compositions, and he changed his personal name . . . to Jianyu 肩愈, meaning 'to stand shoulder to shoulder with Han Yu.'"[18] While initially championing the lineage of Confucius—Mencius—Yang Xiong—Han Yu,[19] by 970 he, too, added Wang Tong: Confucius—Mencius—Xunzi—Yang Xiong—Wang Tong—Han Yu.[20] As with Han Yu, Liu clustered Yang Zhu, Mozi, Laozi, and the Buddha as a group, lamenting that the "great Way," "the Way of the sages," did not shine in the Central States due to the chaos wrought by this group.[21]

By the 1130s and 1140s, another advocate of *guwen* 古文 (ancient-style learning),[22] Sun Fu 孫復 (992–1057), had laid out an expanded lineage for "the Way of Confucius," extending it back to Fu Xi 伏羲: Fu Xi—Shen Nong 神農—Huang Di 黃帝—Yao—Shun—Yu—Tang—Wen—Wu—Duke of Zhou—Confucius:

> However, from Fu Xi on down, there was variation in the level of detail by which institutions and norms were established. Our Sage Teacher Confucius followed after them and revised these institutions and norms, adjusting them to attain their balance, which he wrote down as the Six Classics. Thereupon, in all its glory, the great Way of balance in ordering the realm and managing the state was complete. This is why Confucius was great! He greatly surpassed Fu Xi, Shen Nong, Huang Di, Yao, Shun, Yu, Tang, Wen, Wu, and the Duke of Zhou.

> 然伏羲而下，創制立度或畧或繁。我聖師夫子從而益之損之，俾恊厥中，筆為六經。由是治天下經國家大中之道煥然而備。此夫子所為大也。其出乎伏羲神農黃帝堯舜禹湯文武周公也遠矣。

With Confucius's central position thus in place, Sun proceeded to extend the lineage's continuation in the other direction, through what he terms the "Five Worthies" (五賢):

Alas! Since the passing of Confucius, there have been very few classical scholars who, through study of the Master's Way, have been able to find the door to enter it. The few who have are: Mr. Meng Ke, Mr. Xun Qing, Mr. Yang Xiong, Mr. Wang Tong, and Mr. Han Yu.

噫！自夫子沒，諸儒學其道得其門而入者鮮矣。惟孟軻氏、荀卿氏、揚雄氏、王通氏、韓愈氏而已。[23]

In an inscription for a temple to Mencius in Zou county 鄒縣 (Mencius's birthplace), Sun set out a slightly truncated version of both sets of these lineages, moving the focus to Mencius for his decisive role in tackling the teachings of Yang Zhu and Mozi, which had driven the people out of the Central States to move to the lands of the Yi and Di barbarians:

> Yang Xiong said: "In the past, Yang Zhu and Mozi had blocked the road. Mencius spoke out, and by attacking them cleared the road."[24] Han Yu said: "By my reckoning, Mencius's achievements were not less than those of Yu."[25] Yang Xiong's account of Mencius's achievements is not as profound and to the point as the words of Han Yu. Why? When the flood waters ran in all directions, if Great Yu had not arisen, then throughout the realm the people would have become fish and turtles. When the atrocities of Yang Zhu and Mozi [were rampant], if Mencius had not arisen, then throughout the realm people would have become birds and beasts.

> 揚子雲有言曰古者楊墨塞路。孟子辭而闢之廓如也。韓退之有言曰孟子之功。予以謂不在禹下。然子雲述孟子之功不若退之之言深且至也。何哉。洚水橫流。大禹不作，則天下之民魚鱉矣。楊墨暴行。孟子不作，則天下之民禽獸矣欽定四庫全書。[26]

In two other essays, the Yang, Mo, Lao, Buddha clustering is also tied to the Mencius–Yang Xiong–Han Yu lineage (albeit with the curious addition of Dong Zhongshu 董仲舒 [179–104 BC] in the second essay). In the first passage below, from the essay "Ru ru" 儒辱 (The humiliation of the Confucians), Sun describes how this humiliation began with confusion sowed by Yang Zhu and Mozi, followed by threats from Shen Buhai and Han Fei. Matters became worse, however, beginning in the

Han and Wei periods, when "the followers of the Buddha and Laozi ran amuck throughout the Central States . . . throwing our people into confusion." He continues:

> Generally, when people today get into an argument with someone, even if they come off only slightly second best, they still regard it to be humiliating—how much greater is the humiliation when the person one is quarreling with throws the teachings of our sages into chaos by employing the doctrines of the barbarian philosophers!²⁷ Alas! When there are no sages, then the bizarre and the chaotic will not be subdued. Thus, when Yang and Mo arose, Mencius repudiated them; when Shen [Buhai] and Han [Fei] emerged, then Yang Xiong resisted them; when [the teachings of] the Buddha and Lao[zi] thrived, then Han Yu opposed them. If it had not been for these three gentlemen, then all of the people throughout the realm would have become barbarians!

> 凡今之人與人爭鬥，小有所不勝，則尚以為辱，矧彼以夷狄諸子之法，亂我聖人之教耶。其為辱也大哉。噫！聖人不生怪亂不平。故揚墨起而孟子闢之，申韓出而揚雄距之，佛老盛而韓文公排之。微三子則天下之人胥而為夷狄矣。²⁸

In the second essay, "Reply to Zhang Dong," he similarly relates:

> Alas! For a long time it has been hard to realize this culture of ours. From the Western Han to the Tang, there have been great numbers of learned students and erudite scholars who have bequeathed many writings to posterity. However, most of these writings [concern such matters as] nonexistence and karma [as taught by] Yang, Mo, Lao[zi], and the Buddha. . . . As for those [after Mencius who firmly maintained that] humaneness and rightness/duty must never be departed from, there were only Dong Zhongshu, Yang Xiong, and Han Yu.

> 噫！斯文之難至也久矣。自西漢至李唐其間鴻生碩儒摩肩而起。以文章垂世者眾矣。然多楊墨佛老虛無報應之事。……至于終始仁義不叛不離者，惟董仲舒，揚雄，王通，韓愈而已。²⁹

Another admirer of Mencius and Han Yu—and critic of Yang, Mo, Lao, and the Buddha—was Sun Fu's disciple Shi Jie 石介 (1005–1045).[30] Shi Jie also had a penchant for extending the lineage of Confucius and the Five Worthies to several of his own contemporaries and also to Sun Fu, presumably in order to flatter and curry favor.[31]

3. *Guwen* and the Case of Zhiyuan

In the Northern Song dynasty, "ancient-style learning" (*guwen*) appealed to a broad range of literati and was not the exclusive preserve of those who identified primarily with the teachings of Confucius. The Tiantai cleric Zhiyuan 智圓 (976–1022), for example, was a strong proponent of *guwen*. Together with "literatus monk" Zanning 贊寧 (919–1001) (also ordained in the Tiantai order), Albert Welter identifies Zhiyuan as a prominent member of what he calls "Confucian monks" (*Ruseng* 儒僧). "These were monks who established strong reputations among secular literati for their literary abilities, including an acknowledged expertise over the Confucian classics. The likes of Zanning and Zhiyuan openly accepted the Confucian premises of Chinese society, even going so far as to teach *guwen* principles to members of the Buddhist clergy."[32]

As with other *guwen* proponents, Zhiyuan also invoked genealogical discourse. In the following passage, for example, Zhiyuan employs the analogy of portraiture to convey the life-like quality of the lineage of "the Way of Confucius." Having first established that Confucius received the Way of Tang, Yu, Wen, Wu, and Zhou—which he describes as being as vivid as "a person's visage"—he continues with an account of the lineage after Confucius:

> In the thousand years after Confucius had passed away, those who were able to inherit and carry on his legacy were just Mencius, Xun Qing, Yang Xiong, Wang Tong, Han Yu, and Liu Zongyuan. This was indeed a case of "sketching his visage to convey his spirit!" Those who were students of Shen [Buhai], Shang [Yang], Zhuang [Zhou], Lie [Yukou], [Yang] Zhu, and [Mo] Di, were like [artists who] splash ink to draw a landscape, abandoning themselves to the strange and the occult, indulging in doctrines of passion and caprice.

仲尼既沒千百年間，能嗣仲尼之道者，唯孟軻，荀卿，楊子雲，
王仲淹，韓退之，柳子厚而已。可謂寫其貌傳其神者矣。其申商
莊列朱翟之學者乃潑墨圖山水，縱怪狀鬼神，率情任意之說。[33]

Thus, despite not being a lineage of direct transmission between teacher and immediate disciple, experiencing the spirit conveyed in inheriting and passing on the legacy of Confucius through the writings bequeathed by him and the transmitters of his lineage was just as vivid and immediate. For rhetorical purposes, Zhiyuan then contrasts this with the perverse nature of certain teacher-student relations in which there was a direct line of transmission, associated with such notorious figures as Yang Zhu and Mozi, to make the point that the transmission of the Way could jump several generations and not need to rely on face-to-face lineage transmission. (The subsequent relevance of this for Zhu Xi's *daotong* is explored in chapter 6 of this volume.) Of particular note is that Zhiyuan feels no need to identify the specifics of this heterodox group's perversities—invoking their names suffices to make his point.

In another essay, having first explained that the writings of Laozi, Zhuangzi, Yang Zhu, and Mozi cannot be deemed to be *guwen* writing because they reject rightness, humaneness, ritual, and music, Zhiyuan continues:

> Hence, those who enter into the realm of Lao-Zhuang in their writings are deemed to belong to an adulterated lineage, whereas those whose writings enter the realm of Zhou-Kong are deemed to belong to a pure lineage. The books of [Si]ma Qian and Ban Gu placed Huang-Lao above the Six Classics, demeaned loyal ministers, and glossed over the faults of rulers. Former Confucians deemed them to be adulterated. The books of Mencius and Yang Xiong rejected Yang-Mo, condemned the fighting of the overlords, repudiated the superficial and duplicitous, and esteemed humaneness and rightness. Such was the purity of the writings of former Confucians.

故為文入於老莊者謂之雜宗。於周孔者謂之純。馬遷班固之書，
先黃老，後六經。抑忠臣，飾主闕。先儒文之雜也。孟軻楊雄之
書，排楊墨，罪霸戰，黜浮偽，尚仁義。先儒文之純也。[34]

As to be expected, what distinguishes Zhiyuan's account of the orthodox and the heterodox is that the Buddhists no longer appear in the heterodox lineage together with Yang Zhu and Mozi, their place having been supplanted by Sima Qian (d. 86 BCE) and Ban Gu (32–92).

In the following passage from the same essay, *guwen* is presented as the medium by which the Way is conveyed and transmitted through writing:

> Ancient-style learning refers to taking the Way of antiquity as the authority for establishing one's words and ensuring that one's words elucidate the Way of antiquity. What is the Way of antiquity? It is the Way practised by the sage teacher Confucius. In the past, "Confucius followed Yao and Shun and took the decrees of Wen and Wu as his model"[35] and the Six Classics were complete, and these, in their essentials, are nothing other than humaneness, rightness, and the Five Constants.[36] Humaneness, rightness, and the Five Constants refer to the Way of antiquity. If you are to fix your purpose on this culture of ours, you must meticulously examine the Way of the Five Constants. By not losing the center,[37] one will be able to succeed by adapting to changing circumstances and always conform with the Way. Having attained it in one's mind, then it is expressed in writing and disseminated as teachings.
>
> 夫所謂古文者宗古道而立言。言必明乎古道也。古道者何？聖師仲尼所行之道也。昔者仲尼祖述堯舜，憲章文武。六經大備。要其所歸，無越仁義五常也。仁義五常謂之古道也。若將有志於斯文也，必也研幾乎五常之道，不失於中而達乎變變而通通，則久久而合道。既得之於心矣，然後吐之為文章，敷之為教。[38]

Yu Yingshi 余英時 identifies Zhiyuan as the first figure in the Northern Song to promote *Zhongyong* 中庸.[39] He further argues that in the early Northern Song period the interpretative authority of *Zhongyong* was dominated by followers of Buddhism, with Hu Yuan 胡瑗 (993–1059) being the first Confucian of that period to write a book on *Zhongyong* that had any influence.[40] *Zhongyong*, of course, became central to Zhu Xi's account of *daotong*.[41] Zhiyuan even styled himself as Master Zhongyong (Zhongyongzi 中庸子), and in his *Autobiography of Master Zhongyong* (*Zhongyongzi zhuan* 中庸子傳), he promotes a kind of Buddho-Confucian ecumenicism.[42] This apparently ecumenical agenda ultimately served a distinctly Tiantai goal: to win over the hearts and minds of the educated elite.[43]

In an essay titled "Reply to a Friend's Question" (Dui youren wen 對友人問), Zhiyuan explains why he was qualified to teach the *Nirvana Sutra* even though he had not been personally instructed in that text by a recognized authority. He begins by outlining the following lineage, one that is largely consistent with lineages advocated by Northern Song *guwen* proponents: Duke of Zhou–Confucius–Mencius–Yang Xiong–Wang Tong–Liu Zongyuan–Han Yu.⁴⁴ He describes how even though these figures did not personally receive instruction from the sage or the worthy whose Way (*dao*) they transmitted, in all cases that Way remained the same Way. He continues:

> It is the same with us Buddhists. I have never heard that [the bodhisattva] Mañjuśrī personally instructed Nāgārjuna (second century–third century) in the "single [dharma]-nature tenet." I have never heard that Nāgārjuna personally instructed Huiwen (mid-sixth century) in the "threefold contemplation doctrine." And yet, everyone says that Nāgārjuna took Mañjuśrī as his teacher, and that Huiwen took Nāgārjuna as his teacher. When the Way of Nāgārjuna and Huiwen [was transmitted] to Nanyue [Huisi 慧思; 515–577] and Tiantai [Zhiyi 智顗; 538–597] they greatly expanded it, drawing upon and elaborating its [import]. Still later, Zhang'an [Guanding 灌頂; 561–632] followed this way and wrote the *Da Neipan jing shu* 大般涅槃經疏 (Commentary on the *Nirvana Sutra*). Nearly two hundred years later [it was transmitted] to Jingxi [Zhanran 湛然; 711–782] who finalized its editing,⁴⁵ enabling it to be perfected. When I was looking for commentaries on the *Nirvana Sutra*, I attained the subtle import [of the *Nirvana Sutra* as conveyed through Jingxi Zhanran's edition] by myself. I take Jingxi as my teacher. Who says that [because this was not received through personal instruction, therefore] it was without instruction from the teacher? If the Way can be transmitted through personal instruction [then how is it that] Xun Qing personally instructed Li Si who, on becoming Chancellor to the First Emperor of the Qin, proceeded to burn books and bury scholars? [Chan] master Wuming [d.u.] personally instructed [renegade monk Wei 衛] Yuansong [fl. 561–578], who subsequently toadied Northern Zhou Emperor Wu [r. 561–578] in order to annihilate Buddhism and destroy

the Buddha.⁴⁶ It is hardly the case that personal instruction is capable of transmitting the Way. To me, transmitting means grasping the intention of the ancients and practicing the Way of the ancients. It does not mean seeing someone or hearing their voice.

> 氏亦然也。文殊一性宗不聞面授於龍樹也。龍樹三觀義不聞面授於慧文也。而天下咸云龍樹師於文殊，慧文師於龍樹矣。龍樹慧文之道，至南岳、天台而張大之，引而伸之。後章安宗其道，撰涅槃疏。年將二百至荊溪治定之。然後得盡善矣。吾於涅槃尋疏而自得微旨者。吾師荊溪也。誰云無師授耶。若以面授則可傳道者苟卿面授於李斯而相秦始也，焚書坑儒。亡名師而面授於元嵩而佞周武也。滅釋毀佛。豈面授能傳道哉。吾以得古人之旨，行古人之道為傳授，不以目其人、耳其聲。⁴⁷

Zhiyuan's support for the idea of teacher-student transmission lineages in which the transmission of the Way could jump several generations, and his related critique of face-to-face lineage transmission, served a key rhetorical agenda. As Douglas Skonicki notes, "The Ancient-style Learning claim that the *dao* inhered in and was transmitted through texts comported with Tiantai notions, and provided Zhiyuan with a theoretical framework, popular among Confucian literati, for rebutting Chan arguments concerning the 'mind-to-mind' transmission of Buddhist truth." As a Tiantai monk, "Zhiyuan's dismissal of the necessity of the [face-to-face] teacher-disciple relationship thus may have been intended to undercut the Chan claim to a privileged insight into the Buddhist *dao*."⁴⁸ This emphasis on privileged texts functioning as the medium for the transmission of the Way that inhered in the teachings conveyed in those texts also featured as a key element in Zhu Xi's *daotong* discourse, in particular *Zhongyong* and the famous "sixteen-character teaching" that it transmitted.⁴⁹

Elsewhere, Skonicki maintains that the lineage discourse that incorporated transmission lineages such as the "Five Worthies" began to lose its appeal among the educated elite by the middle of the eleventh century.⁵⁰ Support for Mencius and Han Yu, however, continued to gather momentum. Witness, for example, the following comments by Ouyang Xiu 歐陽修 (1007–1072) written circa 1054: "Mr Han's writings have not been seen in the two hundred years since his passing but now they are very much in vogue."⁵¹ Similarly, the appraisal or encomium (*zan* 贊)

appended to Han Yu's biography (and possibly also penned by Ouyang Xiu) in the *Xin Tangshu* 新唐書 (New history of the Tang), which was completed in 1060, states:

> In the past, when Mencius dismissed Yang Zhu and Mozi, he lived just two hundred years after the time of Confucius. When Han Yu criticized Yang Zhu and Mozi, he lived more than a thousand years [after Mencius]. In rejecting the degenerate and returning to the correct path, his achievements were on par [with those of Mencius] but the effort he made was twice as great, and that is why he greatly surpasses [Xun] Kuang and [Yang] Xiong.
>
> 昔孟軻拒楊、墨,去孔子才二百年。愈排二家,乃去千餘歲,撥衰反正,功與齊而力倍之,所以過況、雄為不少矣。[52]

The institutionalization of this gradual elevation of the status of Mencius and Han Yu was finally realized in 1071 when Wang Anshi 王安石 (1021–1086) added *Mencius* to the examination curriculum and was reaffirmed in 1084 when Mencius became a correlate in the Confucius Temple, alongside Yan Hui; and when Han Yu, together with Yang Xiong and Xunzi, was made an earl (*bo* 伯), one rank below Mencius, and was enshrined among the twenty-two exegetes.[53]

4. The Cheng Brothers and Lineage Discourse

For the Cheng brothers and their disciples, however, it was Mencius alone who was the pivotal link in the orthodox transmission. Cheng Yi's 程頤 (1033–1107) grave epitaph for his elder brother Cheng Hao 程顥 (1032–1085), written in 1085, states:

> When the Duke of Zhou passed away, the Way of the sages was no longer practiced. When Mencius died, the learning of the sages was no longer transmitted. When the Way was no longer practiced, for one hundred generations there was no good rule. When the learning [of the sages] was no longer transmitted, for a thousand years there were no true Confu-

cians.... This gentleman lived one thousand four hundred years after [Mencius] and from the surviving classics he apprehended the learning that had not been transmitted. He was committed to ensuring that it would be this Way that would awaken this people of ours.

周公沒，聖人之道不行；孟軻死，聖人之學不傳。道不行，百世無善治；學不傳，千載無真儒。……先生生千四百年之後，得不傳之學於遺經，志將以斯道覺斯民。[54]

No longer are there any intermediaries in the line of transmission, which proceeds directly from Mencius to Cheng Hao—an account subsequently repeated by Cheng Hao's students.[55] As Peter Bol notes, Cheng Yi "located himself and his brother as the first since Mencius to understand the learning of the sages, and he distinguished his way of learning by calling it Tao-hsueh [*daoxue* 道學]."[56] After his brother's death, Cheng Yi regarded himself as the sole authority over the learning of the sages.[57]

Although lineage discourse remained central to claims of doctrinal orthodoxy in the nascent Daoxue movement, the Cheng brothers and their disciples removed Han Yu from their accounts of the orthodox lineage of transmission. Cheng Yi explains why:

Someone asked Cheng Yi: "What do you think of Han Yu's essay 'On Reading *Mozi*'"?

Cheng Yi replied: "The intention behind the essay was indeed very good, but because it was expressed carelessly there are places where it is wrong. Mencius said that Mozi [maintained that] the affection one has for one's elder brother is just the same as the affection one has for a neighbor's child.[58] Where in the book *Mozi* does it say anything like this? Rather, it is just that Mencius sought to stop this thinking at the very outset, knowing that otherwise it would inevitably lead to this. In the main, when Confucians study the Way, the slightest mistake will lead to profound error. Yang Zhu originally studied *yi* 義 (what is right; duty) and Mozi originally studied humaneness. In what they studied, however, there was a small degree of partiality and so those later influenced by them went so far [as to develop doctrines that amounted to endorsing] that there should be no [distinctions recognizing] fathers or rulers.⁵⁹ Extrapolating that things would come to such a pass [if he did not intervene], Mencius sought to rectify matters at the root. The pleasure that Han Yu derived from countenancing people's [inherently] good mind can indeed be said to [exemplify the qualities of] doing one's best for others and putting oneself in another person's shoes, but the doctrines he endorsed [show that] he erred in failing to understand [the need] to take due care. As for his claim that in regard to 'obeying superiors' and 'being inclusive in one's concern for others' Confucius was the same as Mozi—this is utterly unacceptable. Moreover, students in later times were not the equal of Yang Zhu and Mozi. Yang and Mo originally studied humaneness and rightness, but people who came after them no longer studied humaneness and rightness. [And even though they were partial,] their error was nevertheless pointed out by Mencius. And yet because there was nobody who pointed out [the error] of those who came after them, those people's errors were not seen."

或問伊川曰：「退之讀墨篇如何」？曰。「此篇意亦甚好。但言不謹嚴。便有不是處。且孟子言墨子愛其兄之子猶隣之子。墨子書中何嘗有如此等言。但孟子拔本塞源知其流必至於此。大凡儒者學道差之毫釐繆以千里。楊子本是學義。墨子本是學仁。但所學者稍偏故其流遂至於無父無君。孟子欲正其本，故推至此。退之樂取人善之心可謂忠恕，然持教不知謹嚴故失之。至若言孔子尚同兼愛與墨子同則甚不可也。後之學者又不及楊墨。楊墨本學仁義。後人乃不學仁義，但楊墨之過被孟子指出。後人無人指出。故不見其過也。」⁶⁰

Even a small degree of partiality can lead to disastrous consequences. Here the implication is that if Han Yu's views were not critiqued, then, just as with Yang Zhu's and Mozi's one-sided understanding of rightness and humaneness, this too would have major negative consequences. One hundred years later, this presented Zhu Xi with a dilemma: uncritically accept the views of the Cheng brothers or refuse to accept the thesis that the real root of the problem lay with the Confucians rather than with Yang Zhu and Mozi and instead attempt to provide an alternative explanation.

Conclusion

Beginning in the Song and continuing into the Qing dynasty, the *daotong* concept was employed as a strategy to confirm certain Confucians as true transmitters of the Way and to exclude others on the basis of their being propagators of heterodox teachings. This chapter has provided an overview of four centuries of proto-*daotong* discourse developed before Zhu Xi across a broad range of literary genres—letters, reading notes, essays, prefaces, postfaces, tomb inscriptions, epitaphs, encomia, and commentaries—in which the negative image of Yang Zhu and the cognate Yang-Mo trope were prominent.

The chapter has also identified several key themes that subsequently became central to Zhu Xi's appropriation of the *daotong* concept. The first is the rhetorical strategy of portraying Daoists (variously, Huang-Lao, Lao-Zhuang) and Buddhists as latter-day Yangists and Mohists. This also involved clustering Yang Zhu, Mozi, Laozi, and the Buddha as a group, lamenting that the "great Way," "the Way of the sages," did not shine in the Central States due to the chaos wrought by this group. The promotion of certain figures and exclusion of others was further reinforced by portraying latter-day Yangists and Mohists as belonging to an "adulterated" lineage in contrast to the "pure" lineage of Zhou-Kong. The second is the promotion of a transmission lineage model in which the transmission of the Way did not rely on face-to-face teacher-student transmission. Han Yu's contribution to the development of such a model had an ongoing impact, even if the Cheng brothers and their disciples finally removed Han Yu from their accounts of the orthodox lineage of transmission. Protagonists of *guwen*, or ancient-style learning, also combined lineage discourse with the privileging of certain key texts, such as the Six Classics, as the medium in which the Way of Confucius was preserved and transmitted. Related developments included highlighting the role played by enlightened individuals in understanding those key texts, independent of a lineage of direct transmission between teacher and immediate disciple. Tiantai monk and *guwen* protagonist Zhiyuan contributed significantly to developing this idea and promoted it as part of a broader agenda to develop a kind of Buddho-Confucian ecumenicism. The third is the Cheng brothers' thesis that even a small degree of partiality can eventually have disastrous consequences, a theme that Zhu Xi subsequently came to develop as a pivotal strategy in his exegesis of *Zhongyong*, a text central to the construction of his account of *daotong*.

Notes

1. Thomas A. Wilson, *Genealogy of the Way: The Construction and Uses of the Confucian Tradition in Late Imperial China* (Stanford, CA: Stanford University Press, 1995), 74.

2. *Daotong* has been variously translated as "succession to the Way," "line of continuity with the Way," "transmission of the Way," "legacy of the Way," "orthodox tradition," "tradition of the Way," "interconnecting thread of the Way," and "genealogy of the Way."

3. For example, as with the early Neo-Confucian versions of the *daotong*, modern New Confucian Mou Zongsan's 牟宗三 (1909–1995) revised *daotong* simultaneously served to function as a vehicle for exclusion as well as inclusion. On the one hand, it has been used to privilege one particular lineage in the transmission of the *dao*, the Xiong Shili 熊十力 (1885–1968)—Mou Zongsan lineage; on the other hand, it has been used to exclude figures such as Feng Youlan 馮友蘭 (1895–1990) and He Lin 賀麟 (1902–93) from the New Confucian fold. See Makeham, "The New *Daotong*," in *New Confucianism: A Critical Examination*, ed. John Makeham (New York: Palgrave Macmillan, 2003), 55–78. More recent developments are the focus of chapters "*Daotong* and Chinese Culture" and "*Ruxue*: *Daotong* versus *Zhengtong*" in John Makeham, *Lost Soul: "Confucianism" in Contemporary Chinese Academic Discourse* (Cambridge, MA: Harvard University Asia Center, 2008), 149–67, 192–207.

4. Although the concept is most famously associated with Zhu Xi, recent scholarship demonstrates that the term *daotong* already existed in the Tang dynasty. Christian Soffel identifies an example on a tomb inscription dating from the early Tang period, where it is used as the title of a book, although the content of the book and the term's meaning are unknown. He also identifies examples of the term's use in the Northern and Southern Song (predating Zhu Xi's use) where it has a distinct political sense. He concludes: "Zhu Xi's merit lies in giving the *daotong* thesis wider currency, the subsequent influence of which was immense. Only beginning with Zhu Xi did people use the concise catchword "*daotong*" to promote related doctrines. Before Zhu Xi, although there were scholars who used "*daotong*" to refer to systems of scholarly or political succession, that was sporadic and uncommon." Su Feixiang 蘇費翔 (Christian Soffel), "Zhu Xi zhi qian daotong yi ci de yongfa" 朱熹之前"道統"一詞的用法 [Use of the term "*daotong*" before Zhu Xi], in *Renwen yu jiazhi: Zhuzixue guoji xueshu yantaohui ji Zhuzi danchen 880 zhounian jinianhui lunwenji* 人文與價值——朱子學國際學術研討會暨朱子誕辰880周年紀念會論文集 [Humanities and values: Collected essays from the international symposium on Zhu Xi studies and the meeting to commemorate the 880th anniversary of Zhu Xi's birth], ed. Chen Lai 陳來 and Zhu Jieren 朱杰人 (Shanghai: Huadong shifan daxue chubanshe, 2011), 83–84, 88. See also Christian Soffel and Hoyt Cleveland Tillman, *Cultural Authority and Political*

Culture in China: Exploring Issues with the Zhongyong and the Daotong during the Song, Jin and Yuan Dynasties (Stuttgart: Franz Steiner Verlag, 2012), 90–94. For other Northern Song examples of the term's use, see Cho-ying Li and Charles Hartman, "A Newly Discovered Inscription by Qin Gui: Its Implications for the History of Song *Daoxue*," *Harvard Journal of Asiatic Studies* 70, no. 2 (2010): 387–88, 432.

    5. The letter is reproduced at "Da Zhang Ji shu" 答張籍書 [Reply to Zhang Ji], *Han Changli wenji jiaozhu* 韓昌黎文集校注 [Annotated edition of Han Yu's collected writings], comp. Ma Qixu 馬其昶 and Ma Maoyuan 馬茂元 (Shanghai: Shanghai guji chubanshe, 1986), 131.

    6. "Du Xun," *Han Changli wenji jiaozhu*, 37.

    7. "Song Wang Xiucai xu," *Han Changli wenji jiaozhu*, 261, 262.

    8. It is also worth noting that Han Yu may well have drawn on his friend Li Ao 李翱 (772–841) for these views. In 802 Li had already written the essay, "Fuxing shu" 復性書 [Returning to the nature], in which he outlined how Confucius's Way was transmitted first to his disciples Yan Yuan 顏淵, Zilu 子路, and Zengzi, next to Zisi, then Mencius, and then to Mencius's disciples Gongsun Chou 公孫丑 and Wan Zhang 萬章. Unlike this early, reticent Han Yu, however, Li Ao had no difficulty in presenting himself as the contemporary transmitter of "the Way of the nature and the decree," which, as he informs us, he transmitted via his *Fuxing shu*. See T. H. Barrett, *Li Ao: Buddhist, Taoist or Neo-Confucian?* (Oxford: Oxford University Press, 1992), 110.

    9. "Yuan dao," *Han Changli wenji jiaozhu*, 14, 16, 18.

    10. Han Yu had already listed this group in his "Song Futu Wenchang shi xu" 送浮屠文暢師序 [Valedictory preface for monk Wenchang] composed in 803. In that account, the group transmitted the Way of humaneness and rightness and the teachings of ritual, music, legal codes, and government (*Han Changli wenji jiaozhu*, 253). Sueki Minoru 末岡実 has also pointed out that the category of *shang shang sheng* 上上聖 (top upper-level sages) in the "Gujin ren biao" 古今人表 [Table of figures, past and present] of the *Hanshu* 漢書 [History of the former Han dynasty] also provides a precedent for such a grouping, albeit without Shun. See his "Tōdai 'dōtōsetsu' kokō: Kan Yu o chūshin to shite" 唐代「道統説」小考：韓愈を中心として [A study of the *daotong* doctrine in the Tang dynasty: Han Yu as focus], *Hokkaidō Daigakubu Bungakubu kiyō* 北海道大學文學部紀要 36, no. 1 (1988): 42. Another possible inspiration is *Mencius* 7B38.

    11. The essay thus proceeds to conclude with the recommendation that Buddhist and Daoist priests should be forced to return to secular life, their books burned, and their temples turned into ordinary dwellings.

    12. "Yu Meng Shangshu shu" 與孟尚書書 [Letter to minister Meng], *Han Changli wenji jiaozhu*, 215.

    13. This is also quite different from one of his early pronouncements (written in 798). In responding to Zhang Ji's argument that writing is a better medium in

which to criticize the Daoists and Buddhists, Han Yu claimed to have attained the Way of the sages by himself, quite independent of any transmission lineage, citing Mencius as an example of someone who did not commit to recording his words: "The book *Mencius* was not written by Mencius himself. After he died, his disciples Wan Zhang and Gongsun Chou jointly recorded what he had said to them, and that's that. I, Han Yu, attained the Way of the sages by myself and discoursed on it, and for some years now have been criticising the Daoists and the Buddhists." (孟軻之書，非軻自著，軻既歿，其徒萬章、公孫醜相與記軻所言焉耳。仆自得聖人之道而誦之，排前二家有年矣。) See Han Yu, "Da Zhang Ji shu" 答張籍書 [Reply to Zhang Ji], *Han Changli wenji jiaozhu*, 132.

14. *Pizi wensou* 皮子文藪 [Mr. Pi's literary marsh], *Pi Rixiu wenji* 皮日休文集 [Collected writings of Pi Rixiu], *Sibu congkan* 四部叢刊 [The four divisions collection] edition (hereafter SBCK) (Shanghai: Shangwu yinshuguan, 1919; supplements 1934–36), 3.2b–3a. *Pizi wensou* is a portfolio of writings compiled in 866. See Dingxiang Warner, *Transmitting Authority: Wang Tong (ca. 584–617) and the Zhongshuo in Medieval China's Manuscript Culture* (Boston: Brill, 2014), 181.

15. David McMullen, *State and Scholars in T'ang China* (Cambridge: Cambridge University Press, 1988), 61. Warner, *Transmitting Authority*, 181, maintains it is quite likely that "the petition was never formally submitted to the court, but instead was another of Pi's works that was intended from the start to serve merely as one of his writing samples."

16. *Pizi wensou*, 9.5a.

17. See Zhao Qi 趙岐, *Mengzi tici* 孟子題辭 [Foreword to *Mencius*], in Jiao Xun 焦循, *Mengzi zhengyi* 孟子正義 [Correct meaning of *Mencius*] (Beijing: Zhonghua, 1987), 16.

18. Warner, *Transmitting Authority*, 191. I would suggest, however, that Liu intended the name "Jianyu" to mean "is the equal of Han Yu." See Liu Kai, "Shang Fu Xingzhou shu" 上符興州書 [Letter submitted to prefect of Xingzhou Fu Zhaoyuan 符昭愿], *Hedong ji* 河東集 [The collected writings of Liu Kai], SBCK, 6.16b.

19. "Ying ze" 應責 [Responding to criticism], *Hedong ji*, 1.11b.

20. Liu Kai, "Dongjiao yefu zhuan" 東郊野夫傳 [The yokel from the eastern suburbs], *Hedong ji*, 2.3b.

21. Liu Kai, "Song Chen Zhaohua xu" 送陳昭華序 [Valedictory Preface for Chen Zhaohua], *Hedong ji*, 11.6a.

22. Peter K. Bol describes *guwen* as an intellectual and literary style for the educated elite (*shi*) that emerged in the eighth century and flourished in the eleventh century. Although by the early eleventh century some used *guwen* "to refer to a new variety of non-poetic and non-parallel genres for writing about intellectual and social issues . . . the issue was not the search for a better means of expressing ideas but the values attached to stylistic choice." The *guwen* movement

"was an intellectual movement that saw literary change as integral to changes in public values and whose leading 'thinkers' were literary men." See Bol, *'This Culture of Ours': Intellectual Transitions in T'ang and Sung China* (Stanford, CA: Stanford University Press, 1992), 24, 25, 27.

23. Sun Fu, "Shang Kong Jishi shu" 上孔給事書 [Letter submitted to Steward Kong] in *Sun Mingfu xiao ji* 孫明復小集 [Small collection of Sun Fu's writings], *Wenyuan ge Siku quanshu* 文淵閣四庫全書 [The complete collection of the Four Treasuries—based on the Wenyuan Pavilion copy] (Taipei: Taiwan shangwu yinshuguan, 1983), 1.29a–29b.

24. Yang Xiong, *Fayan* 法言 [Model Sayings], SBCK, 2.3b.

25. Paraphrase of "Yu Meng Shangshu shu," 214.

26. Sun Fu, "Yanzhou Zou xian jian Meng miao ji" 兗州鄒縣建孟廟記 [Inscription for the temple built in honor of Mencius, Zou County, Yanzhou], *Sun Mingfu xiao ji*, 1.33b.

27. Here the reference is to Laozi.

28. "Ru ru," *Sun Mingfu xiao ji*, 1.37a–37b, 38a.

29. "Da Zhang Dong shu" 答張洞書 [Letter replying to Zhang Dong], *Sun Mingfu xiao ji*, 1.32b.

30. "Shang Sun Shaofu shu" 上孫少傅書 [Letter submitted to junior preceptor Sun], *Culai ji* 徂徠集 [Collected writings of Shi Jie], *Wenyuan ge Siku quanshu*, 15.1a–1b.

31. Lei Jiasheng 雷家聖, "Bei Song qianqi, zhongqi Ruxue de duoyuan fazhan: yi Liu Kai daotong shuo yu Sun Fu zunwang lun wei li" 北宋前期、中期儒學的多元發展—以柳開道統說與孫復尊王論為例 [Plural developments among Confucians during the early and middle periods of the Northern Song: the cases of Liu Kai's *daotong* doctrine and Sun Fu's royalism], *Zhongguoshi yanjiu* 76 (2012): 42, 43. As Liu Chengguo 劉成國 shows, this Northern Song practice was not limited to Shi. Liu Chengguo, "9–12 shijichu de daotong 'qianshi' kaoshu" 9－12 世紀初的道統"前史"考述 [An examination of the "prehistory" of *daotong* from the ninth to early twelfth centuries], *Shixue yuekan* (December 2013): 115–16.

32. Albert Welter, *Yongming Yanshou's Conception of Chan in the Zongjing Lu* (New York: Oxford University Press, 2011), 208. For Welter's related study on Zanning, see "Confucian Monks and Buddhist Junzi: Zanning's Topical Compendium of the Buddhist Clergy (Da Song seng shi lüe 大宋僧史略) and the Politics of Buddhist Accommodation at the Song Court," in *The Middle Kingdom and the Dharma Wheel: Aspects of the Relationship between the Buddhist Saṃgha and the State in Chinese History*, ed. Thomas Jülch (Leiden: Brill, 2016).

33. "Xu chuan shen" 敘傳神 [Providing an account of transmitting spirit], in *Xianju bian* 閒居編 [Writings compiled in retirement], preface dated 1016, *Dai Nihon zokuzōkyō* 大日本續藏經 [Kyoto supplement to the canon], CBETA

Chinese Electronic Tripiṭaka Collection edition, Taipei, www.cbeta.org, X56.949, 906b16–19.

34. "Song Shuji xu" 送庶幾序 [Valedictory preface for Shuji], *Xianju bian*, X56.949, 908b8–12.

35. "Zhongyong," *Liji* 禮記 [Book of rites], *Liji zhushu* 禮記注疏 [Book of rites with annotations and sub-commentaries], *Shisan jing zhushu* 十三經注疏 [The Thirteen Classics with Annotations and Sub-Commentaries], comp. Ruan Yuan 阮元 (1764–1849) (Taipei: Yiwen yinshuguan, 1985), 53.12b.

36. Humaneness (仁), rightness (義), ritual propriety (禮), wisdom (智), trust (信).

37. The reason for translating *zhong* in this context as "center" or "middle" rather than "balance" relates to the Tiantai doctrine of the Three Truths. On the Three Truths, see "Introduction," *The Buddhist Roots of Zhu Xi's Philosophical Thought*, ed. John Makeham (New York: Oxford University Press, 2018), 12.

38. "Song Shuji xu," X56.949, 908a16–22.

39. On Qisong's "*Zhongyong jie*" 中庸解 [Interpretation of *Zhongyong*], see Douglas Skonicki, "A Buddhist Response to Ancient-style Learning," *T'oung Pao* 97, no. 1–3 (2011): 21–24.

40. Yu Yingshi, *Zhu Xi de lishi shijie: Songdai shidafu zhengzhi wenhua de yanjiu* 朱熹的歷史世界：宋代士大夫政治文化的研究 [Zhu Xi's historical world: studies of Song dynasty elite literati political culture], vol. 1 (Taipei: Yunchen, 2003), 129–41, 145. See also Hong Shufen 洪淑芬, *Lun Ru-Fo jiaoshe yu Songdai Ruxue fuxing: yi Zhiyuan, Qisong, Zonggao wei li* 論儒佛交涉與宋代儒學復興 — 以智圓、契嵩、宗杲為例 [Confucian-Buddhist interactions and the revival of Confucianism in the Song dynasty: Zhiyuan, Qisong and Zonggao as examples] (Taipei: Daan chubanshe, 2008), 369–413.

41. For details, see Makeham, "Yang Zhu's Role in the Construction of Zhu Xi's *Daotong*" in this volume.

42. *Xianju bian*, X56.949, 894a16–17.

43. On this point, see my introduction to *The Buddhist Roots of Zhu Xi's Philosophical Thought*, 19–21. It is worth noting Skonicki's related observation that Chan monk Qisong's objective in positing a shared *dao* with the *dao* championed by *guwen* learning partisans—the *dao* of the ancient sages—"was not to establish the foundations for a syncretic world view, but rather to demonstrate that the *dao* of the ancient sages was in fact the Buddhist *dao*." Skonicki, "A Buddhist Response to Ancient-style Learning: Qisong's Conception of Political Order," *T'oung Pao* 97, no. 1–3 (2011): 13, 19–20.

44. *Xianju bian*, X56.949, 890a3–a14. The inclusion of Liu Zongyuan was novel.

45. Here the reference is to *Chong zhiding Niepan shu* 重治定涅槃疏 [Finalized revised edition of the *Commentary on the Nirvana Sutra*].

46. The reference is to a memorial submitted by Wei to Emperor Wu. As related by Livia Kohn: "In 567 he had risen to propose a new Buddhist orthodoxy with the people as the flock, the *sangha* as administrators, and the emperor as sacred Buddhist ruler. Because this meant the dissolution of an independent Buddhist organization and the return of all clerics to the laity, Buddhist leaders argued heatedly against it. Emperor Wu of the Northern Zhou, however, liked the idea and honored Wei Yuanzong with a formal title." See *Daoism and Chinese Culture* (St. Petersburg, FL: Three Pines Press, 2001), 177.

47. *Xianju bian*, X56.949, 890a16–b2.

48. Douglas Skonicki, "Viewing the Two Teachings as Distinct yet Complementary: Gushan Zhiyuan's Use of Parallelisms to Demonstrate the Compatibility of Buddhism and Ancient-style Learning," *Journal of Chinese Religions* 38, no. 1 (2010): 3–4, 29.

49. For details, see my chapter, "Yang Zhu's Role in the Construction of Zhu Xi's *Daotong*" in this volume.

50. Douglas Skonicki, "'Guwen' Lineage Discourse in the Northern Song," *Journal of Song-Yuan Studies* 44 (2014): 1.

51. Ouyang Xiu, "Ji jiu ben *Han wen* hou" 記舊本韓文後 [Postface to an old edition of Han Yu's writings], in Zhu Xi, *Changli xiansheng ji kaoyi* 昌黎先生集考異 [Collection of Han Yu's writings], *Zhuzi quanshu* 朱子全書 [Complete works of Zhu Xi], ed. Zhu Jieren et al., 27 vols. (Shanghai: Shanghai guji chubanshe, and Hefei: Anhui jiaoyu chubanshe, 2002), 19:630.

52. See *Xin Tangshu* 新唐書 [New history of the Tang], ed. Ouyang Xiu and Song Qi 宋祁 (Beijing: Zhonghua, 1975), *juan* 101, 5269. Skonicki, "'Guwen' Lineage Discourse," 30, also notes that "a more critical posture towards Han can be traced back to a series of thirty essays from the mid-eleventh century entitled 'Against Han' (Fei Han) written by the Chan monk, and practitioner of *guwen*, Qisong (1007–1072). These essays represent the first comprehensive negative critical assessment of Han Yu in the Northern Song." This did not, however, stop Han Yu's institutional elevation three decades later.

53. Wilson, *Genealogy of the Way*, 41.

54. "Mingdao xiansheng mubiao" 明道先生墓表 [Tombstone epitaph for Mr Cheng Hao], in *Er Cheng ji* 二程集 [Collected works of the two Chengs], 2 vols. (1981; reprint, Beijing: Zhonghua, 2004), 1:640.

55. For example, Liu Li 劉立 (d.u.), Zhu Guangting 朱光庭 (1037–1094) and Fan Zuyu 范祖禹 (1041–1098) in the Preface to "Mingdao xiangsheng xingzhuang" 明道先生行狀 [Record of Mr Cheng Hao's conduct], *Er Cheng ji*, 1:329, 331, 334.

56. Bol, '*This Culture of Ours*,' 304.

57. See the passages cited and translated in Peter K. Bol, "Cheng Yi as a Literatus," in *The Power of Culture: Studies in Chinese Cultural History*, ed. Willard

J. Peterson, Andrew Plaks, Ying-shih Yü (Hong Kong: Chinese University Press, 1994), 177; Bol, 'This Culture of Ours,' 303–304.

58. Reference to *Mencius* 3A5.

59. Reference to *Mencius* 3B9.

60. *Mengzi jingyi* 孟子精義 [Essential meanings of the *Mencius*], in *Lun Meng jingyi* 論孟精義 [Essential meanings of the *Analects* and *Mencius*], *Zhuzi quanshu*, 7:711. Han Yu's essay, "On Reading Mozi" is undated but it would appear to have been written late in his life given the views he expresses are at odds with much of his other writings. In the essay he argues that with respect to several key Mohist doctrines, such as "obeying superiors," "being inclusive in one's concern for others," "honoring the worthy," and "understanding ghosts," Confucius was essentially in agreement with Mozi.

Chapter 6

Yang Zhu's Role in the Construction of Zhu Xi's *Daotong*

JOHN MAKEHAM

Introduction

This chapter examines the role Zhu Xi 朱熹 (1130–1200) accorded Yang Zhu 楊朱 in the construction of Zhu's notion of *daotong* 道統 (succession of the Way). It will show how Zhu's appropriation of the negative image of Yang Zhu (and the cognate Yang-Mo 楊墨 [Yang Zhu and Mozi] trope) was deployed in formulating his particular account of *daotong* and how this was connected with his savage critiques of Daoism and, particularly, Buddhism. The chapter will argue that the critical dimension was integral to Zhu Xi's *daotong* project, a feature that, in turn, drew from four centuries of proto-*daotong* discourse in which the Yang-Mo trope was prominent. For Zhu Xi, identifying "the other," the promoter of "deviant teachings," played a key role in his self-narrative of being the legitimate heir to the transmission of the succession of the true Way

1. Zhu Xi and *Daotong*

Zhu Xi's use of the term *daotong* in the 1189 preface to his commentary on *Zhongyong* 中庸 (Balance as the norm),[1] "*Zhongyong* xu" 中庸序, is perhaps the best known example, although he had already used the term at least as early as 1179 when he referred to Zhou Dunyi 周敦頤 (1016–1073) as having "transmitted the *daotong* with his mind" (心傳道統).² Moreover, it is clear that Zhu had formulated the notion of *daotong* well before this, as is evident in his 1172 preface to *Lun Meng jingyi* 論孟精義 (Essential meanings of the *Analects* and *Mencius*): "Ever since the Qin and Han, no Confucian has been up to the task of participating in and having an insider's understanding of the transmission of this Way of ours" (自秦漢以來儒者類皆不足以與聞斯道之傳). Later in the same preface he refers to "the thread that has not be transmitted for one thousand years" (千載不傳之緒), and the "succession [lit. 'main thread'] transmitted by the enlightened sages" (明聖傳之統).³

In another early example, his 1173 preface to Shi Dun's 石墪 (1128–1182) *Zhongyong jilüe* 中庸輯略 (Short edited collection of commentaries on *Zhongyong*), Zhu outlined the following transmission lineage, in which it is the tradition (傳) of Confucius that was transmitted: Confucius—Zengzi 曾子 (fifth century BCE)—Zisi 子思 (fifth century BCE)—Mencius (fourth century BCE)—Zhou Dunyi—the Cheng brothers (Cheng Yi 程頤 [1033–1107] and Cheng Hao 程顥 [1032–1085]).⁴ Zhu Xi explains that because Zisi feared that the true meaning of what had been transmitted from Confucius would be lost, this had prompted Zisi to compose *Zhongyong*. Thus, it is *Zhongyong* that is privileged here as the textual record of the teachings of Confucius and subsequently transmitted to Mencius, after which the transmission is interrupted until being revived by Zhou Dunyi.

Perhaps the earliest example of Zhu Xi's proto-*daotong* is in a memorial to the emperor in 1162. In Zhu's memorial the famous "sixteen-character teaching"⁵ (which he later made central to his account of the *daotong*) is already identified as the learning "that was transmitted by Yao 堯, Shun 舜, Yu 禹, Tang 湯, Wen 文, Wu 武, the Duke of Zhou 周公, and Confucius" but ceased transmitted after Mencius, until it was eventually recovered by the Cheng brothers.⁶ The passage is also noteworthy on two other accounts. First, it is Zhu's earliest explicit identification of both Cheng brothers as having been the first to have taken up the transmission of the learning that ceased with Mencius. Second, Zhu Xi used *Daxue* 大學 (Great Learning) rather than *Zhongyong* to gloss key terms in the sixteen-character teaching.⁷ Post-1162, however, increasingly it was *Zhongyong* that Zhu Xi employed to gloss key terms in the sixteen-character teaching, as will be made evident later in this chapter.

Two aspects of Zhu's appropriation of the *daotong* conceit are especially pertinent. First, Confucius, Zengzi, Zisi, and Mencius are identified as the last in a long line of early transmitters. By privileging this group, Zhu was able to present the *Analects, Daxue, Zhongyong*, and *Mencius* as an integrated body of texts, premised on a line of transmission of the *daotong* from Confucius to Mencius. The Four Books were published together for the first time[8] in Zhu's 1190 publication *Sizi* 四子 (Four masters), later known as *Sishu zhangju jizhu* 四書章句集注 (Section and sentence commentaries and collected annotations on the Four Books), and consists of *Daxue zhangju* 大學章句 (Section and sentence commentaries on the *Great Learning*), *Lunyu jizhu* 論語集注 (Collected annotations on the *Analects*), *Mengzi jizhu* 孟子集注 (Collected annotations on *Mencius*), and *Zhongyong zhangju*. Although the *Analects* and *Mencius* had been accorded canonical status in the mid-ninth and late-eleventh centuries, respectively, *Daxue* and *Zhongyong* had not. Nevertheless, these two chapters from the *Book of Rites* had attracted the attention of many intellectuals since the mid-Tang. Second, by writing commentaries on these four books and identifying the Cheng brothers (and Zhou Dunyi in many instances as well[9]) as the modern inheritors of the *daotong* transmission, Zhu sought to imply that he, too, was an heir to that transmission.

In 1313, Yuan emperor Renzong 仁宗 (r. 1311–1320) included questions on the Four Books in the civil service examinations and candidates were required to use Zhu's commentaries.[10] As Benjamin Elman has pointed out, however, "The *Tao-hsueh* civil examination orthodoxy [based on the Four Books with Zhu's commentary] . . . did not achieve widespread influence outside the imperial schools and private academies until 1425–50, when the ratio of candidates to graduates for *chin-shih* degrees again approached the high levels of the Northern Sung."[11] Nevertheless, from the mid-fifteenth century until the turn of the twentieth century, the Four Books and Zhu's commentaries continued to be represented in, and therefore sanctioned by, the examination system.

As related in my previous chapter in this volume, "Yang Zhu's Role in Tang-Song Proto-*daotong* Discourse," a key theme to emerge in the Cheng brothers' criticisms of Yang Zhu and Mozi is that even a small degree of partiality or inclination to one side can develop to have disastrous consequences. This theme informs a number of discussions by the Cheng brothers, of which the following by Cheng Yi is typical:

Most Confucians focus single-mindedly on the true Way. This focus admits no error. [If there is any error, then even though] at first it is very slight, eventually [the situation] will be irredeemable. For example, "Shi [Zizhang] is excessive whereas Shang [Zixia] falls short."[12] With respect to the balanced Way of the sages, even though Shi was only a little excessive in being generous, and Shang fell short of being generous only by a little, [excessive] generosity gradually became "inclusive concern," and falling short [of being generous] gradually became "serving one's own interests."[13] Excess and deficiency both came from the Confucians, but in the end they became that of Yang and Mo. As for Yang and Mo, even though they did not go so far as to [develop doctrines that amounted to endorsing] that there be no [distinctions recognizing] fathers or rulers, Mencius extrapolated that it would indeed come to this.

大抵儒者潛心正道，不容有差，其始甚微，其終則不可救。如「師也過，商也不及」，於聖人中道，師只是過於厚些，商只是不及些。然而厚則漸至於兼愛，不及則便至於為我。其過不及同出於儒者，其末遂至楊、墨。至如楊、墨，亦未至於無父無君，孟子推之，便至於此。[14]

In addition to the thesis that even a small degree of partiality can eventually lead to disastrous consequences, Cheng Yi also maintains that the real root of the problem lies with the Confucians and not with Yang Zhu and Mozi per se. In this passage, Cheng Yi claims that "excess and deficiency both come from the Confucians"; that "Yang and Mo originally studied humaneness and rightness"; and that "students in later times were not the equal of Yang Zhu and Mozi" when it came to learning humaneness and rightness.[15] They go so far as to infer that Yang Zhu and Mozi were actually students of Zixia and Zizhang, respectively: "Yangzi seems have come from [the door] of Zizhang and Mozi seems to have come from [the door] of Zixia. Between them, there is excess and deficiency. It can hardly be the case that Zizhang and Zixia were not students of Confucius." (楊子似出于子張，墨子似出于子夏。其中更有過不及。豈是師商不學於聖人之門。)[16]

One hundred years later, this presented Zhu Xi with a dilemma: uncritically accept the views of the Cheng brothers or refuse to accept the thesis that the real root of the problem lay with the Confucians rather than with Yang Zhu and Mozi and instead attempt to provide an alternative explanation. Zhu Xi chose the latter horn of the dilemma.

2. Yang Zhu as Daoist

In his *Lunyu jingyi* 論語精義 (Essential meaning of the *Analects*; preface 1072) Zhu Xi cited comments by Cheng Yi that the real root of the problem lay with the Confucians and not with Yang Zhu and Mozi; he also cited comments by students of the Cheng brothers—Xie Liangzuo 謝良佐 (d. 1120) and Hou Zhongliang 候仲良 (fl. 1110)—who similarly maintained that the genesis of the views of the later followers of Yang Zhu and Mozi (後世楊墨之學) was the teachings of Zixia and Zizhang, respectively.[17] Two years later, however, Zhu started to repudiate this relationship, instead arguing that Yang Zhu's teachings were actually derived from the writings of Lao Dan 老聃 (Laozi) and denying that Yang Zhu and Mozi had been students of Zixia and Zizhang.[18]

In a discussion of Mencius's claim that "Yang Zhu clung to serving one's own interests" (楊子取為我; *Mencius* 7A26), *Zhuzi yulei* 朱子語類 (Topically arranged conversations of master Zhu) records the following exchange:

> [Zhu Xi]: "Yang Zhu was a disciple of Laozi and his learning was focused specifically on 'serving one's own interests.' [The "Yang Zhu" chapter of] the *Liezi* states: 'Bocheng Zigao[19] would not pull out even one hair in order to benefit the whole world. He said: "How could one hair be able to benefit the whole world? If every person were not to pull out one hair, and not [attempt to] benefit the whole world, then the whole world would come to order of itself."'"[20]
>
> [Interlocuter]: "It would seem that Laozi was not the same as Yang Zhu."
>
> [Zhu Xi]: "Laozi's perspective on the affairs of the world was to secure his own comfort at the expense of others. Is not what he said about 'by being pure and still [affairs] will come to order of themselves'[21] just the same as what Yang Zhu [advocated]?"

「楊朱乃老子弟子,其學專為己。列子云:『伯成子羔拔一毛而利天下不為。其言曰:「一毛安能利天下?使人人不拔一毛,不利天下,則天下自治矣。」』」問:「老子似不與楊朱同。」曰:「老子窺見天下之事,卻討便宜置身於安閑之地,云『清靜自治』,豈不是與朱同?」²²

Elsewhere, Zhu similarly drew on passages such as *Daode jing* chapters 7, 13, 16, and 44 to conclude that the doctrine of "serving one's own interests" was based on the teachings of Laozi.²³ In 1177, in responding to a question about whether the doctrines of Yang Zhu and Mozi were derived from the teachings of Zixia and Zizhang, Zhu even endorsed Hu Yin's 胡寅 (1098–1156) identification of Yang Zhu with Laozi's disciple, Yang Ziju 楊子居,²⁴ as related in the "Yuyan" 寓言 (Dwelling Words) chapter of *Zhuangzi*.²⁵

Zhu Xi's students and interlocuters, however, pointed out that if Yang Zhu's teachings were in fact derived from Laozi, then Zhu still needed to explain why Mencius criticized only Yang Zhu and not Laozi, to which Zhu's responded as follows:

People say that Mencius criticized only Yang Zhu and Mozi but not Laozi. What they fail to understand is that Daoist doctrines about self-cultivation are solely "to serve one's own interests." Yang Zhu's doctrine of "serving one's own interests" is [to be concerned] about one's own self and that's it, having no concern for other people.

人說孟子只闢楊墨,不闢老氏,卻不知道道家修養之說只是為己,獨自一身便了,更不管別人,便是楊氏為我之學。²⁶

In other words, Mencius's criticisms of Yang Zhu were actually directed at Laozi.

Indeed, this reference to "Daoist doctrines" is not limited to Laozi—it also includes Zhuangzi and Liezi, as the following passages make clear:

Li Mengxian asked: "Zhuangzi and Mencius were contemporaries. How is it that they never encountered one another and did not know about each other's way?"

[Zhu Xi] replied: "At the time, there was nobody who aligned himself with Zhuangzi's teachings. Zhuangzi lived in a remote location and kept only his own company. Nonetheless, his were nothing other than the teachings of Yang Zhu. It is just that Yang Zhu was boastful and so Mencius strenuously criticized him."

李夢先問:「莊子、孟子同時,何不一相遇,又不聞道相及,如何?」曰:「莊子當時也無人宗之,他只在僻處自說,然亦止是楊朱之學。但楊氏說得大了,故孟子力排之。」[27]

Liezi's and Zhuangzi's [teachings] are based on those of Yang Zhu, and so their writings frequently cite his sayings. *Zhuangzi* says: "A child's love for his or her parents is a matter of fate. This cannot be erased [from the child's] mind." As for a minister's [service] to his ruler, *Zhuangzi* says: "*Yi* (rightness/duty)—it cannot be escaped anywhere in the world."[28] Zhuangzi here seems to regard *yi* between minister and ruler as inescapable and about which nothing can be done, namely that minister must submit to ruler. Much less is there any [sense of] a relationship of mutuality, which in and of itself constitutes a whole. How odd! Accordingly, it was just these sorts of views that Mencius deemed to be [the same as Yang Zhu's teaching of] "having no ruler."

列、莊本楊朱之學,故其書多引其語。《莊子》說:「子之於親也,命也,不可解於心。」至臣之於君,則曰:「義也,無所逃於天地之間。」是他看得那君臣之義,却似是逃不得,不奈何,須着臣服他。更無一個自然相胥為一體處,可怪,故孟子以為無君,此類是也。[29]

It seems that [for Zhuangzi], so long as son and minister say nothing negative about father and ruler, this suffices to evidence *yi* (rightness/duty) on the part of the son and minister. *Zhuangzi* says: "In the world there are two great imperatives: fate and duty. A child's love for his or her parents is a matter of fate. There is nowhere a child can go where this fate does not prevail. As for the minister's [service] to his ruler, there is nowhere he can go where *yi* does not prevail."[30] I once wrote a colophon in which I cited these passages. I took these doctrines to be Yang Zhu's "having no ruler" doctrine. The sense seems to be that there is *yi* only because there is nothing one can do about it. Yet this is to fail to understand that *yi* as principle exists in and of itself.

看來臣子無說君父不是底道理，此便見得是君臣之義處。莊子云；「天下之大戒二：命也，義也。子之於父，無適而非命也；臣之於君，無適而非義也；無所逃於天地之間。」舊嘗題跋一文字，曾引此語，以為莊子此說，乃楊氏無君之說。似它這意思，便是沒奈何了，方恁地有義，却不知此是自然有底道理。[31]

3. Yang Zhu's Values Perpetuated through Buddhism

Despite Zhu Xi's criticisms of what he took to be the expression of Yang Zhu's values in the *Zhuangzi* and the *Liezi*, his real concern was the expression of those values in his own time. For Zhu Xi, it was through Buddhism that Yang Zhu's values continued to be perpetuated:

> My sense is that, in the main, *Liezi*'s language is similar to that of the Buddhist scriptures. I suspect that when the Buddhists first came to China,[32] they largely stole Laozi's ideas to write their scriptures. Their explanation of *kong* 空 (empty; emptiness) is one such example.

列子言語多與佛經相類，覺得是如此。疑得佛家初來中國，多是偷老子意去做經，如說空處是也。[33]

Because Yang Zhu studied under Laozi, the writings of Zhuangzi and Liezi both talk about Yang Zhu. Mencius's criticisms of Yang Zhu were criticisms of Laozi. The Buddhists have a kind of simple level—what Emperor Wu of Liang attained was this simple level. When Buddhists first entered China [the more sophisticated level] did not yet exist. When

Buddhists later came to China, they stole many sayings of the followers of Laozi and Zhuangzi and thus appeared to be sublime.

蓋是楊朱曾就老子學來，故莊列之書皆說楊朱。孟子闢楊朱，便是闢莊老了。釋氏有一種低底，如梁武帝是得其低底。彼初入中國，也未在。後來到中國，却竊取老莊之徒許話，見得儘高。[34]

When Bodhidharma entered [China], he subsequently overturned many established practices [by] preaching Chan, which was even more ingenious than doctrinal learning, maintaining that one could directly proceed by shortcut to enlightenment [without having first to undergo doctrinal learning]. At the beginning, the Buddhists [merely] preached the doctrine of [the operations of] karma in relation to fortune and misfortune, which was enough to dupe foolish ordinary people, and they relied on this to fulfill their scheme to be clothed and fed. They then made those who governed the country expropriate fields to support them, select lands to accommodate them, and so their followers unwittingly became trapped in the realm of "having no father and having no ruler."

及達磨入來，又翻了許多窠臼，說出禪來，又高妙於義學，以為可以直超徑悟。而其始者禍福報應之說，又足以鉗制愚俗，以為資足衣食之計。遂使有國家者割田以贍之，擇地以居之，以相從陷於無父無君之域而不自覺。[35]

This reference to "having no father and having no ruler" is, of course, an allusion to Mozi and Yang Zhu. Thus, by means of appropriating the writings of Laozi and Zhuangzi to embellish their doctrines, the Buddhists were de facto latter-day Yangists and Mohists. Elsewhere Zhu goes a step further, specifically identifying Chan Buddhism with Yangism: "Mencius criticized Yang Zhu and Mozi but not Laozi and Zhuangzi—this is because Yang Zhu and Mozi were Laozi and Zhuangzi. Nowadays, the Buddhists are also of two kinds: Chan learning is Yang Zhu; as for the practice of almsgiving, that is Mo Di. (孟子不闢老莊而闢楊墨，楊墨即老莊也。今釋子亦有兩般：禪學，楊朱也；若行布施，墨翟也。)[36]

4. Buddhism as More Sophisticated than Yang-Mo

Why was Zhu concerned about the influence of Buddhism? As he explains, "Of the heterodoxies harmful to the Way, Buddhism is the worst." (異端之害道，如釋氏者極矣。)³⁷ Zhu Xi deemed Buddhist teachings to be far more sophisticated and insidious than those of Yang Zhu and Mozi. This view had already been expressed frequently and emphatically by the Cheng brothers. In his biographical account of his brother's life, Cheng Yi relates:

> [Cheng Hao] said that after Mencius died, the learning of the sages ceased being transmitted and so he took it upon himself to revive this culture of ours. In his own words: "The Way is not clear because heterodoxies have harmed it. In the past, the harm was superficial and easy to recognize; now the harm is deep and difficult to discern. In the past, people were deceived by taking advantage of their ignorance; nowadays people are won over by taking advantage of their brilliance. . . . Ever since the Way ceased to be clear, perverse and monstrous doctrines have arisen in contestation, blocking people's ears and eyes and drowning the world in filth. The gateway to the sages is obstructed and only by clearing it can the Way be entered."

> 謂孟子沒而聖學不傳，以興起斯文為己任。其言曰："道之不明，異端害之也。昔之害近而易知，今之害深而難辨。昔之惑人也乘其迷暗，今之入人也因其高明。. . . 自道之不明也，邪誕妖異之說競起，塗生民之耳目，溺天下於汙濁。. . . 聖門之蔽塞，闢之而後可以入道。"³⁸

In the following related passage, Cheng Yi provides an unequivocal statement about why he and his brother found Buddhist teachings to be particularly insidious.

> Should you want to examine thoroughly the Buddhist doctrines in order to determine which to accept and which to reject, then you would certainly have already converted to Buddhism even before you'd have been able to complete your investigations! . . . Although most Confucians sooner or later

stray into Buddhism, it is not their intention to do so—and they do so, of course, by dint of circumstance. This is because even though they grow mentally and physically exhausted and wish to cease, they nevertheless feel uncomfortable about doing so and are unable to stop. And so, seeing that the Buddhists have a reasoned set of teachings, circumstances conspire to compel them to follow those teachings.

釋氏之說，若欲窮其說而去取之，則其說未能窮，固已化而為佛矣。　儒者其卒多入異教，其志非願也，其勢自然如此。蓋智窮力屈，欲休來，又知得未安穩，休不得，故見人有一道理，其勢須從之。³⁹

These comments take on an extra resonance given Cheng Yi's statement that "for several decades" his brother Cheng Hao "had drifted among the various schools and wandered in and out of Daoism and Buddhism, before finally returning to the Six Classics."⁴⁰

Following this lead, the following passage appears at the very opening of *juan* 13 in *Jin si lu* 近思錄 (Record of reflection on things at hand), a work jointly compiled by Zhu Xi and Lü Zuqian 呂祖謙 (1137–1181) in 1175:

Master Mingdao [Cheng Hao] said: "[The teachings of] Yang Zhu and Mozi were more harmful than those of Shen Buhai and Han Fei, and [the teachings of] the Buddha and Laozi are more harmful than those of Yang Zhu and Mozi. Yang Zhu's doctrine of looking out for oneself seems to be like rightness/duty and Mozi's doctrine of inclusive concern seems to be like humaneness. In the case of Shen Buhai and Han Fei, [their teachings] were crass and [their fallacies] easy to discern, and so Mencius criticized only Yang Zhu and Mozi. In the case of the Buddha and Laozi, their words come close to principle and are in quite a different league from that of Yang Zhu and Mozi—that is why they are even more harmful.

明道先生曰：楊墨之害，甚於申韓。佛老之害，甚於楊墨。楊氏爲我，疑於義；墨氏兼愛，疑於仁。申韓則淺陋易見，故孟子只闢楊墨，爲其惑世之甚也。佛老其言近理，又非楊墨之比，此所以爲害尤甚。⁴¹

The prominent placement of this passage in *Jin si lu* is significant. Sometime after the publication of *Sizi* in 1190, Zhu Xi emphasized the intended role that *Jin si lu* was meant to play as a foundational text: "*Sizi* is the stairway to the Six Classics; *Jin si lu* is the stairway to *Sizi*."[42]

5. The Consequences of Being Off Target

Elsewhere, Zhu introduced another theme first formulated by the Cheng brothers: that even being a little off target can have dire consequences. In response to a student's question about whether the claim made in *Mencius*[43] that Yang Zhu's and Mozi's doctrines will result in "beasts being led to devour people" was an exaggeration and, in fact, there were no such consequences, Zhu replied:

> Not so. . . . Take for example the fad for "pure talk" in the Eastern Jin period—this was down to Yang Zhu's learning, and Yang Zhu's way was that of Laozi and Zhuangzi. Before long, everything went to wrack and ruin, opening the way for the Di barbarians to throw China into chaos. Was this calamity not even more tragic than the harm done by floods and wild beasts?! Or again, as further proof, take the example of Emperor Wu of Liang's undertaking to serve the Buddha, which resulted in the country turning into ruins. In recent times, take the example of Wang Jiefu [Anshi]. A man of outstanding learning, he dabbled in Daoism and Buddhism, and in matters of government he sought to emulate [the achievements of] Yao, Shun, and the Three Dynasties. However, those who served him were all men of little integrity. He assembled a bunch of worthless scoundrels drawn from across the realm, leaving a calamitous legacy that endures to this day. He never started out intending to open the way for the Di barbarians to throw China into chaos, to "beasts being led to devour people." It is just that if at the very beginning things are not correct, and normative principles are not clear, then in the end matters must come to this.

> 不然。……如東晉之尚清談，此便是楊氏之學，楊氏即老莊之道。少間百事廢弛，遂啟夷狄亂華，其禍豈不慘於洪水猛獸之害！又如梁武帝事佛，至於社稷丘墟，亦其驗也。如近世王介

甫，其學問高妙，出入於老佛之間，其政事欲與堯舜三代爭衡。然所用者盡是小人，聚天下輕薄無賴小人作一處，以至遺禍至今。他初間也何嘗有啟狄亂華，『率獸食人』之意？只是本原不正，義理不明，其終必至於是耳。[44]

Zhu's message is clear: the insidious effects of Buddhism lead to social turmoil and the collapse of political order. In making his criticisms about the dire threat that Buddhism posed to contemporary society, Zhu was reiterating the very same views expressed by the Cheng brothers a century before:

> This doctrine [Buddhism] has already become a trend throughout realm. What can be done to remedy this? There was already Buddhism in ancient times but even at its most prosperous period it was merely a teaching about worshipping images and did little harm. In its mode today, however, it first of all speaks about the nature and the decree, the Way and virtue, and first of all pursues the intelligent. And the more brilliant the talents of a person are, the deeper that person becomes mired in it. My gifts being humble and my qualities slight, there is nothing I can do about it. Yet even if today we had several Menciuses, they too would be helpless. In Mencius' time, the harm done by Yang Zhu and Mozi did not amount to much; compared with the situation today it was negligible. This matter also surely concerns the failure or success of the state. When pure talk flourished, the house of Jin declined, yet the harm done by pure talk was merely through idle talk. That is in no way comparable to the harm being done to the Way today [by profound and sophisticated Buddhist teachings]!

> 此說天下已成風，其何能救！古亦有釋氏，盛時尚只是崇設像教。其害至小。今日之風，便先言性命道德，先驅了知者，才愈高明，則陷溺愈深。在某則才卑德薄無可奈何他。然據今日便有數孟子，亦無如之何。只看孟子時，楊墨之害能有甚！況之今日殊不足言。此事蓋亦繫時之污隆。清談盛而晉室衰，然清談為害卻只是閑言談，又豈若今之害道。[45]

Why such an alarmist tone? Why was Buddhism so feared and loathed—and in Zhu Xi's case, Chan in particular? At the broader socio-institutional level, the proliferation of monasteries with public abbacies in the Northern Song (920–1127) benefitted Chan, enabling it to develop an independent identity and an institutional base. And because Chan masters needed the support of the elite laity if they were to be able to hold abbacies at public monasteries and thereby perpetuate their own dharma transmission families, this encouraged Chan masters to forge close links with the educated elite. This situation prevailed until the transition to the Southern Song in the late eleventh century when public monasteries increasingly became dominated by Huayan and Tiantai schools, and Chan transmission families had to compete with one another to secure the support of the educated elite.[46]

It was against this background that the Caodong lineage-tradition (Caodong zong 曹洞宗) reemerged in the late eleventh century and grew to prominence in the early twelfth century, relying on officials and literati for political and financial support. This competition for literati support was also a factor motivating Dahui Zonggao's 大慧宗杲 (1089–1163; of the Linji tradition) attacks on silent illumination (*mozhao* 默照) Chan, favored by the Caodong tradition. His teachings had strong appeal among the scholar-gentry, to whom he specifically directed some of his teachings. As I have argued elsewhere, "Zhu Xi had become concerned that Dahui was undermining support among the educated elite for Daoxue or more broadly for Confucianism. In particular, he was also concerned that second-generation followers of the Cheng brothers had become vulnerable to Dahui's teachings."[47]

6. *Zhong*: Balance or Middle?

Although Zhu Xi disagreed with the Cheng brothers' claim that Yang Zhu and Mozi had been students of Zixia and Zizhang, he strongly endorsed their thesis about the damaging consequences of partiality or one-sidedness. The *Analects* 11.16 account of Zizhang and Zixia also provided Zhu Xi with an opportunity to connect the idea of impartiality with the concepts of *zhong yong* 中庸 and *zhong* 中 (and, inter alia, connect *Mencius* with *Zhongyong*, a key element in Zhu's *daotong* construct):

> Zigong asked: "Who is smarter, Shi [Zizhang] or Shang [Zixia]?"
>
> The Master replied: "Shi is excessive whereas Shang falls short."

"Then Shi is superior?"
The Master replied: "Excess is just as bad as falling short."

子貢問：「師與商也孰賢？」子曰：「師也過，商也不及。」
曰：「然則師愈與？」子曰：「過猶不及。」

Zhu Xi comments:

> The Way takes *zhong yong* as perfection. Although it seems that the excesses of the smart are superior to the deficiencies of the dull-witted and incompetent, the error in each case is the same. Yin [Tun 尹焞 (1071–1142)] said: "The efficacy of *zhong yong* is supreme! Being in excess and falling short amount to the same. Slight errors lead to huge divergences. Hence, the teachings of the sages consist of nothing other than holding back that which is excessive and drawing forth that which falls short, so that both return to the Way of *zhong*."

> 道以中庸為至。賢知之過，雖若勝於愚不肖之不及，然其失中則一也。尹氏曰：「中庸之為德也，其至矣乎！夫過與不及，均也。差之毫釐，繆以千里。故聖人之教，抑其過，引其不及，歸於中道而已。」[48]

Here Zhu effectively glosses *zhong* to mean being neither in excess nor in deficiency: to be balanced. Elsewhere he also explicitly connects this sense of *zhong* with *Zhongyong*.

Before introducing the key elements in Zhu Xi's exegesis of *Zhongyong* and how this relates to his *daotong* thesis, I will first address a related but more preliminary issue: two seemingly inconsistent accounts of *zhi zhong* 執中. In Zhu's preface to *Zhongyong* he identifies the content of what Yao first transmitted to Shun as the phrase, "properly maintain the balance" (允執厥中), which Zhu praised as "perfect, consummate."[49] The apparent inconsistency is with the account of *zhi zhong* as "adhering to the middle" in *Mencius* 7A26, which I translate based on Zhu Xi's commentary to the passage in *Mengzi jizhu*:

> Mencius said: "Yang Zhu clung to 'serving one's own interests.' If he could have benefitted the realm by pulling out a single hair, he would not have done so. Mozi was 'inclusive in his

concern for others.' If he could have benefitted the realm by wearing himself smooth from crown to heels,[50] he would have done so. Zimo adhered to the middle (執中), which comes close to it, but adhering to the middle without [using] a counterbalance is just like adhering to one [position]. What I detest about those who adhere to one [position] is the harm they do to the Way by promoting one [position] at the expense of the hundred [other positions that arise]."

孟子曰：「楊子取為我，拔一毛而利天下，不為也。墨子兼愛，摩頂放踵利天下，為之。子莫執中，執中為近之。執中無權，猶執一也。所惡執一者，為其賊道也，舉一而廢百也。」[51]

Mencius is critical of "adhering to the middle" because it fails to accommodate changed circumstances. In his *Mengzi jizhu* commentary, Zhu Xi explains that Zimo chose the middle point between the extremes represented by Yang Zhu and Mozi (度於二者之間而執其中). Zhu takes the term *quan* 權 to be the counterbalance of a steelyard (稱錘),[52] "which is how something is weighed so as to attain balance [of the steelyard beam]. Adhering to the middle [point on the beam] without using a counterbalance is to be stuck to a fixed center and not understanding [the need] to change—this too is nothing other than adhering to one [position]." (所以稱物之輕重而取中也。執中而無權，則膠於一定之中而不知變，是亦執一而已矣。)[53]

As to why Zimo's "adhering to the middle" (執中) differs from the injunction to "properly maintain the balance" (允執厥中) as handed down by the three sages Yao, Shun, and Yu, Zhu explains:

By being meticulous in focusing on the subtlety of the mind of the Way, there will be balance in everything one does—and so to "properly maintain" it is not done in vain. In order to adhere to the middle, Zimo dared not go so far as Yang Zhu in [clinging to] serving one's own interests, and he dared not make the same mistake as Mozi in being inclusive in his concern for others; rather, he adhered to a position between them, deeming it to be the middle. Thus, if one follows what the three sages deemed to be *zhong* (balance), then this *zhong* is active, but if one follows what Zimo deemed to be *zhong* (the middle), then this *zhong* is inert. The *zhong* that is active is consistently *zhong* (balanced) without relying upon a counterbalance. As for the *zhong* that is inert, unless one learns from the learning of the sages, then one will be unable to counterbalance it such that one consistently attains balance. *Quan* 權 is the counterbalance of a steelyard (權), as in "counterbalance of steelyard and beam" (權衡).[54] This refers to being able to weigh something and then move [the suspended counterbalance] to and fro [across the beam] so as to reach an equilibrium (平).

蓋精一於道心之微，則無適而非中者。其曰允執則非徒然而執之矣。子莫之為執中，則其為我不敢為楊朱之深，兼愛不敢為墨翟之過，而於二者之間執其一節以為中耳。故由三聖以為中，則其中活；由子莫以為中，則其中死。中之活者，不待權而無不中；中之死者，則非學乎聖人之學，不能有以權之而常適於中也。權者，權衡之權，言其可以稱物之輕重而游移前卻，以適於平。[55]

The *quan* metaphor is here introduced to explain the need to adapt to the exigencies of changed or changing circumstances. Zhu elsewhere uses a simple example to illustrate what he means by *quan*: changing one's garments as the seasons change.[56]

7. Zhongyong

Zhu's most influential and best-known account of *daotong* is in his 1189 preface to *Zhongyong zhangju*, which begins as follows:

> Why was the *Zhongyong* written? Zisi composed it because he was concerned that the transmission of the learning of the Way (*daoxue*) would be lost. This is because, from high antiquity, sages and god-like men continued the work of heaven by establishing an ultimate norm so that the transmission of the *daotong* [always had a point of reference indicating] whence it issued. Thus, as seen in the classics, "properly maintain the balance" is what Yao passed on to Shun; "the human mind is precarious; the mind of the Way is subtle; be meticulous and focused; properly maintain the balance"[57] is what Shun passed on to Yu. The single phrase by Yao is perfect, consummate!

The reason Shun added another three phrases was to explain Yao's phrase. This was to ensure that later it would be as clear as possible.

《中庸》何為而作也？子思子憂道學之失其傳而作也。蓋自上古聖神繼天立極，而道統之傳有自來矣。其見於經，則「允執厥中」者，堯之所以授舜也；「人心惟危，道心惟微，惟精惟一，允執厥中」者，舜之所以授禹也。堯之一言，至矣，盡矣！而舜復益之以三言者，則所以明夫堯之一言，必如是而後可庶幾也。[58]

Zhu then describes the initial transmission of the rule of All under Heaven (天下) between Yao, Shun, and Yu, as well as the transmission of Yu's key admonition to "properly maintain the balance." In turn, this succession was followed by that of Cheng Tang, Wen, and Wu, who served as rulers, aided by Gao Yao, Yi, Fu, Zhou, and Shao, who served them as ministers, and all took their turn in the transmission of the *daotong* (接夫道統之傳). Coming to Confucius, even though he did not hold a position as ruler or minister, his merit in passing on the learning of the sages was even greater than that of Yao or Shun. Of Confucius's students, only Yanzi and Zengzi received his lineage (得其宗), and Zengzi alone passed it on to Confucius's grandson, Zisi. With the rise of "deviant teachings" (異端), that is, the teachings of Yang Zhu and Mo Di, Zisi feared the eventual loss of the truth of what had been passed on, and so he "traced the intent of what had been transmitted since the time of Yao and Shun, tested it against the words he had regularly heard from his teacher [Zengzi], and by further elaborating on the basis of both, he wrote this book [*Zhongyong*] to instruct later students. . . . From this, the transmission was again taken up by Mencius, who was able to elaborate on and elucidate this book so as to continue the succession of the former sages (承先聖之統). But when he died, its transmission became lost." In other words, what ceased to be transmitted after Mencius was the "succession of the Way" passed down by the former sages. All was not lost, however:

This Way of ours had nothing more than words and writing to rely on [for its transmission], and deviant teachings increasingly flourished, such that by the time followers of Laozi and the Buddha appeared, because their teachings increasingly came to approximate what is reasonable, this threw truth into disarray.

Fortunately, however, this book has survived, and so with the appearance of the Cheng brothers it became possible for [these matters] to be investigated and thereby to continue the transmission of the thread that had not been transmitted for [more than] a thousand years, and also making it possible to have a basis on which to repudiate the dissemblance of the two schools [Daoism and Buddhism].

吾道之所寄不越乎言語文字之間，而異端之說日新月盛，以至於老佛之徒出，則彌近理而大亂真矣。然而尚幸此書之不泯，故程夫子兄弟者出，得有所考，以續夫千載不傳之緒;得有所據，以斥夫二家似是之非。⁵⁹

The core teaching that had been transmitted in the succession of the Way was the injunction to "properly maintain the balance."

8. Deviant Teachings

Identifying "the other," the promoter of "deviant teachings" (異端), played a key role in constructing Zhu Xi's self-narrative of being the legitimate heir to the transmission of the succession of the true Way. The "other" was not limited to the Buddhists and Daoists—the latter-day incarnations of Yang and Mo. For Zhu Xi, the other "other" were prominent, rival Confucian scholars and statesmen. In the following model essay for students preparing for the *jinshi* degree examination, Zhu Xi singles out Ouyang Xiu, Su Shi 蘇軾 (1037–1101), and Wang Anshi for veiled criticism:

> When the followers of Yang Zhu and Mozi appeared, Mencius illuminated the Way of Confucius to rectify matters so that later on their doctrines would be unable to be propagated. More than a thousand years later [in the Song period], students all sing the praises of Confucius, yet it is Xun Qing, Yang Xiong, Wang Tong, and Han Yu alone whom they declare to have sounded forth about the Way. With regard to Mencius, however, some criticized him, some saw themselves to be his equal, some could find nothing to praise him for, and still others praised his achievements as being no less than those of Yu.⁶⁰ Since the differences in the orientation [of their

assessments] were as such, when it came for these gentlemen to assess those who came before them,[61] some deemed them to be in a different branch of the same school, some could find nothing to praise them for, and still others deemed them mostly pure but with some slight faults such that they were unable to be included among those who transmitted this Way of ours. With regard to Yang and Mo, some mildly rebuked them for their faults, some could find nothing to praise them for, and still others chose between them to be correlates of Confucius [in the Shrine to Confucius at the State Academy]. The disparity in their evaluations again being as such indeed warrants some explanation.

Confucian learning in our dynasty has thrived greatly, owing to the learning of Master Ouyang [Xiu], Master Wang [Anshi], and Master Su [Shi] being practiced at the court, and the learning of Master Hu [Yuan 瑗, 993–1059] and Masters Cheng [Yi and Cheng Hao] has also been transmitted to students. Nevertheless, [the learning of] Wang and Su fundamentally derived from that of Ouyang, and so there is no great difference between them. [In contrast, the learning of] Master Hu and Master Sun [Fu 復, 992–1057][62] did not suit the times, and [the learning of] Masters Cheng was particularly incompatible with that of Wang and Su. Which of them received the Way of Confucius and which of them lost it? Surely it is not the case that there is nothing that can be deliberated?

The doctrines of Yang and Mo have been extinguished, but surely it is not the case that all the lingering influences of those doctrines have been completely wiped out? In later times, moreover, there have been the doctrines of the Buddhists and Daoists—are they the same as the doctrines of Yang and Mo or are they different? Ever since Yang Xiong, affirmation and condemnation of these two schools would certainly seem to have varied greatly. Who has attained the truth of the matter? Students—go into the particulars of this matter carefully.

楊墨之徒出，孟子明孔子之道以正之，而後其說不得肆。千有餘年，諸生皆誦說孔子，而獨荀卿、揚雄、王通、韓愈號為以道鳴者，然於孟子或非之，或自比焉，或無稱焉，或尊其功以為不在禹下。其歸趣之不同既如此，而是數子者後議其前，或以為同門而異戶，或無稱焉，或以為大醇而小疵，而不得與於斯道之傳者。其於楊墨，或微議其失，或無稱焉，或取焉以配孔子，其取予之不同又如此，是亦必有說矣。本朝儒學最盛，自歐陽氏、王氏、蘇氏，皆以其學行于朝廷，而胡氏、程氏亦以其學傳之學者。然王、蘇本出於歐陽，而其未有大不同者，胡氏、孫氏亦不相容於當時，而程氏尤不合於王與蘇也。是其於孔子之道孰得孰失？豈亦無有可論者耶？楊墨之說則熄矣，然其說之流豈亦無有未盡泯滅者耶？後世又有佛老之說，其於楊墨之說同耶？異耶？自揚雄以來，於是二家是非之論，蓋亦多不同者。又孰為得其正耶？二三子其詳言之。[63]

This essay opens by expressing some concern about Northern Song assessments of Mencius and of other Confucians who came after him, as well as varying assessments of Yang Zhu and Mozi in the Northern Song. Zhu then contrasts the Confucian learning of Ouyang Xiu, Wang Anshi, and Su Shi with that of the Cheng brothers, and pointedly asks: "Which of them received the Way of Confucius and which of them lost it?" The final alignment of Yang and Mo with the Buddhists and Daoists, and the question about "lingering influence of those doctrines," can also be read as a thinly veiled criticism of those who had "lost the Way of Confucius": Ouyang Xiu, Wang Anshi, and Su Shi.

Elsewhere, his many strong, explicit criticisms of Wang Anshi and especially Su Shi support this reading. Consider the following passage in a letter replying to his cousin Wang Yingchen 汪應辰 (1118–1176), written in 1168:

> In your letter you also maintained that Mr. Su [Shi's superficial understanding of Buddhism] was due to the flaws in his behavioral tendencies and that even though he did not understand the Way, he harbored no evil intent; and that, unlike Mr. Wang [Anshi], he did not make outlandish explanations in an attempt to rescue his biased and aberrant learning. In my humble opinion, learning takes understanding of the Way as its foundation. Having understood the Way then one's learning is pure and one's mind is set right. This is evident in the conduct of one's affairs, is given expression in one's words and speech, and regardless of the undertaking, one will always attain what is correct therein. As for Mr. Wang, when he first

began to learn, he was probably [motivated] by the desire to surpass [the achievements of] Yang [Xiong] and Han [Yu], and render obscure the [the achievements of] Yan [Hui] and Mencius [by surpassing them]. At the outset, he surely harbored no evil intent. It was just because his learning was not pure that he was unable to understand the Way, and so his intentions and deeds consequently drifted into the aberrant. Moreover, being opinionated, he attempted to gloss over [his failings] by greatly indulging in outlandish explanations. Although the learning of Mr. Su differed from that of Mr. Wang, he was just the same in failing to understand the Way and so indulging in outlandish explanations. . . . The cunning of [Su Shi's] outlandish explanations, such as his discussion of attaining buddhahood or explaining Laozi, which you referred to in your letter, are however, almost certainly not something that Mr. Wang could have matched.

In learning about how to practice rightness, Yang Zhu was inclined towards "serving one's own interests." In learning about how to be humane, Mo Di drifted into "being inclusive in one's concern for others."[64] It is surely not the case that at the outset their intentions were aberrant. Rather, they simply carried out what they took to be goodness. It is just that at the initial stage there was the slightest mistake, and this is why Mencius anticipated calamitous consequences, deeming that [the tenets of] "having no father" and "having no ruler" [would lead to people throughout the realm] descending to the level of birds and beasts, and so he spoke out and attacked them. In doing so, he was [actually] being very lenient.

It is surely not the case that Mencius had failed to track down the cause [of their aberrance] and hence was at fault for condemning them in such harsh terms. It is indeed the case that, at certain critical junctures of incipient developments, damaging heaven's principles and harming the human mind can lead people to become mired [in aberrance] and yet not be aware of it. This, however, is not like the case of [those who practiced] the methods of [Legalist] *xingming*[65] or [Strategist] deception, the calamitous [consequences] of which were easy to discern. For this reason, in order to nip this thinking in the bud, [Mencius] had no alternative but to be as forceful [in his criticisms as he was]. The *Book of Documents* says: "Fearing Shangdi, I dare not do what is not right."[66] It also says: "If I were to disobey heaven [and not punish those whose acts are egregious], then I would be just as much at fault."[67] Mencius' intentions were nothing other than this. Considered in this light, with regard to the matter before us, whereas Mr. Wang would amount to nothing more than a [latter-day] Shen [Buhai], Han [Fei], Zhang [Yi 儀], or [Gongsun 公孫] Yan, then it stands to reason that Mr. Su's iniquities far exceeded those of Yang and Mo. In my humble opinion, if Mencius were living again today, he would certainly [still] have reason [to condemn Su Shi], contrary to what you claim in your correspondence.

來教又以為蘇氏乃習氣之弊，雖不知道而無邪心，非若王氏之穿鑿附會，以濟其私邪之學也。熹竊謂學以知道為本，知道則學純而心正，見於行事，發於言語，亦無往而不得其正焉。如王氏者，其始學也，蓋欲凌跨揚、韓，掩跡顏、孟。初亦豈遽有邪心哉？特以不能知道，故其學不純，而設心造事遂流入於邪。又自以為是，而大為穿鑿附會以文之，此其所以重得罪於聖人之門也。蘇氏之學雖與王氏若有不同者，然其不知道而自以為是則均焉。…其穿鑿附會之巧，如來教所稱論成佛、說老子之屬，蓋非王氏所及。而其心之不正，至乃謂湯、武篡弒而盛稱句踐，以為聖人之徒。凡若此類，皆逞其私邪，無復忌憚，不在王氏之下。…

楊朱，學為義者也，而偏於為我；墨翟，學為仁者也，而流於兼愛。本其設心，豈有邪哉？皆以善而為之耳。特於本原之際微有毫釐之差，是以孟子推言其禍，以為無父無君而陷於禽獸，辭而闢之，不少假借。孟子亦豈不原其情而過為是刻核之論哉？誠以其賊天理、害人心於幾微之間，使人陷溺而不自知，非若刑名狙詐之術，其禍淺切而易見也。是以拔本塞源，不得不如是之力。《書》曰：「予畏上帝，不敢不正。」又曰：「予弗順天，厥罪惟均。」孟子之心，亦若是而已爾。以此論之，今日之事，王氏僅足為申、韓、儀、衍，而蘇氏學不正而言成理，又非楊、墨之比。愚恐孟子復生，則其取舍先後必將有在，而非如來教之云也。[68]

Here Zhu again deploys the theme of how being even a little off target can have dire consequences: to link Su Shi and Wang Anshi with Yang

Zhu and Mozi, and with Zhu himself assuming the role of a latter-day Mencius. Peter Bol opines that, as with Han Yu 韓愈 (768–824) in his "Yuan dao" 原道 (Tracing the Way to its origins) essay, Zhu Xi "claimed that with Confucius moral authority was transferred from political leaders to scholars. To say that after Mencius the Way 'did not obtain its transmission' (in Han's terms) meant that although there were political authorities in the world (e.g., the Han and Tang rulers), there was no one with moral authority. To say that the Way was recovered by a handful of Song literati was to say that there was now true authority in the world, but that it was still with the literati and not with the ruler."[69] It was, however, one particular lineage of literati that Zhu Xi sought to champion as the legitimate claimants to that authority, a legitimacy vouchsafed by their affiliation with the one true *daotong*.

Conclusion

This chapter has shown that the promotion of certain figures and exclusion of others from privileged versions of just who and what constitutes ideological and doctrinal orthodoxy was integral to Zhu Xi's *daotong* project, a feature that in turn drew from four centuries of proto-*daotong* discourse in which the negative image of Yang Zhu and cognate Yang-Mo trope figured prominently and consistently. Where Zhu's *daotong* conceit differed from earlier proto-*daotong* discourse from Han Yu onward was that calling out "the other," the promoter of "deviant teachings," became central to the construction Zhu Xi's self-narrative of being the legitimate heir to the transmission of the succession of the true Way.

The essay has also identified three other related themes that had already emerged in that long tradition of proto-*daotong* discourse and that subsequently informed Zhu Xi's appropriation of the *daotong* concept. The first is the rhetorical strategy of portraying contemporary Daoists and Buddhists as latter-day Yangists and Mohists. With Zhu Xi (and the Chengs) this became transformed into the thesis that contemporary Buddhist teachings were far more sophisticated and insidious than those of Yang Zhu and Mozi, and accordingly needed to be counteracted. The second is the promotion of a transmission lineage model in which the transmission of the Way did not rely on face-to-face teacher-student transmission, but rather on the understanding of key texts by enlightened individuals.[70] Zhu Xi used this model to insinuate himself into his own account of the *daotong* genealogy;

to privilege the authority of *Zhongyong*, the concepts *zhong* and *yong*, and the "sixteen-character teaching"; and also to establish various intertextual links premised on his interpretation of that teaching. The third is the thesis that even a small degree of partiality or inclination to one side can develop to have disastrous consequences. Zhu developed this thesis to connect the idea of impartiality with the concepts *zhong* and *yong* to claim that the core teaching that had been transmitted in the succession of the Way was the injunction to "properly maintain the balance."

Notes

1. This is how Zhu Xi understood the two concepts in the title.

2. "Zhi Nankang die" 知南康牒 [Non-official document by the prefect of Nankang], in *Zhuzi quanshu* 朱子全書 [Complete works of Zhu Xi], ed. Zhu Jieren 朱傑人 et al., 27 vols. (Shanghai: Shanghai guji chubanshe, and Hefei: Anhui jiaoyu chubanshe, 2002), 25:4582; hereafter *ZZQS*.

3. ZZQS, 7:11–12.

4. ZZQS, 24:3639–40. Part of the preface is translated in Christian Soffel and Hoyt Cleveland Tillman, *Cultural Authority and Political Culture in China: Exploring Issues with the Zhongyong and the Daotong during the Song, Jin and Yuan Dynasties* (Stuttgart: Franz Steiner Verlag, 2012), 53.

5. The sixteen-character teaching is a passage in "Da Yu mo" 大禹謨 [The counsels of Yu the Great], *Shangshu* 尚書 [Book of documents]: "The human mind is precarious; the mind of the Way is subtle. By being meticulous and focused one will sincerely maintain balance." (人心惟危，道心惟微，惟精惟一，允執厥中。) *Shisan jing zhushu* 十三經注疏 [The Thirteen Classics with annotations and sub-commentaries], comp. Ruan Yuan 阮元 (Taipei: Yiwen yinshuguan, 1985), 4.8b. I have interpreted this passage in the way I think Zhu Xi intended the passage to be understood, based on a variety of glosses in his preface to the *Zhongyong* in *Zhongyong zhangju* 中庸章句 [Section and sentences comments on *Zhongyong*], which forms part of *Sishu zhangju jizhu* 四書章句集注 [Section and sentence commentaries and collected annotations on the Four Books], and also in *Zhuzi yulei* 朱子語類 [Topically arranged conversations of master Zhu], comp. Li Jingde 黎靖德 (fl. 1263).

6. "Renwu ying zhao feng shi" 壬午應詔封事 [Sealed memorial in response to the emperor of 1162], ZZQS, 20:571.

7. Zhu Xi asserted that the core tenets of the sixteen-character teaching are given expression in the *Great Learning*'s doctrines of "extending knowledge through the investigation of things," "setting the mind right," and "making one's intentions sincere"; "Renwu ying zhao feng shi," 572.

8. See Zhu Xi, "Shu Lizhang suo kan *Sizi* hou" 書臨漳所刊四子後 [Postface to the edition of the *Four Masters* engraved at Linzhang], recorded in Zhu Xi, *Huian xiansheng Zhu Wengong wenji* 晦庵先生朱文公文集 [Zhu Xi's collected writings], ZZQS, 24:3895–96. The prefatory comments to the "*Daoxue* biographies" section of the *Songshi* 宋史 [History of the Song dynasty], ed. Tuo Tuo 脫脫 et al. (Beijing: Zhonghua shuju, 1985), *juan* 427, 12710, credit the Cheng brothers with having been the first to have combined these four books as a distinct group, and Cheng Yi's biography in *Songshi, juan* 427, 12720, maintains that Cheng Yi had regarded the Four Books to be on par with the Six Classics.

9. See Joseph A. Adler, *Reconstructing the Confucian Dao: Zhu Xi's Appropriation of Zhou Dunyi* (Albany: State University of New York Press, 2014), chap. 2.

10. *Yuanshi* 元史 (History of the Yuan dynasty), ed. Song Lian 宋濂 et al. (Beijing: Zhonghua, 1983), *juan* 81, 2019.

11. See Elman's review of Hoyt Cleveland Tillman, *Confucian Discourse and Chu Hsi's Ascendancy, Harvard Journal of Asiatic Studies* 54, no. 2 (1994): 585.

12. *Analects* 11.16, *Shisan jing zhushu*, 11.5b.

13. *Mencius* 7A26, *Shisan jing zhushu*, 13B.3a–3b.

14. *Er Cheng ji* 二程集 [Collected works of the two Chengs], 2 vols. (Beijing: Zhonghua shuju, 1981; repr. 2004), 1:176.

15. *Mengzi jingyi* 孟子精義 [Essential meanings of the *Mencius*], in *Lun Meng jingyi* 論孟精義 [Essential meanings of the *Analects* and *Mencius*], ZZQS, 7:711.

16. *Mengzi jingyi*, ZZQS, 7:712.

17. *Lunyu jingyi*, in *Lun Meng jingyi*, ZZQS, 7:393

18. "Da Pan Gongshu" 答潘恭叔 [Reply to Pan Gongshu], in *Huian xiansheng Zhu Wengong wenji*, ZZQS, 22:2301. Zhu maintains that during the time of Yanzi 晏子 (sixth century BCE), Mozi's views were already in existence.

19. As related in the "Tiandi" 天地 [Heaven and earth] chapter of *Zhuangzi*, *Sibi beiyao* 四部備要 [The essential collection of the Four Divisions; hereafter SBBY] (Beijing: Zhonghua, 1936), 5.4b, Bocheng Zigao had accepted an appointment to serve under Yao but refused to do so under Shun, and instead chose to retreat from service to till the land.

20. This is a very loose paraphrase of a passage in the "Yang Zhu" chapter of *Liezi* 列子, SBBY, 7.8a–8b.

21. This is an interpretative paraphrase of *Daode jing* 道德經 [The Way and its power], chapter 45, obviously inspired by chapter 57.

22. *Zhuzi yulei*, ZZQS, 16:1962.

23. "Da Qiu Zifu" 答丘子服 [Reply to Qiu Zifu], in *Huian xiansheng Zhu Wengong wenji*, ZZQS, 22:2066–67.

24. The *Zhuangzi* text gives the name as 陽子居.

25. *Lunyu huowen* 論語或問 [Questions and answers on the *Analects*], in *Sishu huowen* 四書或問 [Questions and answers on the Four Books], ZZQS, 6:790–91. In *Zhuzi yulei*, Zhu himself states that "Yang Zhu was a disciple of Laozi"; see ZZQS, 16:1962; 18:3925.

26. *Zhuzi yulei, juan* 126, 3926.
27. "Zhuangzi" 莊子, *Zhuzi yulei*, ZZQS, 18:3901.
28. Both citations are based on passages in the "Renjian shi" 人間世 [The human world] chapter of *Zhuangzi*, SBCK, 2.9a.
29. "Zhuang Lie" 莊列 [Zhuangzi and Liezi], ZZQS, 18:3904.
30. Paraphrase of *Zhuangzi*, 2.9a.
31. "Li xing" 力行 [To carry out strenuously], *Zhuzi yulei*, ZZQS, 14:400.
32. In translating *Zhongguo* 中國 here as "China," rather than as central lands or central states, I am assuming that Zhu was using the term as it was used in the Song period. On this usage, see Ge Zhaoguang 葛兆光, "Songdai 'Zhongguo' yishi de tuxian—guanyu jinshi minzuzhuyi sixiang de yige yuanyuan" 宋代'中國'意識的凸現—關於近世民族主義思想的一個遠源 [The prominence of Song dynasty "China" consciousness: concerning a distant source of modern nationalist thought] (2004), reprinted in Ge Zhaoguang, *Gudai Zhongguo de lishi, sixiang yu zongjiao* 古代中國的歷史、思想與宗教 [The history, thought and religion of ancient China] (Beijing: Beijing shifan daxue chubanshe, 2006), 135–51.
33. *Zhuzi yulei, juan* 126, ZZQS, 18:3926.
34. *Zhuzi yulei*, ZZQS, 18,:3900.
35. *Zhuzi yulei*, ZZQS, 18:3927.
36. *Zhuzi yulei*, ZZQS, 18:3924.
37. *Zhuzi yulei*, ZZQS, 18:3962.
38. Cheng Yi, "Mingdao xiansheng xingzhuang," 1:638. The last sentence is a reference to a passage in Yang Xiong, *Fayan* 法言 [Model Sayings], 2.3b, SBCK: "In the past, Yang Zhu and Mozi had blocked the road. Mencius spoke out, and by attacking them cleared the road."
39. Zhu Xi and Lü Zuxian, *Jin si lu, juan* 13, ZZQS, 13:279.
40. "Mingdao xiansheng xingzhuang," *Er Cheng ji*, 1:638.
41. *Jin si lu*, ZZQS, 13:277.
42. *Zhuzi yulei*, ZZQS, 17:3450.
43. *Mencius* 3B9; cf. 1A.4.
44. *Zhuzi yulei*, ZZQS, 15:1807.
45. *Er Cheng ji*, 1:23.
46. Morten Schlütter, *How Zen Became Zen: The Dispute over Enlightenment and the Formation of Chan Buddhism in Song-Dynasty China* (Honolulu: University of Hawai'i Press, 2010), chaps. 3 and 4.
47. "Introduction," *The Buddhist Roots of Zhu Xi's Philosophical Thought*, ed. John Makeham (New York: Oxford University Press, 2018), 7.
48. *Lunyu jizhu*, ZZQS, 6:161.
49. "Zhongyong zhangju xu" 中庸章句序 [Preface to *Zhongyong zhangju*], *Zhongyong zhangju, Sishu zhangju jizhu*, ZZQS, 6:29.
50. Following Angus C. Graham's translation of this phrase in "The Right to Selfishness: Yangism, Later Mohism, Chuang Tzu," in *Individualism and*

Holism: Studies in Confucian and Taoist Values, ed. Donald J. Munro (Ann Arbor: University of Michigan Press, 1985), 73.

51. *Mencius* 7A26, *Shisan jing zhushu*, 13A.3a–3b.

52. Here Zhu is following Zheng Xuan's 鄭玄 (127–200) gloss, which Griet Vankeerberghen argues is anachronistic. See "Choosing Balance: Weighing (Quan 權) as a Metaphor for Action in Early Chinese Texts," *Early China* 30 (2005–2006): 54.

53. *Mengzi jizhu*, in *Sishu zhangju jizhu*, ZZQJ, 6:346.

54. On these identifications, see Joseph Needham, *Science and Civilisation in China: Volume 4, Physics and Physical Technology, Part 1, Physics* (Cambridge: Cambridge University Press, 1962), 22. He writes that *quan* "means essentially the weight of a steelyard, but occasionally by implication the steelyard itself, and later more commonly came to be used as a verb, to weigh."

55. "Da Song Shenzhi" 答宋深之 [Reply to Song Shenzhi], *Huian xiansheng Zhu Wengong wenji*, ZZQS, 23:2770.

56. *Mengzi jingyi*, ZZQS, 7:810.

57. "Da Yu mo" 大禹謨 [The counsels of Yu the Great], *Shangshu* 尚書 [Book of documents], *Shisan jing zhushu*, 4.8b.

58. "*Zhongyong zhangju* xu," 29.

59. "*Zhongyong zhangju* xu," 30.

60. The "some" here refers to Xun Qing, Yang Xiong, Wang Tong, and Han Yu.

61. That is, when Han Yu assessed Yang Xiong, or when Yang Xiong assessed Xunzi, for example.

62. On Hu Yuan and Sun Fu, see chapter 5 in this volume, "Yang Zhu's Role in Tang-Song Proto-daotong Discourse."

63. "Bailu shutang cewen" 白鹿書堂策問 [Model strategic question essay for students in the White Deer Academy] (ca. 1180), *Huian xiansheng Zhu Wengong wenji*, ZZQS, 24:3579.

64. Note that this letter was composed six years before Zhu started to deny that Yang Zhu and Mozi had been students of Zixia and Zizhang; see the earlier discussion in this chapter.

65. On this concept, see my "The Legalist Concept of *Hsing-Ming*: An Example of the Contribution of Archaeological Evidence to the Re-Interpretation of Transmitted Texts," *Monumenta Serica* 39 (1990–1991): 87–114.

66. *Shangshu*, *Sisan jing zhushu*, 8.2a–2b.

67. *Shangshu*, *Sisan jing zhushu*, 11.6b.

68. Zhu Xi, "Da Wang shangshu (shiyi yue ji wang)" 答汪尚書 (十一月既望) [Reply to Minister Wang (eighteenth day of eleventh month)], *Huian xiansheng Zhu Wengong ji*, ZZQS, 21:1303–1304. Chen Lai 陳來, *Zhuzi shuxin biannian kaozheng* 朱子書信編年考證 [Evidenced-based examination of Zhu Xi's letters, arranged chronologically] (Beijing: Sanlian, 2007), 48, dates this letter to 1168.

69. Peter K. Bol, review of Thomas A. Wilson, *Genealogy of the Way: The Construction and Uses of the Confucian Tradition in Late Imperial China*, *China Review International* 3, no. 2 (1996): 569.

70. As noted earlier, the main exception to this was in 1179 when Zhu referred to Zhou Dunyi as having "transmitted the *daotong* with his mind" (心傳道統). In a text written two years before this, Zhu had also claimed that Zhou Dunyi had received the Way from heaven, without teacher or text as intermediary, after a fourteen-hundred-year hiatus since Mencius. As Joseph Adler, *Reconstructing the Confucian Dao*, 42, notes: "The argument that the Confucian *dao* was directly accessible by sages such as Mencius and Zhou Dunyi, who could then transmit it to others, was a crucial strategy of legitimation for Song Confucians in the face of strong competition from Chan Buddhism for the hearts and minds of literati." The only qualification I would make here concerns Adler's inclusion of Mencius alongside Zhou Dunyi. As noted earlier, in Zhu's 1173 preface to Shi Dun's *Zhongyong jilüe*, Mencius is presented as heir to the transmission of *Zhongyong*, which is privileged as the textual record of the teachings of Confucius.

Chapter 7

Plucking Hairs and Shaving Heads
Li Zhi's Repudiation of Yang Zhu

Esther Sunkyung Klein

Introduction

Li Zhi 李贄 (1527–1602), a notorious iconoclast and individualist, might be expected to share some common ground with Yang Zhu 楊朱 (fourth century BCE) and the "egoism" with which that figure has come to be associated. Li resigned from office to pursue the pleasures of intellectual self-cultivation.[1] Symbolically dodging any claims his family might try to make on him, he even shaved his head and adopted some aspects of Buddhist monastic life—but only those aspects that suited him.[2] He explicitly stated that he was (or wanted to be) loved "for himself" rather than for any of the social roles he would naturally be expected to fill.[3] And he accused all his eminent contemporaries of hypocrisy by pointing out that self-interest played just as strong a motivating role in their lives as it did in the lives of common people.[4] Superficially at least, he seemed like someone who did "hold to the principle of 'doing for oneself'" (取為我), just as the *Mengzi* 孟子 accused Yang Zhu of doing.[5]

Despite this superficial similarity, all of Li Zhi's references to Yang Zhu are negative and disapproving. Could it be that confessing to intellectual kinship with the tradition's most hated egoist was a bridge too far, even for the man who reversed the verdicts on so many of tradition's heroes and villains—one who claimed, provocatively, that a sage would "accord with" (*shun* 順) people's inherent tendency to "satisfy the five senses we were born with" (厚吾天生之五官)?[6] Or did Li Zhi truly draw a principled distinction between his own beliefs and those he ascribed to Yang Zhu? The following investigation will analyze Li Zhi's references to Yang Zhu within the broader context of his life and work. I conclude that while Li Zhi's contemporaries saw him as a Yang Zhu–type figure, Li Zhi himself vehemently denied the comparison and the criticism behind it; from his perspective, his own motivations and overall project were entirely distinct from the ideas and attitudes he associated with Yang Zhu. Far from hesitating to pluck out a single hair for the sake of the world, he considered himself to be one who would shave his entire head—and later slit his own throat. Despite his refusal to conform to contemporary norms of harmonious and prosocial behavior, he did see himself as "doing for the realm" (or indeed for all living beings) and not merely for himself.

The puzzles with which this paper engages have more to do with Li Zhi and his philosophical milieu than they do with Yang Zhu, of whom we have no reliable textual remains. But the two are linked by more than just a few oblique references to plucking hairs. It seems highly likely that Mencius either misunderstood or willfully misrepresented Yang Zhu, creating the distorted image that has come down to us in the tradition. Li Zhi's voluminous writings allow us to form a philosophical portrait of someone who dared to advocate for "the self," albeit as a complex and contested term.

1. Puzzles in Li Zhi's "Self-Evaluation"

Li Zhi's "Self-Evaluation" (Zi zan 自贊), written in 1588 and published in *Fen shu* 焚書 (A Book to Burn), is one of his best-known pieces. It also contains a clear reference to Yang Zhu. It is not easy to make sense of this reference, however, without understanding what the "Self-Evaluation" is intended to accomplish, and that is a difficult task. Much of this section will seem a digression, then, but one that serves to introduce the philosophical complexity of "self-interest" for Li Zhi in ways that will inform the later discussion.

A surface reading of the "Self-Evaluation" might suggest that Li Zhi was writing within a long tradition of disarmingly self-deprecating autobiographical descriptions. Writers within this tradition disingenuously "denounce themselves" for having culturally disesteemed qualities, thus creating an opportunity to implicitly defend, or even praise, these qualities.[7] But by the end, Li Zhi's "Self-Evaluation" is *too* self-denigrating to fit even within this framework. Furthermore, if one traces all the potential allusions and dropped hints, a different pattern emerges: Li Zhi wanted this text to be read, not just as a humble brag but as an attack on his critics. He accomplishes this by reporting other people's critiques of him in a way that systematically undermines those critiques *and* launches a subtle counter-offensive.[8]

To establish that this kind of move is at least plausible for Li Zhi, I briefly mention two other self-descriptions from Li Zhi's oeuvre. The first, the "Sketch of Zhuowu" (Zhuowu lun lüe 卓吾論略), describes what Li Zhi clearly considered to have been genuine errors on his own part, and he does it in the starkest and most minimal of terms:[9] the "Sketch" shows Li Zhi frankly admitting his own wrongdoing, with none of the overblown self-accusation that characterizes the "Self-Evaluation." On the other hand, in the bitterly sarcastic "Response to Zhou Liutang" (Da Zhou Liutang 答周柳塘), Li cites the prominent official Geng Dingxiang's 耿定向 (1524–1597) critiques of him—which he obviously does *not* see as justified—and "admits" to them in an explicitly ironic and mocking tone, quite similar to the one he employs in the "Self-Evaluation" but less elliptical and so easier to interpret:[10] this is Li Zhi firing back at a critic he thinks has badly misunderstood him.

Li Zhi begins the "Self-Evaluation" by aggressively ascribing to himself a whole suite of highly unpleasant character traits: he is "intolerant and rash" (*bianji* 褊急) by nature, "arrogant" (*jingao* 矜高) in appearance, "crude and vulgar" (*bisu* 鄙俗) in speech, "impetuous and foolhardy" (*kuangchi* 狂癡) at heart, and with those closest to him he seems to "love finding fault" (好求其過).[11] These descriptive phrases set up the reader for the puzzle-solving aspect of reading this piece. Each phrase is perfectly understandable as genuine humility when read on a surface level but also uses a specific allusion or association to signal an exculpatory double-entendre specific to Li Zhi's particular character and situation. This is the humble brag at its most extreme.[12]

The next lines set up several apparent contradictions, and this is where Li Zhi shifts into an offensive mode. This passage is also where the Yang Zhu line figures:

志在溫飽，	His will is focused just on keeping warm and well-fed,

而自謂伯夷叔齊；	but he describes himself as Bo Yi or Shu Qi.
質本齊人，	He has the same substance as that man from Qi,
而自謂飽道飫德。	but he describes himself as having partaken fully in the Way and being replete with Virtue.
分明一介不與，	Clearly he would not give so much as a blade of grass to anyone,
而以有莘藉口；	but he uses You Shen as an excuse.
分明豪毛不拔，	Clearly he would not pluck out the smallest hair,
而謂楊朱賊仁。[13]	while yet describing Yang Zhu as a destroyer of benevolence.

With these lines, it is impossible to have it both ways. The reader is left with only two alternatives: either Li Zhi is admitting to being profoundly and self-aggrandizingly hypocritical, or the apparent contradictions are puzzles that Li Zhi challenges his erudite readers to solve.

I would argue that the first half of each line in the above-quoted passage is a doctored version of what Li Zhi's accuser(s) might have charged him with. The second half can be read as Li Zhi's message to the reader that the damning description must be problematic. The overall purpose of each line is to counterattack, demonstrating that Li Zhi's accusers have misunderstood him in particularly stupid or vicious ways.

HIS WILL IS FOCUSED JUST ON KEEPING WARM AND WELL-FED BUT HE DESCRIBES HIMSELF AS BO YI OR SHU QI 志在溫飽，而自謂伯夷叔齊

"Will" or "aspiration," *zhi* 志, is often taken to be quite revealing of one's individual moral character; most striking is the long *Lunyu* 論語 anecdote where the Master invites each of his disciples to "describe your aspirations" (言爾志).[14] In *Lunyu*, the term is frequently used in rhetorical contexts of moral elevation: the observation of a person's *zhi* is taken to be an essential step in judging whether they are filial (*Lunyu* 1.11), and objects of *zhi* in *Lunyu* include things like "learning" (*xue* 學; *Lunyu* 2.4), "benevolence" (*ren* 仁; *Lunyu* 4.4), and "the Way" (*dao* 道; *Lunyu* 4.9, 7.6).[15] Li Zhi's will, however, is said to be fixated on mundane material concerns about clothing and food. The surface suggestion is that Li Zhi is petty or lazy and lacking in moral vision. Aspects of Li Zhi's biography might superficially support this: he retired from his official position to enjoy himself with friends, and he refused to return to his ancestral home to take up the duties of local governance as would traditionally be expected of him (Jiang 2001: 12, 14). Furthermore, he wrote to Deng Shiyang 登石陽[16] in 1585,

> Wearing clothes and eating food constitute "human relations" and "the principle of things." There is nothing more to human relations and the principle of things than dressing and eating.
>
> 穿衣吃飯即是人倫物理；除卻穿衣吃飯，無倫物矣。[17]

"Human relations" (*renlun* 人倫) and "the principle of things" (*wuli* 物理) were weighty Neo-Confucian technical terms,[18] and the claim that they were exhaustively defined by considerations relating to clothing and food would surely strike a committed Cheng-Zhu believer as thoroughly offensive.

The word choice in the "Self-Evaluation" is not quite the same, however. The phrase used there is *wenbao* 溫飽, recalling a claim made in the "Periods of Government" (Zhi qi 治期) chapter of Wang Chong's 王充 (27–ca. 97) *Lunheng* 論衡 that "When starvation and cold both reach an extreme, there are few who can avoid doing immoral things; when extremely warm and well-fed, there are few who can avoid doing good" (夫饑寒並至而能無為非者寡，然則溫飽並至而能不為善者希).[19] There is also a potential ambiguity as to *whose* material comforts Li Zhi is focused on. The natural reading would be "his own," but nothing precludes it from referring to the material comforts *of the people*. The *Guanzi* 管子, in a line from "Shepherding the People" (Mu min 牧民) also quoted by Wang Chong in another chapter but on a similar theme, has it that "when the granaries are full, [the people] understand propriety and restraint; when they have enough clothing and food, they have a sense of honor and shame" (倉廩實，則知禮節；衣食足，則知榮辱).[20] Therefore, if Li Zhi's will is focused not just on enjoying but also on *providing* material necessities, this can potentially be viewed as a fundamental step in a broader project of moral cultivation.

Li Zhi's own family suffered tragedy when in 1564 he had left them near Beijing while he returned to Fuzhou to attend to the (re)burial of his ancestors. He had seen to it that his family was provided with land for farming, but the harvest was extremely meager, and his two younger daughters died while he was away.[21] Li Zhi had therefore personally experienced the disaster that came about through his own *lack* of sufficient concern for material necessities, and this could well have affected his thinking. That the family survived at all in his absence had been due to the assistance of the same Deng Shiyang mentioned previously.

The reference to Bo Yi 伯夷 and Shu Qi 叔齊 that concludes the line might also have multiple layers of meaning. The surface reading would be as an allusion to the fact that Bo Yi and Shu Qi starved to death.[22] Juxtaposing them with Li Zhi's supposed concern about being well fed would make him seem particularly hypocritical. But Li Zhi does not describe himself as "admiring" or "imitating" Bo Yi and Shu Qi; the term he uses is *ziwei* 自謂: "describes himself as." Modesty was never Li Zhi's strong suit, but explicitly claiming to actually *be* a latter-day Bo Yi seems extreme even for him. The key to the puzzle may lie in investigating what particular aspect of Bo Yi and Shu Qi he might be underlyingly pointing at. Here, two possibilities present themselves.

First, Li Zhi would go on (in 1596) to write a "Traditions of Bo Yi" (Bo Yi zhuan 伯夷傳).[23] He would focus here on the long-standing controversy over whether the two brothers were resentful: Confucius 孔丘 (551–479 BCE) allegedly ruled that they were not,[24] but Sima Qian 司馬遷 (b. 145 BCE) had included in their biography a song in which they accuse the Zhou King Wu 周武王 (ca. eleventh century BCE) of "using violence to alter violence, not understanding that this is wrong" (以暴易暴兮，不知其非矣).[25] Zhu Xi 朱熹 (1130–1200) had taken Sima Qian to task for daring to dispute the ruling of the Sage.[26] Li Zhi, characteristically, would revel in expounding on the brothers' many causes for resentment, concluding, "How could anyone minimize such resentment? Our problem today is that scholars do not dare to resent. That's why they accomplish nothing." (此怨曷可少也？今學者唯不敢怨，故不成事)[27] Although the Bo Yi essay postdates the "Self-Evaluation" by eight years, Li Zhi's ideas about Bo Yi and Shu Qi might well have remained consistent, suggesting that the way in which he was claiming to be like them had nothing to do with starvation and everything to do with being (justifiably) resentful.[28]

A second possibility is a bit more obscure. Most of the allusions in the "Self-Evaluation" are creatively repurposed allusions to familiar texts such as the *Lunyu* and *Mengzi*. However, Handler-Spitz et al. point out that "Li also explored both Daoist texts and arcana" and "he peppered his writings liberally with allusions to texts ranging from the familiar to the obscure . . . [exhibiting] a synthesis of divergent religious-philosophical traditions."[29] It seems not impossible, then, that in "describing himself" as a Bo Yi or Shu Qi, he could have had in mind a poem by the Southern Song dynasty poet and Daoist master Bai Yuchan 白玉蟾 (1134–1229). The poem is entitled, "Self-Description" (Ziwei 自謂), and contains the lines, "Others are mixed waters of [pure] Jing and [turbid] Wei; only I have the air of [Bo] Yi and [Shu] Qi" (人自涇渭水，我但夷齊風).[30] While the connection might be coincidental, it is worth noticing that Bai Yuchan (though born on Hainan Island) traced his ancestral home to Fujian province and spent much of his adult life associated with that locality. (Li Zhi's ancestral home was also in Fujian.) The "Self-Description" poem also seems very much in line with Li Zhi's tastes: erudite, complex, allusive, and filled with oblique references to Confucius's disciples. If this connection is genuine, it would imply that the aspect of Bo Yi and Shu Qi being singled out is their purity and singleness of purpose.

One could therefore reinterpret the line as meaning something like, "His will is focused on [the moral perfection that can only come to one who enjoys] life's basic necessities, and [in the purity of this quest] he could be described as a Bo Yi or Shu Qi." Alternatively, "His will is focused on [the frequently overlooked importance] of life's basic necessities, and [on account of this issue, which directly led to tragedy in his own life] he could be described as [overflowing with resentment in the manner of] a Bo Yi or Shu Qi." Or finally, "His will is focused on [stopping at the point of] basic necessities, and [his purity in this] can be described as that of Bo Yi or Shu Qi."

He has the same substance as that man from Qi, but he describes himself as having partaken fully in the Way and being replete with Virtue. 質本齊人，而自謂飽道飫德。

The second apparent contradiction continues the theme of eating and hunger but is much simpler. The first part of the line has Li Zhi describing himself as having "the same substance as that man from Qi." This refers to a parable in the *Mengzi* where a man from Qi tells his wife and concubine that he dines out each day with the wealthy and noble. His wife becomes suspicious because no such people ever visit their house and so one day goes out and surreptitiously follows her husband:

> Not a single person in the city stopped to talk to him. In the end he went to the outskirts on the east side of the city amongst the graves. He went up to someone who was offering sacrifices to the dead and begged for what was left over. This not being enough he looked around and went up to another.
>
> 遍國中無與立談者。卒之東郭墦閒，之祭者，乞其餘；不足，又顧而之他。[31]

The wife and concubine are horribly disappointed when they find out that their husband is in fact no more than a beggar, an eater of leftovers. In the context of the *Mengzi*, the parable is meant to symbolize the fact that pursuing wealth and status results in getting one's hands dirty, morally speaking: "There are few ways to seek wealth and position that do not lead wives and concubines to weep with shame" (人之所以求富貴利達者，其妻妾不羞也，而不相泣者，幾希矣).[32]

How then does Li Zhi resemble the man from Qi? Several possibilities present themselves. Despite his distaste for it, he studied for the civil service examinations and passed them,[33] serving in office for a time before taking early retirement to pursue his studies.[34] He also reports his wife weeping tears of disappointment at his behavior, though for reasons unrelated to his career as such.[35] Another striking line in the *Mengzi* passage is the description of how no one stopped to talk to the man from Qi: he is isolated or alienated from his peers. Li Zhi did have his friends and admirers, but at certain points—particularly while living in Macheng where he was eventually hounded out by hostile partisans of his erstwhile friend Geng Dingxiang—he must have felt the sting of ostracism.[36]

The other half of the line is a striking phrase that (as far as I can tell) appears to be innovative rather than allusive. Li Zhi seems to have been playing with the image of the man eating his fill. The *Mengzi* story sums up the wife's discovery with the words: 此其為饜足之道也.[37] In Lau's translation: "This is how he had his food and drink."[38] But out of context it could also read, "This is the Way that made him full and satisfied." The phrase in the "Self-Evaluation" could be read as a kind of paraphrase: "having partaken fully in the Way and being replete with Virtue" (鮑道飫德). The juxtaposition of *Dao* and *de* also evoke the *Daodejing* 道德經, which Li Zhi also studied intently and for which he even wrote a commentary.[39]

If we again reinterpret the contradictory line in a sympathetic manner it might read, "He [was once] substantially like that man from Qi [in pursuing wealth and position in questionable ways, or in being a terrible disappointment to his wife], but [now] what he fills himself with is the Way and Virtue [and/or the teachings of Laozi 老子]." Or alternatively, "he was [ostracized by his peers] like that man from Qi, but is nonetheless fully satisfied with the Way and Virtue."

CLEARLY HE WOULD NOT GIVE SO MUCH AS A BLADE OF
GRASS TO ANYONE, BUT HE USES YOU SHEN AS AN EXCUSE.
分明一介不與，而以有莘藉口

The third contradiction takes up the theme of moral purity in a slightly different manner, through an allusion to another *Mengzi* story, this one about Yi Yin 伊尹. The apparently accusatory first part of the line attacks Li Zhi for his selfishness: "Clearly he would not give even a blade of grass to anyone." However, the full story as told by Mencius has Yi Yin "ploughing in the wildlands of You Shen" (耕於有莘之野), where he so strictly observed the principles of rightness and the Way that he would not only refuse substantial gifts (such as the chance to rule the realm or a thousand teams of horses) but was similarly scrupulous even in small things: "If it was contrary to rightness or to the Way, he would not give even a blade of grass to anyone, nor would he accept even a blade of grass from anyone" (非其義也，非其道也，一介不以與人，一介不以取諸人).[40] To one who knows the *Mengzi* story, the refusal to give is inextricably linked with the refusal to receive. It is not a matter of selfishness so much as a matter of being deeply principled.[41]

The line concludes, "He uses You Shen as an excuse," You Shen alluding to the place where Yi Yin did his ploughing.[42] The twist in this line may come from the multiple meanings of *jiekou* 藉口, translated above as "excuse"—that is, a not entirely sincere reason one gives for getting out of something one does not want to do. But *jiekou* has an older sense, related to the basic meaning of *jie*: a mat made of grass. It is not a commonly used term in early sources, but an instance in the

Zuozhuan 左傳⁴³ suggests to commentators a meaning of "a support for one's own position," a type of borrowed "padding" for the mouth. In the *Zuozhuan* story, the Jin negotiators, having the *jiekou* provided to them in the form of minor concessions by Qi, need not go back to their ruler empty-handed (bare-mouthed). Furthermore, *jie* on its own is not just any mat but often a mat used for placing sacrificial offerings. This, combined with the previous line, is quite clever, insofar as the blade of grass and woven grass mat are tied together with the fields outside You Shen, all elevated by the image of the sagely Yi Yin. The line can then be reinterpreted as, "He will neither give [nor receive] even a blade grass [if it is not in line with rightness and the Way], and this position of his is supported by the grass mat from You Shen [i.e., the story of Yi Yin's uncompromising virtue]."

CLEARLY HE WOULD NOT PLUCK OUT THE SMALLEST HAIR, WHILE YET DESCRIBING YANG ZHU AS A VIOLATOR OF |BENEVOLENCE. 分明豪毛不拔，而謂楊朱賊仁。

This brings us then to the final line of the puzzle, which is the one related to Yang Zhu. The first part of the line is closely parallel to the previous line: "Clearly he would not pluck out even the smallest hair." This allusion will be familiar to everyone as a reference to the *Mengzi*'s famous description of Yang Zhu: "Yangzi holds to [the path] of doing for oneself: if he could benefit the whole world by plucking out a single one [of his] hairs, he would not do it" (楊子取為我，拔一毛而利天下，不為也; 7A26). But why does Li Zhi write *haomao* 豪毛, "the smallest hair," instead of *yimao* 一毛, "a single hair"? There are various possibilities,⁴⁴ but the most philosophically intriguing comes from a line in *Lunheng*. In multiple chapters throughout the work, Wang Chong refers to the way in which Confucius's editing of the *Chunqiu* 春秋 "selects for inclusion even the smallest hairsbreadth of goodness, and castigates the tiniest sprout of badness" (采毫毛之善，貶纖介之惡).⁴⁵ Note that, as in Li Zhi's text, this line contains a *mao* 毛—*jie* 介 parallel, strengthening the possible connection. Understanding this as the underlying reference also twists the meaning: while seeming to cite his attacker's accusation of Yang Zhu–like selfishness, Li Zhi is actually obliquely comparing himself to the sage Confucius, saying he is not one to root out even the smallest hair *of goodness.*

The second half of the line is more difficult: "describing Yang Zhu as a destroyer of benevolence" is likely a complex allusion conflating two passages in the *Mengzi*. Mencius uses the actual phrase *zei ren* 賊仁 when King Xuan of Qi 齊宣王 (r. 319–301 BCE) asks him whether it was permissible for a subject to assassinate a ruler in the case of King Wu of Zhou. Mencius says that "a destroyer of benevolence is called a bandit; a destroyer of rightness is called a ruffian. Someone who is a bandit and a ruffian is referred to [only] as a male. I have heard of executing a male named Zhou, but have never heard that equated to assassinating a ruler." (賊仁者謂之賊，賊義者謂之殘，殘賊之人謂之一夫。聞誅一夫紂矣，未聞弒君也)[46] But through a line in Yang Xiong's 楊雄 (53 BCE–18 CE) *Fayan* 法言, this kind of "destroyer" can be linked to the figure of the *xiangyuan* 鄉原, which I will translate as "village centrist."[47] Yang Xiong writes, "Wanton flattery is a destroyer of benevolence; wanton defamation is a destroyer of rightness. The destroyer of benevolence closely resembles the village centrist. The destroyer of rightness closely resembles the village scandalmonger." (安響，仁之賊也；安毀，義之賊也。賊仁近鄉原，賊義近鄉訕)[48] Yang Xiong is certainly alluding to another passage in the *Mengzi*, one that explicitly elaborates on the *Lunyu* statement that the village centrist is "a destroyer of virtue" (德之賊):[49]

> If you want to censure him, you cannot find anything; if you want to find fault with him, you cannot find anything either. He shares with others the practices of the day and is in conformity with the sordid world. He appears to be conscientious and faithful and appears to have integrity in his conduct. He is liked by the multitude and is self-righteous.
>
> 非之無舉也，刺之無刺也；同乎流俗，合乎汙世；居之似忠信，行之似廉潔；眾皆悅之，自以為是。[50]

This is exactly how Geng Dingxiang and his friends appear to Li Zhi, as evinced by the many remarks in his correspondence: they play it safe, make themselves look good, and slither away from any critique one tries to pin on them. Without too much of a stretch, such a person could be connected with the traditional image of Yang Zhu. A line from the *Lunheng* makes an even more solid connection: "One who conforms to popular customs *to keep himself safe*—this is the village centrist" (偶俗

全身，則鄉原也).⁵¹ Wang Chong goes on to paraphrase the *Mengzi*'s description: that a village centrist is someone whose conduct is entirely unobjectionable yet is despised by both Confucius and Mencius because (in the words of the *Mengzi*) with such a person "you cannot enter into the Way of Yao and Shun" (不可與入堯舜之道); they "seem like the real thing but are not" (似而非者).⁵²

All of this may seem too much to pack into one line, but Li Zhi had been brooding for a long time over the accusation that he was selfish and arrogant—a Yang Zhu, according to the contemporary understanding of that figure.⁵³ Linking Yang Zhu with the cluster of associations around "the destroyer of benevolence" and thence to the "village centrist" is the kind of philosophical move Li Zhi would make, in that it turns the critique against the critics themselves. *They* are the Yang Zhu and "destroyers of benevolence," in that despite their pleasing words, they will always choose to preserve themselves rather than take risks to do genuine good. The fourth puzzle can therefore be reread as saying, "I am one who would not pluck out the smallest hairsbreadth [of goodness], and I consider [all of you to be as selfish as] Yang Zhu, a destroyer of benevolence [in the manner of the village centrist: prudent for the sake of self-preservation and never doing genuine good]."

This concludes the four "puzzle" lines. The next few lines are also worth looking at in that they continue the theme raised in the Yang Zhu line. The next line solidifies the contrast between Li Zhi himself and the *xiangyuan* who "obsequiously flatter their generation" (閹然媚於世):⁵⁴

WHAT HE DOES, GOES AGAINST THINGS; WHAT HE SAYS CONTRADICTS WHAT IS IN THEIR HEARTS. 動與物迕，口與心違。⁵⁵

Li Zhi writes of himself that he is a contrarian: "what he does, goes against things" (動與物迕). Certainly no one would accuse him of pandering to custom, given his attitude toward his career, his abandonment of familial duty, his admitted enjoyment of brothels, and other instances of what Jiang Jin has described as his "heteropraxy."⁵⁶ It would be natural to read the subsequent companion phrase as "what he says contradicts what is in his heart" (口與心違). Understood this way, however, it is hard to make sense of, except perhaps as a reference to the sly puzzles embedded in the preceding contradictions ("[what] his words [seem to be saying on the surface] contradict [what is actually in his] heart"). Parallelism, however, might also allow us to read the heart(s) in question as belonging not to him but to *things*, that is, to other people:[57] "his words depart from [other people's typical] mental attitudes." If this second reading is grammatically possible, it is certainly not the most obvious interpretation. Still, it fits very well with the remarks that follow and conclude the piece:

> Since his character is like this, the people of the village have all come to hate him. Long ago Zigong[58] asked the master, "How is it if people in the village all hate someone?" The master said, "Still not enough [to go on]." But with someone like this recluse, it is perhaps enough!
>
> 其人如此，鄉人皆惡之矣。昔子貢問夫子曰：「鄉人皆惡之何如？」子曰：「未可也。」若居士，其可乎哉！[59]

The *Lunyu* passage begins with Zigong asking the master if one can judge a person by whether the village people all love him. The master also says in that case that it is "not enough [to go on]." But the conclusion of the same *Lunyu* passage, which Li Zhi has not included, is probably the key to the whole piece. "It is best," says Confucius, "if the good people in the village love him and the bad people in the village hate him" (不如鄉人之善者好之，其不善者惡之). Li Zhi has introduced one final puzzle: he has said that everyone in the village hates him but then also claims that this *is* actually enough to go on, despite the well-known conclusion of the *Lunyu* item he has alluded to. Perhaps he is contradicting Confucius? The better and cleverer solution, however, would be that he is implicitly claiming that all the people "in the village" are, in fact, bad. Then the good people (of whom there are none) would all love him, and the bad people (i.e., everyone) would all hate him; a sage like Confucius would then indeed be able to judge him as morally worthy despite, or even because of, how much he is hated.

2. Frugality versus Stinginess

If I have read the "Self-Evaluation" correctly, it reveals a negative assessment of Yang Zhu. This is borne out by the other two references to Yang Zhu I have been able to locate in Li Zhi's writings.

The first occurs in an essay from *Fen shu* entitled "Zhuge Liang writes to the Last Ruler about Shen (Buhai), Han (Fei), Guanzi, and the Six Strategies" (Kong Ming wei houzhu xie Shen, Han, Guanzi, Liu Tao 孔明為後主寫申韓管子六韜).[60] The essay is too long to discuss in its entirety, but it deals with the delicate issue of amoral strategies for governance. The reference to Yang Zhu is found near the end of the essay, where Li Zhi seems to be expressing his own perspective on the matter:

> I once argued that those who would achieve great things must not be too concerned with pernicious after-effects;[61] in this way there is nothing that cannot be achieved. Lord Shang in Qin and Wu Qi in Chu are examples of this. The Confucians[62] all desire [such success], but they do not realize that it is a doubtful and uncertain matter whether the great achievements in the world can even be accomplished at all by [someone with] an attitude of concern regarding pernicious after-effects.
>
> 愚嘗論之，成大功者必不顧後患，故功無不成，商君之於秦，吳起之於楚是矣。而儒者皆欲之，不知天下之大功，果可以顧後患之心成之乎否也，吾不得而知也。[63]

Li Zhi goes on to discuss Zhuangzi as someone particularly concerned with pernicious aftereffects, focusing on an aspect of Zhuangzi that some scholars have argued has an affinity with Yang Zhu: the refusal to take office.[64]

> These [worriers over][65] pernicious after-effects will certainly be unwilling to achieve great things in the world. People like Zhuang Zhou are of this sort. So it was that he would rather be a turtle dragging its tail in the mud, being unwilling to receive a thousand gold worth of reward; he preferred happiness on the River Hao, being unwilling to take responsibility for [solving] the problems of the state of Chu.
>
> 此後患者必不肯成天下之大功，莊周之徒是已。是以寧為曳尾之龜，而不肯受千金之弊；寧為濠上之樂，而不肯任楚國之憂。[66]

Stitching together several different *Zhuangzi* anecdotes, Li Zhi makes the point that this self-protective attitude prevents anything from getting accomplished. While this might historically have had affinities with a Yangist position,[67] Li Zhi associates it with Zhuang Zhou. It also forms one end of a spectrum, with efficacious amoral strategists on the opposite end. The Confucians seem to occupy a space in between, but Li Zhi does not seem to see it as an optimal mean between the two. Instead, the Confucian position almost comes out as the worst of both worlds: Unlike the Zhuangzi types, Confucians *desire* the responsibility. Unlike the great doers of the world, Confucians are unwilling to proceed boldly, fretting over the possibility of pernicious aftereffects.

As described above, Li Zhi believes this to be an error. Earlier in the essay, he compared amoral strategies to a strong medicine. Strong medicines can be harmful, even poisonous. But sometimes the ailments of the state are such that strong medicines are required.[68] In describing those who had been willing to disregard potential future adverse effects, Li Zhi brings in Mozi and Yang Zhu in the space of a single line:

墨子之學術貴儉，雖天下以我為不拔一毛不恤也，	Mozi's learning and techniques greatly prize frugality, and [his attitude was] "I would not be upset even if the entire world should take me to be an advocate of 'not plucking a single hair.'"
商子之學術貴法，申子之學術貴術，韓非子之學術兼貴法、術，雖大卜以我為殘忍刻薄不恤也	Shangzi's learning and technique prized laws, Shenzi's prized techniques, Han Feizi's prized both laws and techniques, and [their attitude was] "I would not be upset even if the entire world might thereby come to see me as an advocate of cruelty and harshness."[69]

Other contributors to this volume have analyzed the frequent juxtaposition of Mozi and Yang Zhu. Many (though not all) have supported Attilio Andreini's analysis that "the Yang-Mo symbol" has a specific rhetorical purpose, defining a "range of ethical deviance into two dichotomous positions and placing them at the extremes of a moral and ideological scheme in which the *Ru* are located right in the middle."[70] Li Zhi introduces here an interesting twist on this juxtaposition by implying a deeper connection between the two than the standard antithesis of excessive selfishness and excessive altruism. His view appears to be that the frugality (*jian* 儉) advocated by the Mohists[71] could be (mis)interpreted as resulting from the "not plucking a single hair" mentality of Yang Zhu types.

This could be true on two levels. First, what Li Zhi likely had in mind was that people might accuse Mohists of opposing extravagance because they wanted to hoard resources for themselves rather than use them for public benefit. This would be an absurd misunderstanding of Mohism. There is, however, a more sophisticated way that Mohist frugality could be misunderstood as "not plucking a single hair": in opposing excessive expenditures, extravagant music, and costly funerals, the Mohists put the *basic health* of the body politic above the more complex aesthetic and symbolic structures of civilization that the Confucians advocated and upper classes desired.[72] In a superficially similar way, the Yangists would put the basic health of their own bodies above the more complex structures of society, such as bureaucracy, politics, and perhaps even minimal social cooperation. In opposition to both sides, Confucians would advocate for a more complex, aesthetic, and *patterned* (*wen* 文) society.

The alignments suggested by this remark are slightly surprising. We find Mohists and the hard-headed strategists often described as "Legalists"[73] grouped together in opposition to Confucians and people like Zhuangzi. Nor are Yang and Mo placed on equal footing here. Instead, "being seen as a Yang Zhu type" is presented as a bad alternative—so bad that someone overly concerned with negative consequences might hesitate or even decline to continue. The Mohists, however, were bold enough to forge ahead.

One wonders, particularly in connection with the Mohist advocacy of moderate funerals, if the events of 1564 weighed on Li Zhi's thoughts. After the death of his second son (his eldest had died in 1555), he had decided to make a lengthy trip to his ancestral home, with the purpose of giving his great-grandparents a more "suitable" burial. Having recently entered the ranks of officialdom, he could now afford it:

> My great-grandparents passed away more than fifty years ago. I was not able to give them a suitable burial because I was impoverished and had no means to obtain a plot. This is a great violation of custom. . . . I have never heard of anyone who was considered filial because he chose first to protect himself from wind and rain. I fear that Heaven and the spirits above will never be willing to leave an auspicious burial plot for one as lacking in filial piety as I.

> 吾先曾大父大母歿五十多年矣，所以未歸土者，為貧不能求葬地；又重違俗……未聞以卜吉自衛暴露為孝也。天道神明，吾恐決不肯留吉地以與不孝之人。[74]

While he was away attending to this symbolic and quintessentially Confucian filial duty, his younger daughters died—of privation, Li Zhi believed—and his wife and eldest daughter endured terrible hardship on a basic level:

> The year's harvest was extremely meager. The plot of land acquired by the Recluse [i.e., Li Zhi, for the sustenance of his family] barely yielded a few bushels of weeds. The eldest daughter had long endured difficult times. She ate the weeds as if she were eating grain. His second and third daughters were unable to gulp down weeds and soon both, so young, had fallen ill and died.
>
> 歲果大荒，居士所置田僅收數斛稗。長女隨艱難日久，食稗如食粟。二女三女遂不能下咽，因病相繼夭死。[75]

With deliberate irony Li Zhi narrates his return home: the reader knows about the tragedy, while the protagonist does not. He describes how satisfied he feels about having completed the burial arrangements and his filial duty to his ancestors, and how happy he is to return home—only to learn that in his absence, the next generation of his family had been all but wiped out.

Did he regret his choice not to protect his immediate family "from the wind and the rain"? What if he had, in "violation of custom," chosen a path of Mohist frugality with regard to his patriline's funeral arrangements, or if he had not cared about whether he was "considered filial"? Perhaps, as his Yang-Mo line suggests, people would have considered him selfish, unwilling to pluck a hair. Li Zhi does not say it, but between the spare, sorrowful lines of his narrative is the possibility that it was the filial son who was being selfish—or if not selfish exactly, perhaps blinkered, blinded by the flawed ideology of his time and place. "I really am too narrow" (余實窄),[76] he admits. As a result of this experience, he turns away from the societal and familial expectations for someone in his position, not toward to the down-to-earth practicality of the Mohists but to "the mysteries of the Dao" and what he envisioned would be a life of contemplation.

Such an autobiographical interpretation of this line may be a stretch. There is no explicit license in the "Zhuge Liang" essay to read it in a personal sense. So perhaps one should instead read the Yang-Mo connection together with a *Mengzi* passage on ideological "drift" among different strands of thought: "Those who desert Mo will certainly turn to Yang. Those who desert Yang will certainly turn to Confucianism. When they do so, one [should] simply accept them." (逃墨必歸於楊，逃楊必歸於儒。歸，斯受之而已矣)[77] In context, the point of the passage is probably an argument against trying to win adherents through debate.[78] A secondary (but for present purposes more interesting) point is the possible implication that there is a specific directionality in the path from Mo to Yang to Confucianism: that it might represent a moral or philosophical maturation process. Mencius does not give any specifics about why he thinks the process goes in that particular direction (or whether other directions are possible). Nor, for obvious reasons related to his own ideological stance, does Mencius address the potential (and plausible!) closing of the loop: that those who desert the Confucians could end up with the Mohists.[79]

Li Zhi's linking of Mo and Yang is not exactly of this type. He seems to argue, instead, that what is in fact Mohism might be *mis*understood as Yangism, at least in its emphasis on frugality. Being mistakenly seen as a selfish "Yang Zhu" type would count as a *hou huan*, a pernicious aftereffect, placed in parallel with being seen as "cruel and harsh," a risk for Legalist types. The Mohist advocation of frugality, on the other hand, is placed together with Shang Yang, Shenzi, and Han Fei in the realm of (at least potentially) great achievements.

Li Zhi's third reference to Yang Zhu occurs in a very different context: the evaluation of Han Emperor Wen 漢文帝 (b.202 BCE, r. 180–157 BCE) found in his historical commentary *Cang shu* 藏書 (A Book to Keep Hidden). Like the above, it seems also to relate to the question of modest funerals.

Though in many cases *Cang shu* takes issue with established evaluations of historical figures, its biography of Han Emperor Wen seems more or less in line with what one would expect. It is a positive portrayal, a shortened version of the *Hanshu*'s 漢書 "Annals of Emperor Wen" (Wen di ji 文帝紀) including most of Ban Gu's 班固 (32–92) evaluation.[80] At the end of this, Li Zhi appends his own words:

> Scholar Li said: Throughout history, edicts and orders are often very ornamental. Only in the written edicts of Filial Wen did every word come from the lungs and guts. Reading them makes a person deeply joyful. For this reason I recorded them all. Filial Wen was profoundly accomplished in the method

of taking a step back, and so naturally "his heels were sturdy and solid."[81] As a result, his edicts and orders are not vacuous.

李生曰：歷代詔令多文飾，惟孝文詔書，字字出肺腸，讀之令人深快。予故備載之。孝文深得退一步法，自然腳跟穩實，故其詔令不虛也。[82]

The next lines are more difficult, in part because there is some disagreement about how to parse them.

Scholars did not yet understand the solid core of Huang Di and Laozi, describing them as [akin to?] the heterodox Mr. Yang Zhu, [whose ideas] have the potential to bring the world to catastrophe and defeat.

學者未知黃帝老子之實，謂之異端楊朱氏，能令天下禍敗。[83]

In the previous section, Li Zhi had mentioned the possibility of people misunderstanding a Mohist policy as having Yang Zhu–type motivations. Here, he argues against another misunderstanding, a mistaken association between Huang-Lao ideas and the "heterodox" Yang Zhu. The evaluation concludes, colorfully,

Oh! I beg you to look closely at this. Do not just gnaw on the dregs and leavings of your predecessors.

吁！請細觀焉。毋但哺前人糟柏也。[84]

Traditional evaluations of Emperor Wen are so overall positive that it is difficult to identify what Li was thinking of in describing the views of scholars (*xuezhe* 學者). However the *Shiji pinglin* 史記評林 (Forest of comments on the historian's records), which first appeared during Li Zhi's lifetime, does record several comments that hint at what Li Zhi might be talking about. First, it is significant that in the original historical text the posthumously issued "testamentary edict" of Emperor Wen requested that his funeral rites be simplified and abbreviated in numerous ways, with the justification that he did not want to cause hardship to the populace. Li Zhi's interlinear comment on this document reads:

On his own deathbed and still his thoughts are about the people. Truly he was a benevolent person! Truly he was a sage ruler!

身崩而念在民。真仁人哉！真聖主哉！[85]

Huang Zhen 黃震 (1212–1280), as recorded in the *Shiji pinglin*, suggests that the passage about the abbreviated funeral rites is "satirical" (*ji* 譏) and that "later generations, not realizing that it was satirical, turned around and mocked Emperor Wen. How could this be!?" (後世不以為譏而反譏文帝，何哉)[86] The idea that Sima Qian deliberately altered the testamentary edict of an emperor in his own dynasty seems far-fetched, but Huang Zhen's comment might have been the kind of misunderstanding Li Zhi had in mind.

Luo Dajing 羅大經 (1196–post 1252), explaining the short interval between Emperor Wen's death and his burial, wrote,

> This was Emperor Wen's deathbed command. Even though it is not in accord with the Central Way, it shows a unique sort of vision. Emperor Wen's holding these sorts of opinions came entirely from Huang-Lao.

文帝之顧命也。雖未合中道，見亦卓矣。文帝此等見解自黃老中來。[87]

Luo Dajing's comment lacks the strong negativity that Li Zhi attributed to the unnamed scholars (*xuezhe* 學者), but Luo does mildly criticize the ideology behind the deathbed command and does tie it to Huang-Lao and a sense of heterodoxy. These comments establish that the specific subject of Li Zhi's evaluation was indeed the frugality of the mourning rituals prescribed by the dying emperor, even if he meant to apply it more generally as well.

In that connection, then, the comment from the "Zhuge Liang" essay seems relevant. There are always those who want to interpret frugality (of either a Mohist or a Huang-Lao variety) as a sort of selfishness, a statement tantamount to being *wu jun* 無君, as the old Mencian accusation against Yang Zhu would have it.[88] Li Zhi focused on the *shi* 實, the solidity, of Emperor Wen's rule. He pointed out that scholars overlooked the fact that if this was Huang-Lao, it was concretely beneficial to the people when applied by the ruler. He took Emperor Wen as a case study to criticize those who would have knee-jerk reactions against any non-*ru* practice, those who would have the immediate impulse to label economizing reforms as heterodox and dangerous in the *wu jun* way.

Li Zhi may have been straw-manning his opponents, which is to say, he may have just been using Emperor Wen to talk about his own selective employment of Daoist ideas. Despite the difficulty of interpreting the passage, with its ambiguous parsing, it seems clear that to him Yang Zhu nonetheless represents the bogeyman, the logical space that other non-Confucian ideas risk being placed in if they are misunderstood—much to their detriment.

3. Li Zhi and the Problem of Self-Interest

Li Zhi retired from office early, in part because he could not get along with his colleagues and superiors.[89] He devoted his retirement to contemplation but not in the quiet and dignified manner one might expect of an aging Confucian. He refused to go home to his family and play the benevolent patriarch of his local area. He published scathing critiques of prominent people,[90] visited prostitutes and discussed it openly, had an apparently platonic friendship with an aristocratic widow and took another as a student,[91] and shaved his head but not his beard. At least some of these things led to his arrest and imprisonment (like Socrates, he was charged with corrupting youth).[92] Jiang Jin has argued convincingly that it was "Li's heteropraxy, legitimated by his theory of authentic moral self *but not the theory itself*" that "was the immediate and primary cause of his persecution."[93] This contention seems entirely plausible. It was the tactlessness, the gallivanting, the hairstyle, the refusal to fit into a definable place in Ming society that got Li Zhi in trouble. At seventy he wanted to be able, like Confucius, to follow his heart's desire without overstepping.[94] For him, though, that could only have been accomplished if societal boundaries were to have been redrawn. As it was, he overstepped a great deal.

He may not have been more self-indulgent than his peers, but he was more open about it. He is notorious for admitting to selfishness, but his remarks should be taken in context. In one of his increasingly hostile exchanges with Geng Dingxiang, he wrote:

> If we try looking at what you do, there is no considerable difference between you and others. Everyone is like this; I am also like this, and you are too. From the time we come to the age of reason even to this present day, from morning to night we plough in order to get food, buy land in order to plant, build houses in order to find shelter, study in order to pass examinations, hold office in order to win honor and fame, and search for propitious sites in order to provide good fortune for sons and grandsons.
>
> 試觀公之行事，殊無甚異於人者。人盡如此，我亦如此，公亦如此。自朝至暮，自有知識以至今日，均之耕田而求食，買地而求種，架屋而求安，讀書而求科第，居官而求尊顯，博求風水以求福蔭子孫。[95]

Li Zhi's observation, that most people's activity is motivated by self-interest, seems not at all unusual from a present-day perspective. Indeed, in some respects it was not entirely new even in Li Zhi's time. The *Shiji* records the proverb "to the people, food is their heaven" (民人以食為天).[96] What was unusual, though, was to extend this generalization to the intelligentsia who through moral cultivation were supposed to have risen above such concerns. Li Zhi argues that such protestations are profoundly hypocritical.

> The daily round of tasks is done from a calculated concern for oneself and one's family, and with not a jot of consideration for others. Yet as soon as you open your mouth to discuss [moral] learning, you say, "*You* are just looking out for yourself, whereas *I* am doing it for others. *You* are selfish, whereas *I* desire to benefit others. *I* pity my neighbors in the east who may be suffering from hunger; I regret the unbearable cold for my neighbors in the west. Some, like Confucius and Mencius, go out to teach, whereas some [implication: like *you*, Li Zhi] will have nothing to do with others: they are the slaves of self-advantage. . . ." When you look at this, you may see that what you say is not necessarily what you do, and what you do is not necessarily what you say. . . . As I think this over, I feel that you are not the equal of peasants in the marketplace talking about what they do. Those who do business say it is business; those who do farmwork say it is farmwork. Their

talk really has substance, words that are truly virtuous, so that when others hear them, they forget their cares.

> 種種日用，皆為自己身家計慮，無一厘為人謀者。及乎開口談學，便說「爾為自己，我為他人，爾為自私，我欲利他；我憐東家之飢矣，又思西家之寒難可忍也；某等肯上門教人矣，是孔、孟之志也，某等不肯會人，是自私自利之徒也……」以此而觀，所講者未必公之所行，所行者又公之所不講……翻思此等，反不如市井小夫，身履是事，口便說是事，作生意者但說生意，力田作者但說力田，鑿鑿有味，真有德之言，令人聽之忘厭倦矣。[97]

Li Zhi accuses Geng Dingxiang, and probably by extension the whole body of mainstream Confucian followers, of profound hypocrisy. They behave just like everyone else, Li Zhi points out accusingly, but when they open their mouths to speak they portray themselves as being selfless and wholly altruistic.

It is often the case that accusations of hypocrisy arise in situations where the accuser feels attacked by the words or surface pretenses of the accused.[98] Rightly or wrongly, it is clear that Li Zhi felt accused by Geng Dingxiang: he even puts the words into his former friend's mouth. Had he stopped with the observation that almost everyone is on the same level when it comes to self-interest (regardless of moralistic protestations), he might have scored his point more effectively. He goes on, however, to provide his unfortunate correspondent with his own insights on what real goodness would look like:

> Without the phenomenon of "me," I can discard the self; without the phenomenon of others, I can follow others. This is not forced, because I see myself that everyone is a Buddha.

> 無我相，故能舍己；無人相，故能從人。非強之也，以親見人人之皆佛。[99]

These thoughts are philosophically interesting, if a bit idealistic, but Li Zhi has not exactly prepared a fertile ground for them. And Geng promptly responds by accusing Li of a lack of humility.[100]

By admitting to being "like everyone else" in his day-to-day concern for self-preservation, and at the same time claiming special insight into transcending the phenomenon of self, Li Zhi set himself up for a counter-charge of hypocrisy. But Li Zhi's enemies had a simpler course available to them. They could seize upon his early admission—that he was selfish like everyone else—and interpret it as a form of projection: *you* see everyone else as selfish (because you are). This tactic was quite effective and remains part of Li Zhi's reputation to this day: his supposed advocacy of selfishness is furthered by passages such as the one in which he claims that "selfishness is the mind-and-heart of man. Men must be selfish so that what is in their minds can be made known. If there is no selfishness, there is no mind." (夫私者，人之心也。人必有私而後其心乃見。若無私則無心矣)[101]

Conclusion

Li Zhi was (in)famous for the glorification of self—his own self in particular. He was also an independent thinker who never hesitated to reject traditional verdicts. So why was it that he never embraced Yang Zhu's "doing for oneself" (*wei wo* 為我) and indeed firmly rejected it? I would argue that the answer lies in the self-protective aspect of the Yang Zhu figure, as hypothetically reconstructed from references in the *Huainanzi* 淮南子, *Lüshi chunqiu* 呂氏春秋, and *Liezi* 列子.[102] Li Zhi is willing to defend (albeit ambivalently) the despised attitude of "self-affirmation" (*zi shi* 自是)[103] but never uses "Yangist" phrases like "valuing the self" (*gui ji* 貴己), "keeping one's nature whole and protecting one's authenticity" (*quan xing bao zhen* 全性保真), or "not letting things entangle one's person" (*bu yi wu lei xing* 不以物累形).

Li Zhi's "In Memoriam, Master Wang Longxi" (Wang Longxi xiansheng gaowen 王龍溪先生告文) may shed some light on the contrast between his own values and those he associated (perhaps very casually) with Yang Zhu:

> It is strange that people who study the Way suffer from the sickness of loving their own person (*shen* 身) more than they love the Way.

所怪學道者病在愛身而不愛道。[104]

The self-protective strand of Yang Zhu's reputation comes near to Li Zhi's *ai shen* 愛身, as used in this passage. *Shen* 身, plausibly understood as physical self, is not only "loved" by cowardly students of the Way but indeed *begrudged* (to return to an older meaning of the term). Like the village centrist, and like Yang Zhu (who for Li Zhi falls into the same category), they are opposed to self-sacrifice; Li Zhi is not. He goes on:

> Because of this, these [students of the Way] do not comprehend the value of the wisdom entrusted to them by those who came before. Instead, they scheme only for their own profit and interest.
>
> 是以不知前人付托之重，而徒為自私自利之計。

Is Li Zhi being self-contradictory here? Has he not openly said that everyone does what they do out of self-interest? If we read Li Zhi charitably, however, there is a way out of the seeming contradiction. He sets up a contrast between self-interested schemes and the weightiness of precious heritage. The implication is that while self-interest is understandable, there is no way to make moral and spiritual progress if you love yourself more than you love the Way. Not everyone need be a student of the Way, but those who are must devote themselves to it over and above the ordinary self-interested scheming of daily existence. The next lines complicate the matter by introducing two further terms relating to the self:

> Their sickness is that they respect their [own] reputation (*ming* 名) but not their own self (*ji* 己), and so they disregard the fact that their sons and grandsons are sinking into moral decline. Instead they consider it their chief responsibility to steer clear of suspicion and slander. . . . Through such actions they lose their true selves (*shi ji* 失己); they do not actualize themselves (*cheng ji* 成己).
>
> 病在尊名而不尊己，是以不念兒孫陷溺之苦，而務為遠嫌遠謗之圖……是失己也，非成己也。

If *shen* 身 is the bodily self, including the hairs and hands that Yang Zhu refused to give up, *ming* 名 (reputation) is the social self, the self that can be harmed by suspicion and slander. Li Zhi was also reckless toward this aspect of the self, though his voluminous self-justifications show he was not indifferent to it. Both *shen* and *ming* differ from the term that Li

Zhi appears to be placing the highest value on in this passage, *ji* 己. The passage makes clear that this refers to a true or higher self, something one must not lose; the very possibility of losing it shows that it is not being taken as self in the ordinary sense. The other implication is that this self can be "actualized" or "completed" (*cheng* 成). There might be a conflict of interest between caring for one's physical self and caring about the Way, or between protecting one's reputation and pursuing the Way. But between the Way and one's true self, there is no need to choose. One becomes fully oneself exactly by putting the Way above all other considerations. Only once that higher self is completed can one genuinely put it aside (*she ji* 舍己), which ultimately was Li Zhi's goal. It seems a long way from the "doing for oneself" that Li Zhi associated with Yang Zhu, but it is perhaps not so distant from the more defensible version of him that occasionally, throughout the tradition, surfaces in defiance of Mencius's more dominant characterization.

Notes

1. Jiang Jin, "Heresy and Persecution in Late Ming Society: Reinterpreting the Case of Li Zhi," *Late Imperial China* 22, no. 2 (2001): 9, 12.

2. Jiang, "Heresy and Persecution," 14–15, 17.

3. As he wrote to Yang Dingjian 楊定見 (ca. sixteenth to seventeenth century), "People in this world who love me do not love me because I am an official. Nor do they love me because I am a monk. They love *me*." (世之我愛者，非愛我為官也，非愛我為和尚也，愛我也) Li Zhi, "To Yang Dingjian," in *A Book to Burn and a Book to Keep (Hidden): Selected Writings*, trans. Rivi Handler-Spitz (New York: Columbia University Press, 2016), 63–64; Li Zhi, *Li Zhi quan ji zhu* 李贄全集注, 26 vols. (Beijing: Shehui kexue wenxian chubanshe, 2010), 1:157.

4. Discussing the selfish motivations of farmers and scholars alike, he writes, "The daily round of tasks is done for the benefit of oneself and one's family, and not one bit for others" (種種日用，皆為自己身家計慮，無一厘為人謀者) (Li, "Li Zhi and Geng Diangxiang, Correspondence," in *A Book to Burn*, trans. Timothy Brook, 51; *Li Zhi quan ji zhu*, 1:72).

5. *Mengzi* 7A26.

6. "Li Zhi and Geng Diangxiang, Correspondence," 39; *Li Zhi quan ji zhu*, 1:41.

7. Prominent examples include Wang Chong's "Zi ji" 自紀 [Autobiography], Tao Qian's "Wuliu xiansheng" 五柳先生 [Master Five Willows], and Ouyang Xiu's "Liu Yi jushi zhuan" 六一居士傳 (Traditions of recluse six ones], but there are many others.

8. My reading differs slightly from that found in Rivi Handler-Spitz, *Symptoms of an Unruly Age: Li Zhi and Cultures of Early Modernity* (Seattle and London: University of Washington Press, 2017), 48–55, in that I do not think his purported self-description is "simply another mask, a stereotypical, fictionalized image of an eccentric" (55). Rather, I will argue that it has a sustained double meaning that can be excavated through close attention to the pattern of allusions across the entire text.

9. See the excellent discussion of Li Zhi's emotional reaction to his daughters' deaths in Pauline C. Lee, *Li Zhi, Confucianism, and the Virtue of Desire*, SUNY Series in Chinese Philosophy and Culture (Albany: State University of New York Press, 2012), 34–35.

10. Li, "A Response to Zhou Liutang," in *A Book to Burn*, trans. Rivi Handler-Spitz, 65–74; *Li Zhi quan ji zhu*, 1:218–26.

11. *Li Zhi quan ji zhu*, 1:356.

12. In the interest of concision, I will not include a full explication here.

13. *Li Zhi quan ji zhu*, 1:357.

14. *Lunyu* 5.26, with another version in *Lunyu* 10.26.

15. Though there are a few examples of misguided *zhi* (*Lunyu* 14.36), the term tends to have a distinctly positive valence in *Lunyu*, as in the pronouncement that "gentlemen of purpose and people of benevolence would not even seek to preserve their very lives if it came at the expense of benevolence" (志士仁人，無求生以害仁, *Lunyu* 15.9).

16. I.e., Deng Lincai 登林材 (*juren* 1561).

17. Li Zhi, "In Response to Deng Shiyang," in *A Book to Burn*, trans. Pauline C. Lee, 8; *Li Zhi quan ji zhu*, 1:8.

18. When Zhu Xi transformed the "Great Learning" (Daxue 大學) chapter of the *Liji* into one of the Four Books that formed the center of the Neo-Confucian canon, the "investigation of things" (*ge wu* 格物) mentioned there came to be understood as investigating the "principle" (*li* 理) of the things. This was such a key focus of Cheng-Zhu Neo-Confucian endeavor that *Lixue* 理學 (Learning of principle) came, from the mid- or late thirteenth century, to be used as a major alternative to the older term *Daoxue* (Learning of the Way) as a term of Neo-Confucian self-description (John Winthrop Haeger, "The Intellectual Context of Neo-Confucian Syncretism," *Journal of Asian Studies* 31, no. 3 [1972]: 512). *Lixue* places emphasis on the "rationalistic-moralistic" aspects of the Neo-Confucian endeavor, and according to De Bary, it was just these aspects that Li Zhi found most objectionable. See Wm Theodore de Bary, "Individualism and Humanitarianism in Late Ming Thought," in *Self & Society in Ming Thought*, Studies in Oriental Culture 4 (New York: Columbia University Press, 1970), 198. As for *renlun* 人倫, a term associated with the *Mengzi* (e.g., 4B19), even as a general term itself was a key focus of dozens of comments in the *Zhuzi yulei* 朱子語類 (Categorized sayings of Master Zhu), not to mention the specific relationships for which it is a hypernym.

19. Wang Chong, *Lunheng*, 4 vols. (Beijing: Zhonghua, 1995), 53.771–72.

20. Li Xiang, ed., *Guanzi Jiao Zhu* 管子校注, 3 vols. (Beijing: Zhonghua, 2004), 1:2; see also "Criticisms on Confucius" (Wen Kong 問孔), *Lunheng* 28.422, where Wang Chong quotes this line in critiquing Confucius's claim that it is better for the people to go without food than without trust (*Lunyu* 12.7). It is possible that Li Zhi was doing something similar in his "Response to Deng Shiyang."

21. Li Zhi admits that he also took the high road and turned down an offer of special irrigation-related favors from a corrupt local official whose monopolization of water for canal-building projects was a partial cause of the poor harvest. See Li, "A Sketch of Zhuowu: Written in Yunnan," in *A Book to Burn*, trans. Pauline C. Lee, 80–81; *Li Zhi quan ji zhu*, 1:234.

22. The most famous treatment of the two is their chapter in the *Shiji* 史記 (Beijing: Zhonghua, 1959) "Arrayed Traditions of Bo Yi" (Bo Yi liezhuan 伯夷列傳), 61.2121–30, but the core of the story (including their starvation) is drawn from the *Zhuangzi* 莊子 "Yielding Kingship" (Rang wang 讓王) chapter; see Wang Shumin, *Zhuangzi jiao quan* 莊子校詮 (Zhong yang yen jiu yüan li shi yü yen yen jiu suo fa xing, 1994), 28.1164–65.

23. *Li Zhi quan ji zhu*, 2:185; Li, "Biography of Bo Yi," in *A Book to Burn*, trans. Rivi Handler-Spitz, 199–200.

24. *Lunyu* 7.15.

25. *Shiji* 61.2123.

26. E.g., Zhu Xi, *Categorized Sayings of Master Zhu* (*Zhuzi yulei* 朱子語類) (Beijing: Zhonghua, 1986), 122.2952.

27. *Li Zhi quan ji zhu*, 2:185; trans. altered from Li, "Biography of Bo Yi," 200.

28. Further support for this reading can be found in the letter "Bidding Farewell to Justice Minister Geng [Dingxiang]" (與耿司寇告別), where Li Zhi points out that if Bo Yi and Shu Qi lived today, they would certainly be considered too "impetuous and uncompromising" (狂狷) to serve in office, but it is only such people who are truly able to "hear the Way" (聞道). See Li, "Li Zhi and Geng Diangxiang," 60; *Li Zhi quan ji zhu*, 1:67.

29. Li, *A Book to Burn*, xviii.

30. Bai Yuchan, *Bai Yuchan quan ji jiaozhu*, ed. Zhu Yihui (Haikou: Hainan chubanshe, 2004), 137.

31. *Mengzi* 4B33, *Mencius*, trans. D. C. Lau (Harmondsworth, UK: Penguin, 1970), 137.

32. Lau, *Mencius*, 137; trans. slightly altered.

33. The "Sketch of Zhuowu" describes these activities and the ambivalence he felt toward them (*Li Zhi quan ji zhu*, 1:233–34).

34. Jiang, "Heresy and Persecution," 8–9.

35. She weeps because he forbids her to accompany him back to their natal home, robbing her of the chance to see her elderly ailing mother (*Li Zhi quan ji zhu*, 1:234).

36. A vivid description of Li Zhi's social situation in Macheng can be found in William T. Rowe, *Crimson Rain: Seven Centuries of Violence in a Chinese County* (Stanford, CA: Stanford University Press, 2007), 100–105. See also an in-depth analysis in Jiang, "Heresy and Persecution," 21–29.

37. *Mengzi* 4B33.

38. Lau, *Mencius*, 137.

39. I.e., *Laozi jiezhu* 老子解注 (see *Li Zhi quan ji zhu* 14:1–103). For a specific statement by Li on the value of Daoist texts, see also his "A Brief Introduction to a Selection of Daoist Teachings," in *A Book to Burn*, trans. Jennifer Eichman, 265–66; *Dao jiao chao xiao yin* 道教鈔小引, in *Li Zhi quan ji zhu* 3:195.

40. *Mengzi* 5A7.

41. Intriguingly, the refusal to either give or receive is found in a speech ascribed to Yang Zhu in the *Liezi*: "Such were the people of ancient times: if by harming a hair on their heads they could profit the realm, they would not give [that hair], and if the entire realm were offered as their sole possession, they would not take it" (古之人，損一毫利天下，不與也，悉天下奉一身，不取也); Yang Bojun 楊伯峻, ed., *Liezi jishi* 列子集釋 (Beijing: Zhonghua, 1985), 7.230. It does not strike me as likely that Li Zhi had *this* Yang Zhu in mind, though an argument could be made. Rather, the commonality of terminology suggests that the account of Yi Yin in the *Mengzi* and the Yang Zhu of this *Liezi* passage participate in a shared discourse of detachment, one that sees self-sacrifice and pursuit of gain as being both equally problematic. Yi Yin, after some hesitation, decides to reengage with the world when the right opportunity presents itself. The *Liezi*'s Yang Zhu appears to experience a similar hesitation in objecting later in the same passage that "there is no chance at all of the world being saved by a single hair" (世固非一毛之所濟).

42. There is some disagreement in the tradition as the exact identity of You Shen, but Zhao Qi's commentary specifies that it is the name of a polity (*Mengzi zhushu* 5A7.2738).

43. "We, our lord's subjects, led war chariots to plead on behalf of Lu and Wei. If we have the wherewithal for an answer to report back to our unworthy ruler, it is due to your ruler's beneficence. Would we dare to abide by anything but your commands?" (群臣帥賦輿以為魯衛請，若苟有以藉口復於寡君，君之惠也，敢不唯命是聽？); trans. Stephen W. Durrant, Wai-yee Li, and David Schaberg, *Zuo Traditions = Zuozhuan: Commentary on the "Spring and Autumn Annals,"* Classics of Chinese Thought (Seattle: University of Washington Press, 2016), 2:724–25; *Zuozhuan*, "Duke Cheng," 2:3).

44. Including that it could be a reference to the *Liezi* line quoted in n41 above. *Hao* 毫 and *hao* 豪 are very close variants.

45. This line is found verbatim in *Lunheng* 28.406, 55.802, 56.807, and 83.1173 and with only a one-character variant in *Lunheng* 16.191.

46. *Mengzi* 1B8; note that Lau, *Mencius*, 68 uses "outcast" instead of "male" for *fu* 夫.

47. This translation for *xiangyuan* 鄉原 differs from others, which include (most commonly) "village worthy"; see Confucius, *The Analects*, trans. D. C. Lau (Hong Kong: The Chinese University Press, 2000), 175; and "those who make virtue their profession." See Confucius, *The Analects of Confucius*, trans. Simon Leys (New York: W.W. Norton, 1997, 87). My understanding most closely resembles that of Legge: "good careful people of the villages"; See James Legge, *The Chinese Classics: With a Translation, Critical and Exegetical Notes, Prolegomena, and Copious Indexes* (Hong Kong: Hong Kong University Press, 1960), 2:500, and relies on the passage from *Mengzi* 7B37.

48. Yang Xiong, *Fayan yishu* 法言義疏 (Beijing: Zhonghua, 1987), 11.490. Michael Nylan translates the terms as "smugly parochial" (*xiangyuan* 鄉原) and "village gossip" (*xiangshan* 鄉訕). See Yang Xiong, *Exemplary Figures: Fayan*, trans. Michael Nylan, Classics of Chinese Thought (Seattle: University of Washington Press, 2013), 203.

49. *Lunyu* 17.13.

50. *Mengzi* 7B37; Lau, *Mencius*, 203.

51. *Lunheng* "Annoyances and Vexations" (Lei hai 累害) 2.13, emphasis added.

52. *Mengzi* 7B37.

53. He recounts a 1572 conversation with his cherished friend Geng Dingli in which Dingli raised this same part of *Mengzi* 7B37 as an implicit critique of Li Zhi's apparent arrogance. In a way similar to what I think he is doing here, Li Zhi took the opportunity to deflect the criticism onto others (see *Li Zhi quan ji zhu*, 2:22). I have seen no surviving document that literally accuses Li Zhi of resembling Yang Zhu. Either he brought that in himself, in his typical hyperbolic fashion, or he was responding to something that is no longer extant. Geng Dingxiang, however, reproaches him for his selfishness in a variety of ways, including an exquisitely indirect reference to Shun's ability to "set himself aside and follow others" (舍己從人; *Mengzi* 2A8). See "Geng to Li [4]" in Li, *A Book to Burn*, 50–51. For a description of the major bones of contention between Li Zhi and Geng Dingxiang, see Rowe, *Crimson Rain*, 96, 98–100. See also de Bary, "Individualism and Humanitarianism," 200, which discusses the accusations of selfishness leveled against Li Zhi together with his response.

54. According to *Mengzi* 7B37.

55. *Li Zhi quan ji zhu*, 1:357.

56. The main argument developed convincingly throughout Jiang, "Heresy and Persecution" is that it was this heteropraxy (rather than heterodoxy) that eventually got Li Zhi into serious trouble.

57. The meaning of "other people" or "the multitudes" is one possible option for *wu* 物, as in the common expression "benefiting others to the detriment of oneself" 損己利物 (e.g., in *Zhou shu* 周書, comp. Linghu Defen 令狐德棻 [Beijing: Zhonghua, 1971], 46.825).

58. Or the Confucian disciple Duanmu Ci 端木賜 (520–446 BCE).

59. *Lunyu* 13.24.

60. The "Last Ruler" was Liu Shan 劉禪 (r. 223–263), who has the reputation of being weak and not well suited to his position; see *Li Zhi quan ji zhu*, 2:231–32.

61. The use of the phrase *hou huan zhe*—apparently to describe Zhuangzi-type people—a few lines later suggests that perhaps it should be interpreted as a type of person, and that *gu hou huan zhe* should therefore be "heeding the far-sighted worry-warts," or some such.

62. The translation of the word *ru* 儒 has been an issue of some contention for the past few decades. This is in part due to its multiple fields of application and long chronological extension. For simplicity's sake, I opt for "Confucian," but it should be understood that this translation has some drawbacks.

63. *Li Zhi quan ji zhu*, 2:232.

64. This connection was already made by Zhu Xi, who when contrasting Mencius and Zhuangzi pointed out that "Zhuangzi lived in a remote location and kept only his own company. . . . His were nothing other than the teachings of Yang Zhu" (莊子……自說，然亦止是楊朱之學) (see Makeham's essays in this volume).

65. My translation assumes that *hou huan zhe* 後患者 actually refers to those who are concerned about *hou huan* (i.e., 顧後患者), as in the lines immediately preceding. This makes the best sense of the logic of the passage.

66. *Li Zhi quan ji zhu*, 2:232.

67. As suggested by A. C. Graham, "The Right to Selfishness: Yangism, Later Mohism, Chuang Tzu," in *Individualism and Holism: Studies in Confucian and Taoist Values*, ed. Donald J. Munro (Ann Arbor: Center for Chinese Studies, University of Michigan, 1985), 77.

68. Su Shi had employed the same analogy in discussing the techniques of Shang Yang and Sang Hongyang but had come to an opposite conclusion: that such strategies appeared exhilarating and convenient but would ultimately prove fatal, as Cold Food Powder had to He Yan. See Su Shi, *Dongpo zhilin* 東坡志林 (Shanghai: Huadong Shifan Daxue, 1983), 5.107–08.

69. *Li Zhi quan ji zhu*, 2:232.

70. Attilio Andreini, "The Yang Mo 楊墨 Dualism and the Rhetorical Construction of Heterodoxy," *Asiatische Studien—Études Asiatiques* 68, no. 4 (2014), 1115–74.

71. For example, in chapters on "Moderate Expenditure" (*Jie yong* 節用; *Mozi jiao zhu* 6.247–48, 254–56), "Moderate Funerals" (*Jie zang* 節葬; *Mozi jiao zhu* 6.262–68), and "Against Music" (*Fei yue* 非樂; *Mozi jiao zhu* 8.379–83).

72. In connection with this passage, it is particularly interesting to note that the Yang Zhu of the *Liezi* 列子 actually does advocate frugality in funerals, and for reasons that have a distinctly Mohist "feel" (see *Liezi jishi* 列子集釋, 7.222, and Brindley, this volume). Thanks to the anonymous reviewer who noticed this additional point of convergence.

73. The association of Shang Yang 商鞅, Shen Buhai 申不害, and Han Feizi 韓非子 (as well as others) with the term *Fajia* 法家 (Legalism) is made in the *Hanshu* 漢書, "Treatise on the Arts and Literature" (Yi wen zhi 藝文志). See Ban Gu 班固, *Hanshu* (Beijing: Zhonghua, 1962), 30.1735. Kidder Smith, "Sima Tan and the Invention of Daoism, 'Legalism,' et Cetera," *Journal of Asian Studies* 62, no. 1 (February 2003): 141–42 has argued against pushing this association even as far back as the *Shiji*, let alone into the Warring States period.

74. *Li Zhi quan ji zhu*, 1:234; trans. Lee, *A Book to Burn*, 79–80.
75. *Li Zhi quan ji zhu*, 1:235; trans. Lee, *A Book to Burn*, 81.
76. *Li Zhi quan ji zhu*, 1:235.
77. *Mengzi* 7B26; trans. adapted from Lau, *Mencius*, 199.
78. See Defoort, this volume.
79. Though see Andreini, "The Yang Mo Dualism," 1146 for a critical assessment of this possibility.
80. The *Hanshu* version of this chapter (4.105–36) is closely parallel with the *Shiji* version (10.413–37). However, in a departure from Ban Gu's usual practice, the evaluation is entirely different, and it is (only) Ban Gu's evaluation that Li Zhi cites.
81. This is likely *Chan* Buddhist terminology, but the meaning is unclear.
82. Li Zhi, *Cang shu* 藏書 (Beijing: Zhonghua, 1959), 3.35. See also *Li Zhi quan ji zhu*, 4:121, where the comment is placed slightly earlier.
83. Li, *Cang shu*, 3.35. An alternative punctuation can be found in Ling Zhilong 凌稚隆 and Li Guangjin 李光縉, *Bubiao Shiji pinglin* 補標史記評林 [Forest of annotations on the Shiji, supplemented and punctuated], punctuation by Arii Hanpei 有井範平, 5 vols. (Taipei: Diqiu chubanshe, 1992), 11.375. There we find a full stop after *yiduan* 異端. This is grammatically more comfortable but leaves the connection between the two sentences very obscure.
84. Li, *Cang shu*, 3.35.
85. Li, *Cang shu*, 3.34.
86. Ling et al., *Shiji pinglin*, 11.372.
87. Ling et al., *Shiji pinglin*, 11.373.
88. See *Mengzi* 3B9.
89. "Reflections on my Life" (*Gankai pingsheng* 感慨平生), written in 1596, describes how his dislike of "taking orders from another person" (屬人管) had a profound effect on many aspects of his life (trans. Martin Huang in Li, *A Book to Burn*, 186; *Li Zhi quan ji zhu*, 2:109).
90. Most notably, his letters to and about Geng Dingxiang in *Fen shu*.
91. Li Zhi admits to and justifies all these actions and others as well in his "Response to Zhou Liutang," trans. Handler-Spitz in *A Book to Burn*, 65–74; *Li Zhi quan ji zhu*, 1:218–26.
92. According to Zhang Wenda's memorial of impeachment, as preserved in Gu Yanwu's *Rizhilu*: "Young men took delight in [Li Zhi's] unrestrained

wildness and goaded one another to follow suit" (後生小子喜其倡狂放肆，相率煽惑), in Li, *A Book to Burn*, 336; Gu Yanwu, *Rizhilu* 日知錄 (Taipei: Wenshizhe, 1979), 20.540.

93. Jiang, "Heresy and Persecution," 3; emphasis added. Jiang adds that "Li Zhi never attacked the existing political system and showed no interest in any Confucian reformist thinking of the time" (20).

94. As in, for example, *Lunyu* 2.4.

95. Li, "Li Zhi and Geng Diangxiang," 51; *Li Zhi quan ji zhu*, 1:72.

96. *Shiji*, 97.2694.

97. Li, "Li Zhi and Geng Diangxiang," 51–52 (with minor alteration); *Li Zhi quan ji zhu*, 1:72.

98. Numerous examples of this can be found in daily life. The omnivore becomes gleefully outraged at catching the sanctimonious vegetarian sneaking a bite of bacon because the sanctimonious vegetarian has made the omnivore feel defensive. Gentle and forbearing vegetarians, who never try to convert or censure anyone, enjoy a far more charitable reception should they suffer the occasional moment of *akrasia*.

99. Li, "Li Zhi and Geng Diangxiang," 53 (slightly altered); *Li Zhi quan ji zhu*, 1:72.

100. According to Timothy Brook's plausible reconstruction of the order of the exchanges (see "Li Zhi and Geng Diangxiang," 34, 53).

101. Trans. de Bary, "Individualism and Humanitarianism," 200; Li Zhi, *Cang shu*, 32.544. De Bary quotes this in the context of showing Li Zhi's opposition to the idea of "having no mind [of one's own]," which de Bary argues was a Neo-Confucian idea that "meant achieving a state of mind in which one has no self-conscious intent or ulterior motive in doing good." The difficulties and outright contradictions in this supposedly Neo-Confucian idea are beyond the scope of this paper, but they become immediately apparent when revisiting de Bary's sources. In brief, "selfishness" is probably not a good translation of *si* 私 in this context, but I have left it as is, since it is meant only to illustrate how Li Zhi has been interpreted.

102. For example, in Graham, "The Right to Selfishness."

103. See *Li Zhi quan ji ping*, 2:22.

104. Trans. adapted from Handler-Spitz in Li, *A Book to Burn*, 148.

III

From the Qing Dynasty Onward

Chapter 8

The Birth of the Image of the "Egoist-Epicurean Philosopher" Yang Zhu during the Meiji Period

MASAYUKI SATO

Introduction

This chapter aims to investigate how young Japanese intellectuals of the Meiji period (1868–1912) have expounded on Yang Zhu's thought under the scholarly framework of "philosophy."[1] As an academic discipline, philosophy had been imported and was more or less systematically taught at Tokyo University during that time.[2] In other words, the rise of interest in Yang Zhu's "philosophy" paralleled a broader strand of the Meiji intellectual milieu in which the academic discipline of "Chinese philosophy" or "Oriental philosophy" was born and developed from the 1880s onward.

To begin with, around the time of the Meiji restoration in 1867, no traditional Japanese intellectual seems to have shown any specific interest in Yang Zhu himself or his thought. However, Tokugawa intellectuals were likely familiar with the name of Yang Zhu, and to some degree his thought, since Yang Zhu was harshly criticized in the *Mencius*.

Admittedly, the indifference of traditional Japanese intellectuals toward Yang Zhu can also be explained by the fact that the available source material for accessing the actual life and thought of Yang Zhu had been scarce. For instance, in the catalogs of dynastic historical records since the "Treatise on Literature" in the *Book of Han*, no sources can be found under the heading of "Yang Zhu." This suggests that since at least the Later Han period, Yang Zhu's thought was already obscure. Thus, in order to know about Yang Zhu's life (albeit a legendary one) and thought, two kinds of source materials have been available for traditional intellectuals and modern scholars: (1) fragmented passages about Yang Zhu in the *Mencius*, the *Zhuangzi*, *Mr. Lü's Spring and Autumn Annals*, and the *Huainanzi*, among others; and (2) several paragraphs in the chapters "Li ming" 力命 (Effort and Destiny) and "Yang Zhu" in the *Liezi*. Nevertheless, scholars have long suspected that the *Liezi* had been forged in the period of Northern and Southern dynasties.

Indeed, in the eyes of traditional intellectuals who had finished their education in Chinese classics before the Meiji Restoration, Yang Zhu was not worth being studied as one of the major Warring States masters. For example, Hagiwara Yutaka 萩原裕 (1829–1898), who was a successor of the Mito 水戸 school of the Tokugawa period, completely omitted Yang Zhu in his monograph on the thought of Warring States masters, which he published in 1890.[3]

As mentioned previously, the rise of interest in Yang Zhu's "philosophy" paralleled the growth of the academic discipline of "Chinese philosophy" or "Oriental philosophy" mainly at Tokyo University during the 1880s and 1890s. One can observe its birth and significant development in the following two examples. Firstly, the person who believed in the need to set up what we now call the academic discipline of "Chinese philosophy" or "Oriental philosophy" was Katō Hiroyuki 加藤弘之 (1836–1916), the president of Tokyo University. In order to attain this goal, he assigned Inoue Tetsujirō 井上哲次郎 (1856–1944, hereafter "Tetsujirō"), one of the first graduates (1780, Meiji 13), to edit a book entitled *History of Oriental Philosophy*. Soon after that, Tetsujirō started to offer his Oriental philosophy course based on that material.[4]

Second, during the last two decades of the nineteenth century, young graduates trained in the discipline of "philosophy" at the Imperial University (formerly Tokyo University)[5] pursued research in which they eagerly sought out "philosophical" elements in the Chinese intellectual tradition, especially in the texts of the Warring State masters, and accordingly reformulated these elements as the "philosophy" of those masters. Therefore, up until the first decade of the twentieth century, major early Chinese thinkers such as Confucius, Mencius, Xunzi, Laozi, Zhuangzi, and Han Fei were all called Chinese "philosophers" without any hesitation.

In this intellectual trend, Yang Zhu was also transfigured: he was one of the forgotten Warring States masters and had now become a significant "philosopher" on par with those in the Western philosophical tradition.

What comes as a surprise is that among the Meiji discourses about Warring States thinkers, there were more than a few of these who were associated with Yang Zhu.[6] In a word, Yang Zhu was of apparent interest to young intellectuals in that period. Similarly, in the general histories dedicated to "Chinese philosophy" and "Chinese ethics" (*Shina tetsugaku* 支那哲學 and *Shina rinri* 支那倫理) or "Oriental philosophy" and "Oriental ethics" (*Tōyō tetsugaku* 東洋哲學 and *Tōyō rinri* 東洋倫理) in the last few decades of the Meiji period, Yang Zhu was a familiar figure, often called "Master Yang" (Yōshi 楊子). Hence, almost all monographs in the history of Chinese (or Oriental) philosophy of that period (around 1890–1900) contained a section explaining Yang Zhu's thought. Under such a trend, some authors even adopted the term the "Yang Zhu school," representing the distinctiveness of Yang Zhu's "philosophy," which was comparable to that of major Western counterparts such as Aristippus, Epicurus, Spinoza, and Nietzsche.

In order to fully explore this topic, four kinds of source materials during the Meiji period become important tools for analysis: (1) lecture notes by students; (2) lecture transcripts[7] published by lecturers; (3) monographs and essays relevant to Yang Zhu; and (4) articulations relevant to Yang Zhu in the monographs and articles about the general history of "Chinese philosophy/ethics" or "Oriental philosophy/ethics." Our discussion mainly proceeds in chronological order.[8]

In this way, we hope to show how Yang Zhu, whose thought had been underexplored by traditional intellectuals, was gradually elevated, positively or negatively, to be one of the indispensable "philosophers" of the Chinese/Oriental intellectual tradition, one who had a substantial philosophical vision to present for the people living in the Meiji period. As to why Yang Zhu enjoyed so much attention compared with other ancient Chinese thinkers, we may presume two possible reasons. First, some ancient Greek thinkers had advocated "similar" perspectives (at least in the eyes of the Meiji scholars); and second, intellectuals of the Meiji period came to feel that the rise of individualism or antisocial trends was parallel to the prevalence of Yang Zhu's philosophy during the Warring States period. This recognition had driven young Meiji scholars into feeling the necessity to criticize or overcome Yang Zhu's thought, just as Mencius did.

1. The Beginning of the "Discipline of Oriental Philosophy" and the Advent of Yang Zhu as a "Philosopher"

Tokyo University was set up in 1877 (Meiji 10). In the following year, the Faculty of Letters was divided into the Department of History, Philosophy, and Politics and the Department of Japanese and Chinese Classics. Even though we are certain that "philosophy" courses were compulsory for all history, philosophy, and politics majors, it remains unclear whether what we now call "Chinese philosophy" was incorporated into the course content. We can, at least, observe the treatment of Chinese philosophy in a course report by an anonymous author, which has been incorporated into *The Handbook of the Three Faculties of Tokyo University* based on the record of 1883 (Meiji 16). According to the report, we know that Tokyo University started to run lectures on "Chinese philosophy" with some mention of Yang Zhu. The report says:

> The course of philosophy is divided into two subjects: Eastern Philosophy and Western Philosophy. . . . In order to understand [and teach] the mainstream evolution of the former, Chinese Philosophy and Indian Philosophy are the most fundamental topics [in the history of all the Eastern Philosophies]. . . . A large part of the philosophical arguments after the Qin-Han period was based upon those of the Warring States period. Hence, the course [on Chinese Philosophy] starts with the doctrines of Warring States masters such as Confucius, Lao, Yang, Zhuang, and Mo. In order to help students acquire gradual comprehension of the outline of East Asian Philosophy, the course tries to discern right and wrong, the merit and demerit of their doctrines, and to clarify the uniqueness [of each] and their relationship to the doctrines of other schools.[9]

According to my knowledge, which is based on various records of that time, the following three courses associated with ancient Chinese philosophy were offered at the initial stage of Tokyo University: (1) relatively fragmented explanations about Chinese philosophy in courses such as philosophy or sociology offered from December 1882 to October 1883 by Ernest Francisco Fenollosa (1853–1908), an American instructor who had graduated from Harvard University before coming to Japan;[10] (2) a History of Oriental Philosophy course[11] offered from winter 1882 to fall 1883 by Inoue Tetsujirō; (3) a Chinese Philosophy course offered by Shimada Chōrei 島田重禮 (1838–1898) from September 1885 to the spring of 1887.

Even though during his professional stay in Japan Fenollosa did not provide any course specifically on Chinese philosophy, in a lecture on philosophy or sociology (presumably from December 1882 to October 1883) he articulated his ideas about the development of Chinese philosophy.[12] In this lecture, Fenollosa briefly mentioned Yang Zhu's philosophy and its role in ancient Chinese philosophy. Fenollosa believed that philosophy and actual social developments closely influenced each other and progressed dialectically. He believed that "if we can unite the doctrines of Spencer's evolution and Hegel's philosophy, we will have a complete philosophy."[13] He thus saw the unfolding of Chinese philosophy as continuous loops of the dialectic process of thesis, antithesis, and synthesis. Through this theoretical perspective, Fenollosa classified Warring States strands of thought into three schools, for which he had no specific names, instead classifying them with ordinal description such as the "First school," "Second school," and "Third school." The "First school" referred primarily to Confucian philosophers such as Confucius, Mencius, Xunzi, and Yang Xiong 揚雄 (53 BCE–18 CE); the "Second school" consisted of Daoists such as Laozi, Zhuangzi, and Liezi, as well as Han Feizi; Yang Zhu and Mozi belonged to the "Third school." In his view, the "First school" comprised the scholars who sought to establish an ideal government by means of the realization of the principles of humaneness (仁 ren) and justice (義 yi). The "Second school" held a negative view about worldly affairs and aimed at emulating the rationality and laws derived from the patterns of heaven and earth, which supposedly was the translation of the dao 道 for Fenollosa.

The Third school was not a simple synthesis of the previous schools, since the radical egoism advocated by Yang Zhu was different from both. As a developmental stage, Mozi also belonged to the Third school and further synthesized Yang Zhu's egoism and the First school's altruism. Just as the Mohists failed to synthesize the apparently incompatible doctrines of "egoism" and "altruism,"[14] Yang Zhu's principle of "Epicureanism" also failed to become the dominant school of thought. For this reason, Mohism and Yang Zhu fell into immediate decline despite their past popularity.[15]

Inoue Tetsujirō described Yang Zhu in his lecture notes for History of Oriental Philosophy, a course he taught the year before his departure to Europe for six years of overseas study and teaching. As far as we know, this course was the first given on Oriental philosophy by an East Asian scholar who had received modern academic training in philosophy.

As we look into what Tetsujirō taught in his course on Oriental philosophy, although the course name suggests a broad scope of materials covered, the content of what he actually taught focused on early Chinese philosophy, extending only to the Han period. Thanks to the preservation of two lecture notes, we are privy to what he taught in his lectures. According to the notes, Tetsujirō's depiction of Yang Zhu appears in the section titled "General Introduction to Chinese Philosophy," which presumably had been allocated to the second lecture.[16] Tetsujirō divided the development of Chinese philosophy into five stages, of which the second stage features speculation. Commenting on this stage, Tetsujirō said:

> Confucius explained humaneness; Mencius explained humaneness, righteousness, and human nature being good; Xunzi explained human nature as being bad; Lao and Zhuang explained nothingness and wild talk; Yang and Mo raised their own explanations.[17]

Having listed these prominent Warring States thinkers, Tetsujirō indicated the equivalents of their thought and doctrines in Western philosophy. Based on the "Yang Zhu" chapter of the *Liezi*, he characterized Yang Zhu's thought as follows:

> Sixth, the "Yang Zhu" chapter says: "In general, the chance to live is so difficult to encounter and to die so easy . . ." and "what should we do and what should we enjoy during our life? Only to pursue the beautiful and tasteful, only to pursue sound and colors." These opinions are similar to the "hedonism" of figures such as Democritus, Aristotle, and Epicurus as much as they are close to "perception-ism" of figures such as Condillac and Helvétius.[18]

In the last part of the section, Tetsujirō recapitulates prevalent Warring States thinkers' orientations under six positions: Confucius/altruism; Yang Zhu/egoism; Mozi/impartial love; Laozi and Zhuangzi/laissez-faire; Shen Buhai and Han Feizi/interventionism; Guanzi and Shang Yang/utilitarianism.[19] Tetsujirō's construction of Yang Zhu as a "hedonist" and "egoist" seems to have come from Fenollosa's presentation of "Yang Zhu, the Third School" as demonstrating "egoism" and "Epicurean hedonism." While Tetsujirō learned Western philosophy from Fenollosa, Tetsujirō, in turn, might have helped him summarize the main ideas of Warring States as Fenollosa articulated his image of dialectical scholarly division in early Chinese philosophy.

The third scholar who lectured on Chinese philosophy at the Faculty of Letters at Tokyo University was Shimada Chōrei.[20] Shimada had completed his studies before the end of the Tokugawa period. Soon after the Meiji Restoration, he started to teach Chinese classics in his own tutoring school. Accordingly, he was invited to teach at the Faculty of Letters of Tokyo University. That was in 1879 (Meiji 12), just one year before Tetsujirō graduated. Two years later, Shimada was promoted to full professorship.[21]

It is probably due to Tetsujirō's leaving for Europe in 1884 (Meiji 17) that Shimada started teaching the course Chinese Philosophy from September 1885 to the spring of the next year. For the period from 1885 to 1887 he followed Tetsujirō's aforementioned way of instruction, arranging his lectures on the history of Chinese philosophy in chronological order. There were two differences between Tetsujirō and Shimada: (1) Shimada's course took two whole academic years to complete all the lectures; and (2) it covered materials from the beginning of Chinese civilization to the end of the Qing dynasty, whereas Tetsujirō's "History of Oriental Philosophy" had only reached Yang Xiong and the end of the Former Han period.[22] Therefore, Shimada's History of Chinese Philosophy can be considered the first to have been taught at any modern higher educational institution that covered the entirety of Chinese history.

So then, how did Shimada expound on the philosophy of Yang Zhu? In his lecture notes, the name Yang Zhu appears in four units: "Mencius' rebutting heresy" (Feb. 17, 1886), "Yang Zhu and Mo Di" (Feb. 24), "Liezi" (Jun. 2), and "Mozi" (Oct. 8). Compared with Fenollosa and Tetsujirō's expositions, Shimada's understanding of Yang Zhu's thought is represented in the following three points:

Firstly, instead of focusing on the term "profit" (*li* 利), as in the case of Fenollosa and Tetsujirō, Shimada instead took the term "love" (*ai* 愛) to delineate the characteristic of Yang Zhu's thought. In the lecture of February 24, he taught the following:

> Master Yang advised "self-love," whereas Master Mo advocated "impartial love." Due to the observation that people in his day

were confused by reputation and subsequently confused to the point of losing their own feelings, Master Yang suggested that one should value and love oneself so as to correct prevalent deficiencies. He probably did not intend to establish a new school but only wanted to stay away from the world and keep himself pure. His thought was developed into a school of thought by people who imitated him.[23]

Shimada contrasted Yang Zhu's thought with the Mohist position of "impartial love" and "love without difference," thus identifying Yang Zhu's position with "loving oneself"[24] and "self-love" (自愛).[25] In this respect, Shimada's understanding differed significantly from both Fenollosa and Tetsujirō, who employed the expression "benefiting oneself" (利己).

Secondly, Shimada maintained that the argument found in the "Yang Zhu" chapter of the *Liezi* further developed Yang Zhu's idea of "self-love." Shimada pointed out: "Master Lie concentrated on valuing equanimity and an empty heart; he privileged the love for one's own body and aimed at preserving the natural endowments by precluding confusion and attraction caused by external things."[26] Shimada took this as a further development of Yang Zhu's notion of "not letting external things take over one's heart" and stated:

> Master Lie (i.e., Liezi) took Yang Zhu's "loving oneself" as the core and consolidated it with the thought of Laozi and the Yellow Emperor. The content of his thought was to let go of oneself in the void and naturalness. This view can be seen as a strand of retrogressionism.[27]

According to Shimada, Master Lie's idea of "letting go of oneself in the void and naturalness" originated from Yang Zhu's idea of "self-love." From our observation of the available source materials written by Meiji intellectuals about Warring States thought, Shimada was the first scholar who tried to clarify a scholarly linage of Daoism by comparing the fragmentary passages about Yang Zhu in the *Mencius* with the more organized arguments presented in the *Liezi* and the *Laozi*. In other words, Shimada believed that the essential philosophical position of Yang Zhu's thought should be understood within the course of the development of pre-Qin Daoist philosophy.

Thirdly, as mentioned previously, although Shimada himself belonged to the generation of traditional scholars of Chinese classics who did not receive any systematic knowledge or training in philosophy, as in the case of Fenollosa and Tetsujirō, this does not mean, however, that Shimada was unaware of or indifferent to those terms and theories which had developed in the Western philosophical tradition. If we look closely at Shimada's use of terms to evaluate or devaluate the significance of Yang Zhu's thought, he did not hesitate to adopt those Western terms in his lecture. For example, Shimada called Master Lie's thought "naturalistic retrogression," even though not explicitly addressing Yang Zhu's thought. It is worth noting that Shimada also spoke of "retrogression" (*taiho* 退步) and "-ism" (*shugi* 主義), both of which Tokugawa intellectuals had not previously known as conceptual tools for discussing the value and problems of certain kinds of thought. From this we can see that Shimada, who has long been regarded as one of the "typical" traditional scholars of Chinese classics (e.g., by the so-called "Kyoto school" Sinologists during the twentieth century), was reasonably progressive in importing Western terms to explicate the thought of Warring States thinkers, even though he may not have understood Western philosophy in the way Tetsujirō and other young Japanese intellectuals did, not to mention Fenollosa.

Thus far, we have reviewed the accounts of Yang Zhu's thought by Fenollosa, Tetsujirō, and Shimada during the initial stage of the Faculty of Letters at Tokyo University from 1882 to 1885 (Meiji 15 to 18). In the process of shaping the academic discipline and research field of Chinese (or Oriental) philosophy during the middle Meiji period, there was one more important scholar, namely Inoue Enryō 井上圓了 (1958–1919, hereafter "Enryō"), who likewise played an indispensable role in its development. Unlike the three scholars mentioned previously, whose understandings and ideas about Chinese philosophy can only be obtained from unpublished lecture manuscripts compiled mainly by their students,[28] Enryō was the first Japanese (and also the first East Asian) intellectual who published both commercial and scholarly monographs and articles (Enryō also established and managed a publishing company) about issues relevant to Chinese philosophy and ethics based on more or less systematic import of knowledge and intellectual skills of Western philosophy.[29]

Significantly, Enryō's account of Chinese philosophy employed the interpretive framework of the dialectical evolutionary model in which "society" and "philosophy" should interact under the dialectical principle. In this manner of explaining the development of philosophy, we can clearly find Fenollosa's influence. Compared with Tetsujirō's lax attitude of searching for objects of comparison with Western philosophy and

Shimada's rather traditional and philological approach to interpreting the philosophical significance of the Warring States masters, Enryō's account of ancient Chinese philosophy is more or less philosophically sophisticated. One reason for having attained that goal is his adoption of Fenollosa's dialectical model for explaining the development of early Chinese philosophy. In addition, Enryō assumed that a dialectical dynamism of the development of early Chinese philosophy was caused by the philosophical confrontation between Confucianism (Confucius) and Daoism (Laozi). Apparently, such an analytic framework was influenced by Fenollosa's idea that the first school and the second school confronted each other, the dynamism which led to the third school. In this way, Enryō's primary scholarly interest was in clarifying the similarities and differences between the philosophies of Confucius and Laozi. Therefore, there is little mention of Yang Zhu in the "Chinese philosophy" of his *Lectures of Pure Philosophy* (純正哲學講義) published in 1891–92 (Meiji 25–26). Here Enryō first sorted out various strands of thought in the Warring States period and classified Yang Zhu as the "Yang school" (楊家). Concerning his thought, Enryō commented:

> Yang Zhu advocated "loving oneself"; Mozi was for "impartial love"; in opposing Confucianism they each founded the doctrines of their own schools. Mencius strived with all his force to refute them, proclaiming, "whoever can rebut Yang Zhu and Mozi with correct words is the follower of Sage."[30]

In interpreting Yang Zhu's thought, Enryō adopted the term "love" instead of "benefit." This understanding of Yang Zhu's thought was closer to Shimada's construal of "Yang Zhu's self-love" than to Fenollosa's and Tetsujirō's views, which were more focused on the elements of benefit in Yang Zhu's thought—although it was evident that Enryō's understanding of Yang Zhu's philosophy surely was more in line with Fenollosa and Tetsujirō's analytical framework.

2. The Study of Yang Zhu by Young Scholars of Chinese Philosophy in the Meiji Twenties

This section introduces arguments about Yang Zhu by three young "researchers": Takigawa Kametarō 瀧川龜太郎 (1865–1946), Matsumoto

Bunsaburō 松本文三郎 (1869–1944), and Nishiwaki Gyokuhō 西脇玉峰 (dates unknown).[31] Although the department or institute they graduated from was different, they both learned the discipline of Chinese philosophy in the third decade of the Meiji period. Since Fenollosa left Tokyo University in 1886 (Meiji 19) and Tetsujirō also departed to Europe for his oversea studies in 1884 (Meiji 17), only Takigawa of the three young scholars was able to attend Tetsujirō's classes. In terms of age, we may say that Takigawa belonged to Enryō's generation, while Matsumoto and Nishiwaki were a bit younger. Therefore, they trained in a more organized manner with more affluent educational resources than were available when Enryō and Takigawa studied. Such different conditions perhaps facilitated post-Takigawa scholars to produce more detailed and well-articulated arguments than those of the previous generation, whose statements about Yang Zhu were more or less limited to outlining Yang Zhu's thought based upon well-known remarks or passages in the *Mencius*. While the younger scholars tried to introduce Yang Zhu's thought with more care, they also advanced their discussions to assess the strengths and weaknesses of Yang Zhu's thought against its counterparts in Western philosophy, such as Epicurus's (341–270 BCE) school in ancient Greece.

Takigawa published two articles on the subject of Yang Zhu's philosophy: one was "Discussing Yang Zhu" (楊朱を論ず)[32] and the other was "One Aspect of Ancient Chinese Philosophy" (支那古代哲學史一斑). The process of publication of the latter was a bit complicated. This work was initially written as Takigawa's graduation thesis for the Imperial University. After his graduation, it was published in the *Journal of Oriental Studies* (東洋學藝雜誌)[33] as four serial essays, all of which shared the same title and were numbered from one to four. Accordingly, a publisher again combined them into a monograph and published it under the title *History of Ancient Chinese Philosophy* (支那古代哲學史, 2 vols.) without either asking permission or sending a notice to the author. Takigawa felt embarrassed when he happened to find out that his articles had been published as a monograph a few years after its publication as a series.[34]

To my knowledge, the essay "Discussing Yang Zhu," published in 1890 (Meiji 23), was the first essay in print that has "Yang Zhu" in its title. However, its content is centered on Takigawa's general explanation of what he considered the characteristics of Warring States thought. He starts with sorting out features of the Warring States masters and then gives six reasons for why their thought had arisen in that period. Takigawa mentions Yang Zhu twice: in the beginning and closing parts of the essay, respectively. The first mention occurs in his account of the "Yang school":

> [Yang Zhu's] saying is that the life of people is [no more than] like morning dew, in which people just live up their days in pleasure as much as possible, not sacrificing their pleasure to benefiting others.[35]

In the concluding part, based on the "Fan lun" 氾論 (Boundless Discourses) chapter of *Huainanzi* 淮南子, Takigawa explains how Warring States thinkers criticized each other.

> The Mohist came out on the scene by opposing Confucians' teachings of ritual and music. In criticizing Mohism, Yang Zhu put forward [the idea that people need to] preserve nature, maintain the authentic, and not allow [outer] objects to burden one's body. Mencius was for opposing Mohism.[36]

Takigawa's more detailed observations on the philosophy of Yang Zhu can be found in his *History of Ancient Chinese Philosophy*.[37] Under the title of "The School of Yang," the discussion starts with a short introductory remark.[38] The main body of the discussion is divided into two sections: "Yang Zhu's biography" and "the origin of his doctrines," respectively. Takigawa's account of Yang Zhu's teaching starts from page five. In Takigawa's exploration of Yang Zhu's philosophy, the two chapters "Li Ming" and "Yang Zhu" of the *Liezi* serve as the textual basis for investigating features of Yang Zhu's thought.

In the second part, from the side of Confucius and Mencius's philosophical position, Takigawa starts his criticism against a theoretical flaw in Yang Zhu's philosophy, namely its tendency to disconnect individuals from their society. This remark is followed by Takigawa's comparison of Yang Zhu's thought with the hedonism of the Greek philosopher Aristippus (ca. 435–356 BCE) and Baruch de Spinoza's (1632–1677) view of nature. Takigawa assumed that the characteristics of Yang Zhu's philosophy could be summarized into the following three points.

First, the pleasures that he advocated were immediate and sensual, particularly those related to appetites for food and sex. Yang Zhu's hedonism did not include spiritual pleasure, which set him apart from Epicureanism. Second, Yang Zhu's "for oneself" had at its core the notion of individual independence for each person and nonaltruism toward others. In other words, the human world would be well governed as long as everyone takes care of oneself. And third, based on Zhang Zhan's 張湛

reading of the "Li Ming" chapter, Yang Zhu's fatalism was opposed to Mozi's antifatalism. Takigawa was critical of "Yang Zhu's theory because it would discourage people from having the motivation to improve or develop themselves, inevitably making them drift into self-indulgence and self-degradation."[39] Comparing Yang Zhu's and Spinoza's views of nature, Takigawa presumed that the latter could also be regarded as "fatalism." Indeed, nature as the growth and decline of things in Spinoza's view belongs to a realm entirely beyond human knowledge; nonetheless it does not mean that nature remains unknown to humans forever. Takigawa believed that since everything has a cause and a consequence, the unknown realm would become knowable as long as human knowledge sufficiently advances in the future.

In addition to expounding on Yang Zhu's thought and comparing it with Western counterparts, Takigawa also critically assessed its value. His perspective can be summarized in three points. First, as mentioned previously, Yang Zhu's fatalism could make people drift into self-indulgence and self-degradation. Second, similarly, the pitfall of Yang Zhu's hedonism in pursuit of bodily pleasure lies in seducing people into uncontrolled self-indulgence. Third, Yang Zhu's doctrine of "for oneself" "not only failed to retain peace in society but also would corrupt the fundamental principle for making society exist." Indeed, Takigawa employed the term *shakai* 社會 (society), which had not appeared in traditional Chinese classics. Concerning this point, Takigawa even emphasized that "we must abolish Yang Zhu's doctrine of 'not benefitting others even with one single hair.'" According to Takigawa, this is because

> society does not consist of one single person but contains more than one person. Therefore, people [in a society] provide others with many things while receiving things that they lack. Also, people are expected to extend their own love toward others. In doing so, they come to love each other and benefit each other. It is on this basis that a society can attain its consolidation. This can be called "morality."[40]

In this passage, it is worth noting that the term "morality" (*dōtoku* 道德 in the original Japanese) here was not the compound word *daode* 道德 in the traditional sense, which consists of "the Way" (道) and "virtue" (德), but was referring instead to "the ethical foundations for setting up a society"—namely, the term *dōtoku* precisely in the sense of contemporary Japanese usage. Takigawa's argument has shown us the intellectual process by which the formal study of Chinese classics (Takigawa was a graduate from the program in Chinese and Japanese classics) gradually transformed into philosophical discourse. In this case, an argument about Yang Zhu's thought began to be oriented toward addressing a more general issue, namely, "the necessity of a social morality." It is precisely in this sense, albeit negatively, that Meiji intellectuals eventually discovered a "philosophy" in Yang Zhu's argument.

For our exploration, another vital young scholar is Nishiwaki Gyokuhō, who graduated from the Philosophy Academy (Tetsugakukan or Tetsugakkan 哲學館) in 1894 (Meiji 27). The Philosophy Academy was a college-level private school set up by Inoue Enryō in 1887. Since during Nishiwaki's study period several instructors in the Academy (including those who taught Chinese philosophy) were graduates of Tokyo University, Nishiwaki is thought to have received his philosophical training mainly from those instructors who belonged to Enryō's generation.[41]

Nishiwaki's article entitled "A Study of Yang Zhu" (楊朱論) was the second topical article focusing on Yang Zhu. It was published in *Oriental Philosophy* in 1895,[42] eight years after Takigawa had published his "Discussing Yang Zhu" in 1888. The content of "A Study of Yang Zhu" is divided into eight sections: "A concise biography of Yang Zhu," "scholarly lineage," "general introduction," "benefiting oneself," "self-indulgence," "nurturing life," "heavenly mandate," and "conclusion." This argumentative organization of the article was apparently more systematic than that of Takigawa. From such a well-organized arrangement of the discussion, we can assume Nishiwaki's ambition for presenting a more systematic and comprehensive account of Yang Zhu's thought *as a philosophy*.

Nishiwaki's discussion of Yang Zhu's thought was primarily based on his close textual analysis of four chapters of the *Liezi*, namely, "Yang Zhu," "Li ming," "Huang Di" 黃帝 (the Yellow Emperor), and "Shuo fu" 說符 (Explaining Conjunction). His textual sources and comparisons with the hedonism of Aristippus do not differ significantly from Takigawa's view. There is also agreement in indicating the inconsistency between "individual pursuits" and "attainment of social order." Nishiwaki also considered this Yang Zhu's weakness:

> Master Yang's perspective was considerably narrow. He witnessed only one side of society; he did not penetrate the other side of it. In other words, he only understood that there were

individual persons; he ignored the existence of society. Although master Yang's doctrine apparently seemed to be good and virtuous, and thus could be regarded as worth following, it cannot be practiced in the realm of state and society. Indeed, Master Yang's theory can be fulfilled only in such a solitary island as where Robinson Crusoe had to live.[43]

Takigawa and Nishiwaki's critical position toward Yang Zhu was grounded in the belief of the human need for forming a society and state. While Nishiwaki followed Takigawa's viewpoint on Yang Zhu (described in the *Liezi*) being a further development of Laozi's philosophy, he also presumed that there was an inevitable intellectual condition that germinated Yang Zhu's thought. In his eyes, the whole scene of Warring States thought became tied up with the formalization of Confucian thought. Initially, Confucians made an effort to rescue people's minds from "moral corruption."[44] However, they had gradually lost vitality and humanistic motivation, ending up degrading themselves down to merely being slaves of ritual formality. Nishiwaki called such Warring States Confucians "wooden robots."[45] Laozi's denial of humaneness and righteousness and Mozi's condemnation of Confucians were repugnant to those degraded Confucians. Likewise, Yang Zhu's "egoistic hedonism" (利己快樂主義)[46] was also considered to be a reaction against Confucians' superiority and solemnness. Yang Zhu rejected the ethical values of ancient sages that Confucians worshiped, and he moved on to criticize them as unable to understand the root of human nature, mind/heart, and emotions. Yang Zhu thus held that one should not diverge from the original state of one's mind/heart. He also believed that if each individual loved her/himself according to nature and let genuine nature be in charge, the world would be in order.[47]

The next scholar we will discuss is Matsumoto Bunsaburō 松本文三郎. Matsumoto graduated from the Faculty of Letters (philosophy major) at Imperial University in 1893 (Meiji 26). After study in Germany, he was appointed as a professor at Kyoto Imperial University in 1906 (Meiji 39), which was established in 1897 (Meiji 30). In that period, he was well known for his research on Buddhism. Interestingly, however, his *History of Ancient Chinese Philosophy*, which was published in 1904 (Meiji 36) as "monograph-styled" lecture notes at Waseda University, did not contain anything on Buddhism.[48] Although the publication date of Takase

Takejirō's monograph *Philosophies of Yang Zhu and Mozi*, which will be discussed in the next section, was prior to Matsumoto's aforementioned work, it would be wise to discuss Matsumoto's view first and then move to Takase's, both because Matsumoto graduated five years earlier[49] than Takase and because Matsumoto had already started to teach the course History of Chinese Philosophy in places such as the Philosophy Academy and Tokyo Senmon Gakkō (later becoming Waseda University) right after his graduation.

In his *History of Ancient Chinese Philosophy*, Matsumoto's exposition of Yang Zhu's thought is placed under the subject of the "Yang school" (楊家) in "the Second Jingchu (荊楚) School after Laozi."[50] His discussion of Yang Zhu is divided into three sections, none of which has its own sub-topics. Matsumoto tried to assess Yang Zhu's hedonism from the comparative perspective between the Eastern and Western histories of philosophy. He called Yang Zhu's doctrine "egoistic pleasure" (利己的快樂) and saw it as a more radical counterpart to Epicurus's hedonism.[51] Generally speaking, compared to Takigawa and Nishiwaki, Matsumoto invested more effort in articulating the content of Yang Zhu's teachings from a perspective of the history of philosophy, and he thus borrowed more philosophical terms to explain its philosophical traits.[52]

Let us look at Matsumoto's adoption of philosophical terms first. Matsumoto held that Yang Zhu's philosophy "transformed" Laozi's misanthropic thought into an extreme variation of egoism.[53] Soon after that argument, Matsumoto maintained that "the Way of Yang Zhu" (楊朱之道) can be explained with two elements, namely, "absolute egoism" (絕對的利己主義) and "absolute hedonism" (絕對的快樂主義).[54] He also noted that Yang Zhu's teachings lacked the elements of "cosmology" (in Matsumoto's term, *uchū'ron* 宇宙論) and politics seen in the thought of Laozi. Matsumoto wrote:

> The content of Yang Zhu's argument mainly involved moral matters and completely lacked elements of cosmology and political affairs, which constituted the most fundamental parts of Laozi's theory.[55]

Of course, the term "cosmology" (宇宙論) did not appear in traditional Chinese literature.

Next, how did Matsumoto, whether positively or negatively, assess Yang Zhu's philosophy? Matsumoto picked up two elements in Yang

Zhu's philosophy, "hedonism" and "egoism," and critiqued them respectively. Against "hedonism" he argued that in order to enjoy greater pleasure, we often have to miss out on minor pleasures at hand. Against Yang's "egoism," he pointed out that if one chooses not to benefit others with even just a hair of one's own, then one will be treated by others on the same grounds. Therefore, Yang Zhu's egoism ended up being harmful. According to Matsumoto's opinion:

> The inevitable outcome of Master Yang's egoism is that followers of the doctrine end up going against the state's organization. In particular, they discard moral duty such as a sense of loyalty. He insisted that loyalty was not sufficient to bring security to a state.[56]

Here, Matsumoto does not use the term "society" (社會) but rather the expression "the state's organization" (國家の組織), which seems to strongly suggest Matsumoto's critical point against Yang Zhu's egoism: that it may cause the disintegration of human community.

3. Takase Takejirō's *Philosophies of Yang Zhu and Mozi*

The last section of the current chapter examines the part of "Yang Zi's philosophy" in Takase Takejirō's 高瀬武次郎 (1869–1950) monograph *Philosophies of Yang Zhu and Mozi* (楊墨哲學). Takase graduated from the Faculty of Letters (Chinese classics major) at Imperial University in 1898 (Meiji 31) and acquired his doctoral degree in philosophy of pre-Qin masters in 1905 (Meiji 38). Starting from 1907 he taught at Kyoto Imperial University.[57] During the Meiji period, he was in charge of a column of studies of the *Analects* for *Oriental Philosophy*, but later he shifted his publication interest to Wang Yangming and traditional Japanese classics. Apart from the previously mentioned publications, he also published monographs on the philosophies of Laozi and Zhuangzi. In 1910 (Meiji 43) his doctoral dissertation was published as a monograph entitled *History of Chinese Philosophy*.[58] This book has been highly admired as the most "systematic study" of this subject among all general histories of Chinese philosophy of that period.[59]

Takase's *Philosophies of Yang Zhu and Mozi*, published in 1901 (Meiji 35), was the first book published explicitly on Mohism and Yang Zhu's philosophy.[60] It consists of two parts: "Mozi's philosophy" and "Yang Zhu's philosophy," each standing as an independent "sub-monograph" combined into one book.[61] The part on Yang Zhu's philosophy comprises three sections: (1) "The Origin," (2) "Yang Zhu's doctrine," and (3) an "Appendix," which contains a supplemental argument about ancient and contemporary views on egoism. As a scholarly monograph, this book also stands out in four other respects: (1) it has a "bibliography," (2) it provides a comprehensive review on ancient and contemporary views on egoism, (3) it includes a "preface" by Tetsujirō,[62] and (4) all textual quotations are translated into modern Japanese by Takase himself to facilitate accessibility for the readers who were not specialists in classical Chinese texts.

The first part, "The Origin," starts by exploring Yang Zhu's life, scholarly lineage, and relation to Laozi's thought. Concerning the scholarly lineage, Takase put forward a novel perspective: he did not rule out the possibility that Yang Zhu personally received teachings from Laozi. In the *Liezi*, Takase found six points that can be commonly observed in the thought of Laozi: (1) do not show off your inner virtues; (2) do not be misled by appearances; (3) benefit-harm and blessing-condemnation interact like echoes; (4) do good, yet stay away from fame and reputation; (5) only when the reputation of loyalty and justice has come to an end will the relationship between the ruler and the ruled be secured, because as long as the virtues of loyalty and justice prevail, no one needs to admire them; and (6) one cannot get to the right destination when the ways are too varied.

In the second part, "Yang Zhu's doctrine," Takase classified it into the following nine philosophical elements: (1) egoism, (2) hedonism, (3) "discourse on name and substance" (名實論), (4) discourse on nurturing life and celebrating death, (5) discourse on taking pleasure in life, (6) discourse on life and death, (7) discourse on suicide (against suicide), (8) discourse on resting in peace in one's life, and (9) discourse on fatalism.

Compared to the aforementioned scholars' manner of discussion, in which they compared Yang Zhu's thought directly with Western philosophers such as Aristippus and Epicurus, among others, or took up general slogans such as "egoistic utilitarian," "self-love," or "pleasure," Takase's approach seemed to focus more on elucidation of Yang Zhu's philosophy by means of intellectual dialogues or debates with contemporary (i.e., Meiji period) Yang Zhu scholars and intellectuals. In this methodological framework, Takase presented the following three major points in his interpretation of the content and significance of Yang Zhu's philosophy.

First, in order to discuss Yang Zhu's so-called hedonist doctrine, Takase adopted a somewhat different textual source from the scholars we have discussed previously. What Takase thought most of were the following two passages: respectively, (1) "Preserving nature and maintaining the authentic, not allowing objects to burden one's body—that's how Yang Zhu takes his position" (*Huainanzi*, "Fan lun"); and (2) "Inside there is no method of preserving tranquility by Yang Zhu," from a commentary to "Biographies of the Past Worthies from Lingling" (零陵先賢傳) quoted in the "Biography of Liu Ba" (劉巴傳) in the *Records of the Three Kingdoms* (三國志). Scholars up until Takase's time had paid little attention to the latter textual source. In other words, Takase refrained from relying on those repudiations of Yang Zhu's doctrine by Mencius. It is perhaps for this reason that he insistently opposed seeing Yang Zhu as a mere advocate for bodily or extreme pleasures. Concerning this, Takase insisted that Yang Zhu's doctrine included the following three points: (1) Yang Zhu did not advocate actively pursuing pleasure in wine and lust or indulging in nightlife.[63] (2) In general, Yang Zhu valued a naturalistic state as the way to attain pleasure in life. It was in this sense that Yang Zhu saw those who had obtained the Way of nurturing life as "true men." Therefore, Yang Zhu's philosophy does not necessarily encourage active indulgence in one's vulgar dispositions.[64] (3) Yang Zhu did not advise that we should indulge in excessive drinking and eating.[65]

According to Takase, Yang Zhu's doctrines further developed Laozi's spirit into his own "egoistic utilitarianism" and "hedonism." Following Laozi, his doctrines kept the idea of preserving tranquility and innocence. For Yang Zhu, egoism and hedonism were to maintain one's innocence and nature.[66]

Next, Takase also gave an account of Yang Zhu's thoughts on life and death that was almost identical to those of Zhuangzi. In this respect, Takase held that

> Yang Zhu delighted in life, but he was not obsessed with being alive. He was attuned to life and awaited death in equilibrium. He moreover did not discuss the afterlife. One cannot but reserve what has come to one when being alive; and it is beyond one's control when life has parted.[67]

In the above remark Takase does not reveal any opposition to Yang Zhu's hedonism. Nevertheless, in various instances, he criticized Yang

Zhu's thought. This leads us to the second point on Takase's construal of Yang Zhu's thought.

Second, Takase intensely criticized "self-love-ism" (*aiko-shugi* 愛己主義) in Yang Zhu's thought. Takase maintained:

> A person who takes self-love to be the truth is bound to be lacking in loving others in practice and will exclude others out of self-love. It is particularly so when a state is jeopardized, so that the great principle of risking one's life to save one's own country will disappear and the great virtue of so-called loyalty and patriotism will go missing.[68]

According to Takase, the prevalence of "loving and benefiting oneself" (愛己利己) will diminish moral practice that has its root in people's heart of loving others. It is out of this anxiety that he proclaimed, "I so assert: Yang Zhu's egoism is radical individualism; therefore, for the welfare of human society, we must prevent it!"[69]

Third, if we examine Takase's statements with care we will also understand that what prompted his objection was not Yang Zhu's own ideas, but the contemporary (i.e., Meiji period) egoism, which in his eyes was very close to Yang Zhu's "for oneself theory" (為我論) (egoism). In a few places Takase mentions the "egoism" he found in his day.

> When considering the egoism of past and present, East and West, we can notice extreme individualism. Compared with this, Yang Zhu's teachings are still crude. The harm of today's sophisticated egoism is much worse.[70]

Takase also took one instance of "the pitfall of egoism" to illustrate the content of the "egoism" of his day.

> In general, those subscribing to "utilitarian egoism" are base people. They are equal to the so-called "believers in omnipotent scientism." Such people are unable to recognize the element of the "good in human nature," which is endowed with a bright spirit and acute sensibility. Such people also lack the capability of intuition and are unable to experience its mystical wonder.[71]

Interestingly, Inoue Tetsujirō, Takase's mentor, made the same point in his preface to Takase's book, harshly criticizing Yang and Mo's philosophies. Tetsujirō contended:

> Surprisingly, the doctrines of Yang and Mo have nowadays revived in our country. Although such doctrines pervade nationwide not under the name of Yang and Mo, they certainly share some substantive features. Indeed, some [contemporary intellectuals] are even more vehement in following these two: those protagonists who advocate egoism, hedonism, and nativism are like the followers of Master Yang, while those Christians who preach indiscriminating philanthropy are the followers of Mozi.[72]

Tetsujirō's remark was conscious of the revival of doctrines of Yang Zhu and Mo Di in his time in Japan. Even though neither this preface nor Takase's work specifically elucidates what elements addressed in Yang Zhu's doctrine had "nowadays revived in our country," or what kind of "utilitarian egoism" and "omnipotent scientism" in their day actually referred to Yang Zhu's doctrines, we can infer that by comparing ancient and contemporary egoistic doctrines, Takase tried to discern a negative psychological effect of Yang Zhu's doctrine on the mind of the people during his time.

In order to demonstrate this point, Takase took up the perspective of Kato Hiroyuki,[73] whom Takase dubbed "Mr. Natural Law" (大則先生). What Takase criticized was Katō's argument in "Egoist Mind and Altruistic Mind," the first chapter of his book *The Advancement of Morality and Law*.[74] According to Takase's understanding, Katō proposed that all beings, especially humans in relatively perfect societies, have a powerful egoistic mindset. At the same time, Katō denied the value of extreme altruism since it tended to destroy the psychological basis that assured the principle of individual independence. By contrast, Takase had an acute sense of the crisis that the "morality of our country is entirely corrupted, bribery abounds, and people are crazy about seeking their own benefit." In such a social atmosphere, "if one advocates egoism, nativism, and utilitarianism," the society could be exposed to the threat of "carrying wood bricks to put out a fire."[75]

To sum up, Takase maintained that Yang Zhu's thought was inherited from Laozi and in many ways bore a resemblance to that of Zhuangzi.

From his perspective, the manifold correspondence with Zhuangzi was natural since Yang Zhu's thought could be traced to Laozi. In the historical context of early Chinese philosophy, Takase's construal privileged the positions of "preserving nature and maintaining the authentic" and "preserving tranquility." Even though he noticed that there was also a difference between Yang Zhu's individualism and that in the Japanese society of the Meiji period, he twice equated Yang Zhu's doctrine with the "advocacy of indulgence in desire" found in Nietzsche (1844–1900), harshly renouncing both as "moral demons."[76] Such an attitude seems to have been more emotional than rational.

At the time, Takase could hardly bear the prevailing situation where the "individualism" cutting off social members from their bonds with the developing Japanese state integrated. Neither could he the spreading notion of the "social evolutionism" that understood human psychology through the lens of "egoism." The matter must have seemed particularly pressing considering that Takase witnessed Katō, who at the time was the most academically reputable intellectual—he had been the president of both Tokyo University and the Imperial University—optimistically endorsing the claim that "the core of human psyche lies in egoist concern." Takase was convinced that he had to reject this trend of thought precisely in the way Mencius had rebutted Yangism and Mohism. He saw in Katō's endorsement of egoism the revival of Yang Zhu's doctrine.

Yet, why did Meiji intellectuals take Yang Zhu's thought so seriously, whether they looked at it positively or negatively? Many of Yang Zhu's statements have been scattered in fragmented texts and distorted. I would like to propose two observations. First, since all the source materials were provided in classical Chinese, its content was easily accessible for Meiji intellectuals. In particular, in their eyes those classical texts also functioned as good textbooks to understand the thought of their Western (in particular, Ancient Greek) philosophical counterparts. And second, the Meiji intellectuals in general sensed the "individualist" and "anti-society" trends of thought that would start to emerge in the late Meiji period. In their eyes, such trends reflected some sort of a "revival" of Yang Zhu's doctrine that had to be rejected.

Around ten to fifteen years after Takase published *Philosophies of Yang Zhu and Mozi*, the young Chinese revolutionary Gu Shi 顧實 (1878–1956) joined "the Second Revolution" launched by Dr. Sun Yat-sen in 1913. However, Gu Shi ran off to Japan with some disillusioned fellows due to the failure of the revolution. Then he happened to attend

The Birth of the Image of the "Egoist-Epicurean Philosopher" | 249

a class taught by Takebe Ton'go 建部遯吾 (1871–1945) at Seihō Gakkō 政法學校, presently Hōsei University 法政大學. In the class he heard Takebe quoting "Yang Zhu" in *Liezi* when criticizing the government's current situation:

> Presently, people's minds are corrupted in China due to a multitude of [ideas like those of] Yang Zhu. The people are focusing narrowly on their own interests and benefits, indulging in their arrogant and unrestrained decadent ruin-the-country-ism. I earnestly warn the Chinese students not to follow in these footsteps again![77]

As a matter of fact, Takebe had also graduated from the Faculty of Letters (philosophy major) at the Imperial University in 1896 (Meiji 29), between Matsumoto's and Takase's study periods.[78] Takebe may have spent his years learning Chinese philosophy in the same academic atmosphere.

Shocked by Takebe's "very touching" (甚感) speech about the relation of Yang Zhu's doctrine to the corruption of contemporary Chinese minds, Gu Shi began to collect publications on Yang Zhu and studied Takase's *Philosophies of Yang Zhu and Mozi* with care. Thirty years later, he also published his own monograph, *The Philosophy of Yang Zhu* (楊朱哲學), using the term "philosophy." Slightly earlier, in 1928, Jiang Weiqiao/Zhuzhuang 蔣維喬 / 竹莊 (1873–1958) had translated Takase's book into Chinese.[79]

In sum, thanks to the efforts of young Japanese intellectuals trained in the discipline of philosophy during the Meiji period, Yang Zhu was revived through various phases, thus transforming from a neglected figure into a major ancient philosopher of egoistic hedonism. It was also within these intellectual trends that an image of "the philosopher Yang Zhu" was exported back to China from Japan.

Conclusion

This chapter has outlined discourses on Yang Zhu contributed by young (except for Shimada who was born in 1838) intellectuals during two decades in the second half of the Meiji period. In particular, I have tried to describe how Yang Zhu, originally "a forgotten Warring States master," was revived as "a representative philosopher of egoism and hedonism" with great significance to the minds of Meiji intellectuals, whether positively or negatively.

Their discourses on Yang Zhu evolved through four stages. First, Fenollosa and Tetsujirō sought to determine his philosophical position in their sketches of the history of Chinese philosophy, configured as a counterpart to thinkers in the history of Western philosophy. Like other Warring States masters, Yang Zhu's "parallel" intellectual role was "discovered" through these comparisons. Fenollosa took Yang Zhu as belonging to the "Third school," whereas Tetsujirō made the first attempt in Japanese research to expound Yang Zhu's philosophy as the hedonism of Epicurus.

The second stage contained perspectives that unfolded in Shimada's lectures and Enryō's monographs. Compared to Tetsujirō's scholarly attitude, Shimada's research interest primarily lies in explaining Chinese philosophy in its own terms and context. Shimada supposed that Master Lie's idea of "letting go of oneself in the void and naturalness" originated from Yang Zhu's idea of "self-love" (自愛), an expression that he coined. On the other hand, Enryō pointed out that, from the perspective of developments in philosophy, "loving oneself" (愛己) in Yang Zhu and "impartial love" in Mozi were both doctrines put forward in opposition to Confucianism.

The third stage introduced discourses of young researchers who received more professional academic training for discussing philosophical issues in traditional Chinese texts. They were Takigawa, Matsumoto, and Nishiwaki. They all learned philosophy around the Meiji twenties (1887–1897). From Takigawa onward, the focus was on Yang Zhu's statements in the *Liezi*, which were taken as a credible basis for determining his thought; at the same time, they proceeded to compare what they saw in Yang Zhu with Epicureanism, with particular attention to their respective strengths and weaknesses. Discourses started to examine and criticize the elements that led Yang Zhu philosophy away from society and the state.

Takase's study represents the fourth stage. His monograph, *Philosophies of Yang Zhu and Mozi*[80] indicated that the "philosophy of Yang Zi" had become an integral topic in the field of Chinese philosophy. While Takase did not attribute a radical type of bodily hedonism to the most significant element in Yang Zhu's philosophy, he instead worried about its egoistic tendencies. Takase saw Yang Zhu's egoism as one of the origins of Japan's antimorality and antistate egoism, which profoundly worried him.

In the gradual articulations of thought pursued by philosophically trained young Meiji intellectuals, Yang Zhu slowly but surely became an iconic philosopher in the Chinese and East Asian intellectual world. To my knowledge of the studies of Warring States masters by Meiji scholars, Yang Zhu received just as much attention as other early Chinese thinkers. In the second half of the Meiji period, when "Chinese philosophy" started to become an established academic discipline, Confucius drew overwhelming interest among the early Chinese thinkers. Yang Zhu received less attention than Laozi or Xunzi, but perhaps slightly more than Mencius.[81] Indeed, in this intellectual context of the last two decades of the nineteenth century, the image of the egoist-hedonist *philosopher* Yang Zhu came into being.

Notes

1. I wish to thank Dr. Jill Miao-kun Tsai 蔡妙坤 and Chun-Chien Wu 吳君健 for their help in translating and editing, as well as *Dr.* Mizuno Hirota 水野博太 for kindly providing me with his own typed text of the *Takamine manuscript* (of the part of Shimada Chōrei's lecture).

2. During the past ten years, scholars have begun to seriously consider the possibility that Chinese philosophy as an academic discipline might have formed during Japan's Meiji period. See Sang Bing 桑兵, "The Birth of Modern 'Chinese Philosophy'" 近代"中国哲學"発源, *Academic Research* 學術研究 (2010–11): 1–11; Barry D. Steben, "Nishi Amane and the Birth of 'Philosophy' and 'Chinese Philosophy' in Early Meiji Japan," in *Learning to Emulate the Wise: The Genesis of Chinese Philosophy as an Academic Discipline in Twentieth-Century China*, ed. John Makeham (Hong Kong: Chinese University of Hong Kong Press, 2012), 39–72; and John Makeham, "The Role of Masters Studies in the Early Formation of Chinese Philosophy as an Academic Discipline," in *Learning to Emulate the Wise*, 73–102. However, perhaps due to the lack of reliable source materials, none of these have given a definitive sense of what kind of events at Tokyo University facilitated or stimulated the formation of the academic discipline of Chinese philosophy in Japan and how Meiji scholars explored Chinese philosophy-related scholarly subjects in their lectures and writings during the 1880s and 1890s.

3. See Hagiwara Yutaka: *The Outline of Thoughts of the Warring States Masters* 諸子大意 (Tokyo: Iyûsha 亦友社, 1893). Hagiwara was trained in traditional classic studies in the Tokugawa period and then taught Chinese classics as a traditional scholar until the mid-Meiji period.

4. Tetsujirō taught the course "Toyō tetsugaku shi" (History of Oriental philosophy) from the fall of 1882 (Meiji 15) to the summer of 1883. This is the first case of a graduate from the philosophy program at Tokyo University officially giving a course in what we presently call "Chinese philosophy."

5. Tokyo University, established in 1877 (Meiji 10), was renamed the Imperial University. Then it was renamed Tokyo Imperial University due to the establishment of Kyoto Imperial University in 1897 (Meiji 30).

6. The publications about Confucius, compared to other Chinese thinkers, overwhelmingly dominated the commercial publication market in the Meiji period.

7. During the Meiji period, transcripts of lectures were often published as "records of lectures" (*kōgiloku* 講義錄), a form of publication equivalent to what we now call "textbooks."

8. Among the scholars I have listed, only Matsumoto Bunsaburō's (松本文三郎, 1969–1944) monograph was published long after his graduation. In my observation, Matsumoto's ideas about early Chinese philosophy came to be formed and consolidated before he left college and changed little afterward.

9. See "(The Syllabi of) 1883 (Meiji 16) academic year," in *The Handbook of the Three Faculties of Tokyo University* 東京大學法理文三學部一覽 (Tokyo: Maruya Zenshichi 丸家善七, 1884).

10. During his eight-year appointment from August 1878 (Meiji 11) to July 30, 1886 (Meiji 19) at Tokyo University, Fenollosa lectured in five courses, ranging from philosophy, history of philosophy, and financial management (economics) to politics and logic.

11. Inoue Tetsujirō took the post of assistant professor at Tokyo University in March 1882 (Meiji 15) and set off to Germany in February 1884 (Meiji 17).

12. The remarks about Chinese philosophy by Fenollosa were recorded in lecture notes taken by Inoue Enryō.

13. Sugihara Shirō 杉原四郎, "Fenollosa's Lectures at Tokyo University: With Close Focus on the Notes of Sakatani Yoshirō" フェノロサの東京大學講義——阪谷芳郎の筆記ノートを中心として——, *Quarterly Journal of Social Thought* 季刊社會思想 2-4 (1972): 192.

14. It is noteworthy that Fenollosa did not associate Mohism with altruism.

15. The above description is based on the lecture notes of Fenollosa taken by Inoue Enryō. The original note was in English, and its Japanese translations are provided by Shibata Takayuki 柴田隆行 and Rainer Schulzer. See Shibata Takayuki and Rainer Schulzer, trans., "A Japanese Translation of Inoue Enryō's Note" 井上圓了「稿錄」の日本語譯, *Annual Report of the Inoue Enryo Center* 井上圓了センター年報, vol. 19 (September 2010), 139–40, 145–53.

16. I use the text that Mizuno Hirota collated. See Mizuno Hirota 水野博太, "Inoue Tetsujirō's Lectures on 'History of Oriental Philosophy' recorded by Takamine Sankichi" 『三吉遺稿』中の井上哲次郎『東洋哲學史』講義, *Journal of The University of Tokyo Archives* 東京大學文書館紀要 36 (March 2018): 20–49.

17. Mizuno, "Inoue Tetsujirō's Lectures," 28.
18. Mizuno, "Inoue Tetsujirō's Lectures," 29.
19. Mizuno, "Inoue Tetsujirō's Lectures," 29–30.
20. The content of Shimada's lectures on Chinese philosophy has been preserved in Takamine Sankichi's posthumous manuscript (hereafter "*Takamine manuscript*"), the same manuscript that recorded Tetsujirō's lectures on the history of Oriental philosophy. The manuscript has been kept at Kanazawa University Library. Concerning the condition of Shimada's note, see Mizuno, "Inoue Tetsujirō's Lectures," 21.
21. Hagiwara Zentarō 萩原善太郎, "A Concise Biography of Mr. Shimada Chorōei, Doctor of Letters" 文學博士島田重禮君小傳, in *Biographies of Doctors (Distinguished Scholars) in (Japan) Empire* 帝國博士列傳 (Tokyo: Keigyōsha 敬業社, 1890), 47–51.
22. Shimada specified in the report of 1886–1887 that his courses "reached the period of Ming and Qing Dynasties" and the schedule "has been fulfilled." According to the chronological order of the note, in fall 1885 Shimada started his lecture by elucidating the principal virtues in Chinese philosophy, including *ren* 仁, *yi* 義, *zhongxin* 忠信 (loyalty and fidelity), and *xiaoti* 孝悌 (filial piety and fraternity). From February 10, 1886, he moved on to Warring States thinkers. In the academic year of 1887, he started to explicate thought from the Han to Qing dynasties. The whole lecture ended in June of the same year. See *Takamine manuscript*, 103–105.
23. See *Takamine manuscript*, 54.
24. *Takamine manuscript*, 24.
25. The phrases "loving oneself" and "self-love" were expressed as *ga'ai* 我愛 and *ji'ai* 自愛 in the original Japanese. See *Takamine manuscript*, 71.
26. *Takamine manuscript*, 66.
27. *Takamine manuscript*, 66.
28. It is worth noting that the actual content of the arguments about Chinese philosophy made by Fenollosa and Tetsujirō are also accessible in Enryō's notes.
29. For example, "Section Three: Chinese Philosophy" in *An Outline of Philosophy* 哲學要領 (1886; Meiji 19), the sixteenth and seventeenth chapters of *A General Introduction to Ethics* 倫理通論 (1886; Meiji 19), and some relevant statements on Chinese philosophy under the subject of "Eastern philosophy" in *The Lectures of Pure Philosophy* 純正哲學講義 (1891–1892; Meiji 25–26). Now these are all collected in *The Selected Works of Inoue Enryō* 井上圓了選集, ed. the Committee of Essays in Celebration of the Hundred Anniversary, founded by Toyo (Tōyō) University.
30. Inoue Enryō, "Chinese Philosophy" シナ哲學, *Lectures of Pure Philosophy* 純正哲學講義 (*The Selected Works* version 選集版), 90.
31. Takigawa graduated from the Department of Classics (古典講習科) at Imperial University in 1887 (Meiji 20); Matsumoto graduated from the Department of Philosophy at Imperial University in 1893 (Meiji 26); Nishiwaki graduated

from the Tetsugakukan (or Tetugakkan; 哲學館, literally "The Philosophy Academy") in 1894 (Meiji 27). The academy was founded by Inoue Enryō in 1887 (Meiji 20), which developed into the present Toyo (Tōyō) University 東洋大學.

32. Takigawa Kametarō 瀧川龜太郎, "Discussing Yang Zhu with a General Introduction to The Rise of Ancient Chinese Philosophy" 楊朱を論ず：附、支那古代哲學興起之概略, *Journal of the Oriental Studies Association* 東洋學會雜誌 4, no. 2 (1888): 63–68.

33. Takigawa's "One Aspect in Ancient Chinese Philosophy (1–4)" (支那古代哲學史一斑) was published in the *Journal of Oriental Studies* 東洋學藝雜誌, respectively in *Journal of Oriental Studies* 5, no. 78 (1888): 126–39; *Journal of Oriental Studies* 5, no. 79 (1888): 169–80; *Journal of Oriental Studies* 5, no. 80 (1888): 248–56; and *Journal of Oriental Studies* 5, no. 81 (1888): 291–98.

34. Takigawa Kametarō 瀧川龜太郎, *History of Ancient Chinese Philosophy* 支那古代哲學史 (published between 1888 and 1892). This volume is preserved at the Library of the University of Tokyo. On its front page, there is a memo handwritten by Takigawa himself stating that he was unaware of its publication and accidentally came across it at a bookstore.

35. Takigawa, "Discussing Yang Zhu," 65.

36. Takigawa, "Discussing Yang Zhu," 68.

37. All its content had been completed before he graduated from Imperial University in 1887 (Meiji 20). Parts discussing Yang Zhu's thought belong to the first half of the second volume. The amount of argument extends to a total of thirteen pages (twenty-seven pages when folded). In the discussion, scholars and publications cited also included: Zhu Xi 朱熹, *Zhuzi yulei* 朱子語類; Lü Donglai 呂東萊, *Yühai* 玉海; Hu Yuanrui 胡元瑞, *Jiuliu xulun* 九流緒論; Tao Xibao 姚惜抱, *Xibaoxuan shizhong* 惜抱軒十種; and Washizu Kidō 鷲津毅堂, *Shinto yo'in* 親燈餘影.

38. Takigawas's introductory remark is as follows: "The School of Yang (*Yōka* 楊家) originated from Master Yang, whose theoretical position was diametrically opposed against that of the Mohists. Yang's doctrine once flourished. However, we find no names of advocates of Yang's doctrine transmitted to later periods."

39. Takigawa, *History of Ancient Chinese Philosophy*, 27.

40. Takigawa, *History of Ancient Chinese Philosophy*, 18–19.

41. Among them, Uchida Shūhei 內田周平 (1854–1944) was one of the representative scholars of Chinese philosophy who taught at the Philosophy Academy. Uchida in his youth learned German at *Hongō jinshin gijuku* 本鄉壬申義塾, a private language school. Its funder was Ôkuma Shun'kichi 大熊春吉 (1840–1914). Uchida then entered the Faculty of Medicine at Tokyo University in 1877. However, he withdrew in December 1884 and enrolled in the Faculty of Letters (Chinese philosophy course) (文科大學支那哲學選科) at Tokyo University and graduated in 1886. After graduation, Uchida started his career by teaching Confucianism, Chinese philosophy, and aesthetics at the Philosophy Academy.

42. Nishiwaki Gyokuhō 西脇玉峰, "A Study of Yang Zhu (I)" 楊朱論, *Oriental Philosophy* 東洋哲學 2 (1895): 56–65; Nishiwaki Gyokuhō: "A Study of

Yang Zhu (II)" 楊朱論 (承前), *Oriental Philosophy* 5 (1895): 203–213. *Oriental Philosophy* was a journal founded by Enryō.

43. Nishiwaki, "A Study of Yang Zhu (II)," 212. Robinson Crusoe is the protagonist of *The Life and Strange Surprising Adventures of Robinson Crusoe* by Daniel Defoe (1660–1731). The novel was translated into Japanese with the title *A Story of Drifting in the Wild Ocean* (*Hyōkō kiji* 漂荒紀事) in the 1850s.

44. Nishiwaki, "A Study of Yang Zhu (I)," 60.
45. Nishiwaki, "A Study of Yang Zhu (I)," 60.
46. Nishiwaki, "A Study of Yang Zhu (I)," 60.
47. Nishiwaki, "A Study of Yang Zhu (I)," 61.
48. Matsumoto Bunsaburō 松本文三郎, *History of Ancient Chinese Philosophy* 支那古代哲學史 (Tokyo: Waseda University Press, 1904).
49. Matsumoto at a young age published essays such as: "Reading Dr. Motora's *Ethics*" 文科大學教授元良博士の倫理學を讀む, *Rikugō zasshi* 六合雜誌 152 (1893); "Features of Oriental Ethics" 東洋倫理の特質, *Education Bulletin* 教育公報 228 (1899); "On Utilitarianism" 實理主義に就いて, in *Ethics Studies* 倫理研究, ed. East Asian Association (Tokyo: Kōdōkan 弘道館, 1901). As indicated in these publications, young Matsumoto's interest in ethics was of no doubt.
50. Matsumoto, *History of Ancient Chinese Philosophy*, 193–206.
51. Matsumoto, *History of Ancient Chinese Philosophy*, 196. Here, Matsumoto's explanation does not mention Aristippus.
52. Matsumoto maintained that "no matter when or where in the history of (world) philosophy, no other philosophers insisted on hedonism in a manner more intense than Master Yang. . . . Although the doctrine of Master Yang was not so profound to the point of being worth following, we cannot but admit that it caused a notable change in the course of the development of philosophy" (Matsumoto, *History of Ancient Chinese Philosophy*, 196). Here, the term "philosophy" (*tetsugaku* 哲學 in the original text) appears twice.
53. Matsumoto, *History of Ancient Chinese Philosophy*, 94.
54. Matsumoto, *History of Ancient Chinese Philosophy*, 205.
55. Matsumoto, *History of Ancient Chinese Philosophy*, 195.
56. Matsumoto, *History of Ancient Chinese Philosophy*, 203.
57. Yoshida Kōhei 吉田公平, "A Note for a Biography of Takase Takejirō: The Scholars of Classical Chinese at Tōyō University: Part 1" 高瀨武次郎年譜稿：東洋大學の漢學家たち（その一）, *Annual Report of the Inoue Enryo Center* 井上圓了センター年報 15 (2006): 161–324.
58. Takase Takejirō 高瀨武次郎, *History of Chinese Philosophy* 支那哲學史 (Tokyo: Bunseidō 文盛堂, 1910).
59. Akatsuka Kiyoshi 赤塚忠, "Introduction" 序論, in *General Introduction to (Chinese) Thought* 思想概論, ed. Akatsuka et al. (Tokyo: Taishûkan shoten 大修館書店, 1968), 9.
60. In addition, Takase gave an oral presentation under the heading "Yang Zhu's Statements on Egoism" at a periodical meeting of the Association

for Canonical Classics (經研會) in March 1990, a year before publication. See Association for Canonical Classics, ed., *A Collection of Philological and Historical Studies of the Classical Canons* 經史說林 (Tokyo: Gen'gendō shobō 元元堂書房, 1907), appendix, 3. Unfortunately, the volume does not contain the content of Takese's presentation.

61. Takase's arrangement of putting the two philosophies of Mozi and Yang Zhu into a single book was, of course, not incidental, if we take into consideration the fact that Takase was a practitioner of Yangming Confucian doctrine.

62. The content of the preface provides a crucial clue as to why Takase wrote a monograph devoted to Yang Zhu's philosophy. This will be explained later in the chapter.

63. Takase, *History of Chinese Philosophy*, 52.
64. Takase, *History of Chinese Philosophy*, 57–58.
65. Takase, *History of Chinese Philosophy*, 63.
66. Takase, *History of Chinese Philosophy*, 34.
67. Takase, *History of Chinese Philosophy*, 54.
68. Takase, *History of Chinese Philosophy*, 36.
69. Takase, *History of Chinese Philosophy*, 29.
70. Takase, *History of Chinese Philosophy*, 29.
71. Takase, *History of Chinese Philosophy*, 35.
72. "Prelude by Inoue Tetsujirō," in Takase, *History of Chinese Philosophy*.
73. Katō served as president twice during the beginnings of Tokyo University (1877–1886; Meiji 10–19) and its restructuring period into the Imperial University (1890–1893; Meiji 23–26).

74. Katō Hiroyuki 加藤弘之, "Egoist Mind and Altruistic Mind" 利己心與利他心, *The Advancement of Morality and Law* 道德法律之進步 (Tokyo: Keigyōsha 敬業社, 1894).

75. Takase, *History of Chinese Philosophy*, 100.

76. Takase argued as follows: "Nietzsche is also a devil against morality. Whose duty is exterminating these devils?" (ニーチェもまた道徳の惡魔なり。惡魔を退治するは其れ誰の任ぞや) See Takase, *History of Chinese Philosophy*, 60. It is also worthy of attention that the year 1900 (Meiji 34) when Takase finished the draft of *The Philosophies of Yang Zhu and Mozi* was exactly the year of Nietzsche's death.

77. With respect to Gu Shi's review and his publication motivations during his study period in Japan, see Gu Shi 顧實, "Author's Preface" 自序, *The Philosophy of Yang Zhu* 楊朱哲學, in *Gu Shi's works on Chinese studies, no. 5* 顧實所著國學院叢書之五 (Nanjing: Dongfang yeyao shuju 東方醫藥書局, 1931). A reprinted version was published by Yuelu shuyuan (嶽麓書院) (Changsha) in 2011.

78. More specifically, Matsumoto also graduated as a "philosophy major."

79. Takase Takejirō 高瀬武次郎, *Philosophies of Yang Zhu and Mozi* 楊墨哲學, trans. and comp. Jiang Zhuzhuang 蔣竹莊 (Shanghai: Shangwu yinshuguan, 1929).

The Birth of the Image of the "Egoist-Epicurean Philosopher" | 257

80. To the best of my knowledge, no book exclusively addressing Yang Zhu has been published in Japan.

81. In my impression, the attention Meiji intellectuals devoted to Yang Zhu seems about equal to Mozi, Han Feizi, and Zhuangzi. This suggests that whenever Meiji intellectuals configured their history of Chinese philosophy, they always kept Yang Zhu in mind.

Chapter 9

Struggling between Tradition and Modernity
Liang Qichao's Portrayal of Yang Zhu
in the Early Twentieth Century

Xiaowei Wang

Introduction

The twentieth century was when China went from being the "world" to merely a "nation."[1] The drastic change of the geographical and political perception of China led to a revision of traditional ideas that were believed to hold universal value. Against this background, the reevaluation of a supposedly pre-Qin figure became particularly interesting in revealing how the paradigm shift subverted the conventional criteria of value. In this chapter, I examine how Liang Qichao 梁啟超 (1873–1929), a leading intellectual in the early twentieth century, made his contribution to the revision of Yang Zhu 楊朱 (approximately 400 BCE),[2] the long-standing "heretic" in Chinese intellectual history. By retracing Liang's early portrayal of Yang Zhu, I present how Yang Zhu gained his modern image as a valuable ancient Chinese philosopher after thousands of years of being considered mostly negative or irrelevant. I also show how, by introducing Yang Zhu in this way, modern intellectuals negotiated the meanings of imported modern concepts.

Liang lived in an era when China's last empire was coming to an end and when the Chinese had to accept the geographical and political reality of China being only one nation among many.[3] The notion of "nation" was then and has remained a complicated and controversial issue.[4] China was not only contracted from "all under heaven" to one nation; it was also among the weaker ones. It was against this background that Chinese intellectuals started to build imaginations of a united Chinese nation and to construct narratives that could strengthen it in order to save it from decay. Liang was one of the leading figures who contributed greatly to this "nation-building" project.[5] In this process, his ideology was shaken and reshaped by both the upheaval of Chinese history and the new ideas he had gained.

Although the studies of Liang Qichao are numerous, research on his views on Yang Zhu is scarce. Most research on this topic has been conducted by the Fudan historian He Aiguo. His paper on Liang's changing views on Yangism from the 1890s to the 1920s claims that Liang's attitude turned from negative to positive in a four-stage evolution.[6] In other writings, He also points out that Yang Zhu turned from a "beast" to a philosopher who advocated "rights" because of Western influence in the twentieth century.[7] The current chapter focuses on Liang's writings in a shorter period, namely between 1896 and 1904. This coincides with two of He's stages: Liang's "period of self-strengthening" (*weixin shiqi* 維新時期) and "period of renovating the people" (*xinmin shiqi* 新民時期), when Liang's opinions on Yang Zhu gradually turned from negative to slightly positive due to Western influence. Instead of seeing Liang's views on Yang Zhu as a linear developmental course from negative to positive, this chapter presents a detailed examination of Liang's construction of Yang Zhu's theory and his use of terms. It argues that from 1896 to 1904 Liang wavered between a positive and negative evaluation, against the background of the national crisis, and struggling between conventional education and new insights from the West. Liang's depiction of Yang Zhu in this period is much more complicated than a mere transformation from a traditional understanding to a modern understanding incited by the introduction of Western ideas. Instead, the two evaluations are parallel and intertwined, which in the end leads to a portrayal that has an unsolved tension.

Despite the mostly unfavorable portrayals in pre-Republican China, views on Yang Zhu took a sudden turn in the twentieth century and became relatively positive.[8] One of the major figures who contributed to this change was Liang Qichao. Being one of the most influential intellectuals in Republican China, Liang had a profound influence on Yang

Zhu's modern image. Liang's writings from the 1890s to the 1920s express his multiple interpretations of Yang Zhu, which were usually affected by the new theories he had absorbed and by his shifting interests during that period. Yang Zhu was seen in different texts as a heretic, a Daoist master, a philosopher, a Darwinist, a naturalist, and a materialist.[9] Most importantly, Liang was probably the first Chinese intellectual to establish Yang Zhu as a philosopher advocating the notion of "rights." This portrayal foreshadowed the later discussion of Yang Zhu as a representative of individualism in the May Fourth period. However, how Liang constructed Yang Zhu's theories and how he integrated Yang Zhu into his own narratives have been largely overlooked. The discussion here is divided into two parts concerning the two aspects that constantly competed with each other in Liang's understanding of Yang Zhu. In the first part, we see how Liang accused Yang Zhu of being the "villain" whose theories debilitated China even though Yang Zhu's theories could be justified. In the second part, the discussion concentrates on how Liang incorporates Yang Zhu in the discourse of "rights."

From "Heretic" to "Egoist"

According to Mencius, Yang Zhu's teachings were so influential that his words filled the world.[10] Today it is almost impossible to find texts that provide solid evidence for Yang Zhu's historical existence or theories. Nonetheless, current scholarship still considers Yang Zhu the founder of Yangism and labels him with tags such as egoist, hedonist, and individualist. This contemporary conception of Yang Zhu, however, is largely determined by reconstructions of Yang Zhu's theories in the twentieth century. Despite the few texts attributed to Yang Zhu, twentieth-century Chinese intellectuals still evinced a keen interest in the long-lost theories of this alleged master. Their interest in reconstructing a coherent theory of Yang Zhu's thought was affected by the sparse textual evidence, the premodern portrayals, and their own agendas in that specific period of Chinese history. As a result, the usually negative portrayals of Yang Zhu as a "heretic"[11] in premodern times were replaced by slightly more positive images associated with Western ideas.[12]

Unlike the other ancient masters whose thoughts were preserved in books allegedly written by themselves or their disciples, Yang Zhu's ideas had merely been transmitted in some short comments and anecdotes scattered among early texts,[13] with the exception of the "Yang Zhu" chapter in the *Liezi*. Among the extant texts that are related or attributed to Yang Zhu, the *Mencius*, and the *Liezi* are crucial in the modern construction of Yang Zhu's theories. Concerning the content of Yang Zhu's theories, the *Mencius* presents a long-standing image that affected the portrayal of Yang Zhu in later generations:

> Yang holds the notion of "for oneself" (*wei wo*), which amounts to a denial of one's ruler; Mo holds the notion of "impartial care" (*jian ai*), which amounts to a denial of one's father. [Those who] deny one's ruler or one's father are beasts.
>
> 楊氏為我，是無君也；墨氏兼愛，是無父也。無父無君，是禽獸也。(*Mencius* 3B9)
>
> Yangzi chooses "for oneself"; if by pulling out a single hair he could have benefited the world, he would not have done it. Mozi chooses "impartial care"; if by rubbing his whole body smooth from head to heel he could have benefited the world, he would have done it.
>
> 楊子取為我，拔一毛而利天下，不為也。墨子兼愛，摩頂放踵利天下，為之。(*Mencius* 7A26)

These statements stress three traits of Yang Zhu's doctrines: the notion of "for oneself" (*wei wo* 為我), his unwillingness to pull out a single hair to benefit the world, and the oppositional relation between the teachings of Yang Zhu and Mozi. Yang Zhu's unwillingness to pull out a single hair is also echoed in the *Liezi*:

> Yang Zhu said: ". . . If no one loses a single hair, and no one benefits the world, the world will be in good order."
>
> 楊朱曰：……人人不損一毫，人人不利天下，天下治矣。(*Liezi* "Yang Zhu")

Apart from this, the *Liezi* also presents other dimensions of Yang Zhu's teachings. While the authenticity and dating of the *Liezi* is highly controversial,[14] it is seen by many modern intellectuals as the only chance to take a better look at Yang Zhu's doctrines. It not only contains an entire chapter titled "Yang Zhu" but also mentions Yang Zhu in five out of eight chapters in total. The *Liezi* portrays Yang Zhu as one of Laozi's disciples. His thought was usually understood as a promotion of "indulgence in desires" (*zong yu* 縱慾) because of the short lifespan of human beings. The expression *zong yu*, however, had the specific meaning of world-weariness in modern times and was mostly constructed by modern intellectuals.[15] Another *Liezi* chapter, "Yellow Emperor" 黃帝, tells an anecdote of Laozi criticizing Yang Zhu for being arrogant, which also occurs in the *Zhuangzi* chapter "Dwelling Words" 寓言 with a person called Yang Ziju 陽子居. This anecdote is usually taken as supporting evidence that Yang Zhu was a disciple of Laozi, confirming the association between Yang Zhu and the Daoist lineage.[16] The statements attributed to Yang Zhu in the "Yang Zhu" chapter are often abstract and open to interpretation. An example is the statement that compares the states of life and death among the prominent figures of Yao, Shun, Jie, and Zhou:

In life they were Yao and Shun, in death they are rotten bones; in life they were Jie and Zhou, in death they are rotten bones.

生則堯舜，死則腐骨；生則桀紂，死則腐骨。

This statement has often been quoted in academic discussions involving Yang Zhu. Its implied pessimism gained a popular interpretation in the late Qing and early Republican periods, which established Yang Zhu as someone who was world-weary (*yanshi* 厭世) and hence tended to indulge in desires.[17] Republican intellectuals such as Kang Youwei 康有為 (1858–1927), Liang Qichao, and Gao Xu 高旭 (1877–1925) all expressed opinions about Yang Zhu's indulgence in desires.[18]

In the late Qing dynasty, these materials related to Yang Zhu were often taken as textual sources for constructing Yang Zhu's lineage and his theories. While there was a gap between traditional and modern readings, the tradition lingered on in his representation. This combination of old and new was most visible in the weakening connection between Yang and Mo as opposing villains and their replacement by the poisonous thoughts of Yang and Lao.

The Shifted Focus from "Yang-Mo" to "Lao-Yang"

For a long time in Chinese intellectual history, Yang Zhu and Mozi were seen as the two representative heretics in the dominant Confucian cultural sphere. "Yang-Mo" had been the rhetorical trope that signified social threats that should be attacked.¹⁹ In the late Qing and early Republican era, under the themes of self-strengthening and saving the nation, the association between Yang and Mo was weakened. The "Yang-Mo" trope was largely replaced by the "Lao-Yang" category.²⁰ Along with some of his contemporaries, Liang contributed to this shift.

All in all, the "Yang-Mo" trope that had driven the discourse on Yang Zhu for thousands of years lost its appeal to leading late-Qing intellectuals such as Kang and Liang. Under the theme of nationalism, the relevance of the "Yang-Mo" trope diminished while the "Lao-Yang" category became more prominent. Liang's early views in this respect echo his teacher Kang Youwei. In their construction of a Chinese intellectual history, they both tended to stress the "Lao-Yang" category, whereas the "Yang-Mo" trope was no longer appealing to them. One can even say that Kang and Liang may have consciously tried to undermine the conventionally negative "Yang-Mo" trope.²¹ In his epilogue to *A Reading List of Western Learning*, Liang criticizes Lao-Yang for poisoning the Chinese mind, adding that "the teaching of Mozi should be revived" (墨子之學當復興).²²

The traditional "Yang-Mo" trope and its long-standing opposition lingered on in Liang's writings. But with Mozi's improving image in the late-Qing dynasty, Liang's use of the trope shows some deviation from the conventional use. Liang seldom brings up the connection of Yang Zhu and Mozi as fixed opponents. The first time is in *On Changing Trends*, when Liang tries to summarize Yang Zhu's theories. Although he does not directly state that Mozi's theories should be considered utilitarian, he contrasts Yang Zhu's theories with Jeremy Bentham's (1748–1832) and John Stuart Mill's (1806–1873) utilitarianism (*gonglizhuyi* 功利主義),²³ and then states:

> Thus, there was Mohism [representing] the learning in the north and Yangism [representing] the learning in the south. The two learnings are at the extreme point of the two sides. Their teachings are the complete opposite of each other.
>
> 故北學之有墨，南學之有楊，皆走於兩極端之頂點，而立於正反對之地位。²⁴

The second time is when Liang points out the central shortcoming of the pre-Qin schools, which is the lack of logic in the teachings of the pre-Qin period. Liang used Mencius's criticism against Yang Zhu and Mozi as an example to argue that equating Yang Zhu's notion of "for oneself" with "a denial of one's lord" and Mozi's notion of "impartial care" with "a denial of one's father" show the lack of logic in Mencius' criticism.[25] Another occasion is when Liang promotes the doctrines of Mozi, he claims that "Yang Zhu's theories are going to bring China to its end" (楊學遂亡中國).[26]

The "Poisonous" Thoughts of Lao and Yang

As Chinese culturalism was replaced by nationalism,[27] "nation" became the core criterion of the new value system. Laozi and Yang Zhu were then blamed by the late-Qing intellectuals for the weak state of China. Liang's understanding of these two figures reflects both his engagement with his contemporaries and his interpretation based on the Western theories that he knew. Before 1902, Liang's comments on Laozi and Yang Zhu were shaped by Darwinist ideas, whereas after 1902, Liang tried to offer an academic explanation of the cause of Laozi and Yang Zhu's theories based on a geographical reading.

Liang's consciousness of the existence of nations and how to strengthen them was gradually formed over the years. Before Liang gained consciousness of the world and China as a nation, he had been just one young Chinese person receiving a conventional education without the slightest concern for the existence of other countries. The year 1890 was a turning point for Liang. He not only broadened his views of the world at this time but also experienced the beginnings of an inner struggle between his conventional education and the "new" thoughts gained from his contemporaries and from Western and Japanese sources. After failing the imperial examination,[28] Liang passed through Shanghai where he picked up a world map, and only then did he realize the existence of other nations.[29] In the autumn of the same year, Liang met reformer Kang Youwei who later became his mentor and provided the basis for Liang's intellectual thought. According to Liang, it was in this year that he was shocked out of his complacency and gained an apprehension of the national crisis.[30] In the following years, Liang studied under the instruction of Kang and helped him propagate the idea of "self-strengthening." It was also in this period that Liang broadened his intellectual contacts. In 1895 Liang became friends with Tan Sitong 譚嗣同 (1865–98) and gained an understanding of Tan's theory of "Renxue" 仁學 (The study of *ren*). The next year, he read Yan Fu's 嚴復 (1854–1921) translation of Thomas Henry Huxley's (1825–95) *Evolution and Ethics*, which gave him a taste of Darwinism. Some scholars argue that 1898 was another turning point for Liang, since it was after this year that Liang gained access to the enormous collection of Japanese translations of Western theories.[31] In 1898 Kang and Liang initiated the Hundred Days' Reform (*bairi weixin* 百日維新), or Wuxu Reform (*wuxu bianfa* 戊戌變法). When it failed, Liang fled to Japan, where he met Meiji intellectuals such as Fukuzawa Yukichi 福澤諭吉 (1835–1901) and Katō Hiroyuki 加藤弘之 (1836–1916), whose ideas helped Liang gain his conception of nationalism. Although Liang rarely makes explicit reference to these writers, there are instances in his writings that resemble their thought. The intellectuals mentioned previously helped Liang shape his belief in strengthening China. This belief dominated Liang's views in the first decade of the twentieth century and determined his views on Yang Zhu.

In a time focused on strengthening and saving the nation, self-reflection was part of that endeavor. As Joseph Levenson stated, "China was not only somehow weak, they felt, but somehow wrong."[32] Since the genuine principles of Chinese culture had been distorted, it was the reformers' task to identify the "wrong" and restore the "right." With Yang Zhu being a long-standing target of criticism in Chinese intellectual history, it should not be a surprise that he still bore that mark in the late Qing. According to He Aiguo, Yang Zhu's modern image emerged as part of the "Yang-Mo" trope. The resemblance shared by Mozi's doctrines and Catholicism turned Yang Zhu the lesser of two evils when considered in the frame of Yang and Mo.[33] But I would argue that the connection between Yang Zhu and Mozi had weakened after the Self-Strengthening Movement (also known as the Western Affairs Movement, *yangwu yundong* 洋務運動, ca.1861–1895) and the Hundred Days' Reform (1898), which both promoted science and religion, thus shedding a new and positive light on Mohism.[34] Yang Zhu, however, along with Laozi, became the new target blamed for China's downfall by intellectuals such as Zhang Zhidong 張之洞 (1837–1909), Bi Yongnian 畢永年 (1869–1902), and Kang Youwei.[35]

Liang's comments on Laozi and Yang Zhu seem to have been shaped by Darwinism. Before 1898, the Darwinist concept of "grouping" (or "integrating," *qun* 群) and "struggling" (or "competition," *jingzheng* 競爭) were believed to be two central principles that allowed any animate and inanimate thing to exist and endure. This conviction regarding the cosmological order thence led to his vision of sociopolitical order. He believed that when two groups struggled against each other, the most cohesive group would prevail. Thus, in the case of two "nation-groups" (*guojia qun* 國家群), the one with a higher level of sociopolitical integration would prevail.[36] Chinese society was weak because it had been working with "egoistic methods" (*dushu* 獨術), while "collective methods" (*qunshu* 群術) made a society successful.[37]

This intellectual background was then reflected in Liang's views on Yang Zhu. In line with Kang, he took the category of Lao and Yang as the target of his criticism.[38] His views on the "poisonous" thoughts of Lao and Yang are stated as self-evident: they were seen as the causes of the resigned and selfish personality of the Chinese. These qualities are the exact opposite of what Liang believed could make China strong. This "Lao-Yang" category first appeared in his epilogue to *A Reading List of Western Learning*, published in 1896. In this text, Liang makes the short comment that the Chinese mind "has been poisoned by the doctrines of Lao and Yang for two thousand years" (二千年實陰受其毒).[39] Another example can be found in Liang's 1900 article "Reproaching the bystanders." Here he criticizes Laozi and Yang Zhu as the teachers of those who stood by as long as the subjugation of the nation would not harm them.[40] In Liang's 1898 article "On Dynamism," he calls Laozi and Yang Zhu "the fellows of quietude and for oneself" (柔靜為我之徒).[41] Liang, moreover, takes Tan's theory of "Renxue" to promote the quality of being dynamic instead of static. For Liang, "dynamism" is a cosmological principle that leads to changes and ultimately to a better world. With this premise, Lao and Yang's "quiet" (*roujing* 柔靜) personalities stand for the exact opposite. Their doctrine of "for oneself" is another quality that Liang felt the need to attack. His strategy of dealing with the national crisis was to promote a sense of unification of the Chinese people, a theme from his early writings. The obvious opposition to the doctrine of "for oneself" may have contributed to Liang's disapproval of Lao and Yang.

In 1902 Liang started to construct a theory that was supposed to explain the "poisonous" nature of Lao and Yang's theories. The two serials, namely, *On Changing Trends in Chinese Scholarship and Thought* and *Discourse on the New Citizen*, both published in 1902, witness a shift in Liang's use of the "Lao-Yang" category. From the previous short comments, his criticism moves toward his assertion of the "world-weary" quality of Lao and Yang's thought.[42] This poisoning quality contains different aspects. In *On Changing Trends*, Liang contrasts Lao and Yang's "world-weary spirit" with Jeremy Bentham's utilitarianism.[43] Whereas in the *Discourse on the New Citizen*, Liang blames Yang Zhu's "flowing poison" (流毒) for the "world-weary" nature of his doctrine, which was detrimental to preserving one's rights (*quanli* 權利).[44] In *On Changing Trends*, Liang explains that the two core ideas of Yang Zhu's doctrines, "the doctrine of 'for oneself'" (or "ego-centrism," *weiwozhuyi* 為我主義) and "the doctrine of 'indulging in pleasure'" (or "hedonism," *zonglezhuyi* 縱樂主義) were caused by this "world-weary worldview" (*yanshiguan* 厭世觀).[45] These assertions were based on his discussion of the ancient masters in his efforts to practice "a genuine conservatism."

In 1902, Liang also wrote an article in which he argues that what determined the general trends of the world was not military force or political power but what he called "the power of scholarship" (*xueshu shili* 學術勢力).[46] Liang was convinced that it was with such power that an individual could determine the fate of a nation and that a nation could determine the general trends in the world.[47] Therefore, an authentic Chinese intellectual history had to be constructed, or what he calls "genuine conservatism" (*zhen shoujiu* 真守舊):[48]

> From now and in the coming twenty years, I do not worry that foreign scholarly thought will not be imported. I only worry that the scholarly thought of our own nation will not flourish. . . . In general, if a nation stands between heaven and earth, it must have characteristic traits that keep it standing. If one wants to improve one's nation, one must refine and develop these traits.
>
> 自今以往二十年中，吾不患外國學術思想之不輸入，吾惟患本國學術思想之不發明。……凡一國立於天地，必有其所以立之特質。欲自善其國者，不可不於此特質焉，淬屬之而增長之。[49]

In pursuit of this "genuine conservatism," Liang explains Yang Zhu's world-weariness in relation to the geography of the ancient masters.[50] With Liang's newfound interests in geography,[51] he associates Yang Zhu's theories with the master's geographical location. *On Changing Trends* introduces a classification of the ancient masters based on their southern or northern origins and proposes a relationship with their doctrines. In order to make this classification, Liang distinguished between two ancient civilizations: the Yellow River civilization and the Yangtze (Yangzi) civilization.[52] These were the basis of different schools belonging to the northern group (*beipai* 北派) and southern group (*nanpai* 南派), respectively.[53] Liang divided nineteen ancient masters[54] into these two groups and claimed that the climate and the geography of northern and southern China determined the dispositions of these masters. The harsh climate and infertile lands in the north had the effect that the doctrines of this group tended to be more "practically oriented" (*wu shiji* 務實際), while the warm climate and fertile lands in the south cultivated the "world-weary" doctrines of the other group.[55] He then made a diagram listing the twenty-two opposing traits of both groups, which can be seen as a general opposition between "favoring action" (*zhu dong* 主動) versus "favoring quietude" (*zhu jing* 主靜).[56] Yang Zhu is put into the division of "the Southern group" and represents a branch that originated with Laozi. As this classification offers a geographical explanation of Yang Zhu's "world-weary worldview," it also explains the cause of the doctrines of "for oneself" and "indulging in pleasure," both of which were purely negative from the standpoint of Confucian orthodoxy as well as the perspective of nationalism.

Although Liang did not show any inclination toward either the southern or the northern group, he still felt the need to make a clear distinction between Yang Zhu's doctrine of "indulging in pleasure" and Bentham's utilitarianism that is beneficial to the nation. In *On Changing Trends*, he coined the term "indulging in pleasure" (*zongle* 縱樂) as a core idea of Yang Zhu, which is slightly different from Kang's use of "indulging in desires" (*zong yu* 縱慾). This is probably because of Liang's positive understanding of "indulging in desires." This can be deduced from a quotation he made in 1902 of the following statement by Kang Youwei:

> Saving the nation and saving the world both depend on "indulging in desires." This is the case when one indulges in his "mind of not being able to bear the sufferings of others."
>
> 救國救天下，皆以縱慾也。縱其不忍人之心則然也。[57]

For Liang, "indulging in desires" was not necessarily a bad thing as long as the "desire" was good for the nation and the world. The reason why Liang felt the urge to clarify the distinction between "the doctrine of indulging in pleasure" and utilitarianism might be due to the resemblance between the term that he coined and the Japanese translation of "utilitarianism" as "the doctrine of taking pleasure in profit" (*lelizhuyi* 樂利主義)

or "the school of happiness" (*kuaile pai* 快樂派). The shared character "*le* 樂*"* in the two concepts may have given the impression that Yang Zhu's theory shared similarities with Bentham's. However, in Liang's opinion, Bentham's utilitarian theories were in line with Katō Hiroyuki's theory of "the mind of loving the self" (*aiji xin* 愛己心) and "the mind of loving others" (*aita xin* 愛他心).[58] It also resonated with Kang's positive understanding of "indulging in desires,"[59] whereas "indulging in pleasure" was something Liang deemed negative. Liang claims that Yang Zhu's doctrines and utilitarianism are "completely different" (迥殊科矣). In contrast to the utilitarians that were beneficial to the nation,[60] "those who hold the doctrine of world-weariness are all sinners of the society and sinners of the world" (凡持厭世主義者，皆社會之罪人，天地之罪人也).[61]

As shown above, Liang cultivated a sense of the nation over the years, and nationalism became dominant in his evaluation of ancient Chinese thought. Under this frame, Yang Zhu was blamed for China's weakness. Even though Liang tried to explain the reasons for his thoughts in an academic context, his judgment was still overshadowed by his nationalist ideas. The Chinese empire was gone; a Chinese nation was forming. If for Mencius, Yang Zhu was someone who "denied one's lord," for Liang, Yang Zhu was someone who "denied one's nation."

2. From an "Egoist" to a "Philosopher"

In a time when the idea of "the nation being subjugated and the race being exterminated" (亡國滅種) was prevalent in the discourse of late-Qing intellectuals, the expression "the slaves whose nation was subjugated" (亡國奴) was coined to warn about China's dangerous situation. The narrative about "slaves" (奴隸) was then taken up by intellectuals to indicate the situation in which the Chinese were not entitled to participate in political affairs. In Liang's discussion, the Chinese were not only "slaves" politically but also intellectually,[62] the cause of which could be traced to the ancient masters Laozi and Yang Zhu, whose ideas cultivated the meek philosophy of China. In 1902, Liang wrote the *New Citizen* to promote a renovation of the Chinese from "slaves" to "citizens" (國民). In his understanding, the Chinese did not have the consciousness of a nation and did not act for the good of the nation. What they showed was not only indifference to the national crisis but also an abysmal lethargy that expressed itself as an "inveterate spirit of resignation and submissiveness."⁶³ In this renovation, the concept of "rights" was crucial in turning the Chinese into modern citizens who were conscious of the nation and strived to strengthen it. It was against this background that Yang Zhu was included in Liang's discussion of "rights."

The current widely accepted Chinese translation of "rights" is the compound of *quanli*. However, there was a process before this indigenous term began to be seen as an equivalent of the Western concept of "rights." The earliest use of *quanli* can be found in the *Xunzi*. There the expression refers to the power and profit that inspired immoral intentions:

> The gentleman knows that whatever is incomplete and unadulterated does not deserve to be considered beautiful . . . For this reason, power and profit cannot sway him, and the masses cannot shift him.
>
> 君子知夫不全不粹不足以為美也……是故權利不能傾也，群眾不能移也。⁶⁴

Although before the Han dynasty, *quanli* sometimes meant "weighing the benefits and harms," from the Han dynasty on, it generally referred to power and profit,⁶⁵ which had an immoral connotation in Confucian discourse.⁶⁶

By the latter part of the nineteenth century, more specifically in 1864, however, the expression was endowed with new meanings. In 1836, Henry Wheaton had published his *Elements of International Law*, which was later translated into Chinese by the American missionary W. A. P. Martin (also known as Ding Weiliang 丁韙良, 1827–1916) and published in 1864 under the title *General Laws of the Myriad Nations* (*Wanguo gongfa* 萬國公法). In this book, the word most frequently used to translate "rights" is *quan* 權, although sometimes that term is also used to mean "authority." *Quanli* was also introduced as a direct translation of "rights," which gradually became more important than *quan*. While in Chinese contexts, *quan* often meant power, in Martin's translation, the *quan* of a state can be read as "the *quan* a state has to equality or independence whether or not it is equal or independent"; in other words, *quan* is what "states ought to have."⁶⁷ Stephen Angle notices that it is also in the *General Laws* that the indigenous term *quanli* undergoes two kinds of transformations: the first is from "power and profit" in a negative sense to a positive one and the second is the occasional use of *quanli* as the direct translation of "rights."[68]

Liang also saw the complexity in the term. More importantly, the nuanced connotations of *quanli* in different contexts affected the association he made between Yang Zhu and *quanli*. From Liang's reading of Yang Zhu, we can trace the transformation of the term *quanli* from its traditional meaning of "power and profits" to the "authority" of the people and ultimately to become an equivalent of the Western concept of "rights."

Reading Yang Zhu with "Power and Benefit"

Liang's first uses of *quanli* appear in the "General Discussion on Reform" (Bianfa tongyi 變法通議), a famous serial published in 1896–97. An example is where he warns that

> Nowadays, the reason why they get to hold so much power over and take so much benefit from China is that we are weak and foolish. . . . The Western officials who (claim to) make plans for China actually simply do this to protect the power and benefits (*quanli*) of their own states.
>
> 今夫彼之所以得操大權、占大利於中國者，以吾之弱也愚也[...]西官之為中國謀者，實以保護本國之權利耳。[69]

His use of *quanli* before 1899 does not sound very different from its traditional meaning of "power and profit." While Liang tended to promote the *quanli* of the state and condemn the actions that reduced it, he still rejected the *quanli* of individuals. His association of Yang Zhu with the notion of *quanli* was based on this view. It is reflected in his criticism of Yang Zhu and his followers. In "On Dynamism" (1898) he wrote:

> Confucius guarded against being centered on oneself, whereas Yang was "for oneself." And this is how the benevolent and non-benevolent are distinguished. Nowadays everyone is obsessed with the imperial examinations (*kemu*) and (obtaining) power and profit (*quanli*), discreetly waiting for the day when the beans are peeled off and the melons are distributed.

This is because they have nothing but the word "self" filling their chests.

夫孔氏戒我，而楊氏為我，此仁不仁之判也。乃今天下營營於科目，孳孳於權利，伈伈俔俔於豆剖瓜分之日，不過"我"之一字橫梗胸臆。⁷⁰

In this statement, *quanli* still connotes its traditional meaning and is criticized. So is Yang Zhu, as the representative of those who pursue *quanli*. Liang's earliest connection between Yang Zhu and *quanli* was thus based on the negative connotation of obtaining *quanli*. The doctrine of "for oneself" was interpreted as the ideology of those who pursued power and profit for their own benefit. Even though Liang's later understanding of *quanli* evolved, this early connection of 1898 was preserved until 1902.

Reading Yang Zhu with the Democratic Concept of "People's Authority"

In the 1890s, "rights" discourse prospered in China. The word *minquan* 民權 (*minken* 民権 in Japanese) was first coined in Japan in the late 1870s and soon after used in Chinese by two diplomats. It was not widely adopted in China until late in the 1890s. Angle believes that the best translation for *minquan* is "people's authority" since this word was mostly used by reformers to argue for the authority of the people to engage in public undertakings,⁷¹ which can be seen in Liang's discussion of *minquan* in the passages quoted below. If *minquan* refers to the *quan* (authority) of the collective, the use of *zizhu zhiquan* 自主之權 (the right to self-mastery) highlights the *quan* (authority or rights) of individuals. The latter expression was used in *General Laws* as a translation for "independence," the literal meaning of the term being "the power to rule oneself."⁷² In the 1880s, Kang's discussion of this notion was already closely linked to equality and the right to self-mastery.⁷³ Liang's discussion of *minquan* and *zizhu zhiquan* are also in line with the reformers of his time.

In 1896, Liang started to use expressions such as *minquan* or *zizhu zhiquan* to discuss the sort of authority or rights that should be legitimately enjoyed by the people. Instead of seeing the tension between the *quan* of the collective and the *quan* of individuals, he now saw the *quan* of individuals as a means to realize the *quan* of the collective. He defined *zizhu zhiquan* as "each person doing all he ought to do, and receiving all the benefits he ought to receive" (各盡其所當為之事，各得其所應有之利).[74] He also stressed that power or authority (*quan*) consisted of obligations (or affairs, undertakings, *shi* 事) as well as benefits (*li* 利).[75] Although his definition seemed to only stress one's obligations and benefits, it still implied the power or authority gained from fulfilling one's obligations by managing one's affairs or engaging in one's undertakings. Liang explained that since the emperor fulfilled all the obligations, he also enjoyed all the benefits. However, it was not the emperor alone who ought to fulfill all the obligations and enjoy all the benefits; the obligations and benefits should also be fulfilled and enjoyed by the people.[76] Thus, his definition of "people's authority" or "the right to self-mastery" aimed at people's power (or rights) in political participation through elaborating on the relation between engaging in public affairs and the benefit to be gained from it. Although the character that stands for benefit or profit (*li* 利) is not included in either *minquan* or *zizhu zhiquan*, Liang's definition suggested its association with *quan*. However, before 1898, his use of *quan* almost exclusively emphasized the authority one has over one's private and public affairs. While *zizhu* 自主 is often understood as self-mastery, what Liang stressed was self-rule, that is, people participating in the public processes of government.

The word *quanli* did not appear in Liang's writings until 1899. Influenced by a social Darwinist worldview, he deemed "struggling" (*jingzheng*) a crucial part of the claim and preservation of individual *quanli*.[77] Angle offers a definition for Liang's notion of *quanli* at this stage: "the abilities and interests that one should legitimately be able to enjoy."[78] In the same year, Liang wrote "On Might as Right" 論強權, expanding on his understanding of the notion. First, he claims that "there is no such thing as rights in the world. There is only power. Power is benefit." (天下無所謂權利，只有權力而已，權力即利也)[79] Second, for Liang, the *quanli* of liberty was not something people were born with but something that needed to be claimed and struggled for.[80] The ambiguity he attributed to the term "rights" (*quanli* 權利), "power" (*quanli* 權力), and "benefit" (*li* 利) suggests a close association between the actions of benefiting, empowering, and claiming rights.

This positive understanding of claims to *quanli* is exhibited in Liang's views on Yang Zhu's notion of "for oneself" and his insistence on not losing a single hair. Liang now associates Yang Zhu's doctrine with the active struggle for one's *quanli*, which will end up strengthening the *quan* of Chinese people:

In the past, China's Yang Zhu established his teaching based on the notion of "for oneself" and said: "If no one pulls out a single hair, and no one benefits the world, the world will be in good order." I used to seriously doubt the validity of these words and to seriously hate these words. It was not until I read the books of the British and German philosophers that I realize that so many of them advocate things that are similar to what Yang Zhu advocated. And their theories are so well developed that they can strengthen the group and allow the citizens to achieve civilization. The politics of Western states/nations is built upon the concept of people's rights (*minquan*), and the reason why people's authority is stable is that all the citizens struggle for their rights (*quanli*) without taking even a single step back. This is how, by not pulling out a single hair, everyone benefits the world through benefiting the self.

昔中國楊朱以爲我立教，曰："人人不拔一毫，人人不利天下，天下治矣。" 吾昔甚疑其言，甚惡其言，及觀英、德諸國哲學大家之書，其所標名義與楊朱吻合者，不一而足，而其理論之完備，實有足以助人群之發達，進國民之文明者。蓋西國政治之基礎在於民權，而民權之鞏固由於國民競爭權利寸步不肯稍讓，即以人人不拔一毫之心，以自利者利天下。[81]

Yang Zhu's doctrine of "for oneself" is interpreted as "benefiting the self" (*li ji* 利己), which suggests an intention of struggling for one's rights. This intention is beneficial in equipping the Chinese with "people's rights." This association was possible because of Liang's layered construction of the term. "Benefiting" (*li* 利) did not only refer to acquiring benefits but also to claiming one's "rights." If an individual did not have the intention to benefit himself, he was deliberately giving up his "rights," his responsibilities, and his footing.[82] Yang Zhu was thus portrayed positively as someone whose doctrine was beneficial to claiming the *quanli* of individuals, which would contribute to the empowering of the *quan* of the people.

Reading Yang Zhu with "the Consciousness of Rights"

In 1902 Liang started to publish his critical serial *New Citizens* to advocate a renovation of the people, or to promote what he called the "new citizens" of China. After explaining the necessity of renovating the people, Liang wrote sixteen chapters between 1902 and 1906 to elaborate on the different aspects of the ideal personality of this new citizen. In one of these chapters, "Lun quanli sixiang" 論權利思想 (On the consciousness of rights), he introduced the expression "consciousness of rights," the awareness to actively claim and preserve one's rights.[83] Once again, Liang found his way to Yang Zhu.

In Liang's description, the consciousness of rights is an abstract idea that can be imagined through the parallel of one's physical integrity. The consciousness of rights, or to be more precise, the consciousness of the existence and the protection of rights, is exactly like the consciousness of one's physical integrity and the instincts to protect that integrity. Liang explains that unlike animals that only have instincts to preserve the integrity of their "physical sustainability" (*xing er xia zhi shengcun* 形而下之生存), human beings also have instincts to preserve their "mental sustainability" (*xing er shang zhi shengcun* 形而上之生存). Angle argues that this idea was probably inspired in Liang by Rudolf von Jhering's (1818–92) distinction between one's "physical life" and "moral existence."[84] Liang explains that one's instinct to "preserve one's life" (*bao shengming* 保生命) is helpful for keeping intact one's "physical sustainability," whereas one's instinct to preserve one's rights is helpful for keeping intact one's "mental sustainability." This latter instinct is the consciousness of rights. When one's "physical sustainability" is violated, one will instinctively feel pain. Likewise, when one's "mental sustainability" is violated, those who have the consciousness of rights will also instinctively feel pain.[85] Thus, the preservation of rights is extrapolated from Liang's description of the protection of physical integrity.

On top of this, Liang's understanding of the relation between a citizen and a nation was also filled with body metaphors. The theme of the *New Citizen* is Liang's promotion of new "citizens" (*guomin*) in place of the "slaves" that the Chinese people used to be. Liang's understanding of the relationship between *guomin* (citizens) and *guo* (states) exhibits resemblance to Johann Kaspar Bluntschli's (1808–81) organic theory of the state.[86] Bluntschli believed that the state is "an organic, masculine, moral person, having both spirit and body."[87] In such a state, "the citizen was nothing, except as a member of the State. His whole existence depended on and was subject to the State."[88] This organic theory of state echoes in Liang's own writing: "The state is formed by its citizens. A state has its citizens is as a body has four limbs, five organs, tendons, and blood." (國也者，積民而成。國之有民，猶身之有四肢五臟筋脈血輪也)[89] This is how Liang connects citizens and states as limbs and organs belonging to one body.

With the consciousness of rights closely related to physical integrity and the new citizen related to the state by way of the body metaphor, Yang Zhu's defense of physical integrity seemed like a pertinent analogy to articulate vividly the consciousness of rights and the relation between the rights of individuals and the rights of the state:

> Yang Zhu says: "If no one loses a single hair, and no one benefits the world, the world will be in good order." I used to loath his statement, but when I think of it today, I realize there is some insight in it. . . . Even an extremely mean and unworthy person would not care about one hair and haggle over it. It is not the hair he is fighting for. He is fighting because his ownership over that hair was challenged. This ownership is the authority.[90] This is to expand the category of consciousness of rights and extend its content to its outermost limits. When rights of singular parts are put together, rights of the whole body will be constituted. When each individual's consciousness of rights is compiled together, this forms the whole nation's consciousness of rights. Thus, in order to cultivate this consciousness, it has to start from the individuals.
>
> 杨朱曰："人人不损一毫，人人不利天下，天下治矣。"吾畴昔罪深恶痛恨其言，由今思之，盖亦有所見焉。……夫人雖至鄙吝，至不肖，亦何至愛及一毫，顧斤斤焉爭之者，非爭此一毫，爭夫人之損我一毫所有權也。所有權即主權。是推權利思想充類至義之盡者也。一部分之權利，合之即為全體之權利，一私人之權利思想，積之即為一國家之權利思想。故欲養成此思想，必自個人始。[91]

In this passage, *quanli* refers to both the rights of individuals and of states. With inspiration from Jhering and Bluntschli, Yang Zhu's extreme emphasis on physical integrity is reinterpreted by Liang as an appeal for protecting the integrity of the rights of individuals, which will accumulate into the integral rights of states. It is through this process of contemplation that Yang Zhu is depicted as a Chinese philosopher who had the consciousness of rights.

Although Yang Zhu had already appeared as one of the major ancient Chinese philosophers in several histories of Chinese philosophy written by Japanese intellectuals, based on my research so far, Liang was the first Chinese intellectual who called Yang Zhu a philosopher, and he associated him with the concept of "rights" as early as 1902. Before Liang, there were already some Japanese intellectuals who had written their own histories of Chinese philosophy (*Shina tetsugaku shi*) in which Yang Zhu is listed as one of the major Chinese philosophers. In Matsumoto Bunzaburō's 松本文三郎 (1869–1944) history published in 1898, Endō Ryūkichi's 遠藤隆吉 (1874–1946) history published in 1900, and Takase Takejirō's 高瀨武次郎 (1869–1950) *Philosophy of Yang and Mo* published in 1902, Yang Zhu is included in all of these Japanese intellectuals' constructions of Chinese philosophy.[92] It is difficult to ascertain which of these books Liang read, but he differed from these Japanese scholars in his association of Yang Zhu with the concept of "rights." In "On the Consciousness of Rights," following his articulation of this association, Liang calls Yang Zhu a philosopher for the first time:

> That is to say, Yang Zhu was actually a philosopher who advocated rights.
>
> 然則楊朱者，實主權利之哲學家。[93]

Despite this positive association of Yang Zhu with the notion of rights, Liang still could not fully embrace his ideas as being beneficial to the nation. The other aspect Liang attributed to Yang Zhu still overpowered this new reading. Liang remained convinced that Yang Zhu's theory was not good for the nation because Yang Zhu did not fully understand the consciousness of rights.

> Yang Zhu was not someone who understood the truth of rights. He only knew that rights should be preserved and not lost, but he did not know that rights only emerged on the premise of being aggressive. Indulgence, entertainment, spontaneity, and world-weariness are all executioners of rights. But Yang Zhu advocated these things to pursue rights. What he did does not differ much from expecting to live forever while drinking poison. This is why although Yang's learning prevails in our nation, (the Chinese people were) only subjugated to the flowing poison of "no one benefiting the world," while the ideal of "no one losing a single hair" was not realized. That is caused by the weak consciousness of rights.

楊朱非能解權利之真相者也，彼知權利當保守而勿失。而不知權利以進取而始生，放佚也，娛樂也，任運也，厭世也，皆殺權利之劊子手也。而楊朱昌言之，是以求權利，則何異飲鴆以祈永年也。此吾國雖盛行楊學，而惟熏染其人人不利天下之流毒，而不能實行其人人不損一毫之理想也。權利思想薄弱使然也。

The above statement shows Liang's reservations about fully embracing Yang Zhu's theory. Even though Liang believes that Yang Zhu was a philosopher who understood the need to preserve rights, Yang Zhu did not understand the method of preserving them. This is how Liang incorporates his convoluted understanding of Yang Zhu that is shaped by both tradition and modernity: Yang Zhu's theory is against the nation and beneficial to the nation at the same time.

Conclusion

Liang's early reading of Yang Zhu is the product of its specific time in Chinese history, when intellectuals felt the need to shuffle what they had in mind and adjust these ideas to gain a better understanding of themselves and the world. Liang's portrayal of Yang Zhu reflects a triple influence: from the conventional education he received, the foreign knowledge he acquired, and the specific background of his time. Under these influences, Liang's portrayal of Yang Zhu became a compound formed by traditional and modern understandings. The shifted paradigm turned the Yang Zhu who was against a lord to someone who was against the nation, while the introduction of Western concepts shed new light on Yang Zhu and turned him into a philosopher who advocated rights. In Liang's study of Yang Zhu, on the one hand, he absorbed knowledge that he considered beneficial to the nation and adjusted his reading of the classics; on the other hand, he understood the new knowledge based on his own intellectual background, which facilitated the introduction of Western concepts. Liang's wavering between the positive and negative reading of Yang Zhu between 1896 and 1904 shows his inner struggle between the new ideas he was attracted to and the conventional ideas he was accustomed to. This struggle allowed Liang to find value in what had been generally condemned for thousands of years. Although he saw Yang Zhu as someone responsible for the weak state of China, his theorization of the geographical explanation of Yang Zhu's doctrine ameliorated Yang Zhu's negative image. This theorization initiated a trend of explaining Yang Zhu's world-weariness with the environment he was in, which was carried on by Wu Yu 吳虞 (1872–1949), Hu Shi 胡適 (1891–1962), Jiang Weiqiao 蔣維喬 (1873–1958), and Chen Cisheng 陳此生 (1900–1981). The association of Yang Zhu's doctrine with rights also shows Liang's struggle in accepting the Western concept of rights. Since this association was mostly in service of Liang's nation-building project, it was not preserved in his writings of the 1920s, when Liang's focus became more academically oriented.[94] However, Liang's association might have triggered the May Fourth portrayal of Yang Zhu as an individualist and explains the tendency of reinterpreting Yang Zhu with modern concepts such as rights, liberty, and individualism in later academic writings, which contributed to Yang Zhu's contemporary image.

Notes

1. This research was supported by the FWO project G060817N: "Mozi and Yang Zhu from Heretics to Philosophers: Caught in Another Web? The Genealogy of 'Chinese Philosophy' in Three Major Steps."

2. Depending on the texts, he is also referred to as Yang Sheng 楊生, Yangzi 楊子, or Yang Ziju 陽子居.

3. Joseph Levenson declares that China's shift from tradition to early modernity was marked by a shift from the traditional concept of "all under heaven" (*tianxia* 天下) to a modern concept of "all nations." See Joseph Levenson, "The Genesis of Confucian China and Its Modern Fate," in *The Historian's Workshop*, ed. L. P. Curtis Jr. (New York: Knopf, 1970), 288. See also Joseph Levenson, *Confucian China and Its Modern Fate: A Trilogy* (Berkeley and Los Angeles: University of California Press, 1968), 103.

4. See, among others, Julia Schneider, "Early Chinese Nationalism: The Origins under Manchu Rule," in *Interpreting China as a Regional and Global Power*, ed. Bart Dessein (New York: Palgrave Macmillan, 2014), 13–18. For the first definition of "nation," see the *Oxford Advanced Learner's Dictionary*, 9th ed. (Oxford: Oxford University Press, 2020).

5. Shen Songqiao 沈松僑, "Jindai Zhongguo de 'guomin' guannian, 1895–1911" 近代中國的"國民"觀念, 1895–1911 [The concept of "citizen" in modern China, 1895–1911], in *Higashi Ajia ni okeru kindai shogainen no seiritsu* 『東アジアにおける近代諸概念の成立』 (Kyoto: International Research Center for Japanese Studies, 2005), 190–91. There is also an English translation of this paper: see Sung-chiao Shen and Sechin Y. S. Chien, "Turning Slaves into Citizens:

Discourses of *Guomin* and the Construction of Chinese National Identity in the Late Qing Period," in *The Dignity of Nations: Equality, Competition, and Honor in East Asian Nationalism*, ed. John Fitzgerald and Sechin Y. S. Chien (Hong Kong: Hong Kong University Press, 2006), 49–69.

6. He divides these four stages as *Weixin shiqi* 維新時期 [The period of self-strengthening], *Xinmin shiqi* 新民時期 [The period of renovating the people], *Xinwenhua yundong shiqi* 新文化運動時期 [The period of the new culture movement], and *Dongfang wenhua fuxing yundong shiqi* 東方文化復興運動時期 [The period of the reviving eastern culture movement]. See He Aiguo 何愛國, "Shibian yu xueshu: Liang Qichao de Yang xue sanbian" 世變與學術：梁啟超的楊學三變 [The relation between the changing world and the scholarly thoughts: the three-stage evolution of Liang Qichao's views on Yangism], *History Research and Teaching*, no. 3 (2014): 10–18.

7. See He Aiguo 何愛國, "Cong 'qinshou' dao 'quanli zhexuejia': Lun Yang Zhu xuepai xin xingxiang de jindai goujian," 從禽獸到權利哲學家論楊朱學派新形象的近代構建 [From "beast" to "philosopher of rights": On the reconstructions of Yangism in the modern era], *Lishi jiaoxue wenti* 歷史教學問題, no. 5 (2015): 11–19. See also He, "Qingji minchu Yang Zhu sixiang de huohua" 清季民初楊朱思想的活化 [Reinterpretation of Yang Zhu thought in the late Qing dynasty to early Republic of China], *Lishi jiaoxue wenti* 歷史教學問題, no. 1 (2015): 81–149.

8. For the pre-Republican portrayals of Yang Zhu, see He, *Xiandaixing de bentu huixiang: Jindai yangmo sichao yanjiu*, 現代性的本土迴響：近代楊墨思潮研究 [Local echoes of modernity: A study of Yang Zhu and Mozi thought in Modern China] (Guangzhou: Shijie tushu chuban Guangdong, 2015), 42–48; He, "Cong 'qinshou' dao 'quanli zhexuejia,'" 11–13; Li Yucheng 李玉誠, "Yang Zhu 'yiduan' xingxiang de lishi shengcheng," 楊朱'異端'形象的歷史生成 [The emergence and evolution of Yang Zhu as heretic symbol], *Shehui kexue luntan* 社會科學論壇 3 (2017): 51–61. See also Defoort in this volume.

9. From 1898 to 1922, Liang's writings referring to Yang Zhu display a group of interpretations that constantly change. For Liang, Yang Zhu is a heretic against Confucianism ("An Explanation of Mencius," 1898), a thinker who contemplates life and death ("The Deceased in the 20th Century"), a master who establishes a school based on the notion of "for oneself" ("Contradictory and Complementary Principles of Ten Types of Morality," 1900), a hedonistic Daoist (*On Changing Trends in Chinese Scholarship and Thought*, 1902), a philosopher who advocates rights and liberty but lacks the notion of civic virtue (*Discourses on the Making New of the People*, 1902), a Darwinist who promotes the "greater self" or "group" ("My Views on Life and Death," 1904), a master whose thoughts could destroy China ("Master Mozi's Thoughts," 1904), a naturalist ("An Overview of the Schools Succeeded Lao, Kong, and Mo," 1920), an extreme individualist (*The Political Thoughts in Pre-Qin*, 1922), and a materialist (*The Indian Buddhism*, 1925). See Liang Qichao 梁啟超, *Liang Qichao quanji* 梁啟超全集 [The collected

works of Liang Qichao], ed. Zhang Pinxing 張品興 (Beijing: Beijing Publishing House, 1999).

10. Irene Bloom, trans., *Mencius* (New York: Columbia University Press, 2011), 70.

11. Although the popular view of Yang Zhu being a heretic against the Confucian tradition has been around for quite some time, there are some scholars who point out the nuances of Yang Zhu's images in different periods of Chinese intellectual history. See Carine Defoort, "Five Visions of Yang Zhu: Before He Became a Philosopher," *Asian Studies* 8, no. 2 (2020): 235–56. See also Li, "Yang Zhu 'yiduan' xingxiang de lishi shengcheng," 60. See also Wei Yixia 魏義霞, "Kang Youwei shijie zhong de Yang Zhu" 康有為視界中的楊朱 [Kang Youwei's views on Yang Zhu], *Jianghuai luntan* 江淮論壇 (April 2017), 40–45.

12. See more on the modern portrayals of Yang Zhu in He, "Cong 'qinshou' dao 'quanli zhexuejia,'" 11–19. See also He, "Qingji minchu Yang Zhu sixiang de huohua," 81–149.

13. Some scattered statements about Yang Zhu can be found in the *Mencius* 孟子, *Zhuangzi* 莊子, *Han Feizi* 韓非子, *Lüshi chunqiu* 呂氏春秋, *Huainanzi* 淮南子, and *Liezi* 列子.

14. Many scholars have questioned the date, the author, and the content of the text. See also Brindley's paper in the current volume. The *Liezi* is considered by many scholars to be a pseudograph, and there are abundant studies on this matter. See Liu Gusheng 劉固盛 & Li Haijie 李海傑, "Laoxue shi zhong de Yang Zhu sixiang—jian lun *Liezi* shu fei wei" 老學史中的楊朱思想——兼論《列子》書非偽 [The thought of Yang Zhu in the history of Laozi learning: Along with a discussion of the authenticity of *Liezi*], *Hunan Daxye xuebao* 湖南大學學報 32, no. 1 (2018): 35–42.

15. He Aiguo proposes that the criticism against Yang Zhu's indulgence in desires emerged from ancient times. However, "desires" in premodern texts usually refer to the physical and material pleasures, whereas "indulging in desires" in modern texts is explained as a trait of the worldview defined by world-weariness. He points out that the premodern criticisms are usually based on the so-called Yangist texts that did not refer to Yang Zhu. Although there is no direct evidence in the "Yang Zhu" chapter to prove that Yang Zhu promoted indulgence in desires, the sayings of the other figures in this chapter (such as Guan Zhong 管仲, Gongsun Zhao 公孫朝, and Gongsun Mu 公孫穆) attest to this. See He Aiguo, *Xiandaixing de bentu huixiang: jindai yangmo sichao yanjiu*, 58.

16. This incorporation of Yang Zhu into the Daoist lineage emerged much earlier than the late Qing dynasty. See Defoort, "Five Visions of Yang Zhu: Before He Became a Philosopher."

17. For a more nuanced account of Yang Zhu's thought presented in the *Liezi*, see Brindley, this volume.

18. He, *Xiandaixing de bentu huixiang: jindai yangmo sichao yanjiu*, 58. See also, He, "Qingji minchu Yang Zhu sixiang de huohua," 82.

19. Defoort, "Five Visions of Yang Zhu: Before He Became a Philosopher."

20. Influenced by Western ideas, modern intellectuals started to gain a positive image of Mozi and blame Laozi and Yang Zhu for the selfish and resigned personality of the Chinese. Kang Youwei, Liang Qichao, and Bi Yongnian 畢永年 (1869–1902) all criticized the teachings of Laozi and Yang Zhu as the "poison" that had polluted the Chinese mind. See He, "Cong 'qinshou' dao 'quanli zhexuejia,'" 16.

21. Kang tends to praise Mozi's theories for the resemblance between Mozi's doctrine of "impartial care" (*jian ai*) and Confucius's "humaneness" (*ren*). See Wei Yixia, "Kang Youwei dui Mozi sixiang de taidu yu qushe" 康有为对墨子思想的态度与取舍 [Kang Youwei's attitudes towards Mozi and his acceptance and rejection of Mozi's theory], *Heilongjiang Social Science* 141, no. 6 (2013): 3. By contrast, Kang's views on Yang Zhu are generally negative. See Wei, "Kang Youwei shijie zhong de Yang Zhu," 43.

22. Liang, "*Xixue shumu biao* houxu" 《西學書目表》後序 [The epilogue of *A Reading List of Western Learning*], in *Liang Qichao quanji*, 1:86.

23. Bentham and Mill were seen by Liang as the two representative utilitarianists. See Liang, "Lelizhuyi taidou bianqing zhi xueshuo," 4:1045.

24. Liang, *Lun Zhongguo xueshu sixiang bianqian zhi dashi* 論中國學術思想變遷之大勢 [On changing trends in Chinese scholarship and thought], in *Liang Qichao quanji*, 3:574.

25. Liang, *Lun Zhongguo xueshu sixiang*, 580.

26. Liang, *Zi Mozi xueshuo* 子墨子學說 [The doctrines of Master Mozi], in *Liang Qichao quanji*, 3158. Liang's negative comment on Yang Zhu in this text probably shows the influence of Yang Du 楊度 (1875–1931). In 1904, Liang published *Zhongguo Wushidao* 中國武士道 [Chinese Bushido]. Yang Du wrote a preface for this book and harshly criticized Yang Zhu for destroying China. See "Yang Xu" 楊敘 [Yang's preface], in *Zhongguo Wushidao*, *Liang Qichao quanji*, 1378–83.

27. Joseph R. Levenson, *Liang Ch'i-Ch'ao and the Mind of Modern China* (Cambridge, MA: Harvard University Press, 1953), 109.

28. Liu Pansui 劉盼遂, "Liang Rengong xiansheng zhuan" 梁任公先生傳 [Liang Rengong: A biographical sketch], in *Zhuiyi Liang Qichao* 追憶梁啟超 [Remembrances of Liang Qichao], ed. Xia Xiaohong 夏曉虹 (Beijing: Zhongguo guangbo dianshi chubanshe, 1996), 7.

29. The world map Liang purchased was *Yinghuan zhilüe* 瀛寰志略, a world map compiled by Xu Jiyu 徐繼畬 in 1840. See Liang, "Sanshi zishu" 三十自述 [Autobiography at the age of thirty], in *Liang Qichao quanji*, 957–58.

30. Chang Hao, *Liang Ch'i-ch'ao and Intellectual Transition in China, 1890–1907* (Taipei: Rainbow Bridge, 1971), 59–60. See also Liang Qichao, "Shikezhai

jiyan jixing xu" 適可齋記言記行序 [Preface to jottings on the talk and doings in the *Shikezhai*], in *Liang Qichao quanji*, 89.

31. See the division of the different stages of Liang's thought in Levenson, *Liang Ch'i-Ch'ao and the Mind of Modern China*. See also Liang's metaphor that describes his feelings of reading the translated books: "It was like catching a beam of sunshine in a dark room, or having a cup of warm rice wine when you were starving" (如幽室見日，枯腹得酒"), in "Lun xue Ribenwen zhi yi" 論學日本文之益 [On the benefit of learning the Japanese language], in *Liang Qichao quanji*, 324. The translation of this quote is based on the translation in Tang Xiaobing 唐小兵, *Global Space and the Nationalist Discourse of Modernity: The Historical Thinking of Liang Qichao* (Stanford, CA: Stanford University Press, 1996), 14.

32. Levenson, *Confucian China and Its Modern Fate: A Trilogy*, 81.

33. He, "Cong 'qinshou' dao 'quanli zhexuejia'," 16.

34. He, "Cong 'qinshou' dao 'quanli zhexuejia,'" 16.

35. He, "Cong 'qinshou' dao 'quanli zhexuejia,'" 16.

36. Chang, *Liang Ch'i-ch'ao and Intellectual Transition in China*, 96–104.

37. "*Shuoqun* xu" 說群序, in *Liang Qichao quanji*, 93. See more on Liang's explanation of "egoistic methods" and "collective methods" in Chang, *Liang Ch'i-ch'ao and Intellectual Transition in China*, 104–106.

38. Back in 1891, in the school regulations Kang wrote, he had pointed out that Lao and Yang's teachings had degraded the Confucian tradition and made their followers egocentric (*dushan* 獨善) and profit-seeking (*yingsi* 營私) individuals. See Kang Youwei, "Changxing xueji" 長興學記 [The school regulations of *Changxing*], in *Kang Youwei quanji* [The collected works of Kang Youwei], ed. Jiang Yihua 姜義華 & Zhang Ronghua 張榮華, vol. 1 (Beijing: Zhongguo renmindaxue chubanshe, 2007), 345.

39. Liang, "*Xixue shumu biao* houxu," 86.

40. Liang, "He pangguanzhe wen" 呵旁觀者文 [Reproaching the bystanders], in *Liang Qichao quanji*, 445. This also echoes Kang's criticism of those who were influenced by "the poison left by Yang Zhu" (楊朱之貽毒) and "sat by in leisure when the nation was subjugated and the race was exterminated" (坐視亡國滅種而從容). See Kang Youwei, *Mengzi wei* 孟子微 [Comments of Mencius], in *Kang Youwei quanji*, 5:497–98.

41. Liang, "Shuo dong" 說動 [On dynamism], in *Liang Qichao quanji*, 176. This is also in accordance with Bi Yongnian's 畢永年 (1869–1902) statement: "Lao and Yang poisoned China with (their ideas of) quietude and non-action" (老楊以柔靜無為毒中國). See Bi Yongnian, "Cun hua pian" 存華篇, in *Zhongguo jindai qimeng sichao* 中國近代啟蒙思潮 [The Chinese modern enlightenment], ed. Ding Shouhe 丁守和 (Beijing: Shehui kexue wenxian chubanshe, 1999), 275.

42. Although Kang also defined Yang Zhu's theory with the term "world-weariness," Kang did not elaborate on this opinion.

43. Liang, *Lun Zhongguo xueshu sixiang*, in *Liang Qichao quanji*, 3:596.
44. Liang, *Xinmin shuo* 新民說 [Discourse on the new citizen], in *Liang Qichao quanji*, 673.
45. Liang, *Lun Zhongguo xueshu sixiang*, 573.
46. Liang, "Lun xueshu shili zhi zuoyou shijie" 論學術勢力之左右世界 [On the power of the intellectual thoughts to determine the world situation], in *Liang Qichao quanji*, 557.
47. Liang, "Lun xueshu shili zhi zuoyou shijie," 560.
48. Liang, *Xinmin shuo*, 657. From now on, I will refer to this book as *New Citizen*.
49. Liang, *Lun Zhongguo xueshu sixiang*, 562.
50. Before Liang, Fujita Toyohachi 藤田豊八 (1869–1929) and Bunzaburō Matsumoto 松本文三郎 (1869–1944) both made their own classifications of the Chinese philosophers based on their Southern or Northern origin. Their classifications are different from Liang's. See more in Ning Tengfei 寧騰飛, "Liang Qichao 'Kong bei Lao nan' shuo de jianli ji qi yiyi" 梁啟超"孔北老南"說的建立及其意義 [On the establishment and significance of Liang Qichao's "Northern Confucius and Southern Laozi" theory], *Shixue yuekan* 史學月刊, no. 2 (2019): 117.
51. Inspired by Ukita Kazutami 浮田和民 (1859–1946) and Shiga Shigetaka's 志賀重昂 (1863–1927), Liang published four articles discussing the relationship between geography and civilization, Asian geography, Chinese geography, and European geography in 1902. For more about Liang's interests in geography, see Ning, "Liang Qichao 'Kong bei Lao nan' shuo de jianli ji qi yiyi," 121.
52. Although Liang did not refer to Shiga Shigetaka, he was probably inspired by the latter. See Ning, "Liang Qichao 'Kong bei Lao nan' shuo," 121.
53. This classification was probably inspired by Ukita Kazutami, since Ukita elaborated on a relation between the geography and the ideology of a civilization. See Ning, "Liang Qichao 'Kong bei Lao nan' shuo," 122.
54. The nineteen masters include Confucius, Mencius, Xun Qing 荀卿, Guan Zhong 管仲, Zou Yan 鄒衍, Shen Buhai 申不害, Shang Yang 商鞅, Han Fei 韓非, Li Kui 李悝, Mo Di 墨翟, Song Xing 宋銒, Deng Xi 鄧析, Hui Shi 惠施, Laozi, Zhuangzi, Liezi, Yang Zhu, Xu Xing 許行, Qu Yuan 屈原. The Northern group includes masters such as Confucius 孔子, Mencius, Xunzi, Guanzi 管子, Zou Yan 鄒衍, Shen Buhai 申不害, Shang Yang 商鞅, Han Fei 韓非, Li Kui 李悝, Mo Di 墨翟, Song Xing 宋銒, Deng Xi 鄧析, and Hui Shi 惠施. Whereas the Southern group includes Laozi, Zhuangzi, Liezi, Yang Zhu, Xu Xing 許行, and Qu Yuan 屈原. See Liang, *Lun Zhongguo xueshu sixiang*, 570.
55. Liang, *Lun Zhongguo xueshu sixiang*, 570.
56. Liang, *Lun Zhongguo xueshu sixiang*, 570–71.

57. Liang, "Lelizhuyi taidou bianqing zhi xueshuo" 樂利主義泰斗邊沁之學說 [The doctrine of Bentham, the master of utilitarianism], in *Liang Qichao quanji*, 1049.

58. For Katō, "the mind of loving the self" is what makes "the mind of loving others" possible. See Liang, "Lelizhuyi taidou bianqing zhi xueshuo," 1049.

59. Liang, "Lelizhuyi taidou bianqing zhi xueshuo," 1049.

60. Liang, "Lelizhuyi taidou bianqing zhi xueshuo," 1045.

61. Liang, "Xuelang heshang yulu erze" 雪浪和尚語錄二則 [Monk Xuelang's two sayings], in *Liang Qichao quanji*, 2:402.

62. Shen, "Jindai Zhongguo de 'guomin' guannian," 193.

63. See Shen, "Jindai Zhongguo de 'guomin' guannian," 193; Chang, *Liang Ch'i-ch'ao and Intellectual Transition in China*, 196.

64. "Quan xue" 勸學 [An Exhortation to Learn], *Xunzi* 荀子.

65. Jin Guantao 金觀濤 and Liu Qingfeng 劉青峰, "Jindai Zhongguo quanli guannian de qiyuan he yanbian," 近代中國權利觀念的起源和演變 [The origin and the evolution of the concept of rights in modern China], in *Guannianshi yanjiu: Zhongguo xiandai zhongyao zhengzhi shuyu de xingcheng* 觀念史研究：中國現代重要政治術語的形成 [On the history of concepts: The formation of the key political terms in modern China], (Beijing: Falü chubanshe, 2010), 114.

66. Stephen C. Angle, *Human Rights and Chinese Thought: A Cross-Cultural Inquiry* (New York: Cambridge University Press, 2003), 109.

67. Angle, *Human Rights and Chinese Thought*, 107–108.

68. Angle, *Human Rights and Chinese Thought*, 109.

69. Liang, "Bianfa tongyi" 變法通議 [General discussion on reform], in *Liang Qichao quanji*, 16.

70. Liang, "Shuo dong," 176.

71. Angle, *Human Rights and Chinese Thought*, 128–33.

72. Angle, *Human Rights and Chinese Thought*, 130.

73. Angle, *Human Rights and Chinese Thought*, 132.

74. Liang, "Zhongguo jiruo youyu fangbi" 中國積弱由於防弊 [On how China got weak due to being defensive, in *Liang Qichao quanji*, 63.

75. Liang, "Zhongguo jiruo youyu fangbi," 64–65.

76. Liang, "Zhongguo jiruo youyu fangbi," 65.

77. See Chang, *Liang Ch'i-ch'ao and Intellectual Transition in China*, 193–94.

78. Angle, *Human Rights and Chinese Thought*, 143.

79. Liang, "Lun qiangquan" 論強權 [On might as right], in *Liang Qichao quanji*, 352.

80. Liang, "Lun qiangquan," 353.

81. Liang, "Shizhong dexing xiangfan xiangcheng yi," 十種德性相反相成義 [Contradictory and complementary principles of ten types of morality], in *Liang Qichao quanji*, 431.

82. Liang, "Shizhong dexing xiangfan xiangcheng yi," 431.
83. Liang, "Lun quanli sixiang," 671.
84. See Rudolf von Jhering, *The Struggle for Law*, trans. John J. Lalor (Chicago: Callaghan and Company, 1915), 31.
85. Liang's concept of "the consciousness of rights" was inspired by Jhering's notion of "feeling of right" (*Rechtsgefühl*). See Jhering, *The Struggle for Law*, 28–29.
86. By 1901, Liang had already written "Guojia sixiang bianqian yitong lun" [On the differences and similarities of the evolution of the state theories] to discuss Bluntschli's theory of state. In 1903, Liang wrote "Zhengzhixue dajia Bolunzhili zhi xueshuo" [The theory of Bluntschli, a master of political science] to elaborate Bluntschli's theory of state. See also Shen, "Jindai Zhongguo de 'guomin' guannian," 195.
87. Brian C. Schmidt, *The Political Discourse of Anarchy: A Disciplinary History of International Relations* (New York: State University of New York Press, 1998), 50.
88. Johann Kaspar Bluntschli, *The Theory of the State* (Kitchener, ON: Batoche), 40.
89. Liang, *Xinmin shuo*, 655.
90. The statement "this ownership is the authority" is a footnote Liang adds to explain the meaning of "ownership." *Zhuquan* 主權 is usually taken as an equivalent of sovereignty that indicates the power to govern a country in contemporary Chinese-English dictionaries; in Liang's early writings, that is not always the case. Usually, Liang's use of *zhuquan* connotes one's ownership that justifies one's authority in dealing with his possessions. The subject that enjoys *zhuquan* is not necessarily a state. For instance, in the quoted statement, the subject that possesses *zhuquan* can be an individual.
91. Liang, "Lun quanli sixiang," 673.
92. Takase Takejirō 高瀨武次郎, *Youboku tetsugaku* 楊墨哲學 [Philosophy of Yang and Mo] (Tokyo: Kinkōdō shōseki 金港堂書籍, 1902). See the paper by Masayuki Sato in the current volume.
93. Liang, "Lun quanli sixiang," 673.
94. Liang's association between Yang Zhu and rights was repeated in some of the journal articles published under a few anonymous authors between 1902 and 1920.

Chapter 10

Feng Youlan and Yang Zhu
The Shifting Discursive Space (1920-80)

XIAOQING DIANA LIN

Introduction

Yang Zhu is often considered a contributor to the Chinese sense of the self—not an autonomous self but one that guards against the pressures of an all-enveloping social web.¹ Yang's proclivity for discussing the body and self apart from society has long been associated with Daoism.² Cui Shu 崔述 (1740-1816), a Qing dynasty scholar known for his skepticism toward Confucian classics, argued that *Laozi* reflected the viewpoints of Yang Zhu. He believed that this was because Yang Zhu's followers forged the *Laozi*.³ Yan Fu believed that both Zhuang Zi and Yang Zhu emphasized free spirit and a transcendence of the division between self and other, and that Zhuang Zi could actually be Yang Zhu.⁴ Kang Youwei designated Yang Zhu a disciple of Laozi.⁵ In 1932, one year after Feng Youlan's *History of Chinese Philosophy*, vol. 1 (1931) was published, Gu Jiegang 顧頡剛 (1893-1980) argued that Yang Zhu influenced *Laozi* because Lao Dan 老聃 lived in the Warring States era when Yang Zhu was influential.⁶ Gu did not attempt to build a scholarly genealogy of Daoism that rationalized Yang Zhu's role in it.

In his discussions of Yang Zhu, Feng Youlan 馮友蘭 (1895-1990) focused on the association between Yang Zhu and Daoism.⁷ In his review monograph on Yang Zhu's work and the schools of thought associated with Yang, Sun Daosheng 孫道昇 (1908–1955), a prominent scholar of an impressive array of works on Chinese philosophy, cited Gu Shi 顧實 (1878–1956), who is briefly discussed in part 2 below, and Feng Youlan as representative figures who associated Yang Zhu with Daoism in the early twentieth century.[8] Feng built a genealogy of Daoism in his *History of Chinese Philosophy*, vol. 1, linking the rise of Daoism with hermits at the time of Confucius, who Feng believed preceded Yang Zhu and Laozi. Feng argued that while the hermits practiced a life of keeping themselves intact, Yang Zhu developed a systematic rationale for such a way of life.[9] In the 1930s Feng further elaborated on the link between the hermits of Confucius's time and the early Daoists. These articles included "Xian Qin zhuzi zhi qiyuan" 先秦諸子之起源 (The origins of the pre-Qin schools of thought) (1936) and "Yuan ming fa yinyang daode" 原名法陰陽道德 (Tracing the roots of the School of Names, the Legalists, the School of Yin and Yang, and the Daoists) (1936).[10]

In his 1923 PhD dissertation, Feng placed Laozi before Yang Zhu. However, after his return to China, Feng consistently placed Yang Zhu prior to Laozi under the conviction that *Laozi* was not written by Lao Dan 老聃 of the Spring and Autumn era but was forged by someone in a later age.[11] Even though Yang Zhu's role as the founder of Daoism is nowadays generally considered debatable,[12] Feng's argument that Yang's thought developed a more systematic framework for Daoism remains a significant contribution to Yang Zhu and Daoist studies.

Feng Youlan sought to develop a philosophical system, at once modeled on the Neo-Confucian worldview that extended from self-cultivation to pacification of the universe, as in the *Great Learning* (*Daxue* 大學), and also based on a rational system in which human nature is inherently amoral and thought value-neutral.[13] Yang Zhu, along with the other early Daoists Laozi and Zhuangzi provided a critical starting point for Feng's discussion of a rational self, free of ethical concerns. Feng's understanding of the self was also influenced by the changing society in which he lived and by new ideas he drew on, such as Marxist dialectical materialism and new interpretations of Daoism in early twentieth-century China. Changes in Feng's perception of the self also affected his interpretation of Yang Zhu.

Daoism, with its amoral approach to life, played a crucial role in Feng's philosophical system, enabling him to develop a rationale for self-development that transcends societal or ethical concerns and a final alignment with heaven and earth as life's goal. Yang Zhu provided a systematic explanation of why one should value life and oneself. Central to the reasoning was Yang's refusal to lose a hair to save or gain a city. Feng quoted from *Han Feizi* to argue that Yang Zhu or a "follower of Yang" was a person who "has slight regard for mere things and holds life as something important," and furthermore "does not allow outside things to entangle his person."[14] Feng also quoted *Huainanzi*, which attributes to Yang Zhu such values as "completeness of living, preservation of what is genuine, and not allowing outside things to entangle one's person" (全生保真不以物累形).[15]

Feng's approach to Yang Zhu varied greatly from his writings in the 1920s to his new edition of *History of Chinese Philosophy*, vol. 1, in 1980. Changes in his conception of the individual, new scholarship and interpretations, and his relation to society impacted Feng's assessment of Yang Zhu. One can divide his treatment of Yang Zhu into five stages. The first was Yang Zhu in his 1923 PhD dissertation, where Feng tried to approach Yang's thought as comparable to hedonism but adopted a nonjudgmental approach to it. Yang Zhu. He was a good example for Feng's view on the relevance of philosophy in a world dominated by science and to put Feng's array of philosophical approaches on display. At this point, Feng's interest was in a comparative study of epistemology: he believed that different approaches to knowledge were the ultimate reason for cultural and social differences around the world—that different philosophical outlooks on life and nature accounted for the development of science or the lack of it. For Feng, an epistemological study of how different philosophers have approached knowledge would help explain the differences between the East and the West.

The second stage was in the first half of the 1930s, where Feng depicted Yang Zhu as egoistic, representing a self-contained system. In the wake of the May Fourth movement and a subsequent Doubting Antiquity movement after 1923, challenges to Confucian orthodoxy led to a flourishing of works on other thinkers of the Spring and Autumn period and Warring States era, and many new interpretations of Yang Zhu emerged in the 1920s and 1930s. Feng's work was part of this movement reinterpreting Yang Zhu. In his *History of Chinese Philosophy*, vol. 1, published in 1931, Feng studied Yang Zhu's idea of self-preservation as a balanced approach to life. Also, the *History* debuted as Feng's course lectures at National Tsinghua University after he started teaching there in 1928. It was more scholarly than his dissertation: it built an extensive genealogy of Daoism and did a systematic textual study of ancient sources that could be attributed to Yang Zhu.

The third stage was in the 1940s, when Feng increasingly treated Yang Zhu's self as private, selfish, or partial. Feng reinterpreted Yang Zhu as immoral in his *Xinyuandao* 新原道 (A new treatise on the nature of Dao) (1945) because Yang Zhu's thought would block individual involvement in society. The book was written as the war between China and Japan was still going on. The urge for individual contribution to national salvation drove Feng to an intellectual criticism of Yang Zhu's lifestyle. Feng even praised Laozi and Zhuangzi for self-negation because that enabled the individual to align with the world outside the self.

From 1949 to 1964 was the fourth stage, when a Marxist dialectical and materialist approach had increasing influence on Feng's writings. After China became communist in 1949, the Chinese communist government sought to replace historical analysis with class analysis. Feng sought resistance and compromise through reconciling both approaches. Feng's discussion of Yang Zhu sought a finer discussion of the lineage of Daoism established by Yang Zhu while linking Yang to the declining slave-owning class.

During the fifth stage, represented in his new edition of *History of Chinese Philosophy*, vol. 1, published in 1980, Feng dismissed Yang Zhu as a self-indulgent hedonist, evoking the term "hedonism" from his dissertation of 1923. Pressures to adopt the class-struggle approach over the years and the social and intellectual redemption Feng sought because of his alliance with the Gang of Four during the last years of the Cultural Revolution led to his more radical denunciation of Yang Zhu. The label of "hedonism" that he assigned to Yang Zhu's thought was no longer neutral but a livid condemnation.

The changes in Feng's critique of Yang Zhu reflect shifts in his views of the individual and its relationship to society. The following is a chronological discussion of Feng Youlan's critique of Yang Zhu from the 1920s to 1980, which also corresponded with Feng's shifts of intellectual perspectives from Confucianism to Marxism.

1. Yang Zhu in A Comparative Study of Life Ideals (1923)

One of Feng's earliest discussions of Yang Zhu was in his PhD dissertation, "A Comparative Study of Life Ideals," which he completed at Columbia University under the supervision of John Dewey in 1923. Feng saw Yang Zhu's epistemology as based on a universe operating by mechanistic laws irrespective of human volition and human action and without bearing on the afterlife. Therefore, one should simply practice hedonism and maximize pleasure in life.

Feng's dissertation was inspired by the May Fourth movement of 1919 and the subsequent debates in China that dichotomized science and metaphysics. Hoping to reconcile science and Confucian traditions, Feng tried to show that philosophy differed from science in its purpose but was equally important: while science searched for truth, philosophy searched for the good. Feng also sought to show that each philosophy was limited in its pursuit, hence the need for a comparative study of world philosophies. This reflected another important aspect of his early thinking: Chinese and Western philosophies are comparable in their limited coverage, and Chinese philosophy is a part of world philosophy. These points were reflected in his dissertation.

Feng's dissertation was a showcase of philosophical perspectives on life from the East and the West.[16] Published in 1924 as *A Comparative Study of Life Ideals*, it divided global thinking into three different approaches toward nature: pessimism about the world, optimism that human efforts could enhance the current world, and visions of perfection for this world. Feng later added two chapters to the work's Chinese edition in 1926, which provided a synthesis of the various schools of thought.[17]

In prioritizing human volition in the study of philosophical differences, Feng differed markedly from John Dewey's pragmatism, which built a continuum between thinking and praxis. Feng's dissertation reflected influence from Henri Bergson, who emphasized the importance of intuition and consciousness in a scientific world. In the article "Bergson's Philosophical Methods," published in the journal *New Tide* in 1921, Feng depicted Bergson's emphasis on intuition and consciousness as modern and compatible with science. Feng's dissertation was also a follow-up to his 1922 article titled "Why China Has No Science," where he argued that China did not have science because the Chinese were not interested in it. The Western distinction between humans and nature had led Europeans to the knowledge and conquest of nature—yet these elements were absent from Chinese culture, where people sought harmony with nature. Hence there was no motivation to seek external knowledge such as science.[18] Feng thereby reduced the lack of scientific development in recent Chinese history to a matter of volition.

In Feng's classification of the three visions toward nature—pessimism, optimism, and vision of perfection—Yang Zhu was classified into the second group: the optimistic school believing that humans, despite their imperfect nature, could enhance the current world. Before discussing Feng's treatment of Yang Zhu in his dissertation, we need to outline Feng's arguments about these three approaches to nature. He titled the first group, which included Zhuangzi, Plato, and Schopenhauer, "the idealization of nature and the way of decrease." This group thought "the present world, or the present state of the world, is the consequence of some original mistake, something that fundamentally ought not to be."[19] Feng characterized the second group "the idealization of art and the way of increase," which included Yang Zhu, Mozi, Descartes, Bacon, and Fichte, as those who saw the potential to build the world into a paradise through human endeavor.[20] Here, Feng referred to the natural world as "nature" and the world modified by human effort as "art."[21] The first two groups differed in their views toward nature and human effort: group one treated nature as all-encompassing with little room for human endeavor, and group two tried to maximize human effort to triumph over the forces of nature. Feng characterized the third group as "the idealization of the continuity of nature and art and the good of activity," where nature and human effort were happily reconciled. Feng included in this group Confucius, Aristotle, Neo-Confucians, and Hegel.[22]

Feng's thesis was to show that all philosophies had their drawbacks because they idealized "certain features of experience in order that it may become a standard of life. No wonder that philosophers were always blinded by that which they realized."[23] Feng argued that these limitations would render all philosophies compatible in their imperfection. Feng also used his thesis to distinguish between philosophy and science: "So far as truth is also good, let science continue its work. At the same time let philosophy continue to search for *the* good."[24]

Feng saw Yang Zhu as a successor to the Daoist School. Feng discussed Yang Zhu in comparison with Laozi, who was not discussed in his dissertation but who would likely have been placed in group one: Feng saw both as proceeding from a perspective that "nature is not benevolent." He argued that two different interpretations would ensue from this view: either "Nature is spontaneity itself, so it has no desire or wish to be benevolent," or "Nature is not benevolent, because it is a blind physical force. It produces the world, not at all by design or will, but simply by necessity or chance."[25] Feng argued that Yang developed a hedonistic attitude toward life based on the latter line of thought: because nature is a blind physical force and life is short, humans should maximize happiness and avoid pain in this world.[26] Feng treated Yang Zhu and Zhuangzi as inheriting two different aspects of Laozi's argument. Zhuangzi inherited nature as spontaneity.[27] Feng speculated that after Laozi's death, his disciples split into two groups, one represented by Zhuangzi, the other by Yang Zhu. This resembled Socrates's case, whose followers divided into three schools, two of which, the Cynics and Cyrenaics, were diametrically opposite.[28]

Yang's mechanistic view of the universe meant that life was short, with no promise of an afterlife. Feng quoted Yang Zhu in *Liezi* as saying, "During life, there is the difference of intelligence and dullness, honor and meanness; but in death there is the equality of rottenness and putrefaction." So the only thing humans can do is to "hasten to enjoy life and pay no attention to death."[29] Concerns such as fame and reputation should be irrelevant, and only immediate tangible pleasures are worth pursuing.[30] Since the worst consequence of any social behavior is death, and one no longer exists after death, this consequence did not matter.[31] Feng concluded that Yang Zhu agreed in detail with the Cyrenaics and with the Epicureans only in principle. The Cyrenaics taught that corporeal pleasures were superior to mental ones and corporeal sufferings worse than mental ones. Epicurus said that since "all good and all evil is in sensation, and since death is only the privation of sensation," death was of no concern to him.[32] Yang showed great contempt for social norms because "there was nothing naturally and intrinsically just, or honorable, or disgraceful; but that things were considered so because of law and fashion," which, according to Herodotus, were the "consent of the fools."[33] Yang Zhu's solution was to claim that all should seek only immediate pleasure, and the world would then be in an ideal state. Yang Zhu's was a naïve artistic endeavor, seeking pleasure in life because lofty pursuits would not impact the order of things.[34]

Feng also pointed out that Yang's idea of the individual was based on the principle of complete disregard for society. Feng quoted from Anton Forke's translation of the "Yang Zhu" chapter in the *Liezi*, specifically, a passage where Qin Guli 禽滑釐 asked Yang Zhu if he would pluck out a hair to save the world and Yang refused.[35] Feng says that this was often cited as an example of Yang Zhu's egoism, such as in Mencius's remark that "The doctrine of the philosopher Yang was each one for himself. Though he might benefit the whole world by plucking out a single hair, he would not do it."[36] Feng further remarked on Qin Guli's conversation with Yang Zhu and subsequently with Mengsun Yang 孟孫揚:

> [A]lthough Yang Chu's doctrine is egoistic, this passage does not necessarily show that effect. The general trend of the argument shows that even if Ch'in-tse (Ch'in Ku-li) would offer the whole world to Yang Chu himself for one of his hairs, Yang Chu still would not make the exchange. Thus this passage is simply an extreme statement of the teaching that we should not inflict any amount of pain upon ourselves, no matter how great the remote future gain is.[37]

In the above quotations, Feng acknowledges two types of interpretations of Yang Zhu: Yang Zhu as an egoist and Yang Zhu who would not inflict pain on himself to gain anything from others. In his later works, Feng adhered to the dual interpretation that Yang would not give up his hair to benefit the world or benefit from getting the whole world. It is one of the most consistent arguments he makes about Yang Zhu. It seems that although Feng labeled Yang Zhu a hedonist, he thought of Yang Zhu as much more than an advocate of purely selfish and sensual desires, and rather as someone with a systematic rationale of the individual.

Although Feng used hedonism to describe Yang Zhu's vision on humans, he did not make a systematic comparison between Yang Zhu and the Cyrenaics and Epicureans. The discussion of Yang Zhu was, to Feng, a discussion of how desires were justified in Chinese history. Even though Feng was not for the hedonism as described in the *Liezi*, he argued for the legitimacy of desires, as shown in his article "Why China Had No Science" that Chinese philosophy might be short on clear thinking but it was compensated for by more rational happiness. Feng also quoted Bertrand Russell in a positive way, who said that Chinese people seemed to be rational hedonists, differing from Europeans through the fact that they prefer enjoyment to power.[38] Ultimately, Feng's focus was on how epistemology guides individual behavior in life in order to prove the importance of philosophy alongside science. Yang Zhu's vision of the world as a mechanistic one led to Yang Zhu's call for complete self-protection and a hedonistic lifestyle. It was a good example to illustrate how different attitudes toward nature and life shaped philosophies worldwide, and for Feng to show how all philosophies in the world were comparable in their incomplete perspectives on the world. Feng did not intend to delve much into Yang Zhu's hedonism as a philosophy.

2. Yang Zhu in *A History of Chinese Philosophy* (1931, 1934)

Feng developed a more systematic discussion of Yang Zhu's view on life in his *Zhongguo zhexueshi* 中國哲學史 (A history of Chinese philosophy, vol. 1, 1931, vol. 2, 1934). This was different in several significant ways from his dissertation. First, Feng created a more formal Daoist genealogy, and Yang Zhu changed from being a disciple of Laozi to the founder of Daoism. The sequence of Daoist masters became Yang Zhu—Laozi—Zhuangzi. Second, in his identification of Yang Zhu's writings, Feng shifted from *Liezi* to *Lüshi chunqiu* 呂氏春秋 (Master Lü's Spring and Autumn Annals, ca. 293 BCE), *Han Feizi* 韓非子 (Han Fei, 280-233 BCE), and *Huainanzi* 淮南子 (Liu An, 179-122 BCE, Duke of Huainan in the Western Han Dynasty). Feng decided that *Liezi*, purportedly the work of Lie Yukou 列禦寇 (450-375 BCE), was written by someone from the Wei (220-266 CE) and Jin (265–420 CE) dynasties, and relegated *Liezi* to his discussion of neo-Daoism in the Wei and Jin dynasties. Feng identified the materialistic and mechanistic aspects of certain *Liezi* chapters, as in his dissertation. However, he now stated that this Yang Zhu figure was not the historical one and that he fit well "with the Wei and Chin emphasis on 'abandonment' and 'comprehension'" since it was not the work of Liezi but "the product of some unknown Wei or Chin writer."[39]

The drastic changes in Feng's interpretation of Yang Zhu in 1931 from his 1923 dissertation were primarily due to the changing Chinese intellectual landscape. The May Fourth movement destroyed Confucian orthodoxy in China. Many Chinese scholars such as Kang Youwei, Liang Qichao, Hu Shi, Jiang Weiqiao 蔣維喬, and Chen Cisheng 陳此生 reexamined ancient sources on Yang Zhu, including reassessing the authenticity of *Liezi*. They reinterpreted Yang Zhu from a selfish hedonist, an image often derived from *Liezi* and Mencius, to a more positive figure who celebrated the preservation of life. Some, such as Liang Qichao, even linked Yang Zhu with modern ideas of rights.[40] In the process, as the negative image of Yang Zhu in *Liezi* was questioned, more sources were tapped to render a different Yang Zhu whose arguments would lend support to modern-day conceptions of the human being. The Doubting Antiquity (疑古) movement led by Gu Jiegang certainly also promoted explorations of new interpretations of Yang Zhu. Articles on

Yang Zhu were published in vol. 4 of *Gushi bian* 古史辨 (Debates on ancient history), in 1933.[41]

In the surging scholarly interest in Yang Zhu and exploration of classical sources that could have included Yang's work,[42] Gu Shi 顧實 (1878–1956) is regarded by several contemporary Yang Zhu scholars such as Gao Huaping 高華平 and He Aiguo 何愛國 as one of the first to identify a broader range of ancient sources associated with Yang Zhu, including chapters from the *Lüshi chunqiu* such as "Taking Life as Basic" 本生, "Honoring Life" 貴生, "Valuing the Self" 重己, "Essential Desires" 情慾, "Fulfilling the Number" 盡數, and "Placing the Self First" 先己.[43] Gu Shi's authoritative *The Philosophy of Yang Zhu* was published in 1931,[44] the same year as Feng Youlan's first volume of *A History of Chinese Philosophy*. However, Gu did publish two articles on Yang Zhu in 1928,[45] the same year when Feng started teaching at Tsinghua University and compiling the lectures on Chinese philosophy that became the two-volume *History of Chinese Philosophy*. Gu concurred with Hu Shi in the charge that *Liezi* was a forgery. To restore the true character of Yang Zhu and Yang's appreciation of life, Gu cited a more comprehensive range of sources attributed to Yang Zhu in that 1928 article, including chapters from the *Lüshi chunqiu* ("Taking Life as Basic," "Valuing the Self," and "Honoring Life") and chapters from *Zhuangzi* ("Yielding the Throne" 讓王 and "Robber Zhi" 盜跖).[46] Gu Shi's work on Yang Zhu may have helped direct Feng Youlan's attention to *Lüshi chunqiu* and *Zhuangzi* chapters hitherto not associated with Yang Zhu as sources of Yang Zhu's writings.

It is possible that Feng's genealogy of the Daoist school was influenced by a debate between Hu Shi and Liang Qichao and subsequent intellectual debates about Laozi. After the publication of Hu Shi's *An Outline of the History of Chinese Philosophy* (1919),[47] Liang Qichao gave a critical review of it in an open lecture in Beiping on March 4, 1922, in particular addressing Hu's study of Laozi. Hu continued an argument upheld by Qing scholars such as Wang Zhong 汪中 and Cui Shu that Laozi preceded Confucius. Liang disagreed, citing sources from *Mencius*, *Laozi*, *Zhuangzi*, *Records of the Grand Historian*, and *Book of Rites*, among others, to prove that *Laozi* was a work of the late Spring and Autumn Period and Laozi came after Confucius. Liang later turned the lecture into an article, "Ping Hu Shizhi Zhongguo zhexueshi dagang" 評胡適之中國哲學史大綱 (On Hu Shi's *An Outline of the History of Chinese Philosophy*). It was serialized in *Morning News Supplement* 晨報副刊 and ignited a highly influential scholarly debate on Laozi, with over forty articles published on Laozi in the 1920s and 1930s, most of which were collected in volumes 4 and 6 of *Gushi bian*,[48] edited by Feng Youlan's close friend Gu Jiegang. (Feng and Gu's friendship dated back to undergraduate years at the Philosophy Department of Peking University, where they were one year apart.) Multiple articles on Laozi in the *Gushi bian* were written by the Doubting Antiquity group started in 1923 and headed by Gu Jiegang, who postulated that *Laozi* was written in the late Warring States period or even during the Han dynasty, around the time of *Xunzi* and *Huainanzi*.[49] Therefore, it would not be a surprise if Feng Youlan was influenced by Liang Qichao and Feng's antiquity doubting colleagues and friends. In his *History of Chinese Philosophy* (1931), Feng placed Confucius before Laozi and sparred with Hu Shi on whether Confucius preceded Laozi.[50] Feng Youlan's late placement of *Laozi* in history led to his placement of Yang Zhu as the founder of Daoism.

Another difference between Feng's *History* and his dissertation is that Feng gave a more comprehensive study of Yang Zhu's philosophy as a way of life in the former. Again, this was in accord with the overall intellectual milieu where Yang Zhu received much more positive treatment and more attention to his appreciation of life (贵生). Nationalism could be another factor motivating Feng to use Yang Zhu to justify the importance of valuing life. Feng focused on Yang's egoism as a way of life, which stood for complete self-protection from the universe at large. Feng would exhaust all aspects of Yang Zhu's description of the self and discuss them as a way of life. He quoted from *Lüshi chunqiu* (chap. 17/7, "No Duality" 不二), which states that Yang Zhu "valued self" (*gui ji* 貴己), from *Han Feizi* (chap. 50) that Yang Zhu had "slight regard for mere things and holds life as something important," and from *Huainanzi* (chap. 13) that Yang Zhu argued for "completeness of living, preservation of what is genuine, and not allowing outside things to entangle one's person."[51] Feng concluded that

> according to this *Han-fei-tzŭ* quotation, a follower of Yang, even were he to be given the world as a return for pulling out one of his hairs, would not do so. Such a person "has slight regard for mere things and holds life as something important"; he "does not allow outside things to entangle his person." This is because the world, though large, is still something external, whereas a hair, though small, is still part of one's own person and life. Therefore the former may be regarded lightly, whereas the latter should be looked upon as important.[52]

Feng had made a similar observation regarding Yang Zhu toward the end of his dissertation, although he had not elaborated on it: Yang would not benefit the world nor benefit from the world with one hair. In a note of explanation in his *History of Chinese Philosophy*, vol. 1, Feng elaborated a bit more on this duality of Yang's idea by commenting on his colleague Gu Jiegang's interpretation of Mencius's judgment of Yang Zhu. Gu believed Mencius could have meant that Yang Zhu took self-preservation as a principle and not just selfishness, and that Mencius agreed that Yang Zhu "would not do it even if he would benefit from the world through plucking one hair." Feng disagreed with Gu's novel interpretation of Mencius. But while Feng still believed that the latter had stated that Yang Zhu would not benefit the world by plucking one hair, he admitted that Yang Zhu himself might also have expressed the unwillingness to benefit from the world by plucking a single hair.[53]

Yet another change from his dissertation was the reinterpretation of Yang Zhu from a hedonist to someone who gingerly balanced enjoyment of life and self-preservation. Feng commented that no writings from the pre-Qin era testify to Yang Zhu as a hedonist, as found "in the chapter bearing his name in the *Lieh-tzŭ*; a chapter that, therefore, cannot be attributed to him even though hints of such hedonistic thought may be found scattered in other writings of the Warring States period"[54] (from *Lüshi chunqiu*, "Essential Desires" 情慾). Feng reiterated that Yang Zhu's self-protection was not selfish but a matter of principle: he would do nothing that would benefit others just as he would not benefit from others. Almost as a corrective to his analysis of Yang Zhu in his PhD dissertation, Feng argued that Yang Zhu's emphasis was not on the complete satiation but the reasonable satisfaction of one's desires. He quoted the following passages

> Heaven has generated mankind endowed with longings and desires. These desires have their natural tendencies (*qing* 情). The natural tendencies have their restraints. The Sage cultivates these restraints to halt his desires, and, therefore, does not allow his natural tendencies to run to excess. . . . By acting in accordance with the principle of valuing life, one keeps control over one's natural tendencies. By not acting in this way, one loses control over them.

天生人而使有貪有欲，欲有情，情有節。聖人修節以止欲，故不過行其情也。……由貴生動則得其情矣，不由貴生動則失其情矣。[55]

Therefore, desires were normal and should be allowed to exist. Feng quotes from the same chapter the claim that if one could not hear, see, or eat what one desired, it would be no different from death, thus showing that sentiments and desires differentiated life from death.[56] The key here is to have restraints on desires so that one's natural tendencies do not run to excess. Feng's study of Yang Zhu in 1931 was his first serious treatment of the idea of the self in Chinese thought.

Despite the value conferred on Yang Zhu's self in Feng's subsequent discussion of Yang Zhu and Daoism in the 1940s, Yang Zhu would receive a more negative treatment because of his insistence on self-preservation.

3. Yang Zhu in *Xinyuandao* 新原道 (*A New Treatise on the Nature of Dao*) (1945)

In the late 1930s and 1940s, Feng published six works written during the Sino-Japanese War (1937–45). This *Zhenyuan liushu* 貞元六書 (Purity descends, primacy ascends: Six books) (1938–46) represented the magnum opus of his philosophical thought. *A New Philosophy of Principle* (*Xinlixue* 新理學), the first volume and the philosophical underpinning of the other works, was written in Nanyue 南嶽, Hunan Province. Tsinghua University had temporarily relocated there during the Sino-Japanese War in 1938 before moving to Kunming 昆明 in Yunan Province. As reflected in his preface to *New Philosophy of Principle*, wartime nationalism created the urgent need to complete his philosophical framework to guide China's revitalization.[57] Nationalism called for self-sacrifice and active engagement of the individual in a social cause. Yang Zhu's insistence on self-preservation as a principle became morally reprehensible in the wartime situation.

In *A New Treatise on the Nature of Dao* (*Xinyuandao* 新原道) (1945), the fifth volume in the series, Feng saw Yang Zhu as not just egoistic but also selfish and unethical. Feng was not only examining Yang's philosophical outlook but also morally berating Yang. Feng was drawing close to Mencius, quoting Mencius's attacks on Yang Zhu that accused the latter of "blocking humaneness and justice" (充塞仁義, *Mencius* 3B9). Feng now concurred with Mencius that Yang and his followers were obstructing the moral order.[58] Regardless of Yang's aims, Feng argued that what Yang did was incompatible with the Confucian ideal of self-sacrifice in the name of justice.[59] By the 1940s, Feng wanted to see a more socially connected self.

The second change in Feng's critique of Yang Zhu was his elevation of Laozi and Zhuangzi for their self-negation. Thus far, Feng had treated Yang Zhu's life-preservation as a positive trait; now, he considered cherishing life (*zhong sheng* 重生) a passive approach to living. Feng said Yang would practice avoidance (*bi* 避) to dodge being hurt by people or things: avoiding the world, avoiding fame, avoiding punishments, and so on. Those who were good at nourishing life (*yang sheng* 養生), Feng said, did not dare to commit big crimes nor do too much good and had to stay between good and not good.[60] Yang's avoidance blocked one from reaching beyond oneself. Compared with Yang, Feng saw Laozi and Zhuangzi developing Daoism on a new level. Feng considered Laozi a representative of the second stage of Daoism, erasing the distinction between the human body and the universe; Zhuangzi represented the third and highest stage of Daoism because of his dialectical merger of humans and the universe.[61] Feng decided that Zhuangzi developed selfishness to such an extreme that it in fact annihilated selfishness. "Early Daoists were selfish. But selfishness gone extreme would go to its opposite and vanquish selfishness" (初期的道家是自私的自私之極反而克去了自私).[62] Self-negation was superior to egoistic self-preservation because it allowed a merger of the individual and society.

By the 1940s, Feng had established a new self-cultivation system that went beyond Confucian morals and linked the individual with a transcendent universe: a combination of Daoist cosmos, Confucian self-endeavor, and Yang Zhu's self. In *A New Treatise on the Nature of Man* (*Xinyuanren* 新原人) (1943), the fourth volume in the six-volume series, Feng created a universal system of meaningful human life in four stages: the natural stage (*ziran jingjie* 自然境界), the utilitarian stage (*gongli jingjie* 功利境界), the ethical stage (*daode jingjie* 道德境界), and finally the stage of individual alignment with heaven and earth (*tiandi jingjie* 天地境界).[63] The ultimate goal of the self was the last stage, namely alignment with the universe. Yang Zhu provided partial prototypes for the first two stages: a primordial stage where individuals lived in a natural state of being, and a utilitarian stage where individuals were pitched against society. But Feng cast aside Yang Zhu in the two higher stages. His ultimate goal was what Feng called a rationalized life that enabled "the merger between finite humans and the infinite universe" (自同於大全).[64] For Feng, this resembled a *tathatā* experience in Buddhism (*bhūtatathatā, zhenru* 真如, the true state of the world) and the Daoist state of *dao*, as in "the sage has no self" (聖人無我).[65] Feng also compared the experience to Mencius's noble spirit or *qi* that enables one to completely identify with the universe (*haoran zhi qi* 浩然之氣) and the Confucian state of humaneness (*ren* 仁).[66]

In his *A Short History of Chinese Philosophy: A Systematic Account of Chinese Thought from Its Origins to the Present Day* (1947), Feng continued to discuss Yang Zhu along the same lines as in *A New Treatise on the Nature of Dao*. He criticized Yang Zhu for his life preservation and avoidance of danger.[67] He reiterated the two sides of Yang's philosophy about principled self-preservation, not benefiting the world nor benefiting from the world in exchange for one hair.[68] Feng went on to quote the "Yang Zhu" chapter of *Liezi*, showing that even though it might not present Yang Zhu's own words, it summed up the two aspects of his theory mentioned previously.[69] He criticized Yang Zhu as passively seeking a way to avoid endangering life, and he concluded that if a man could not see things from a higher point of view, nothing would guarantee him protection from danger and harm. Here he emphasized again the need to think beyond the self and the practice of self-negation.[70]

In conclusion, by 1943, Feng Youlan had formed a new conceptual framework of the ideal human being, with Yang Zhu's self as the starting point, but with the expectation that human life would go through stages of cultivation and ultimately align with a transcendent universe. Yang Zhu's self was incorporated into Feng Youlan's philosophical system. Still, it was morally reprehensible because of its principled refusal to be connected to society at large and could not serve as the end of the human self.

4. Yang Zhu in *A History of Chinese Philosophy* (New Trial Edition) (1962–64)

The communist takeover of China in 1949 had a tremendous impact on Feng Youlan's philosophy. Marxist dialectical materialism and its emphasis on class struggle pushed Feng to a Marxist class analysis of Yang Zhu, reflected in his new trial editions of *History of Chinese Philosophy* (1962–64). China's intellectuals now had to break from self-cultivation, connect with social reality, and judge ideas by their social outcome. This last aim was meant to deemphasize historical continuity. Feng Youlan became interested in Marxism in the 1930s because it enabled him to situate Chinese philosophy in a global social framework.[71] However, the 1950s state stipulation for class analysis was much more difficult for him to accept than Marxist dialecticism or historical materialism. In this version, Feng insisted on building a more elaborate genealogy of Daoism, despite its irrelevance to communist Chinese society. But he also tried to situate Daoism in a Marxist class framework.

Feng consistently pushed his scholarly boundaries in the 1950s to build intrinsic connections within scholarship. During the political movements in the early 1950s, Feng was criticized numerous times for his past idealist stance in philosophy. But at the slightest relaxation of the political atmosphere, he would always fight back to assert the authority of his traditional Chinese thought. In 1956, Feng wrote a self-criticism and denounced his writing as idealistic and complying with the exploiting class.[72] However, in early 1957, he argued that Chinese tradition, even though originating from the exploiting classes, might still be valuable to the present. Feng's argument followed the Twentieth Communist Party Congress of the Soviet Union in February 1956, where Khrushchev had denounced Stalin, and the tense political atmosphere seemed momentarily calm.[73]

After the Three Years' Famine (1959-61), political radicalism momentarily lessened in 1962. Feng attempted to rewrite his *History of Chinese Philosophy* by incorporating a class approach. However, as soon as he published the first volume of the new trial edition (*xinbian shigao* 新編試稿) of *History of Chinese Philosophy* in 1962, the book was attacked for its affirmation of the validity of Confucian values in communist China. Feng hastily revised it.[74] The revised first volume was published along with the second in 1964, and the 1962 new trial edition of the first volume was not included in collections of Feng's works.

The trial edition associated Yang Zhu with the declining aristocratic class. Feng said that Yang Zhu's predecessors

> referred to themselves as "gentry who avoided the world." It shows they still regarded themselves as the gentry who were either declined nobility or closely related to the declined nobility from the Spring and Autumn era. They lost their

former political and social positions but were not ready to give up their manner of behavior in the past and work for the newly risen landlord class. Hence, they retreated to an hermetic life and some did minor work for a living. They comforted themselves with the idea that they would now live a comfortable life and avoid the dangers of the world. On the other hand, they also envied the new power holders and often expressed some cynicism. They resented new things, which had cost them their social status. But they were not completely satisfied with the old things because the latter had not prevented their decline. Theirs was the consciousness of the declining aristocratic class. At the time of Confucius, such passive hermits were just passively taking care of themselves and did not have a systematic theory yet. The founder of such a systematic theory was Yang Zhu.

他們自稱為避世之士，可見他們都還以士自居。在春期戰國時代，這些士，或者其本身就是當時的沒落貴族，或者與沒落貴族有密切的聯繫.他們失掉了原來有的政治社會地位，但是又不甘心放棄原來的架子，為新興的地主階級服務.於是他們就隱居起來，有的從事一些輕微活動，以維持生活.他們一方面安慰自己說，這樣可以過一種安逸的生活，避免社會上各種風險，一方面對於當時新興的有權有勢的人，又不免心懷忌妒，經常發出一種"憤世嫉俗"的言論.他們厭惡當時新的東西，因為正是哲學東西使他們失去了原來的地位.但是對於舊的東西，他們也不完全滿意，因為這些東西並沒有是他們免於沒落。這就是當時沒落貴族階級的意識.在孔子的時候，此等消極的"隱者"亦只消極的獨善其身而已，對於其如此的行為，還沒有一貫的學說，以為其理論的根據。首先創立這樣一貫學說的人是楊朱。[75]

Against the Marxist class background, however, Feng also built a more elaborate Daoist lineage: from Yang Zhu, through Peng Meng 彭蒙 (ca. 370-310 BC), Tian Pian 田駢 (ca. 370-291 BC), and Shen Dao 慎到 (ca. 395-315 BC), to Laozi and Zhuangzi. In his *History of Chinese Philosophy* (1931), Feng had classified Peng Meng, Tian Pian, and Shen Dao as part of the "hundred schools of thought" parallel to Yang Zhu during the Spring and Autumn era.[76] The new Daoist lineage may have been informed by Feng's colleague Meng Wentong's Yang Zhu studies in the 1940s that argued for an inherent connection between Yang's and these three thinkers' work through intertextual studies.[77] However, unlike Meng Wentong's earlier work on Yang Zhu, Peng Meng, Tian Pian, and Shen Dao that focused on an inherent connection of ideas between these thinkers, Feng Youlan applied class analysis to their thought.[78]

Feng's new genealogy of Daoism consisted of four stages: Yang Zhu—Peng Meng, Tian Pian, and Shen Dao—Laozi—Zhuangzi. This new categorization of the Daoist school provided a more nuanced discussion of the different approaches to self-preservation of the Daoists. Still, this analysis also associated Daoism with the ideas of the declining slave-owning class. Peng Meng, Tian Pian, and Shen Dao specifically championed "abandoning knowledge and self-judgment" (棄知去己), so that one would become as ignorant as "a piece of clay with no personal opinions to accord with the Dao" (塊不失道; cf. *Zhuangzi* "Tianxia" 天下 [The World]), which was the mentality of the declining slave-owning class.[79] As Feng put it:

> Daoism went through four stages, from Yang Zhu, through Peng Meng, Tian Pian, and Shen Dao to Laozi and finally to Zhuangzi. It was no accident that its self-interest threaded through all Daoist schools because Daoism was a typical reflection of the declining slave-owning aristocratic class who lost everything except their bodies and lives, which they subsequently decided were the essential things in life.... Because they had declined, they advocated reducing or curbing one's desires. This is just as the fable says: the grapes are sour because you cannot reach them. Therefore, they would say: not plucking one hair, not benefiting the world. Their hair could not be exchanged for bringing great benefits to the world; much less could it save the world. By the time of Zhuangzi not only did the world (society) become irrelevant, but heaven and earth (the material world) became nothing. Such was the ultimate development of their sour grapes logic.

> 楊朱，彭蒙，田駢，慎到，老子，莊子，代表道家哲學思想發展的四個階段。道家哲學是沒落的奴隸主貴族意識的集中反映.為我的思想貫穿於道家各派之中，這不是偶然的.沒落貴族失掉了原來所有的一切，所留下的只是自己的身體和生命，除此之外，沒有別的東西可以保全的了.於是他們就認為自己身體和生命是人生最重要的東西。富貴功名之類，本來都是身外之物，就是給我，我

也是不要的 [...] 由於他們沒落了,追求物質享樂的慾望得不到滿足, 因此又提倡寡欲, 節欲.這正是像童話中所說的, 吃不著葡萄的人說葡萄酸。於是他們就說, 不拔一毛, 不利天下.其實他們的一毛本來換不到天下之大利, 更救不了天下.到了莊子不僅天下(社會) 是無足重輕的, 就是天地（物質世界）也歸結於虛無了, 這是葡萄酸的最後發展.[80]

In his *History of Chinese Philosophy* (1931), Feng had used sources such as the "Tianxia" (The World) chapter in *Zhuangzi* and chapters in the *Lüshi chunqiu* to interpret Peng Meng, Tian Pian, and Shen Dao as self-abandoning and refusing to rely on sages. On this basis, he saw them as resembling *Zhuangzi*, especially in the "Qiwu lun" 齊物論 (Making Things Even) chapter.[81] Feng's inclusion of them now as a stage in Daoism was based on their supposed attempts to abandon the self to keep themselves free from trouble. Feng interpreted their self-abandonment as a perfect example of how the declining slave-owning class tried to avoid persecution. He dismissed their attempt as "pathetic" (寒傖).[82] Feng argued that Yang Zhu also wanted to use self-interest to solve social problems, according to the "Robber Zhi" 盜跖 chapter in *Zhuangzi*. However, social progress needed the collective pursuit of social good. Self-interest does not encourage cooperation and is not proactive: it reflects a declining social class.[83]

Feng argued that politically, Yang Zhu's notion of self-interest might have meant a passive resistance to and noncooperation with the exploiting class. The question would be which exploiting class would they refuse to cooperate with. From the hermits to the Daoists, the exploiting class that Yang Zhu and his school would not cooperate with was the newly risen landlord class. Feng said that Confucians and Legalists were all representatives of the new landlord class, and Confucius, Mencius, and Han Fei all attacked the self-interest of hermits and Daoists. Zilu 子路 criticized a hermit who, "to keep his purity, disrupted the basic human relationship" between the ruler and subject (欲洁其身而乱大伦) (*Analects* 18.7), because the subject refused to serve his ruler. Mencius also said that Yang Zhu's "all for himself" (*wei wo*) ignored the monarch (*Mencius* 3B9). Han Fei said that those who emphasized life over things should be punished politically. The Legalists and the Confucians, despite their differences, were both newly risen social forces and opposed the old social forces: the slave-owning class. So, by opposing the new landowning social classes, Yang Zhu's self-interest had no progressive value at the time, and it hurt society.[84] Here, Feng used Confucian and Legalist approaches to carry out a class criticism of Yang Zhu.

Feng made some studious evaluation of Yang with his Marxist materialist or class analysis. Whether the Yangists represented materialists or idealists, they seemed to have an atheist tendency and some materialist elements in their attitude toward life, which seemed to contradict their class background. However, Feng argued that early Daoists had a passive approach to life despite their atheist and materialist tendency. What their atheism expressed was despair for the future. Their sudden decline in the fierce class struggles and loss of their ruling status led them to abandon their traditional beliefs in gods and ghosts. The Yangist belief that there is no consciousness after death mostly originated from this despair. The ideas in "Robber Zhi" on the surface represented happiness but were filled with pessimism.[85]

The 1962 and 1964 new trial editions of *History of Chinese Philosophy* marked Feng's formal conversion to applying Marxist class analysis to assessing Chinese thought in history. However, Feng still tried to provide a nuanced analysis of individual masters.[86] It was an awkward combination of scholarship and class analysis, hoping that scholarship would exist concomitant with the constraining class framework.

5. Yang Zhu in *A History of Chinese Philosophy* (New Edition, 1980)

Feng's new edition of *A History of Chinese Philosophy* was his last attempt to delineate a Chinese philosophical framework. Due to his involvement with the Gang of Four (1974–76), Feng was put under house arrest at the end of 1976 and regained his freedom only in 1982. The new edition of *A History of Chinese Philosophy* was Feng's attempt to redeem himself and, in a freer political and intellectual atmosphere, combine Marxist approaches, including class analysis, with intellectual continuity with the past and new insights he gained in the communist era. The seven-volume edition was published volume by volume. The first was published in 1980 and the last was completed shortly before Feng passed away in 1990. Because the volumes were published so far apart, they also represented different intellectual styles. Volume 1 still retained a relatively strong element of Marxist class analysis, while the seventh volume was so openly critical of Mao Zedong that initially it could not be published in Mainland China. It was published first in Hong Kong in 1992, as a stand-alone work titled *Zhongguo xiandai zhexueshi* 中國現代哲學史 (Contemporary Chinese philosophy).

Because Yang Zhu was discussed in the first volume of Feng's new edition, Marxist class analysis still heavily influenced Feng's depiction. Compared to the above attempt to reconstruct a viable study of Yang Zhu and Daoism in 1964, by 1980, Feng's Marxist analysis rendered Yang Zhu a marginal figure in Chinese thought. In 1964, Yang Zhu had eight pages, and Peng Meng, Tian Pian, and Shen Dao six pages in the new trial edition.[87] Now Yang Zhu received four pages, and Peng Meng, Tian Pian, and Shen Dao together received one page in the 1980 new edition.[88] Laozi and Zhuangzi received a similar treatment in both editions, with much more extended coverage than Yang Zhu.[89]

Feng continued to affirm Yang Zhu as the founder of Daoism and credited Yang with originating the idea of "all for himself." Feng's interpretation of Yang Zhu continued to draw from early sources such as *Mencius*, *Huainanzi*, and *Lüshi chunqiu*.[90] One apparent change here in terms of sources was that, even though Feng discredited the *Liezi* "Yang Zhu" chapter as the actual writing of Yang Zhu, he argued that some of the ideas in the *Liezi* chapter might reflect truly on Yang Zhu or might have initially developed from Yang Zhu's ideas. He quoted the "Yang Zhu" chapter of *Liezi*, "If nobody plucks a hair, and nobody benefits the world, the world will be governed" (人人不拔一毛人人不利天下天下治矣), taking it as Yang Zhu's worldview and political stance.[91]

It may sound surprising that Feng was much more dismissive of Yang Zhu in his Marxist class analysis in the 1980 new edition than in his 1964 new trial edition since the political and intellectual atmosphere was more relaxed in 1980 compared with 1964. However, that might not have been so for Feng. Fresh out of the Cultural Revolution and punished for being on the wrong side of history in the last two years of it, Feng described Yang Zhu's "all for himself" as the slave-owning class's noncooperation and open confrontation with the rising landlord class.[92] He interpreted Yang Zhu's description of a fulfilled life as class resistance against the landlord class. Yang described life as consisting of six desires, "which, when all fulfilled, is optimal; when half-fulfilled, is incomplete; and when unfulfilled, is a forced life" (所謂全生者六欲皆得其宜也. 所謂虧生者. 六欲虧得其宜也所謂迫生者. 六欲莫得其宜也). The last is "worse than death" (迫生不如死) (*Lüshi chunqiu* "Gui sheng").[93] Feng commented:

> From a class-struggle point of view, Yang Zhu said that he would rather die than bow to the newly risen landlord class and allow shame to be put on him by the latter. This is how

the declining slaveowners tried to resist the newly risen landlord class with death.

從階級鬥爭的情況看這也，就是說寧可死也不願意向新興地主階級屈服不接受地主階級給予他們的恥辱。這是沒落奴隸主以死為反抗的思想。[94]

While acknowledging Yang Zhu's concepts of the self and life as cornerstones in Chinese thought, Feng was no longer able to see them as positive contributions to Chinese philosophy. Yang Zhu's isolated self now signaled the declining slave-owning class and its struggles against the newly risen landlord class.[95] Finally, Feng criticized Yang Zhu's idea of only safeguarding one's own life and body and satisfying one's desires. He reverted to his dissertation's discussion of Yang Zhu in the *Liezi* and his association with hedonism. He weighed in on Yang's words about curbing one's desires and said they might have led others to develop over-indulgence because of Yang's emphasis on 'all for oneself.' Feng quoted from the "Shen wei" 慎為 (Being Attentive to Aims) chapter in *Lüshi chunqiu* and "Robber Zhi" in *Zhuangzi*, to illustrate a tendency toward self-indulgence during the Spring and Autumn era, which was also reflected in the "Yang Zhu" chapter in *Liezi*. These, Feng said, were not Yang Zhu's ideas. Nonetheless, they were a development of Yang Zhu's "all for himself," which could develop into cherishing life (*gui sheng* 貴生) but also its opposite, courting death (*zhao si* 找死), through over-indulgence.[96]

Feng's negation of Yang Zhu's thought signified how Marxist dialectical materialism had come to dominate Feng's philosophy and how much Feng wanted to distance himself from the position of Yang Zhu. The inevitable symbiotic and interactive relationship between the individual and society in Marxist dialectical materialism rendered Yang Zhu's stand-alone self rather meaningless.

Conclusion: The Idea of the Self and Feng Youlan's Treatments of Yang Zhu

Yang Zhu remained a subject of Feng Youlan's intellectual interest throughout his academic life. Central to this interest was Yang's unabashed regard for the self. Initially, Feng studied Yang Zhu's mechanistic worldview in his PhD dissertation (1923), concluding that it resulted in hedonist sensual pleasure. In subsequent works, with new scholarship and fresh interpretations of

Yang Zhu, and against a background of China slipping into war and rising nationalism, Feng paid more attention to the kind of life implied by Yang Zhu's ideas. In 1931 and 1945, Feng criticized Yang's passive approach to life and his focus on life-preservation for failing to connect the individual with society. Yang did not provide a viable way of life for China at war. After China became communist, Marxist dialectical materialism negated Feng's Confucian and Daoist blend of individual self-cultivation. While he tried to reconcile general scholarship with a class analysis in the new trial edition of 1964, the Cultural Revolution and Feng's personal experience, first as a subject under criticism and then as a collaborator with the Gang of Four in the Cultural Revolution, led to more thorough implementation of Marxist dialectical materialism in the 1980 new edition, where not only Yang was identified with the declining slave-owning class, but his philosophy of the self was also casually dismissed as "hedonist." Yang Zhu still registered a place in Daoism, but his value was quite gone.

Throughout, Feng seems to have been both fascinated and repelled by Yang Zhu. Feng attributed Yang Zhu a central role in forming the Daoist school and highlighted his ideas of the self and the human body. These notions were important to Feng because the discourse of the self was also central to Confucian thought. Feng's championing of individual alignment with the universe, the highest stage of his human cultivation, originated from earlier life stages partially based on Yang Zhu's self, which stood apart from society and social rituals. Feng both borrowed from Yang Zhu and was repelled by Yang's exclusive focus on the individual. The Confucian emphasis on individual behavior's social relevance became especially relevant during the tumultuous years of the 1930s and 1940s when China was embroiled in war with Japan. National salvation made Yang Zhu's isolated self almost detestable, although Yang's idea of self-preservation was worthy of note. After 1949, Marxist class analysis and Marxist emphasis on judging ideas by their relevance to contemporary society rendered Yang Zhu quite irrelevant. While Feng refrained from mounting a full Marxist attack on Yang Zhu in 1964, by 1980, Feng dismissed Yang's self-preservation. He saw Yang's principle of cherishing life as automatically moving toward its opposite, courting death.

Notes

1. An example of representative discussions of Yang Zhu and the Chinese self would be the arguments made by John Emerson and Angus Graham. For

Emerson, Yang Zhu was the first in Chinese history to highlight the importance of the body, which had been alienated from the individual by constrictive rituals. However, Emerson argues, Yang Zhu never succeeded in establishing the autonomous individual or the free citizen. His thought would best be called "privatism" rather than "individualism." See John Emerson, "Yang Zhu's Discovery of the Body," in *Philosophy East and West* 46, no. 4 (October 1996): 533, 534, 537, 540, 550. From a slightly different perspective, Angus Graham questioned whether Yang Zhu could be considered an egoist in the Western sense of the word, "whether Chinese thought ever poses the problem of philosophical egoism as it is understood in the West," and whether *wei wo* should be translated as egoism instead of selfishness. "But one has the impression that Chinese thinkers perceive persons as inherently social beings who are more or less selfish rather than as isolated individuals who will be pure egoists unless taught morality." And Graham wonders whether the Mohists—and by connection, the Yangists—would have any conception of an absolute egoism, and instead would possess varying degrees of selfishness and unselfishness. "Perhaps philosophical egoism is conceivable only in a highly atomized society such as our own, perhaps it is not conceptually coherent at all. . . . [W]e may doubt whether a theoretically pure egoism would be conceived by individuals so closely cemented by kin relations as the ancient Chinese." A. C. Graham, *Disputers of the Tao: Philosophical Argument in Ancient China* (La Salle, IL: Open Court, 1989), 63. Both Emerson and Graham considered Yang Zhu's self as a social construct set apart from the collective. Instead of egoism or individualism, it was more privatism or degrees of selfishness, a final confirmation of the self against the pressures of an all-enveloping social web.

2. In chapter 1, "Five Pre-Republican Portrayals of Yang Zhu," Carine Defoort discusses how *Liezi* (ca. 300 AD) shaped Yang Zhu into a Daoist figure, an interpretation perpetuated in the Song Dynasty and continued in late Qing by Kang Youwei. In chapter 6, "Yang Zhu's Role in the Construction of Zhu Xi's *Daotong*," John Makeham depicts Zhu Xi's association of Yang Zhu with Daoism or even Buddhism in the Song dynasty. See also Graham, *Disputers of the Tao*, 170–211.

3. Gu Jiegang 顧頡剛, "Cong Lüshi chunqiu tuice laozi chengshu niandai" 從呂氏春秋推測老子成書年代 [Surmising the date of Laozi from *Lüshi chunqiu*], *Shixue nianbao* 史學年報, no. 4 (1932): 31.

4. Yan Fu, *Yan Fu ji* 嚴復集 [Collection of Yan Fu], ed. Wang Shi 王栻 (Beijing: Zhonghua, 1986), 1125, 1138. Quoted in Yan Deru 顏德如, "Yan Fu yu ziyouzhuyi zai Zhongguo de shibai" 嚴復與自由主義在中國的失敗 [Yan Fu and the failure of liberalism in China], at https://www.aisixiang.com/data/77663.html (accessed on July 3, 2021).

5. Wei Yixia 魏義霞, "Kang Youwei shijie zhong de Yang Zhu" 康有為視界中的楊朱 [Yang Zhu in the views of Yang Youwei], *Jianghuai luntan* 江淮論壇, no. 4 (2017): 40–45. For a more elaborate discussion of Kang's view toward Yang Zhu, see Defoort, "Five Pre-Republican Portrayals of Yang Zhu."

6. Gu, "Cong Lüshi chunqiu," 31–36.

7. Chai Wenhua 柴文華 and Zheng Qiuyue 鄭秋月, "Lun Feng Youlan de zaoqi daojiaguan" 論馮友蘭的早期道家觀 [On Feng Youlan's early views on Daoism], in *Zhexue yanjiu* 哲學研究, no. 6 (2006): 47.

8. Sun Daosheng 孫道昇 (1934), *Yang Zhu de zhuzuo jiqi xuepai kao* 楊朱的著作及其學派考 [A study of Yang Zhu's work and the schools of thought that are associated with Yang] (publisher unknown), 6. The book has been republished by Beijing Zhongxian tuofang fazhan youxian gongsi 北京中獻拓方科技發展有限公司 in 2007.

9. Feng Youlan, *Zhongguo zhexueshi*, vol. 1 中國哲學史 (上) [History of Chinese philosophy, from now on *Zhongzheshi*], in Feng Youlan, *Sansongtang quanji*, dierban 三松堂全集第二版 [Complete collection of the owner of the House of Three Pines, from now on SSTQJ, 2nd ed.] (Zhengzhou: Henan renmin chubanshe, 2000), 2:371–78.

10. Feng Youlan, "Xianqin zhuzi zhi qiyuan" 先秦諸子之起源 [The origins of the pre-Qin schools of thought], in Feng Youlan, *Sansongtang xueshu wenji* 三松堂學術文集 [Collected works of the master of the House of Three Pines] (from now on, SSTXSWJ) (Beijing: Beijing daxue chubanshe, 1984), 369–73; Feng Youlan, "Yuanming fayinyang daode" 原名法陰陽道德 [Tracing the origins of the School of Names, the Legalists, the School of Yin and Yang, and the Daoists]," in SSTXSWJ, 374–85.

11. See Fung Yu-lan, *A History of Chinese Philosophy* (from now on, *HCP*), trans. Derk Bodde (Princeton, NJ: Princeton University Press, 1952), 1:8n2.

12. The unearthing of a briefer version of *Laozi* on bamboo strips, which dated back to the mid–Warring States era around the fourth century BC from a tomb coded Guodian #1 in Shayang County, Hubei Province in 1993 helped confirm that *Laozi* as a work existed around that time, if not earlier. Even though, as Scott Cook comments, these bamboo strips "present as many questions as they answer. . . . Supposing that the wording, passage divisions, and even passage order of the Guodian 'Laozi' materials reflect an older or more 'original' text, that still does little to help us decide whether they reflect the text as it existed in its entirety or simply selections therefrom. . . . What we do know for certain is that at least the basic philosophy of the Laozi had already taken shape by the end of the fourth century BC, and that a sizable portion, if not the vast majority, of its passages had come to be transmitted in written forms closely resembling those of the received text." Scott Cook, *The Bamboo Texts of Guodian* (Ithaca, NY: Cornell University Press, 2012), 216. For Cook's discussion of the Guodian discoveries, see 195–223.

13. See Xiaoqing Diana Lin, *Feng Youlan and Twentieth Century China: An Intellectual History* (Leiden: Brill, 2016).

14. Fung Yu-lan, *HCP*, 1:134. See also Feng Youlan, *Zhongzheshi*, 1:370.

15. Fung Yu-lan, *HCP*, 1:134.

16. Fung Yu-lan, *A Comparative Study of Life Ideals: The Way of Decrease and Increase with Interpretations and Illustrations from the Philosophies of the East*

and West (PhD diss., Columbia University, 1923; Shanghai: Commercial Press, 1924). The publication was the dissertation itself. It was standard practice for Columbia University to require students to publish their dissertations before they could be formally awarded the PhD degree. As Feng himself stated, because he published his dissertation after returning to China, his degree was conferred afterward, and he did not receive his diploma in person. That was why Feng was conferred an honorary doctorate by Columbia University in 1982 to make up for the convocation ceremony that Feng missed in 1924. See Feng's acceptance speech at the honorary doctorate conferment ceremony at Columbia University on September 10, 1982, Chinese Scholar Honored," in *Columbia University Record*, Sept. 17, 1982, pp. 1, 6.

The spelling of Feng's name in English is inconsistent in different publications. In the two volumes of Feng's *A History of Chinese Philosophy* translated by Derk Bodde, Feng's name is written as family name first. In his dissertation, Feng wrote his family name last.

17. Feng Youlan, *Zhongguo zhexue* (Chinese philosophy) (1926), in SSTQJ, 2:38–242.

18. Feng Youlan (Yu-Lan Fung), "Why China Has No Science—An Interpretation of the History and Consequences of Chinese Philosophy," *International Journal of Ethics* 32, no. 3 (Apr., 1922), 237–263.

19. Fung, *A Comparative Study*, 12.
20. Fung, *A Comparative Study*, 78–156.
21. Fung, *A Comparative Study*, 7–11.
22. Fung, *A Comparative Study*, 154–240.
23. Fung, *A Comparative Study*, 241.
24. Fung, *A Comparative Study*, 249.
25. Fung, *A Comparative Study*, 78–79.
26. Fung, *A Comparative Study*, 78–95.
27. Fung, *A Comparative Study*, 14–16.
28. Fung, *A Comparative Study*, 81–82.
29. Fung, *A Comparative Study*, 82. Quote from the chapter on Yang Zhu in *Liezi* as translated from Forke, *Yang Chu's Garden of Pleasure* (London: John Murray, 1912), 40–41. In his dissertation discussion of Yang Zhu, Feng quoted eleven times from Anton Forke's translation of *Liezi*, "Yang Zhu" chapter, in his *Yang Chu's Garden of Pleasure*. He also had three quotes from Lionel Giles's *Taoist Teachings from the Book of Lieh Tzu* (London, 1912). Feng relied primarily on Lionel Giles's translation of chapters 1 to 6, and chapter 8 of *Liezi*, and Anton Forke's translation of the Yang Zhu chapter (chapter 7) in *Liezi* in his dissertation discussion of Yang Zhu. Although he questioned the genuineness of *Liezi*, Feng said the Yang Zhu chapter itself reflected Laozi's view on nature as a materialistic mechanism. Feng commented that many chapters in *Liezi* con-

tained Zhuangzi's teachings on nature as spontaneous and copied from *Zhuangzi*, whereas others reflected the view of nature as a materialistic mechanism, such as in the chapter "Effort and Destiny" (*Li ming* 力命) in *Liezi*. Although he could not confirm Yang Zhu as the author, Feng decided its viewpoint resembled that in the *Liezi* "Yang Zhu" chapter.

30. Fung, *A Comparative Study*, 82–85.
31. Fung, *A Comparative Study*, 85–90.
32. Fung, *A Comparative Study*, 89–90.
33. Diogenes Laertius, *The Lives and Opinions of Eminent Philosophers*, translated by Charles Duke Yonge (London, 1915), 91. Quoted in Fung, *A Comparative Study*, 84–85.
34. Fung, *A Comparative Study*, 91–93.
35. Forke, *Yang Chu's Garden*, 53–54. Quoted in Fung, *A Comparative Study*, 91.
36. *Mencius* 7.26, quoted in Fung, *A Comparative Study*, 91.
37. Fung, *A Comparative Study*, 91.
38. Feng, "Why China Has No Science," 260–61.
39. Fung, *HCP* 2:190–204.
40. Kang Youwei portrayed Yang Zhu as an opponent to Confucius but did not explore many new sources on Yang. See Carine Defoort's chapter 1 of this volume, "Five Pre-Republican Portrayals of Yang Zhu." For general surveys of the Yang Zhu studies scene in early twentieth-century China, see He Aiguo 何愛國, "Cong 'qinshou' dao 'quanli zhexuejia': Lun Yang Zhu xuepai xin xingxiang de jindai goujian" 從禽獸到權利哲學家論楊朱學派新形象的近代構建 [From "beast" to "philosopher of rights": On the reconstructions of Yangism in the modern era], *Lishi jiaoxue wenti* 歷史教學問題, no. 5 (2015): 11-19. He Aiguo 何愛國, "Qingji minchu Yang Zhu sixiang de huohua" 清季民初楊朱思想的活化 [Enlivened reinterpretations of Yang Zhu from the Late Qing to the Early Republic], *Lishi jiaoxue wenti* 歷史教學問題, no. 1 (2015): 81-90, 149. He Aiguo 何愛國, "Shibian yu xueshu: Liang Qichao de Yang xue sanbian" 世變與學術：梁啟超的楊學三變 [World changes and scholarship: the three-stage evolution of Liang Qichao's views on Yangism], *History Research and Teaching*, no. 3 (2014): 10-18. Xiaowei Wang's "Struggling between Tradition and Modernity: Liang Qichao's Portrayal of Yang Zhu in the Early 20th Century," chapter 9 of this volume, discusses Liang Qichao's association of Yang Zhu and the modern idea of rights.
41. See Feng Cao 曹峰, "Ershi shiji guanyu Yang Zhu de yanjiu yi Meng Wentong, Guo Moruo, Hou Wailu, Liu Zehua dengren wei zhongxin" 20世紀關於楊朱的研究：以蒙文通、郭沫若、侯外廬、劉澤華等人為中心 [Researches on Yang Zhu in the twentieth century: Centered on Meng Wentong, Guo Moruo, Hou Wailu and Liu Zehua], *Shehui kexue* 社會科學, no. 9 (2019): 107.
42. Feng Cao, "Ershi shiji," 105-117.

43. Gao Huaping 高華平, "Lun Lüshi chunqiu dui xian Qin baijia de xueshu piping" 論呂氏春秋對先秦百家的學術批評 [On the scholarly criticism of Pre-Qin hundred schools of thought in the *Lüshi chunqiu*], *Jinan xuebao* 暨南學報 [Philosophy and social sciences], no. 3 (2018): 57. He Aiguo argues that Gu Shi identified a wider array of ancient sources with Yang Zhu than before. Sources Gu used included *Zhuangzi, Mencius, Xunzi, Han Feizi, Lüshi chunqiu, Huainanzi, Records of the Grand Historian, Discourses on Salt and Iron*, and the *Shuo Yuan*. See his "Qingji minchu Yang Zhu sixiang de huohua," 82.

44. Gu Shi 顧實 (1931), *Yang Zhu zhexue* 楊朱哲學 [The philosophy of Yang Zhu] (Changsha: Yuelu Shushe, 2011).

45. Gu Shi 顧實, "Yang Zhu xuean" 楊朱學案 [Yang Zhu as a case study], *Hujiang daxue yuekan* 滬江大學月刊 17, no. 13 (1928): 54–63. Gu Shi, "Yang Zhu Xueanxu" 楊朱學案續 [Yang Zhu as a case study, continued], *Hujiang daxue yuekan* 滬江大學月刊 17, no. 14 (1928): 39–49.

46. Gu Shi, "Yang Zhu Xueanxu." Also, Gu Shi's new sources overlapped with new Yangist sources identified in Graham, *Disputers of the Tao*, 55; quoted in Defoort, "Five Pre-Republican Portrayals of Yang Zhu." Graham's discussion of Yang Zhu cited Feng Youlan's discussion of Yang and Yang's followers, and some of his sources from *Lüshi chunqiu* overlapped with Feng's. See Graham, *Disputers of the Tao*, 430–31. Comparable pages in Feng, *HCP*, 1:133–34, 137–40.

47. Hu Shi, *Zhongguo zhexueshi dagang* 中國哲學史大綱 [An outline of the history of Chinese philosophy] (Shanghai: Shangwu chubanshe, 1919).

48. Liang Qichao 梁啟超, "Liang Qichao de Laozi yanjiu" 梁啟超的老子研究 [Liang Qichao's study of Laozi], at http://f.ttwang.net/RoomFile/NewsShow.aspx?RoomId=2811&NewsId=2618 (accessed on July 3, 2021).

49. For instance, Liu Guangsheng 劉光勝, "Cong xingu dao shigu Zhongguo gushi yanjiude jiben qushi" 從信古到釋古中國古史研究的基本趨勢 [From belief in antiquity to interpreting antiquity: the general trends in Chinese studies of ancient history], at http://m.aisixiang.com/data/80891.html (accessed on July 5, 2021). Also, see Feng Cao, "Three Dimensions of Yang Zhu Research in the Twentieth Century: Hu Shi, Meng Wentong, and Guan Feng," chapter 11 in this volume.

50. For instance, "Hu Shi yu Feng Youlan" [Hu Shi and Feng Youlan], at http://www.guoxue.com/master/fengyoulan/fyl16.htm (accessed on July 3, 2021).

51. All three quotes from Fung, *HCP*, 1:134.

52. Fung, *HCP*, 1:134.

53. *Zhongzheshi*, 1:370–71. See also Fung, *HCP*, 1:134. Both the Chinese original and Bodde's interpretation were based on the 1934 edition of vol. 1 of Feng Youlan's *Zhongzheshi*, which was first published in 1931. Hence both the Chinese and English versions included a comment on Gu Jiegang's article published in 1932.

54. Feng, *Zhongzheshi*, 1:369.

55. Feng, *Zhongzheshi*, 1:374; trans. from Fung, *HCP*, 1:138.

56. Feng, *Zhongzheshi*, 1:374; see also Fung, *HCP*, 1:138–139.
57. Feng Youlan, *Xinlixue* 新理學 [A new philosophy of principle], in SSTQJ, 3rd ed., 5:9.
58. Feng Youlan, *Xinyuandao* 新原道 [A new treatise on the nature of dao], in SSTQJ, 3rd ed., 5:790–91.
59. Feng, *Xinyuandao*, 788.
60. Feng, *Xinyuandao*, 789.
61. Feng, *Xinyuandao*, 789.
62. Feng, *Xinyuandao*, 791.
63. Feng Youlan, *Xinyuanren* 新原人 [A new treatise on the nature of man] (1943), in SSTQJ, 3rd ed., 5:555–756.
64. Feng, *Xinyuanren*, 632.
65. Feng, *Xinyuanren*, 634–38.
66. Feng, *Xinyuanren*, 633, 637.
67. Fung Yu-lan, *A Short History of Chinse Philosophy: A Systematic Account of Chinese Thought from Its Origin to the Present Day* (New York: Free Press, 1948), chap. 6.
68. Fung, *A Short History*, 62.
69. Fung, *A Short History*, 63.
70. Fung, *A Short History*, 67.
71. Lin, *Feng Youlan and Twentieth Century China*, 85–92.
72. Feng (1956), "Guoqu zhexueshi gongzuodi ziwo pipan" 過去哲學史工作底自我批判 [A self-criticism of my previous work in the history of philosophy], in SSTQJ, 2nd ed., 14:932–53.
73. On January 7, 1957, Feng published an article titled "*Zhongguo zhexue yichande jicheng wenti*" 中國哲學遺產底繼承問題 [On the inheritance of China's philosophical legacy], in *Guangming Daily*, SSTQJ, 1st ed., 12:103. Multiple communist hardliner colleagues immediately refuted him. For the political background of Feng's writings in the 1950s; see Lin, *Feng Youlan and Twentieth Century China*, chap. 3.
74. Feng Youlan, *Zhongguo zhexueshi xinbian shigao* 中國哲學史新編試稿 [A history of Chinese philosophy, new trial edition], in SSTQJ, 1st ed., 7:118–19, 639. Only the 1964 two-volume new trial edition, and not the 1962 vol. 1 of the new trial edition, is included in SSTQJ, first through third editions.
75. Feng Youlan, *Zhongguo zhexueshi xinbian shigao* 中國哲學史新編試稿 [A history of Chinese philosophy, new trial edition] (from now on, *Shigao2*), in SSTQJ, 2nd ed. (Zhengzhou: Henan renmin chubanshe, 2000), 7:165.
76. Feng, *Zhongzheshi*, 387–99.
77. Cao, "Researches on Yang Zhu in 20th Century," 108–110.
78. Feng, *Shigao2*, 164–72, 178–82.
79. Feng, *Shigao2*, 169.
80. Feng, *Shigao2*, 170.

81. Feng, *Zhongzheshi*, 387–92.
82. Feng, *Shigao2*, 178–81.
83. Feng, *Shigao2*, 170.
84. Feng, *Shigao2*, 170–71.
85. Feng, *Shigao2*, 171.
86. Lin, *Feng Youlan*, 132–33.
87. Feng, S*higao2*, 164–72, 178–84.
88. Feng Youlan, *Zhongguo zhexueshi xinbian* 中國哲學史新編 [New edition of the *History of Chinese Philosophy*] (from now on, *Xinbian*), in SSTQJ, 2nd ed., 8:233–38.
89. Treatment of Laozi and Zhuangzi in Feng, S*higao2*, 241–74 and 345–81, respectively. Treatment of Laozi and Zhuangzi in Feng, *Xinbian*, 266–300, 342–74, respectively.
90. Feng, *Xinbian*, SSTQJ, 8:233–36.
91. Feng, *Xinbian*, SSTQJ, 8:236–37.
92. Feng, *Xinbian*, SSTQJ, 8: 236.
93. Feng, *Xinbian*, SSTQJ, 8: 235.
94. Feng, *Xinbian*, SSTQJ, 8: 235.
95. Feng, *Xinbian*, SSTQJ, 8: 236-37.
96. Feng, *Xinbian*, SSTQJ, 8: 237.

Chapter 11

Three Dimensions of Yang Zhu Research in the Twentieth Century

Hu Shi, Meng Wentong, and Guan Feng

Feng Cao

Introduction

Among ancient Chinese thinkers, the fate of Yang Zhu has proven especially dramatic.[1] In eras that accorded prestige only to Confucian teachings, Yang Zhu became a symbol of extreme selfishness, unwilling to shoulder any social responsibility, and the supreme representative of egoism and hedonism in Chinese history. Yet in early modern times, with the continuing decline of traditional society and the large-scale introduction and absorption of Western thought, Yang Zhu transformed again to become the ancient figure with the most modern set of ideas. His thought was seen to be of value to the salvation of the Chinese nation and people: where at first he was seen in an extremely negative light, his public image eventually became wholly positive. Behind the process of this stunning transformation there must have been profound historical causes. This chapter examines Hu Shi's 胡適 (1891–1962), Meng Wentong's 蒙文通 (1894–1968), and Guan Feng's 關鋒 (1919–2005) studies of Yang Zhu, seeking to illuminate the various dimensions of their analyses of Yang

Zhu as well as the rationales of the transformation of Yang Zhu's image in the twentieth century. It also inspects the strengths and weaknesses of their respective methods.

1. Hu Shi: Yang Zhu Can Promote China's Progress

Reversing the historical judgment of Yang Zhu is one of the major events that followed modern revitalization of the study of pre-Qin thought. Yet the renaissance or flourishing of Yang Zhu studies happened first in Japan. The invention of labels such as "egoism" (*lijizhuyi*) and "hedonism" (*kuailezhuyi*), the comparison of these teachings with ancient Greek thought, a positive interpretation of these teachings, and the view that they possess a spirit of altruism, freedom, and independence were all pioneered by late Meiji-era Japanese scholars.[2] In China, around the turn of the early twentieth century, scholars then began appraising Yang Zhu in a new way. This evaluation was in part the product of Japanese and Western influence. Renewed examination of pre-Qin thinkers, including Yang Zhu, began from an academic perspective rather than from Confucian morals. This was also, however, closely related to the modern transformation of traditional Chinese thought and culture. That is to say, this new evaluation of Yang Zhu was not entirely neutral. It was intimately connected with the circumstances of Chinese society at the time. While it deployed the concepts and labels of Western learning, the objects and methods of study were greatly influenced by historical circumstance and political aims. We might say that Hu Shi's study of Yang Zhu possessed this characteristic.

Prior to Hu Shi, Liang Qichao 梁啟超 (1873–1929) and other scholars had already embarked on robust discussion of Yang Zhu. On this, He Aiguo has provided valuable analysis, arguing that the changes in scholarship followed changes in the world. Liang Qichao's view of Yang Zhu progressed in three steps, from complete rejection and abhorrence of Yang's teachings to a simplistic view of Yangism as a valuable means to save the nation, and then again to deeper contemplation of the commonalities with Western ideas and spirit.[3] From these three developments we see that Liang's novel explication of Yang Zhu, despite its sequential transformations, was nevertheless unchanging in its basic purport. Throughout, his views are judgments of whether Yang Zhu's teachings were able to save the nation. Liang sought in Yangism intellectual resources that would advance China's Westernization. Beneath his evaluation lies an inexorable practical concern with whether China would be able to integrate with the West.

Taking this as the context to examine Hu Shi's study of Yang Zhu, it is easier to see the origins of his approach and major views. Chronologically speaking, Hu entered scholarship on Yang Zhu at the second stage of Liang's work. In 1917, Hu submitted his doctoral dissertation in America, *The Development of the Logical Method in Ancient China*.[4] This work gives a comprehensive overview of pre-Qin thought through the study of logical concepts, and yet it does not discuss Yang Zhu. However, Hu's 1918 lectures on the history of Chinese philosophy, given as a professor at Peking University, show that he had already assigned Yang Zhu his own chapter in that history.[5] Interestingly, according to the table of contents of Hu's lectures, Yang Zhu is placed in the eighth chapter, while the lecture transcripts themselves place him seventh. From this we see that Yang's place in Hu's history of philosophy was still in flux. When Hu formally published his *Outline of the History of Chinese Philosophy* (*Zhongguo zhexueshi dagang* 中國哲學史大綱) the following year,[6] the finalized chapter on "Yang Zhu" found its place as the seventh chapter, and its content was much expanded from the earlier lecture.[7]

From no mention in the dissertation of 1917 to some initial discussion of Yang Zhu's importance in 1918, Hu then produced a full examination of Yang Zhu in 1919. In this we see the deep influence of contemporary academic trends on Hu Shi's study of Yang Zhu. For one thing, China's very first *History of Chinese Philosophy*, published in 1916, had already accorded a section to Yang Zhu in its chapter on Daoism.[8] Hu Shi would not have missed this. Moreover, many scholars at that time, like Liang Qichao, had produced a great deal of discussion on Yang Zhu that appraised him very highly. Hu Shi would not have overlooked this, either. Thus, within a mere three years after returning to China from America, Hu must have poured tremendous energy into study of Yang Zhu, thereby very quickly becoming a new paradigmatic figure in Yang Zhu research. Here I focus on his *Outline of the History of Chinese Philosophy*.

As I see it, Hu Shi's view of Yang Zhu in this book has three distinctive characteristics. First, it carries forward lofty appraisals of Yang Zhu from the late Qing and early Republican periods. At that time, even Liang Qichao, despite his exaltation of the Yangist spirit, saw the world-weary, hedonist portrayal of Yang in the "Yang Zhu" chapter of the *Liezi* as decadent and objectionable. Hu Shi saw the *Liezi*'s "Yang Zhu" chapter to be "on the whole seemingly reliable" (大體似乎可靠) as a historical testimony and took it as the principal resource in his exploration of Yang Zhu's thought.⁹ He provided a sympathetic interpretation of it and believed that even if Yangist teachings had negative elements, they were natural products of the disorder and suffering of that time. Thus, Yang inherited Laozi's "naturalism," which sought to break down all cultural institutions and return to a state without knowledge or desire. At the same time, Hu saw the Yangist rejection of names and reputation, or "no-names ideology" (無名主義), as closest to Western nominalism: "names" are no more than empty titles created by humans, with no corresponding reality.¹⁰ Yang Zhu thus "recognized only the importance of the individual, and ignored human ethical relations" (只認個人的重要，輕視人倫的關係), and so the tendency toward individualism was to be expected.¹¹ In contradistinction to other scholars, Hu Shi saw all of Yang Zhu's teachings as having a reasonable side to them.

Second is Hu Shi's use of evolutionary theory in vindicating Yang Zhu's teaching of "being for oneself" (為我). While these ideas appear in the 1918 lecture manuscript, they are greatly expanded upon in the published *Outline*. Prior to this, Liang Qichao had discussed the rationality of "benefiting oneself" (利己) from the perspective of survival of the fittest within competition among states. Although Hu Shi accepted this idea, he strove to locate philosophical grounds for it so as to provide a more substantive and principled account. For example, Hu Shi draws on the "Yang Zhu" chapter of the *Liezi* in the following passage:

> The most adaptable organism is the human. For humans, their teeth and nails are inadequate to defend themselves, their skin is inadequate to protect them, their natural tendencies are inadequate to avoid harm, and they have no fur or feathers to ward off the cold. They must rely on fostering other things to nourish themselves. They deploy their wisdom rather than relying on strength; and thus wisdom is of great value to them as preserving themselves is of great value to them, and their strength is of little worth as antagonism toward others is of little worth.
>
> 有生之最靈者，人也。人者，爪牙不足以供守衛，肌膚不足以自捍禦，趨走不足以逃利害，無毛羽以御寒暑，必將資物以為養性。任智而不恃力，故智之所貴，存我為貴；力之所賤，侵物為賤。¹²

Hu subsequently points out that this turns on the principle of natural selection. Plants and animals all have a natural tendency for self-preservation, and it is the need for self-preservation that drives biological evolution. Because of this, Yang Zhu's egoism is not synonymous with harming others to benefit oneself. It is worth noting that Hu Shi goes on to add a whole bunch of ideas that do not appear in the "Yang Zhu" chapter of the *Liezi* itself, but that can largely (if not entirely) be drawn from it and that are quite reasonable and appealing. These include that the human being is an organism that needs to "preserve itself" (存我), but it is also a communal organism and thus generates ideologies of caring for one's community such as protecting one's family, society, and nation. Thereby, the self-interest of "preserving oneself" turns out not to conflict with caring for one's community, and one cannot reject individual consciousness and individual rights on the basis of the community and collective consciousness.

Third, Yangist teachings facilitate the modern enlightenment of the Chinese people. Following his explication of Yangism through evolutionary theory, Hu Shi goes on to discuss the characteristics of ancient Chinese society, which include a "caring for the community-ism" (愛群主義) that oppressed the "being for oneself-ism" (為我主義), so that the communal consciousness surpassed individual consciousness. If we want to view Hu Shi as a flagbearer of the New Culture movement, we can also find evidence of this in his exposition of Yangist teachings. A major characteristic of the New Culture movement was the analysis, criticism, and reform of Chinese national character so as to adapt to, accommodate, and emulate the "advanced" (先進) form of civilization represented by Western cultures. Hu Shi's analysis of Yang Zhu accords precisely with this demand of his times, and it led in the direction of the New Culture movement.

After elaborating on the factors that caused ancient China's ideology of caring for the community to oppress the ideology of being for oneself, Hu Shi immediately shifts into fierce criticism of traditional Confucian thought, authoritarianism, and familism. In *Outline* he writes,

> Looking at society's promotion of "dying for one's husband," "dying for one's ruler," "dying for the state," and other such customs, which it exalted as moral acts, we thereby see the causes of intolerance toward the ideology of preserving oneself. In fact, the idea of preserving oneself was originally a natural biological tendency. In itself there is nothing immoral about it.

試看社會提倡的'殉夫'、'殉君"殉社稷'等等風俗，推尊為道的行為，便可見存我主義所以不見容的原因了。其實存我觀念本是生物天然的趨向，本身並無甚麼不道德。[13]

On the one hand, this is a reasonable rectification of the notion of "benefitting oneself." On the other hand, it is criticism of and a clarion call against ritual, feudal ethics. Whereas overly realist, critical, and impassioned content had previously been considered inappropriate to a work of the history of ancient philosophy, these are precisely the distinctive qualities of Hu Shi's book. From this we see the strong colors of that period in Hu Shi's history of philosophy.

In this way, within the torrent of modern scholarship rectifying the name of Yang Zhu, Hu Shi takes a philosophical approach to systematically and comprehensively explain how Yang Zhu possesses a positive and progressive spirit and is the embodiment of an independent personality. Following May Fourth, an important part of the New Culture movement pushed for the destruction of traditional culture and institutions, advocating liberation of thought, independence and individuality, and freedom and equality. Hu's *Outline of the History of Chinese Philosophy* clearly starts down this road.

2. Meng Wentong: Reconstructing the Yangist Genealogy

From the aforementioned scholarship by Hu Shi we see that examination of Yang Zhu in the early twentieth century, while having some academic components, often affixed labels from Western thought to Yang, drawing simplistic analogies between his thought and Western notions of freedom, equality, and independence. In doing so, they attributed messages to Yang Zhu that he could not possibly have spoken himself. The aims of that scholarship carried an intense sense of societal responsibility, calling on people to save the nation and cultivate a new national character. This greatly reduced the academic nature of these studies.[14] After the 1920s and 1930s, passion for saving the nation through the spirit of early philosophers began to decline, and purely academic examination of the intellectual trends of ancient Chinese thought began to be recognized. Of course, this was also a product of Western influence, and it was especially closely related to the positivist method founded on skepticism. This kind of investigation required comprehensive and systematic analysis and explication of the original character, context, and influence of historical figures and their thought on the basis of fully collecting and respecting textual records and thereafter seeking to draw out strands of thought and lines of intellectual development.

The most exhaustive and meticulous examination of the textual records and scholastic lineage of Yang Zhu was given by Meng Wentong. Meng's "Study of Yangism" (*Yang Zhu xuepai kao*),[15] authored in the 1940s, comprises a "Study of Yang Zhu" (*Yang Zhu kao*) and a "Study of Huang-Lao" (*Huang-Lao kao*). The academic significance of this work has two sides to it. The first is its collection and organization of textual records of Yang Zhu, which is unsurpassed to this day. The second is the construction through careful analysis of a genealogy of Yangism, which ultimately connects it with Huang-Lao Daoism.

Although Meng Mo (Meng Wentong's son) writes in *A Short Biography of Mr. Meng Wentong* (*Meng Wentong xiansheng xiaozhuan* 蒙文通先生小傳) that Meng Wentong "differed starkly in his interests from the trend of Doubting Antiquity" (與疑古者流迥異其趣),[16] there was in fact an intimate connection between Meng Wentong and the school of Doubting Antiquity.[17] At the very least, in certain basic views on Yang Zhu, Meng Wentong did not at all oppose the conclusions drawn from textual analysis that the school of Doubting Antiquity put forth. First, Meng was influenced by them in matters of dating the textual formation of the *Laozi*. He also did not endorse Laozi as a historical figure who at some particular time and place in the late Spring and Autumn period wrote down the five thousand characters of the *Laozi*. Meng instead believed that the *Daodejing* could have appeared only in the mid- to late Warring States period, sometime prior to the *Han Feizi* 韓非子. Nonetheless, due to the excavation of the Guodian *Laozi*, we now tend to reject this conclusion. Yet at that time, this was indeed the conclusion reached after serious discussion by a large group of scholars, which approval was followed by many other academics. Additionally, on the subject of the authenticity of the "Yang Zhu" chapter of the *Liezi*, Meng also aligned with the school of Doubting Antiquity in not including it within the scope of credible textual resources.

Unlike Liang Qichao and Hu Shi, Meng Wentong abstained from discussing the relationship of Yang Zhu's teachings of benefiting oneself with independence of personality, equality of human rights, personal freedom, and so on. His study sets out from the perspective of intellectual history and begins from the following question:

> Records of Mr. Yang's teachings are scarce, and their later transformations cannot be verified. Unable to clarify these teachings as we can with other thinkers such as Mozi, how could we see that they flourished throughout the world [as claimed in *Mencius* 3B9]?
>
> 楊氏之言不多見，後之流變亦不可考。未能如墨氏之顯，則安見其言之盈天下？[18]

That is, considering that Yang Zhu's historical influence was once so significant, we should not fail to give sufficient attention to him today simply because of a lack of historical records. We instead ought to trace whatever strands of evidence we have in tracking the transformation of these ideas. Meng begins from the notion of "valuing oneself" (貴己) attributed to Yang Zhu in the "Bu er" 不二 (No Duality) chapter of *Lü's Spring and Autumn Annals* along with the description of Yang Zhu as "preserving the wholeness of one's nature and protecting what is genuine" (全性保真) in the "Fan lun" 汎論 (Boundless Discourses) chapter of the *Huainanzi*. From these he first concluded that the aims of Yang Zhu's advocacy of "being for oneself" were primarily connected with the cultivation of life (*yang sheng* 養生). Following this meticulous analysis, Meng connected Yang Zhu with the trajectory of the thought of Zhan He 詹何, Zihuazi 子華子, Wei Mou 魏牟, Chen Zhong 陳仲, Peng Meng 彭蒙, Tian Pian 田駢, Shen Dao 慎到, and others, ultimately constructing a lineage of the inheritance and development of Yangism and connecting this genealogy with Huang-Lao Daoism.

In existing records, the connection of Yang Zhu with Zhan He and Zihuazi is relatively easy to establish. The idea of "esteeming one's life" (尊生) attributed to Zhan He in the "Holding to the One" 執一 chapter of *Mr. Lü's Spring and Autumn Annals* and the "Rang wang" 讓王 (Yielding the Throne) chapter of the *Zhuangzi* along with the idea of "preserving the wholeness of one's life" (全生) attributed to Zihuazi in the "Gui sheng" 貴生 (Honoring Life) and "Shen wei" 審為 (Being Attentive to Aims) chapters of the *Lü's Spring and Autumn Annals* allow us to establish genealogical connections from Yang Zhu to Zhan He and Zihuazi.

The idea of the cultivation of life certainly connects with attitudes toward one's natural dispositions and desires. Meng Wentong believed that later followers of Yang Zhu created their own branches of this school of thought. Giving particular attention to the discussions of "indulging one's inborn disposition and nature" (縱情性) and "restraining one's inborn disposition and nature" (忍情性) in the "Fei shier zi" 非十二子 (Against the Twelve Masters) chapter of the *Xunzi*, Meng then combined these with material from the *Guanzi* 管子, the *Strategies of the Warring States* (*Zhanguo ce* 戰國策), and the *Han Feizi*. He thereby argued that "the Yang Zhu school clearly includes the two camps of 'indulging one's inborn disposition and nature' and 'restraining one's inborn disposition and nature'" (楊朱一派顯有"縱情性"、"忍情性"之二派). He additionally declared that "Tuo Xiao 它囂 and Wei Mou, who were for 'indulging one's inborn disposition and nature'" ('縱情性'的它囂魏牟), "also carried forward one line of Yang Zhu's teachings" (亦楊朱一系之學), while "Chen Zhong and Shi You 史鰌, who were for 'restraining one's inborn disposition and nature,' also constituted a line of Yang Zhu's teachings" ('忍情性'的陳仲、史鰌亦楊朱之學者).[19]

Meng recognized that valuing one's life does not necessarily exclude valuing moral rightness. Yang Zhu does not avoid discussion of humaneness and rightness. It is just that his views of humaneness and rightness were not endorsed by Mencius and were thus subjected to criticism. From the *Zhuangzi* we see that Bian Sui 卞隨 and other figures in the "Rang wang" (Yielding the Throne) chapter represent the camp of restraining one's essential disposition and nature, accepting Confucius and endorsing humaneness and rightness, while the "Dao Zhi" 盜跖 (Robber Zhi) chapter represents the camp of indulging one's essential disposition and nature, rejecting humaneness and rightness and ridiculing Confucius. Meng believed that such *Zhuangzi* chapters as "Rang wang" may have been Yangist works mistakenly included in the compilation of the text. He also saw the camp of indulging one's essential disposition and nature as having subsequently developed in ways that brought them close to Zhuangzi's thought. In their treatment of humaneness and rightness, the northern Daoists represented by Yang Zhu and the southern Daoists represented by Laozi and Zhuangzi were diametrically opposed. From this Meng Wentong derived his famous distinction of northern Daoism from southern Daoism; and this distinction was also the starting point of his research into Huang-Lao Daoism. We can say it is precisely through Meng's study of Yang Zhu that academic interest in the connection of Daoists with humaneness and rightness began, and from this they came to see the inclusion of humaneness and rightness and participation in government affairs precisely as the major characteristics of Huang-Lao Daoism.

Supported by his distinction between northern and southern Daoism, Meng Wentong further extended Yang Zhu's influence upon Jixia 稷下

Daoism. Through Tian Pian's advocacy of "following one's nature and letting things take their course" (因性任物) and "adaptive transformation" (變化應求) described in the "Zhi yi" 執一 (Holding on to the One) chapter of *Lü's Spring and Autumn Annals*, Meng asserts, "this is Tian Pian's as well as Zhan He's and Wei Mou's Way (*dao*) of preserving the wholeness of one's life and cultivating one's longevity of years" (是田駢亦詹何、魏牟全生養年之道也).[20] Following this, Meng argued at great length that the four chapters of the *Guanzi* are works of Tian Pian and Shen Dao. The Way of "responsively going along with things" (因循) promoted in the "Xin shu" 心術 (Arts of the Mind) and "Bai xin" 白心 (Purifying the Mind) chapters of the *Guanzi* is precisely an extension and advancement of Yang Zhu's advocacy of "refusing to pluck a single hair to benefit the world" (拔一毛而利天下不為). The "Wei de" 威德 (Awesome Potency) chapter of the *Shenzi* 慎子 states, "The people's relation to sages is that they nurture themselves, rather than that they make sages nurture them [the people]. Thus sages do not undertake any action." (百姓之於聖人也，養之也，非使聖人養己也。則聖人無事矣.) This echoes the spirit of the "Xin shu" ideal in which "without harming or causing turmoil in the world, the world is ordered" (不亂於天下而天下治). We can connect Yang Zhu's "refusal to pluck a single hair to benefit the world" to this notion that "If the [people of the] world order themselves rather than calling on sages to nurture them, what use could there be for sages to benefit the world?" (天下自治，非使聖人養己，則安用聖人之利天下哉?)[21] The *Guanzi*, *Lü's Spring and Autumn Annals*, and the "Jie bi" 解蔽 (Dispelling Ignorance) chapter of the *Xunzi* describe Tian Pian and Shen Dao as emphasizing both "responsively going along with things" as well as "modeling/laws" (*fa* 法). This aligns their position with the emphasis on integrating the Way with models/laws in Huang-Lao teachings. The teachings of Tian Pian and Shen Dao originated from Yang Zhu and were brought together at Jixia. Thus Meng concluded that through Tian Pian and Shen Dao's "advocacy of Huang-Lao theory herein had its start" (黃老之論於是始倡).[22]

> The teachings of Yang Zhu as carried forward in Tian and Shen had become more profound in meaning and more expansive in application. Huang-Lao arose from this, and was close to Legalism.
>
> 楊朱之學，逮乎田、慎，義益邃而用益宏。黃老既由此出，且以法為鄰.[23]

Finally, Meng Wentong also drew Shen Buhai and Liezi into the system of Yangist thought. Especially for Liezi, he discussed this in terms of the lineage:

> Liezi preceded Yang Zhu, and thus Yang's teachings have their origin in the [*Zhuangzi*'s] "Lie Yukou" and laid the foundation for Huang-Lao views.

列子先於楊朱，則楊氏之學，源於《列禦寇》，而下開黃老.[24]

> Wei Mou, Chen Zhong, Zhan He, Zihua, Tian Pian, and Shen Dao all belong to the school of Yang Zhu, while Liezi seems to be the source of Yang Zhu's thought.

魏牟、陳仲、詹何、子華、田駢、慎到，皆楊朱之流派，而列子者，倘又楊朱之遠源也.[25]

We find, then, that in stark contrast to Hu Shi and others, Meng Wentong strove to return to the texts and ideas themselves. The figures drawn into Meng's construction of the Yangist lineage are often those that had been marginalized in previous studies of Daoism. This was due to the fact that after the Wei-Jin period, Lao-Zhuang Daoism had become the main form of Daoism, whereas the Huang-Lao teachings that had flourished in earlier Warring States and Qin-Han times had gradually declined and thereafter received little attention. Another aspect of this situation, though, is that there is a paucity of historical materials that pertain to these figures. Any surviving records are pitifully scarce and extremely scattered. Huang-Lao Daoism became a prevalent object of study only from the 1970s onward, with the discovery of unearthed texts such as the Mawangdui silk manuscripts and Shanghai Museum bamboo slips, which provided an abundance of new historical resources. In the first half of the twentieth century, by contrast, scholars relied only on extremely fragmented and limited materials in tracing a relatively comprehensive and academically reasonable line of intellectual development beginning from Yang Zhu. They also thereby pioneered the fundamental framework of the study of Huang-Lao thought. Meng Wentong's contribution to this was unparalleled. Today, a surge of excavated texts and other new materials provide us much greater scope and potential in explicating this line of intellectual development and framework of study. Yet, this remains an extension of Meng Wentong's view sketched in earlier era.

3. Guan Feng: Yang Zhu as Representative of Small Producers

Following 1949, the academic world in Mainland China underwent dramatic shifts. Everything was directed by Marxism. Yet, in terms of Yang Zhu study, the overall orientation remained an extension of May Fourth and the New Culture movement. If during the New Culture movement the aim of studying and elevating his thought was to connect it with the Western spirit of freedom, equality, and independence, we see no major substantive change in this regard following 1949. Personal freedoms swept through China following May Fourth as an ideological torrent that transcended party consciousness. Thus, both during the Republican period and after 1949 people generally held affirmative outlooks on personal liberty and the strengthening of individual subjective consciousness. What differed was that following 1949 the Western spirit that Yang Zhu was used to be connected with was not the same. The contemporary discourse that Yang served had changed, and his image was further developed through a materialist, populist, and revolutionary outlook. Study of this aspect of things is best represented by the first volume of Hou Wailu's 侯外廬 (1903–1987) *General History of Chinese Thought* (*Zhongguo sixiang tongshi* 中國思想通史) and the pre-Qin volume of Liu Zehua's *History of Chinese Political Thought* (*Zhongguo zhengzhi sixiang shi* 中國政治思想史). Out of considerations of length, these are not further discussed here.[26]

For political reasons, research on Yang Zhu by highly active scholars from the time of the Cultural Revolution such as Guan Feng, Yang Rongguo, and others goes largely unmentioned today. Yet their research was in fact extremely distinctive, and for a time it was hugely influential. If we discard those scholarly positions that are founded on political judgments and view their scholarship as phenomena of intellectual history, we can also see them as presenting a distinctive dimension of research on Yang Zhu that had a certain rationale within a certain period. We should also note that the work of these scholars, although carrying an intensely political mark, was not entirely unacademic. For example, Yang Rongguo saw Yang Zhu as a pioneer of Daoist thought predating Laozi and Zhuangzi and at the same time viewed Yang Zhu as founder of the School of Names

(名家), believing that Yangist ideas such as "the importance of life" (重生) and "non-action" had been inherited by Zhuangzi, while the logical aspect of his thought was inherited by Hui Shi 惠施.[27] This analysis has a certain academic quality to it. Meanwhile, Guan Feng applied class analysis to Yang Zhu, seeing him as representative of small producers, thereby opening up new aspects for studying Yang Zhu. Focusing on the case of Guan Feng, this chapter discusses how he used the theory of class analysis to examine Yang Zhu's thought.

Guan Feng's study of Yang Zhu appears mainly in two essays, "A Preliminary Examination of the Outer and Miscellaneous Chapters of the *Zhuangzi*," published in *Philosophical Researches* in 1961, and "On Mozi and Yangism," published in the sixth edition of *Journal of Chinese Literature and History* in 1965.[28] The former evaluates the properties of textual records but adds to this the basic views of class analysis, while the latter presents systematic analysis of the ideas of Yangism and their formative factors on the basis of comparison with Mohism.

"A Preliminary Examination of the Outer and Miscellaneous Chapters of the *Zhuangzi*" argues that the outer and miscellaneous chapters of the *Zhuangzi* are not works of Zhuangzi himself and "include works of leftist followers of Laozi, works of followers of the camp of Song Xing and Yin Wen, works of followers of Zhuangzi, and works of followers of Yang Zhu"(其中有老子後學左派的作品，有宋鈃、尹文學派後學的作品，有莊子後學的作品，有楊朱後學的作品).[29] Specifically, Guan Feng believed the "Dao Zhi," "Rang wang," and "Yu fu" 漁父 (Old Fisherman) chapters were works by the followers of Yang Zhu. He first drew on materials related to Yang Zhu from *Mencius* 3B9, 7A26, and 7B26, "Xian xue" 顯學 (Eminent Learnings) in the *Han Feizi*, "Li zheng" 立政 (Establish Government) and "Jiu bai jie" 九敗解 (Explanation of Nine Types of Loss) in the *Guanzi*, "Bu er" in *Lü's Spring and Autumn Annals*, and the "Fan lun" chapter of the *Huainanzi*. From these he concluded that Yangism's distinctive characteristics are not only a rejection of self-sacrifice for one's ruler but also a vision of one's own life being more important than anything else. Yangist teachings once held wide sway, to the extent that they challenged Confucianism and Mohism as one of the three most influential teachings throughout the world. While the Confucians advocated "caring intimately for family" (親親) and the Mohists rejected "caring intimately for family" but advocated "care of all" (兼愛), the Yangists rejected "caring intimately for family" and advocated "being for oneself" (為我). Yet these three schools were all a type of "salvationism" (救世主義). Yang Zhu's "egoism"

(為我主義) was a positive and proactive vision of world salvation, not a negative and passive one of eremitism. As long as all people saw "their own lives as most important and external things as unimportant" (輕物重生), they would not compete over external objects, and the world would be ordered and at peace. However, the Wei-Jin period did not have the intellectual foundation for developing such thought. Followers therefore mostly passively withdrew from the sociopolitical realm and did not advance Yangist salvationism.

In these views, Guan Feng did not move beyond the basic positions on Yang Zhu that had been predominant since the early twentieth century, and he thus presented little that was not already known. What is particularly intriguing is that he did not see the "Yang Zhu" chapter of the *Liezi* as a forgery, since the gist of that text aligns closely with his description of the pre-Qin thinkers more broadly. So then, what was the foundation of Yang Zhu's thought? Guan Feng's analysis on this point was first of its kind:

> Such thinking reflects precisely the appearance of the thought of the free small producer in the process of transformation from slave society to feudal society that occurred at the turn of the Spring and Autumn to the Warring States. One of the crucial aspects of the shift from slave institutions to feudal institutions in ancient China was the appearance of private ownership of land, which made land a commodity. In the process of the formation of the feudal landlord class, there concurrently appeared a great number of free small producers, although they could not but quickly bankrupt and fall into serfdom following the consolidation of land ownership.

> 這種思想，正是反映了春秋戰國之交，在奴隸社會向封建社會轉化過程中出現的自由小生產者之思想。我國古代由奴隸制向封建制的轉化，其關鍵之一便是土地私有制的出現，土地變成商品。因此，就在地主階級形成過程中，同時出現了大量自由的小生產者，雖然他們不能不很快地隨著土地集中過程而破產，淪為農奴。[30]

It hardly needs mentioning that this kind of view was produced in great numbers after 1949. Following the division of the evolution of Chinese society into five major social forms, we have the Spring and

Autumn and Warring States periods as a point of transformation from slave institutions to feudal institutions. The modes of thinking about land allocation and personal relations accordingly saw tremendous changes. Guan Feng defined Yang Zhu and his followers as a large group of free small producers who appeared in the process of formation of the class of feudal landowners.

> The principal need of such small producers, in the process of the consolidation of land ownership and continuous extended warfare, was to protect their own economic and political status. The "egoism" of "not giving" and "not taking" is precisely a theoretical expression of this demand on this class.
>
> 這種小生產者，在土地集中過程和長期不斷的戰爭中，主要的要求，就是保持自己的經濟地位和政治地位，"不與"、"不取"的"為我主義"，正是這個階級的階級要求之一種理論表現。[31]

In accordance with the mechanistic materialism commonly espoused after 1949, in which social ideology is determined by society's existence and individual thought is always a reflection of one's class identity, Guan Feng gave Yang Zhu the label of "small producer" (小生產者). In "On Mozi and Yangism," Guan proposed that although Mozi discussed "care for all" and Yang Zhu discussed "being for oneself," both represented the small producers.

> Directed at the situation of "reciprocal infringement" of that time, Mozi proposed "mutually care for all and mutually benefit one another," while Yang Zhu proposed "being for oneself" in the sense of "not giving" and "not taking." Both have in mind the interests of the independent small producer. However, the former more strongly reflects the qualities of the independent small producers as a laborer, while the latter more strongly reflects the qualities of the independent small producers as property owners.
>
> 針對當時"交相侵"的情況，墨子提出"兼相愛、交相利"，揚朱提出"為我"即"不取"、"不予"，都是從獨立小生產者的利益出發的；不過前者更多地反映了獨立小生產者作為勞動者一方面的品質，後者更多地反映了獨立小生產者作為私有者一方面的品質。[32]

> Yang Zhu's individualism is precisely a reflection of the economic status of independent small producers who neither seek to exploit others nor admit of others' exploitation.
>
> 楊朱的個人主義正是獨立小生產者即不剝削人、也不受人剝削這種經濟地位的一種反映.³³

Like "care for all," "being for oneself" was also a vision of equality among small producers. In this way, Guan Feng offered a unique explanation of how Yang Zhu related to Mozi and why his ideas possess a quality of equality.

Guan Feng further pointed out that such small producers, following the rise of the feudal landlord class representative of this new power dynamic, were situated within a process of continuous breakdown, and thus as the "Zhong ji" 重己 (Valuing the Self), "Ben sheng" 本生 (Taking Life as Basic), "Gui sheng," and "Shen wei" chapters of *Lü's Spring and Autumn Annals* show us, the later Yangists were certain to move toward hedonism, since this group already had no prospects. Those small producers had no hopes for their future due to these institutional changes, so they decided to give up fighting and hard work to indulge in pleasure.

On the basis of this line of reasoning, Guan Feng proposed that the "Dao Zhi," "Rang wang," and "Yu fu" chapters of the *Zhuangzi* were all works of later Yangists and all have a common affinity for "seeing one's life as most important and seeing things as unimportant" and "preserving the wholeness of one's nature and protecting what is genuine." Yet each has its own tendencies as well. For example, the "Dao Zhi" chapter reflects "the deep loathing of bankrupt small producers toward the exploitive class of landlords" (破產的小生產者對地主剝削階級的刻骨仇恨).³⁴ In this group of later Yangists, "the vision of great order throughout the world in which all people neither give nor take" (人人不取、不予而天下大治的理想)³⁵ had already vanished because the class of small producers was already on the verge of collapsing. For this reason, the "Dao Zhi" chapter most archetypically reflects the tendency toward hedonism.³⁶ The first passage of the "Rang wang" chapter recounts,

> The world is most important, and yet this man would not accept the injury of his life [for its sake]; how much less would he have allowed any other thing to harm him! Only he who does not care to rule the world is fit to be entrusted with it.

夫天下至重也，而不以害其生，又況他物乎！唯無以天下為者，可以托天下也。[37]

We see here the connection with Yang Zhu's advocacy of "valuing oneself," "viewing one's life as most important and other things as unimportant," and "egoism." We also see Yangism's inheritance of Laozian thought. Yet this chapter likewise could be deemed "a work representative of the Yangist small producers of the Warring States" (代表戰國小生產者的楊朱一派所作), since it describes an economic situation of "sixty acre households" (六十畝), which "is precisely the ideal for a yeoman and small landholder" (正是自耕農、小土地所有者的理想).[38] As for the "Yu fu" chapter, although the tones of reclusiveness are thick, these can be seen as derivative of the notion of "preserving the wholeness of one's nature and protecting what is genuine." By the late Warring States period, "one camp of later Yangists tended toward reclusiveness" (楊朱後學一派趨向隱逸) and "that there was another camp that tended toward nourishing one's life and even hedonism is understandable" (另一派趨向養生乃至縱慾一樣是可以理解的). Guan Feng thereby concluded, "This is a work of the Yangist camp that tended toward reclusiveness in the late Warring States period" (它是戰國末期楊朱後學趨向隱逸的一派所作).[39]

Under the influence of the particular political environment that followed 1949, Mainland academia was certain to follow mechanistic and rigid forms of Marxist theory in digesting the pre-Qin philosophies. This was an unavoidable part of that historical situation, and Guan Feng is merely one relatively paradigmatic figure representing this. On the one hand, we take his views as products of a particular era, so as to understand and describe them objectively. Yet on the other hand, from an academic point of view, although Guan Feng's position was deeply colored by mechanistic materialism, by analyzing people's thought from the perspective of societal and economic development and changes in personal relationships, we also find undeniable lines of rational analysis here.

Moreover, Guan Feng's identification of the "Dao Zhi," "Rang wang," and "Yu fu" chapters of the *Zhuangzi* as Yangist works, along with his belief that later Yangism included a hedonist and an exclusivist camp, not only exerted a certain influence in their time. Removing the Marxist labels of that era, his views retain a certain value in terms of textual analysis. For example, the renowned British Sinologist A. C. Graham affirmed Guan Feng's view of these three chapters as being Yangist works,[40] and he viewed them as a fundamental contribution of Yangism. We might say that Graham's depiction of Yangism is to a large extent constructed on these three chapters of the *Zhuangzi*.⁴¹ He also added the "Shuo jian" chapter of the *Zhuangzi*, which Guan Feng did not include among the Yangist texts. Graham saw this as "a Yangist warning against injury of life by pointless bloodshed."⁴² Although Graham did not define Yang Zhu as a small producer, he did see the Yangists as an eremitic intellectual movement, in line with Guan Feng. However, Graham differed from Guan in dating the formation of the "Dao Zhi" chapter much later. Graham saw the "Dao Zhi" chapter's portrayal of the thought of Shen Nong as a movement within Yangism around the time of the founding of the Qin and Han dynasties. This group loathed excessive punishments and was inclined toward a utopian vision of the past. Graham had earlier made a very detailed analysis of the *Pheasant Cap Master* (*Heguanzi* 鶡冠子), which he believed to include three kinds of ideal states. The last of these is reflected in the "Shi bing" 世兵 (Arms of the Age) and "Bei zhi" 備知 (Complete Knowledge) chapters. In contrast to other chapters of the *Pheasant Cap Master* that are devoted to constructing political order, these two embody an intellectual movement that venerates the past. Like the "Dao Zhi" chapter of the *Zhuangzi*, they were composed and compiled around the time of the founding of the Qin and Han dynasties. Here Graham repeatedly mentions Yangism.

> This must have been a time of unique disillusionment. The united empire so eagerly awaited had at last come, proved to be an unprecedented tyranny, and collapsed almost at once to throw the world into worse chaos than ever. Disdain for all organized government, derision of the sage emperors, nostalgia for the time before the Yellow Emperor invented war, became common ground for the Primitivist, for the Yangist author of 'Robber Chih,' and even for the once semi-Legalist author of *Ho-kuan-tzu*.⁴³

Graham believes that after the experience of two crises, the *Pheasant Cap Master* gave up the former two ideals of the state and "joined the Taoists and Yangists in looking back with nostalgia to the primordial age when there was no government at all."⁴⁴

It needs to be said that prior to Guan Feng many scholars had already examined the connection between Yangism and the "Dao Zhi" and "Rang wang" chapters of the *Zhuangzi*. For example, Meng Wentong's

"Study of Yangism" proposed that the "Rang wang" chapter may have been a Yangist work mistakenly included by those compiling the text. Meng saw such figures as Bian Sui in "Rang wang" as representing the Yangist camp of "restraining one's essential disposition and nature," and saw the "Dao Zhi" chapter as representing the Yangist camp of "giving free reign to one's essential disposition and nature." Both were branches of Yangist teachings, with the latter being closest to Zhuangzi's beliefs. Hou Wailu put forth similar views.[45] But Guan Feng explicitly identified the "Dao Zhi," "Rang wang," and "Yu fu" chapters as from Yangist thought, and A. C. Graham went further by adding the "Shuo jian" chapter. Graham may have been influenced by Meng Wentong and Hou Wailu as well, but the primary influence here seems to have been Guan Feng. Graham retained the fruits of Guan Feng's textual investigation while removing the method and conclusions of his class analysis.

Afterword

The "revival" of Yang Zhu was a major event in twentieth-century thought and in academic history. To a large extent, the academic history of the twentieth century is a constitutive component of intellectual history more broadly. Although there was much change in political conditions and methods of academic inquiry, the early and latter parts of the twentieth century, did not substantively differ in placing Yang Zhu in service of modernity. Thus, although this chapter sees Hu Shi and Guan Feng as representative of the different orientations of two sequential stages of twentieth-century study of Yang Zhu, in a certain sense they also belong to the same group.

Meng Wentong differs from this. Although his study of Yang Zhu became possible only with the popularity of positivism in the twentieth century, his organization, investigation, and analysis of textual materials did not conflict with traditional scholarly methods. In contrast to the orientations represented by Hu Shi and Guan Feng, Meng Wentong can fully be said to represent a different dimension of Yang Zhu research. Although we cannot say there are no reasonable components to the scholarly methods that Hu Shi and Guan Feng represent, we find that if we do not add personal emotions and political views, then relatively neutral, sober, and objective scholarly analysis tells us clearly that Meng Wentong's academic rigor was superior.

Notes

1. This paper was translated by Bobby Carleo.
2. See the contribution of Masayuki Sato in this volume.
3. He Aiguo 何愛國, "Shi bian er xue bian: Liang Qichao de Yangxue san bian" 世變與學術：梁啟超的楊學三變 [Things change and studies change: Liang Qichao's three changes of Yangism], in *Xiandaixing de bentu huixiang: Jindai Yang Mo sichao yanjiu* 現代性的本土迴響：近代楊墨思潮研究 [Local echoes of modernity: A study on the modern thought trends of Yang Zhu and Mozi] (Guangzhou: Shijie tushu chuban, 2015), 66–86. See also Wang's paper in the current volume.
4. Published as Hu Shih, *The Development of Logical Method in Ancient China* (Shanghai: The Oriental Book Company, 1922).
5. See *Zhongguo zhexueshi dagang juan shang (jiangyigao)* 中國哲學史大綱卷上(講義稿) [Outline of the history of Chinese philosophy volume one (lecture manuscript)], volume five of *Hu Shi quan ji*, ed. Zheng Dahua, 44 vols. (Hefei: Anhui jiaoyu chubanshe, 2003), 545–723. Therein, "Yang Zhu" is the seventh chapter, 648–55.
6. Hu Shi's *Zhongguo zhexueshi dagang* [Outline of the history of Chinese philosophy] was first published in 1919 (Shanghai: Commercial Press).
7. Hu Shi, "Yang Zhu" 楊朱, *Zhongguo zhexueshi dagang* [Outline of the history of Chinese philosophy] (Dongfang chubanshe, 1996), 155–62.
8. Xie Wuliang 謝無量, "Yang Zhu" 楊朱, *Zhongguo zhexue shi* 中國哲學史 [History of Chinese philosophy] (Taipei: Taiwan Zhonghua, repr. 1970), 134–36. Xie Wuliang had studied in Japan, and this work very likely was influenced by various histories of Chinese philosophy and works on Chinese intellectual history.
9. However, by the time of writing his notes to the reprint of *Outline of the History of Chinese Philosophy* in 1958 (at which point he retitled the work *History of Ancient Chinese Philosophy* (*Zhongguo gudai zhexueshi*), Hu Shi had already come to completely reject the reliability of the "Yang Zhu" chapter of the *Liezi*. See Zheng Dahua, ed., *Hu Shi quan ji*, 35:537.
10. We should point out that Hu Shi's understanding of nominalism here is mistaken. Nominalism is entirely different in orientation from this "anti-name ideology."
11. Hu, *Zhongguo zhexueshi dagang*, 158.
12. Hu, *Zhongguo zhexueshi dagang*, 158.
13. Hu, *Zhongguo zhexueshi dagang*, 159.
14. Of course, we cannot say that late Qing and early Republican-era scholarship on Yang Zhu has only an intellectual or ideological quality and no academic quality at all. However, the ideological quality is clearly much stronger than its academic quality. A related situation is discussed in "Yang Zhu yanjiu gaikuang ji qi tedian" 楊朱研究概況及其特點 [Overview of scholarship on Yang Zhu and its distinctive characteristics], the second appendix to Liu Peide 劉佩

德, *Liezixue shi* 列子學史 [History of Liezi's thought] (Beijing: Xueyuan chubanshe, 2015).

15. Meng Wentong, *xian Qin zhuzi yu lixue* 先秦諸子與理學 [Pre-Qin thinkers and study of principle] (Guilin: Guangxi shifan daxue chubanshe, 2006), 108–130.

16. Meng Mo 蒙默, *Meng Wentong xiansheng xiaozhuan* 蒙文通先生小傳 [A short biography of Mr. Meng Wentong], in Liu Mengxi 劉夢溪, ed., *Zhongguo xiandai xueshu jingdian* 中國現代學術 [Scholarly classics of Chinese modernity], volume on Liao Ping and Meng Wentong (Shijiazhuang: Hebei jiaoyu chubanshe, 1996), 324.

17. See Lu Xinsheng 路新生, "Shi lun yigushixue dui Meng Wentong de yingxiang: yi Meng Wentong de Zhongguo chuanshuo shidai gushi yanjiu wei li" 試論疑古史學對蒙文通先生的影響：以蒙文通的中國傳說時代古史研究為例 [A exploratory account of the influence of the school of skepticism of ancient history on Meng Wentong: the case of Meng Wentong's study of the ancient history of China's mythical age], *Jilu xuekan* 2010 (3): 34–41.

18. Meng, *xian Qin zhuzi yu lixue*, 108.
19. Meng, *xian Qin zhuzi yu lixue*, 112, 110, 112.
20. Meng, *xian Qin zhuzi yu lixue*, 115.
21. Meng, *xian Qin zhuzi yu lixue*, 123.
22. Meng, *xian Qin zhuzi yu lixue*, 123.
23. Meng, *xian Qin zhuzi yu lixue*, 128.
24. Meng, *xian Qin zhuzi yu lixue*, 130.
25. Meng, *xian Qin zhuzi yu lixue*, 130.

26. See also Feng Cao, "Yang Zhu Research in the Twentieth Century: With a Focus on Guo Moruo, Meng Wentong, Hou Wailu, and Liu Zehua," *Contemporary Chinese Thought*, 50, no. 3–4 (2019): 144–63.

27. See Yang Rongguo 楊榮國, "Yang Zhu sixiang" 楊朱思想 [The thought of Yang Zhu] in *Zhongguo gudai sixiang shi* [Intellectual history of ancient China] (Beijing: Renmin chubanshe, 1963), 197–207.

28. Guan Feng, "Zhuangzi waizapian chutan" 莊子外雜篇初探 [A preliminary examination of the outer and miscellaneous chapters of the *Zhuangzi*], *Zhexue yanjiu* 哲學研究 [Philosophical researches] 2 (1961): 70–85; "Lun Mozi yu Yang Zhu xuepai" 論墨子與楊朱學派 [On Mozi and Yangism], in *Zhonghua wenshi luncong* 中華文史論叢 [Journal of Chinese literature and history] 6 (1965): 41–55.

29. Guan, "Zhuangzi waizapian chutan," 70.
30. Guan, "Zhuangzi waizapian chutan," 83.
31. Guan, "Zhuangzi waizapian chutan," 83.
32. Guan, "Zhuangzi waizapian chutan," 50.
33. Guan, "Zhuangzi waizapian chutan," 50.
34. Guan, "Zhuangzi waizapian chutan," 84.
35. Guan, "Zhuangzi waizapian chutan," 83.

36. In "On Mozi and Yangism," Guan Feng clearly indicates the "Dao Zhi" chapter to be a work of the late Warring States period. Following the disintegration and collapse of the small producers, Yangists began to turn toward ideas of nourishing one's life and giving free rein to one's desires. Many passages of *Lü's Spring and Autumn Annals* present this camp's advocacy of nourishing one's life, while the "Dao Zhi" chapter of the *Zhuangzi* represents the hedonist camp.

37. Trans. follows James Legge.

38. Guan, "Zhuangzi waizapian chutan," 84.

39. Guan, "Zhuangzi waizapian chutan," 85.

40. A. C. Graham, *Disputers of the Tao* (La Salle, IL: Open Court, 1989), n55. However, Graham did not clearly indicate where Guan Feng puts forth this view, indicating merely that it was proposed "in 1962." I suspect Graham here is referencing Guan's "Zhuangzi waizapian chutan," published in 1961.

41. See "Retreat to Private Life: The Yangists," in Graham, *Disputers of the Tao*, 53–64.

42. Graham, *Disputers of the Tao*, n55.

43. A. C. Graham, "A Neglected Pre-Han Philosophical Text: 'Ho-kuan-tzu,'" *Bulletin of the School of Oriental and African Studies* 52, no. 3 (1989): 529.

44. Graham, "A Neglected Pre-Han Philosophical Text," 529.

45. Hou Wailu, *Zhongguo sixiang tongshi* 中國思想通史 [A general history of Chinese thought], vol. 1 (Beijing: Renmin chubanshe, 1995), 348.

About the Contributors

Erica F. Brindley is Professor of Asian Studies, History, and Philosophy at the Pennsylvania State University. She studied Chinese history, philosophy, and Classical Chinese at Princeton University and National Taiwan University. Her fields of interest include early Chinese thought and intellectual history, along with ancient and medieval Chinese history with a focus on the southern frontier and Southeast Asia. She is the author of three books: *Individualism in Early China* (Hawai'i University Press, 2010), *Music, Cosmology, and the Politics of Harmony in Early China* (SUNY Press, 2012), and *Ancient China and the Yue* (Cambridge University Press, 2015). She has also co-edited four special volumes on Asian thought and history: *China's South and Beyond: The Southeast Asian Maritime Zone (SEAMZ) in Premodern History* (Crossroads, 2021), *Asian Empires and Imperialism* (Verge, 2016), *Maritime Frontiers in Asia: Sino-Viet Relations in the 2nd Millennium CE* (Asia Major, 2014), and *Heng Xian and Early Chinese Philosophy* (Dao, 2013). She co-edits the new series Cambridge Elements: Ancient East Asia for Cambridge University Press.

Feng Cao is a Yangtze River Scholar and Professor in the Faculty of Philosophy, Renmin University. He studied history at Shanghai University and Fudan University and received his PhD from Tokyo University. Cao's research focuses on early Chinese philosophy, with a notable specialization in Daoism and the study of excavated documents. His recent monographs are T*he Excavated Manuscripts of Huang-Lao Thought in Recent Years* 近年出土黄老思想文献研究 (Zhongguo shehuikexue chubanshe, 2015) and *A Study of Ancient Chinese Political Thought of "Name"* 中国古代"名"的政治思想研究 (Shanghai guji chubanshe, 2017).

About the Contributors

Yao-cheng Chang is a PhD candidate in Chinese Studies at KU Leuven (University of Leuven), Belgium. He received his BA and MA in Philosophy from Taiwan University (NTU). His primary research interest focuses on interpretations of early Chinese texts. He is currently working on a dissertation that traces the early Chinese conception of sight and hearing as a tool to resolve doubts, especially in the context of proving or disproving the existence of ghosts (*gui*) and immortals (*xian*).

Carine Defoort is Professor in Chinese Studies at KU Leuven (University of Leuven), Belgium. She studied Sinology and Philosophy at KU Leuven, National Taiwan University, and the University of Hawai'i. Her fields of interest are, primarily, early Chinese thought and, secondarily, the modern interpretation of that thought in the twentieth century. She has served as editor of Contemporary Chinese Thought (Taylor & Francis, 1997–2020) and co-edited *The Mozi as an Evolving Text: Different Voices in Early Chinese Thought* (Brill, 2013) and *Having a Word with Angus Graham: At Twenty-Five Years into His Immortality* (SUNY Press, 2018). She is author of *The Pheasant Cap Master (Heguanzi): A Rhetorical Reading* (SUNY Press, 1997) and various articles on the legitimacy of Chinese philosophy, the early concepts of "regicide" and "benefit," the Shizi, the Zhuangzi, the Mozi, and Yang Zhu.

Esther Sunkyung Klein is Senior Lecturer at the Australian National University in the School of Culture, History, and Language. She received her PhD in East Asian Studies from Princeton University. Her monograph, *Reading Sima Qian from Han to Song* (Brill, 2019) traces changes in readers' understanding of Sima Qian's authorial role. In addition to research on the Shiji, she has published on a variety of topics in Chinese philosophy, including the composition and early reception of the Zhuangzi, Wang Chong's epistemology, and Xu Heng's cultural translation of Zhu Xi's thought. Her current research explores the intersection between pre-modern Chinese philosophy and historiography across a broad chronological sweep.

Ting-mien Lee is Assistant Professor in the Department of Philosophy and Religious Studies at the University of Macau. Lee received her BA in Chinese Literature from Taiwan University (NTU) and MA in Philosophy from KU Leuven (University of Leuven), Belgium. She completed her PhD in Sinology at KU Leuven. Her main research interests lie in classical Chinese philosophy and the study of Chinese philosophy in contemporary China. Lee is guest editor of the special issue *The "Victory of Confucianism" Revisited in Contemporary Chinese Scholarship* (*Contemporary Chinese Thought* 51.2 [2020]) and co-editor of *Mo Zi Research in the People's Republic of China* (Contemporary Chinese Thought 42.4 [2011]). She has published various articles on classical Chinese philosophy as well as on contemporary Chinese studies of classical Chinese philosophy, with a particular focus on political strategy and rhetoric.

Xiaoqing Diana Lin is Professor of History in the Department of History, Philosophy, Political Science and Religious Studies at Indiana University Northwest, USA. Her fields of research interest include modern Chinese cultural, political, and intellectual history, along with social media and contemporary Chinese society and culture. Lin is the author of the *Feng Youlan and Twentieth Century China: An Intellectual Biography* (Brill, 2016) and *Peking University: Chinese Intellectuals and Scholarship* (SUNY Press, 2005).

John Makeham is Professor Emeritus at both La Trobe University and The Australian National University. His research specialization is the intellectual history of Chinese philosophy. He has particular interest in Confucian thought throughout Chinese history and in the role played by Sinitic Buddhist thought as an intellectual resource in pre-modern and modern Confucian philosophy. He is editor of the Brill book series Modern Chinese Philosophy and one of the editors of the new Brill book series East Asian Buddhist Philosophy. His most recent publication is *The Awakening of Faith and New Confucian Philosophy* (Brill, 2021).

Masayuki Sato is Professor in the Department of Philosophy, National Taiwan University. His main research interests include early Chinese political concepts, the philosophy of Xunzi, and the birth and evolution of "Chinese philosophy" as a field of research in modern Japan. He is the author of five monographs, including *The Confucian Quest for Order: The Origin and Formation of the Political Thought of Xun Zi* (Brill, 2003), *Xunzi Studies and Research on Xunzi's Philosophy: Reflection on the Past, Current Image and Future Design* (Taipei: Wanjuanlou, 2015 [in Chinese]), and *The World Order after Zhou-Lu Regime in Early China: A Comparative*

Study of Political Philosophies of the Xunzi and Mr. Lü's Spring and Autumn Annals (National Taiwan University Press, 2021 [in Chinese]), along with over 70 scholarly articles about aforementioned topics.

Xiaowei Wang is a PhD candidate in Chinese Studies at KU Leuven (University of Leuven), Belgium. Her dissertation focuses on the paradigm shifts of twentieth-century Chinese philosophy. Currently, she is working on a project that examines how the bookless master Yang Zhu was reconstructed as an early Chinese philosopher by modern Chinese intellectuals in their construction of Chinese philosophy.

Index

archery. See *she*
authorship, 57, 74n2, 76n24, 80, 85, 88–90, 98–99n20, 100n28, 101n33–34, 126, 282n14, 314–15n29, 336

ba 霸 (hegemon, overlord), 62, 140, 146
Bai Yuchan 白玉蟾, 197
Ban Gu 班固, 146, 208
Bao Jiao 鮑焦, 84–85
bao zhen 保真 (preserve the genuine, protecting one's authenticity), 2, 24, 214, 291, 299, 326, 334–35
being and becoming, 10–14
benefit. See *li*
Bentham, Jeremy, 264, 268–70, 283n23
Bi Yongnian 畢永年, 17n21, 266, 283n20, 284n41
bian 辯 (dispute, debate, argument), 6, 11, 22, 25, 26, 66, 79, 82–94 passim, 97n10, n13, 100n25; *bianzhe* 辯者 (disputers), 21–23, 80–86; *hao bian* 好辯 (fond of disputation) 22, 85
bing shu 兵書 (military texts, strategic manuals), 51, 52
Bluntschli, Johann Kaspar, 276–77
boshi 博士 (Academicians, Erudites), 141–42

Bo Yi 伯夷, 92, 116–17, 118, 120, 130n16, 194, 196–97, 218n22
Bocheng Zigao 伯成子高, 30–31, 68, 165, 186n19
bu de yi 不得已 (being compelled to, not having any other option), 26, 58, 66–67
bu yi wu lei xing 不以物累形 (not let one's body be ensnared by things), 2, 24, 214, 291, 299
Buddha, 28, 137–38, 142–45, 149, 153, 171–72, 178, 182, 213
Buddhism, Buddhists, 7–8, 12–13, 25–32 passim, 41–42, 136–41, 145–49, 153–61 passim, 168–73, 179– 81, 184, 189, 191, 241, 303; Chan / Zen, 25, 148, 149, 158n43, 159n 52, 169, 173–74, 189n70; mendicant orders, 25

Cang shu 藏書 (A Book to Keep Hidden), 208
carpe diem, quick enjoyment, 106–113, 116, 127, 128, 129n4, 132n49
Carpenter Chui 工倕, 86, 92
Chen Cisheng 陳此生, 17n21, 280, 297
Cheng brothers (Cheng Hao 程顥 and Cheng Yi 程頤), 7, 28, 150–53, 162–65, 170–72, 174, 179–81, 184; Cheng Yi 程頤, 25, 32, 41–42n49

346 | Index

Chunqiu 春秋 (Spring and autumn annals), 200. See also *Lüshi Chunqiu*
Chunyu Kun 淳于髡, 56
citizens (*guomin* 國民), 270–71, 275–77, 312n1
Confucius. *See* Kongzi
consuming pleasures / sustaining pleasures, 107
Cui Shu 崔述, 289, 298

Daodejing 道德經, 199, 325. *See also* Laozi
Daoism, Daoist, 12–13, 20, 25, 30, 35, 90, 105, 137, 165–66, 197, 211, 231, 236, 292, 297, 302–311, 329; Daoists and Buddhists, 7–8, 13, 27–29, 138–40, 153, 155n11, 155–56n13, 161, 171–72, 179–81, 184; Yang Zhu as, 10, 13, 19, 24, 35, 37, 165–66, 234, 261, 263, 281n9, 282n16, 289–90, 297, 299, 305–306, 309, 311, 312n2, 325–30
daotong 道統 (succession of the Way), 7–8, 13, 26–27, 29, 34, 37, 135–89 passim
Daoxue (Learning of the Way), 151, 174, 177, 217n18
Dark Learning. See *Xuan xue*
Darwinism, 261, 265–66, 274, 281n9
Daxue 大學 (Great Learning), 162–63, 185n7, 217n18, 290
de 德 (virtue, charisma, potency), 32–33, 52–53, 62, 83, 92, 125, 138–39, 173, 194, 197, 201, 239
death. See *si*
Deng Shiyang 登石陽, 195–96
Deng Xi 鄧析, 86, 94, 285n54
destiny. See *ming*
Dong Zhongshu 董仲舒, 143, 144
Duanmu Shu 端木叔, 125, 130n18, 131n43

dushu 獨術 (egoistic methods), 267, 284n37

egoist, egoism, 1, 6, 8, 9, 19, 28, 30, 36, 49, 83, 91, 118, 130n19, 191, 231–33, 241–51, 261, 270, 291, 296, 299, 301–302, 312n1, 319, 320, 323, 331, 333, 335
empty signifier, 27–28, 33
Endō Ryūkichi 遠藤隆吉, 278
Epicurean thought, 19, 128–29n2, 231, 233, 238, 295–96
expediency. See *quan*

fate. See *ming*
Fayan 法言 (Model Sayings), 26, 90, 95n2, 136–37, 187n38, 201
Fen shu 焚書 (A Book to Burn), 192, 203, 222n90
Feng Youlan 馮友蘭, 3, 8–10, 13, 154n3, 289–311 passim
Fenollosa, Ernest Francisco, 230–37, 250, 252n10, n12–13, 253n28
filiality, filial piety. See *xiao*
five senses. See *wu guan*
Fo 佛. *See* Buddhism, Buddhists
freedom, 6, 105, 109–113, 115, 117, 122–28, 320, 324–25, 330
frugality, 35, 203, 205–208, 210, 221n72
Fukuzawa Yukichi 福澤諭吉, 266

Gao Xu 高旭, 17n21, 263
ge wu 格物 (investigation of things), 185n6, 217n18
Geng Dingxiang 耿定向, 193, 198, 201, 213, 220n53, 222n90
Gongsun Chao 公孫朝, 121, 131n31, 282n15
Gongsun Long 公孫龍, 86, 94, 97n9, n13
Gongsun Mu 公孫穆, 121, 131n31, 282n15

Gongyang zhuan 公羊傳 (Gongyang commentary on the Spring and Autumn annals), 64
Graham, A. C., 3, 10, 41n38, 67, 100n29, 101n34, 105, 108, 126, 311–12, 316n45, 335–37, 340n40
Great Yu 大禹. *See* Yu 禹
Gu Jiegang 顧頡剛, 17n21, 43n78, 289, 297, 299–300, 316n52
Gu Shi 顧實, 17n21, 248–49, 290, 298, 315–16n42
Guan Feng 關鋒, 3, 8, 10, 13, 319, 330–37, 340n36
Guan Yin 關尹, 31
Guanzi 管子 (Master Guan), 11, 203–204, 232, 285n54, 327, 328; ch. 1 "Shepherding the People" 牧民, 195; ch. 4 "Establish Government" 立政, 331; chs. 36–37 "Arts of the Mind" 心術, 328; ch. 38 "Purifying the Mind" 白心, 328; ch. 65 "Explanation of Nine Types of Loss" 九敗解, 331
Guan Zhong 管仲, 115, 120, 124, 282n15, 285n54
gui ji 貴己 (value oneself, honoring the self), 2, 19, 24, 214, 299, 326, 335
guojia qun 國家群 (nation-groups), 267
guojiao 國教 (state religion), 36
guwen 古文 (ancient-style learning/writing), 7, 142, 145–49, 153, 156–57n22, 158n43

Han Emperor Wen, 141, 208–211
Han Feizi, *Han Feizi* 韓非子, 2, 5–6, 11–13, 38n3, n6, 70, 79–93 passim, 98–99n20, 101–102n37, 205, 222n73, 231–32, 257n81, 291, 297, 315–16n42, 325, 327; ch. 41 "An Inquiry about Disputes" 問辯, 93; ch. 47 "Eight Theories" 八說, 22, 93, 100n28; ch. 50 "Eminent Learnings" 顯學, 2, 24, 299, 331
Han Yu 韓愈, 7, 17n21, 27–28, 32, 42n52, 96n8, 136–45, 149–53, 155–56n13, 159n52, 179, 184
Hanshu 漢書, 24, 51–52, 95n2, 155n10, 208
hedonist, hedonism, 1, 3, 6, 9–10, 19, 35–36, 49, 105–132 passim, 232–33, 238–51 passim, 255n52, 261, 268, 281n9, 291–97, 300, 310–11, 319–21, 334–35, 340n36
Heguanzi 鶡冠子 (Pheasant Cap Master), 336
heretic, 20, 25, 28, 31–34, 259, 261–63, 282n11
hermits. *See* recluses
Hou Ji 后稷 (Lord of Millet), 25, 32
Hou Wailu 侯外廬, 17n21, 330, 337
Hua Jiao 華角, 84–85, 93
Hu Hong 胡宏, 28, 40, 42, 97
Hu Shi 胡適, 8, 10, 280, 297–99, 319–25, 329, 337
Hu Yuan 胡瑗, 147
Huainanzi, *Huainanzi* 淮南子 (The Master of Huainan), 2, 13, 24, 38n3, 97n13, 100n28, 101n33, 129n13, 214, 228, 291, 297, 299, 309, 315–16n42; ch. 2 "Activating the Genuine" 俶真, 24; ch. 11 "Placing Customs on a Par" 齊俗, 94, 95n2; ch. 13 "Boundless Discourses" 氾論, 24, 238, 245, 326, 331
Huang Zhen 黃震, 210
Huang Di 黃帝 (Yellow Emperor), 142, 209, 234, 240, 263, 336
Huang-Lao 黃老 (Yellow Emperor and Laozi), 136–38, 146, 153, 209–210, 325–29

Hui Shi 惠施, Huizi 惠子, 86, 94, 97n9, 13, 285n54, 331
Hundred Days' Reform (*bairi weixin* 百日維新), 266
Huxley, Thomas Henry, 266
hypocrisy, 191, 194, 196, 212–14

inclusiveness, impartiality. See *jian*
individualism, individualist, 1, 3, 8–10, 15n3, 19, 191, 229, 246–48, 261, 280, 281n9, 311–12n1, 322–24, 334
indulgence, 6, 106–107, 110–14, 122, 124, 131n32, 145–46, 239–40, 245, 248–49, 268–70, 278, 292, 310, 326–27, 334. See also *zong yu*
Inoue Enryō 井上圓了, 235, 240, 253–54n31
Inoue Tetsujirō 井上哲次郎, 40n32, 228, 231, 247, 252n11
internal and external. See *nei wai*
intertextuality, 91, 185, 306

Ji Kang 嵇康, 128, 132n48
jia 家 (lineage), 4, 23–25, 35–37, 135, 137–53, 184, 244, 263, 282n16, 305–306, 325–26, 329
jian 兼 (inclusiveness, impartiality), 114, 119
jian ai 兼愛 (inclusive care, impartial love, care of all), 5, 23–24, 31–34, 41n47, 48–49, 57, 61, 77n33, 79, 95n1, 130n19, 152, 160n60, 164, 171, 175–77, 182–83, 232–34, 250, 262, 265, 283n21, 331–34
jianbai 堅白 (hard and white), 23, 82, 86, 92–94, 97n13, 98n16
Jiang Weiqiao 蔣維喬, 17n21, 249, 280, 297
Jie-Zhi 桀跖 (Tyrant Jie and Robber Zhi), 83–84, 92, 98n19, 99n22

Jin si lu 近思錄 (Record of reflection on things at hand), 171–72
jingzheng 競爭 (struggle, competition), 266, 275

Kang Youwei 康有為, 5, 12–13, 34–37, 263–66, 269, 283n20, 297, 315n39
Katō Hiroyuki 加藤弘之, 228, 247–48, 256n73, 266, 270, 286n58
King Wu of Zhou 周武王, 53, 68–69, 74, 77n43, 159, 196, 201
Kong-Mo 孔墨, 37, 84, 93

Lao-Yang 老楊, 263–67
Lao-Zhuang 老莊, 146, 153, 329
Lao Dan 老聃, 31, 97n9, 165, 289, 290
laws, 84, 109, 205, 231, 293, 328
le 樂 (joy, pleasure), 109, 111, 113, 114, 122, 152, 204, 242, 268, 269, 270, 279, 306–307; *le sheng* 樂生 (joy-in-life), 106, 110, 112, 117, 119
Legalism, Legalists, 90, 182, 206, 208, 222n73, 307, 328, 336
li 利 (benefit, profit), 60, 61, 66, 77n41, 85, 113–14, 119, 131n26, 233, 274–75, 307, 322, 333; others, 30, 68, 111, 212–13, 220n57; the self, 30, 68, 112, 212–13, 215, 234, 241–42, 246, 275, 322; all under Heaven/the world (*tianxia* 天下), 23, 30, 35, 48, 57, 58, 61, 64, 68, 77n41, 95n1, 165–66, 175–76, 200, 219n41, 262, 275, 277–79, 307, 309, 328
Li Zhi 李贄, 7–8, 13, 191–216, 220n53, n56, 222–23n92, 223n93, n101
Li Zhu 離朱, 82, 86, 92

Liang Qichao 梁啟超, 8, 9, 259–61, 263–80, 283n20, 297–99, 320–22
Lie Yukou 列禦寇, 145, 297, 329
Liezi / *Liezi* 列子, 2–3, 5–6, 12, 16n19, 24, 29–31, 35–37, 41n38, 68–70, 72, 99, 105–109, 115, 119, 126–32, 141, 165–68, 214, 219n41, 221n72, 228, 231, 232, 234–35 238, 240, 244, 250, 262–63, 285n54, 295–98, 303, 309–310, 314–15n29, 321–23, 325, 329, 332, 338; ch. 2 "Yellow Emperor" 黃帝, 240, 263; ch. 6 "Effort and Destiny" 力命, 228, 238–40, 315n29; ch. 8 "Explaining Conjunction" 說符, 130–31n26, 240
Liu Kai 柳開, 142
Liu Ling 劉伶, 128, 132n48
liu yi 六藝 (six arts, classicism), 51
Liu Zehua 劉澤華, 330
Liutao 六韜 (Six Bow Cases), 51–54, 75n14
long life, natural lifespan, 113, 115–18, 122–23, 127, 131n43
Lord Shang, Shang Yang, *Shangjunshu* 商君書, 102n37, 204, 208, 221n68, 222n73, 232, 285n54
Lu Jiuyuan 陸九淵, 17n21, 28
Lu Xun 魯迅, 1
Lü Zuqian 呂祖謙, 171
Lunheng 論衡, 13, 38n6, 39n23, 71, 90, 95n2, 195, 200, 201
Luo Dajing 羅大經, 210
Lüshi Chunqiu 呂氏春秋 (Mr. Lü's Spring and Autumn Annals), 2–3, 12, 24, 39n13, 53, 71, 76n23, 128, 214, 228, 297–300, 307, 309, 328, 340n36; ch. 1/2 "Taking Life as Basic" 本生, 2, 23, 298, 334; ch. 1/3 "Valuing the Self" 重己, 2, 23, 298, 334; ch. 17/7 "No Duality" 不二, 24, 299, 326, 331; ch. 2/2 "Honoring Life" 貴生, 2, 23, 298, 309, 326, 334; ch. 2/3 "Essential Desires" 情欲, 2, 23, 298, 300; ch. 3.2. "Fulfilling the Number" 盡數, 298; ch. 3.3 "Placing the Self First" 先己, 298; ch. 17/8 "Holding on to the One" 執一, 326, 328; ch. 21/4 "Being Attentive to Aims" 審為, 2, 23, 310, 326, 334

materialist, materialism, 19, 261, 281n9, 290, 292, 297, 303–304, 308, 310–11, 314n29, 330, 333, 335
Matsumoto Bunsaburō 松本文三郎, 236–37, 241–43, 250, 252n8, 253–54n31, 256n78, 278, 285n50
May Fourth period, 9–10, 12, 261, 280, 291, 293, 297, 330
Mencius, *Mengzi* 孟子; 1A5, 55–56; 1A6, 55; 1A7, 54, 62; 1B10, 55; 1B11, 55; 2A2, 32; 3A5, 32, 160n58, 2B13, 53; 3B9, 22, 23, 26, 48, 57, 65, 66, 85, 87, 90, 95n2, 97n10, 130n19, 160n59, 262, 301, 307, 326, 331; 4A17, 56; 7A26, 23, 39n13, 48, 57, 86, 87, 90, 95n1–2, 165, 175, 200, 262, 331; 7B26, 21, 27, 35, 86, 90, 97n10, 331; 7B37, 32
mendicant orders. *See* Buddhism
Meng Wentong 蒙文通, 8, 10, 305–306, 319, 324–30, 336–37
Mengsun Yang 孟孫陽/楊, 31, 43n69, 115, 129n11, 296
Mengzi. *See* Mencius
Mill, John Stuart, 264, 283n23
ming 命 (destiny, fate), 6, 24, 109, 113, 123, 167–68, 173
ming 名 (name, reputation), 53, 83, 87, 105, 108, 112, 113, 119, 121–23, 130–31n26, 215, 244, 322

Mozi, *Mozi* 墨子 Mo Di 墨翟, 2–11 passim, 23–25, 29–33, 35, 37, 42n52, n54–55, 48–51, 57–58, 60–61, 65–74, 76n26, 79, 82, 84–86, 94, 95n1–3, 100n25, 137–43, 146–47, 150–53, 160n60, 163–66, 169–76, 179, 181, 184, 186n18, 187n38, 188n64, 205, 231, 232, 236, 239, 241, 247, 250, 257n81, 262–66, 283n20–21, 294, 326, 333–334
music. See *yue*

nation, 10, 12–13, 259–60, 264–71, 276, 278–80, 284n40, 292, 319–20, 323–24
nationalism, 19, 264–66, 269–70, 299, 301, 311
naturalist, 19, 235, 245, 261, 281n9, 322
nature (human). See *xing*
nei wai 內外 (internal and external), 6, 105, 115, 121–24
New Culture movement, 323–24, 330
Nishiwaki Gyokuhō 西脇玉峰, 237, 240–41, 242, 250, 253–54n31

oriental philosophy (*Tōyō tetsugaku* 東洋哲學), 227–29, 235
Ouyang Xiu 歐陽修, 8, 28, 149–50, 179–81

Peng Meng 彭蒙, 305–307, 309, 326
philosopher (Yang Zhu as), 2, 4–5, 8–10, 12–13, 36–37, 229, 249, 251, 259–61, 277–79, 296
Pi Rixiu 皮日休, 141
pleasure-pain dichotomy, 107
poisonous, 205, 263, 267
pretense (false, fake). See *wei*

Qian Mu 錢穆, 82, 87–89, 91, 98n16, 100–101n32

Qin Guli 禽滑釐, Qinzi 禽子, 31, 69, 296
qingtan 清談 (pure conversations), 24, 172–73
quan xing 全性 (keep one's nature intact), 2, 24, 214, 326, 334–35
quan 權 (counterbalance, right, power, expediency), 48, 50–52, 55–64, 67, 72–73, 176–77, 271–72, 277; *quanli* 權利 (rights), 268, 271–79; *minquan* 民權 (people's rights), 273–75; *zizhu zhiquan* 自主之權 (right to self-mastery), 273–74
qun 群 (group), 266–67
qunshu 群術 (collective methods), 267

reality. See *shi*
recluses (hermits), 31, 41–42n49, 117, 203, 290, 305, 307
reformer, 5, 20, 34–36, 42n67, 265–66, 273, 323
relaxation, 109–113, 117
ren 仁 (humaneness, benevolence), 22, 26–27, 31–33, 48–49, 52–57, 62, 83, 92, 130n25, 139–41, 144, 146–47, 152, 171, 183, 194–95, 200–201, 231, 272–73, 301–303
reputation. See *ming*
resignation (attitude), 271, 283
resign/retire from office, 8, 30, 68, 120, 191, 195, 198, 211, 267
rights. See *quan*
Ruan Ji 阮籍, 128, 132n48

sage 聖, 32, 43n70, 48, 74, 77n43, 120, 128, 140, 192, 200, 203, 210, 236, 300, 303, 336; Seven Sages of the Bamboo Grove, 128
selfishness, self-interest. See *li*
Self-strengthening Movement (*Yangwu yundong* 洋務運動), 266

sex, sensual pleasures, 6, 106–107, 111, 114, 121–22, 126, 238, 296, 310
Shang Yang. *See* Lord Shang
she 射 (archery), 33
Shen Buhai 申不害, 143–46, 171, 183, 203–205, 222n73, 232, 285n54, 329
Shen Dao 慎到, 86, 94, 305–307, 309, 326, 328–29
shi 實 (reality, solidity), 71–72, 105, 119, 209–210, 244
Shi 釋. *See* Buddhists
Shi Kuang 師曠, 82, 92, 94–95
Shi Qiu 史鰌 (Shi Yu 史魚), 80, 83
Shiji pinglin 史記評林 (A Collection of Comments on the *Shiji*), 209–210
Shiji 史記, 24, 97n13, 100, 212, 218n22, 222n73
Shimada Chōrei 島田重禮, 231, 233–36, 250, 253n20, n22
Shina 支那; *Shina rinri* 支那倫理 (Chinese ethics), 229; *Shina tetsugaku* 支那哲學 (Chinese philosophy), 229, 278
Shu Qi 叔齊, 120, 194, 196–97, 218n28
Shun 舜, 94, 120, 130n24, 139, 142, 147, 162, 172, 175–78, 202, 220n53, 263
si 死 (death), 27, 64, 105, 110–12, 115–118, 124, 126, 140–41, 263, 309–10
si 肆 (letting go, untethered), 105, 109–110, 112, 114, 122, 124, 180, 222–23n92
Sima fa 司馬法 (Sima's Principles of War), 51–60 passim, 72
Sima Qian 司馬遷, 147, 196, 210
slavery, 10–11, 13, 212, 241, 270, 276, 292, 306–307, 309–311, 332–33
starvation, 110, 117, 120, 195, 196, 218n22, 284n31

Su Shi 蘇軾, 8, 179–83, 221n68
suicide, 64, 69, 244
Sun Daosheng 孫道昇, 290
Sun Fu 孫復, 17n21, 142–45
state religion. See *guojiao*

Takase Takejirō 高瀨武次郎, 241–50, 255–56n60–62
Takebe Ton'go 建部遯吾, 249
Takigawa Kametarō 瀧川龜太郎, 236–42, 250, 253n31
Tan Sitong 譚嗣同, 265, 267
Tian Pian 田駢, 305–307, 309, 326, 328–39
Tiantai 天台, 145, 147–149, 153, 158, 174
Tokyo University, 9, 227, 228, 230, 233, 235, 237, 240, 242, 248, 251–56
tongyi 同異 (same and different)
trope (rhetorical), 4–5, 12–13, 25–41 passim, 80–81, 86–87, 91, 96, 135–36, 153, 161, 184, 26–64, 266

untethered (approach to life)
utilitarianism (*gonglizhuyi* 功利主義), 232, 244–47, 264, 268–70

Wang Anshi 王安石, 8, 17n21, 39n14, 150, 172–73, 179–81, 183
Wang Chong 王充, 39n23, 96n8, 195, 200–202, 216n7
Wang Tong 王通, 141, 142, 145, 179, 188n60
Wang Yangming 王陽明, 28, 33, 96n8, 243
wei 偽 (false, pretense, fake), 6, 105, 114–15, 119–20, 127, 130n22
wei wo 為我 (for oneself, all for himself, serving one's own interests), 1–2, 5, 8, 19, 23, 25, 33–36, 48–49, 57, 79, 82–83, 86,

wei wo (continued) 118, 130n19, 164–66, 175–77, 182, 191, 200, 214, 216, 238–39, 246, 262, 265, 267–69, 272–75, 281n9, 307, 309–310, 312n1, 322–23, 326, 331–34

Wheaton, Henry, 271

world weary. See *yan shi*

wu fu 無父 (no father, denial of one's father, turning one's back on one's father), 23, 48, 152, 164, 169, 182–83, 262, 265

wu guan 五官 (five senses), 192

wu jun 無君 (no lord, denial of one's lord, turning one's back on one's ruler), 23, 48, 152, 164, 167–69, 182–83, 210, 262, 265

Wu Yu 吳虞, 17n21, 280

Wuxu Reform (*Wuxu bianfa* 戊戌變法), 266

wuyong 無用 (fruitless, useless), 80–86, 91–93

xiao 孝 (filiality, filial piety), 58, 74, 83–85, 93, 194, 206–209

xing 性 (inborn nature), 2, 3, 24, 82, 83, 84, 93, 109, 111, 113, 114, 121, 129n13, 148–49, 173, 214, 322, 326–28

xiulian 修煉 (longevity practices), 24

Xuan xue 玄學 (Dark Learning), 132n48

Xunzi, *Xunzi* 荀子, 11, 13, 38n6, 137, 139, 141–42, 150, 188, 228, 231, 232, 271, 285n54, 299; ch. 6 "Against the Twelve Masters" 非十二子, 24, 327; ch. 8: "The Teachings of the Ru" 儒效, 94; ch. 21 "Dispelling Ignorance" 解蔽, 24, 328

Yan Fu 嚴復, 17n21, 266, 289

Yan Pingzhong 晏平仲, 124

yan shi 厭世 (world weary), 9, 263, 267–70, 278–80, 282n15, 284n42, 321

Yan Yuan 顏元, 28, 40n36

Yang Rongguo 楊榮國, 330

yang sheng/xing 養生/性 (nurture one's life/inborn nature), 2, 49, 110, 114, 115, 124, 131n41, n43, 302, 322, 326, 335, 340n36

Yang Shi 楊時 (Guishan 龜山), 31–32, 39n18, 41n49

Yang Xiong 揚/楊雄, 24, 26–28, 96n8, 136–37, 139, 142–46, 148, 150, 179–82, 188n60–61, 201, 231, 233

Yang-Mo 楊墨, 4–8, 12–13, 21–22, 25–37, 48–51, 57–58, 65–67, 70–74, 79–103, 135–37, 139–41, 143–47, 150–53, 161, 163–66, 169–74, 178–84, 187n38, 188n64, 205–207, 231, 236, 247, 262–66

Yanzi 顏子 (Yan Yuan/Hui 顏淵/回), 25, 32, 115, 150, 155n8, 178

Yao 堯, 120, 130n24, 139, 142, 147, 162, 172, 175–78, 186n19, 202, 263

yi mao 一毛 (one hair, a single hair), 23, 30, 35–36, 48, 68–69, 73, 111, 140, 165–66, 175–76, 192, 197, 200, 205–206, 219n41, 239, 262, 274–75, 277–78, 296, 300, 306–307, 309, 328

Yi Yin 伊尹, 199–200, 219n41

yi 義 (righteous, duty), 13, 22, 26, 27, 32, 33, 48–49, 52–53, 65, 83–84, 89, 92–93, 111–13, 121, 139, 141, 144, 146–47, 149, 151–52, 167–73 passim, 182–83, 199, 201, 231, 301

yiduan 異端 (heretic, heresy, deviant teachings), 20, 28, 31–32, 34, 96n8, 161, 178–79, 184, 259, 261, 263, 282n11

Yu Yingshi 余英時, 147

Yu 禹 (Great Yu, Yu the Great 大禹), 25, 26, 30, 31, 32, 68–69, 74, 77n43, 138–39, 142–43, 145, 162, 176–79
yue 樂 (music), 81, 106, 125, 146, 155n10, 206, 238; *Yue fu* (Han-period ballads, Han Bureau of Music), 106

Zeng Can 曾參 or Zhengzi 曾子, 80, 82, 83–85, 87, 92–93, 96n6, 98–99n20, 137–38, 155n8, 162–63, 178
Zhan Li 展李, 117, 118, 130n16
Zhan He 詹何, 326, 328, 329
Zhang Zai 張載, 28, 41
Zhang Zhidong 張之洞, 17n21, 266
Zhao Wen 昭文, 94
Zhiyuan 智圓, 145–49, 153
zhi zhong 執中 (adhere to the middle, maintain balance), 48, 175–79, 185
Zhongyong 中庸 (Balance as the norm), 147, 149, 153, 161–63, 174–75, 177–78, 185, 189n70
zhong 中 (middle, balance), 13, 48, 49, 142, 147, 158n37, 164, 174–79, 185n5
Zhou Dunyi 周敦頤, 28, 162, 163, 189n70
Zhu Xi 朱熹, 7–8, 25, 96n8, 135–36, 138–39, 147, 149, 152–54, 161–85, 196, 217n18, 221n64
Zhuang Zhou 莊周, 3, 204
Zhuangzi chs. 1–7 "Inner Chapters" 內篇, 88, 99n24, 100n27–28, 100–101n32–34; chs. 8–22 "Outer Chapters" 外篇, 87–88, 98n20, 99n24, 100n27–28, 100–101n32–34, 331; chs. 23–33 "Miscellaneous Chapters" 雜篇, 88, 99n24, 100n27–28, 100–101n32–33, 331; ch. 2 "Making Things Even" 齊物論, 94, 307; ch. 3 "Nourishing Life" 養生主, 115; ch. 8 "Webbed Toes" 駢拇, 23, 81, 87–88, 92; ch. 10 "Ransacking Coffers" 胠篋, 23, 77n34, 81, 87–88, 92; ch. 11: "Preserving and Accepting" 在宥, 92; ch. 12 "Heaven and Earth" 天地, 41n43, 81, 87–88, 93, 186n19; ch. 17 "Autumn Floods" 秋水, 97n13; ch. 18, "Utmost Joy" 至樂, 114; ch. 24 "Ghostless Xu" 徐無鬼, 23, 97n9; ch. 27 "Dwelling Words" 寓言, 166, 263; ch. 28 "Yielding the Throne" 讓王, 2, 23, 218n22, 298, 326–27, 331, 334–37; ch. 29 "Robber Zhi" 盜跖, 2, 23, 298, 327, 331, 334–37, 340n36; ch. 30 "Discourse on Swords" 說劍, 2, 23, 336–37; ch. 31 "Old Fisherman" 漁父, 2, 23–24, 331, 334–35, 337; ch. 33 "The World" 天下, 24, 98n16, 306, 307
Zhuzi yulei 朱子語類 (Categorized Sayings of Master Zhu), 165, 185n5, 217n18, 254n37
Zichan 子產, 121–22, 126, 131n31, 132n48
Zigong 子貢, 174–75, 203
Zihuazi 子華子, 326
Zimo 子莫, 48, 176
Zisi 子思, 36, 137–38, 155n8, 162–63, 177–78
Zixia 子夏, 25, 164–66, 174–75, 188n64
Zizhang 子張, 25, 164–66, 174–75, 188n64
zong yu 縱慾 (indulging in desires), 35, 248, 263, 269–70, 282n15
Zuozhuan 左傳 (Zuo's Commentary on Spring and Autumn Annals), 200

www.ingramcontent.com/pod-product-compliance
Lightning Source LLC
Chambersburg PA
CBHW031704230426
43668CB00006B/102